There is currently much interest in the history of interpretation, reader-response and the sociology of sacred texts – in what the text does as much as what it means. Isaiah, 'more evangelist than prophet' according to Jerome and others, provides an ideal case study, because of his profound influence on the language and imagery of Christianity. With illustrations from art, music, literature and the media as well as commentaries, sermons and official church pronouncements, Professor Sawyer shows how Isaiah has been used in all kinds of context, from the cult of the Virgin Mary, mediaeval passion iconography and antisemitic propaganda to Christian feminism and liberation theology. This first attempt at a comprehensive critical study of an essential part of biblical interpretation will provide a model for further research, and ensure that commentaries will never be the same again.

THE FIFTH GOSPEL

THE FIFTH GOSPEL

Isaiah in the history of Christianity

JOHN F. A. SAWYER

Honorary Senior Research Fellow in Hebrew and Biblical Interpretation
Religious Studies Department, Lancaster University

CAMBRIDGE
UNIVERSITY PRESS

Published by the Press Syndicate of the University of Cambridge
The Pitt Building, Trumpington Street, Cambridge CB2 1RP
40 West 20th Street, New York, NY 10011–4211, USA
10 Stamford Road, Oakleigh, Melbourne 3166, Australia

© Cambridge University Press 1996

First published 1996

Printed in Great Britain at the University Press, Cambridge

A catalogue record for this book is available from the British Library

Library of Congress cataloguing in publication data
Sawyer, John F. A.
The fifth gospel: Isaiah in the history of Christianity / John F. A. Sawyer
p.   cm.
Includes bibliographical references and indexes.
ISBN 0 521 44007 6 (hardback)   ISBN 0 521 56596 0 (paperback)
1. Bible. O.T. Isaiah – Criticism, interpretation, etc. – History.
I. Title.
BS1515.2.S35   1995
244´.106´09 – dc20   95–22281 CIP

ISBN 0 521 44007 6 hardback
ISBN 0 521 56596 0 paperback

For
Alexander
Hannah
Sarah
Joseph

Lighten the darkness, O Lord
Lighten the heaviness, O Lord
Make us heavy with thee, O Lord
And we shall bring forth thy glory

Jerusalem 1961

Contents

Plates

14. 'Jesse tree' from Lambeth Bible, twelfth century (Lambeth Palace Library).
15. Brougham Triptych, Antwerp, sixteenth century (reproduced by permission of the Dean and Chapter of Carlisle to whom the Triptych is currently on loan).
16. 'Christ in the Wine-Press', stained glass window, sixteenth century, Conches (B. Acloque/© ARCH.PHOT. Paris/SPADEM).
17. Claus Sluter, 'The prophet Isaiah' on 'Moses' Fountain', Chartreuse de Champmol, Dijon, fourteenth century (B.Acloque/© ARCH.PHOT. Paris/SPADEM).
18. Matthias Grünewald, *Bearing the Cross* 1526 (Staatliche Kunsthalle, Karlsruhe).
19. Sixth Station ('Veronica wipes Christ's face') from J. van Hulst, *Stations of the Cross*, 1886–9, Church of SS Nicholas and Barbara, Amsterdam (now destroyed) (photo: Stichting Kerkelijk Kunstbezit in Nederland, Utrecht).
20. Lukas Cranach, *Isaiah's Vision*, woodcut from the Bible of Nikolaus Wolrab, Leipzig 1541 (Schmidt, *Die Illustration der Lutherbibel* 1522–1700, p. 221).
21. L. Evetts, stained glass window, 1979, St Silas Church, Byker, Newcastle upon Tyne (photo: Rev. Ian Falconer).
22. Konrad Witz, *Die Synagoge*, fifteenth century (photo: Öffentliche Kunstsammlung Basel, Martin Bühler).
23. Frontispiece of Paul Weidner's *Loca praecipua*, Vienna 1559 (by permission of the Houghton Library, Harvard University).
24. Woodcut from N. Reusner, *Emblemata*, Frankfurt 1581 (Heidelberg Universitätsbibliothek, Sign.: G 9506; Henkel-Schöne, cols. 1857–8).
25. Woodcut from J. Mannich, *Sacra Emblemata LXXVI*, Nuremberg 1625 (Herzog August Bibliothek, Wolfenbüttel, Sign.: 389.1 Theol.; Henkel-Schöne, cols. 1024–5).
26. Drawing by Jakob Jordaens, *Isaiah's satire on the sculpting of idols*, seventeenth century (ENSB–A).
27. Jan Brueghel the Elder, *The Preaching of the Prophet Isaiah*, seventeenth century, Alte Pinakothek, Munich (photo: Artothek, Munich).
28. William Blake, *The Book of Urizen* (1794), Plate 1 (The Keynes Family Trust, on deposit at the Fitzwilliam Museum, Cambridge).

Preface

In its earliest form *The Fifth Gospel* was a series of public lectures given in Bangor in 1987 and I would like to begin by thanking Max Wilcox, at that time Head of the Religious Studies Department at the University College of North Wales, and his colleagues for giving me the opportunity to start working on this project. A version of part of chapter 7 was published in *Ritual and Remembrance. Responses to Death in Human Societies*, ed. Jon Davies (Sheffield 1994), and part of chapter 13 in *Currents in Research. Biblical Studies* 3 (1995).

I am grateful to the staff of many libraries for the help they have given me, in particular, the university libraries at Newcastle, Durham, Lancaster, Edinburgh and Utrecht, Durham Cathedral Library, the Warburg Institute and the Courtauld Institute in London, and the Stichting Kerkelijk Kunstbezit in Nederland in Utrecht. I would like to express my gratitude to Newcastle University for granting me a sabbatical in 1991–2, and to the Leverhulme Trust for generously funding it, as well as to the British Academy and the US National Endowment for the Humanities for making possible a stimulating visit to Berkeley in the Summer of 1994. My thanks are also due to the Dean of St Paul's and 'Peaceable Kingdom' artist Karen van Heerden for material they kindly supplied, and to the editorial staff at Cambridge University Press, especially Alex Wright.

I have been greatly helped by the suggestions and criticisms of colleagues, students, friends and relations, among whom I would like to say a special word of thanks to Jon Davies, Graham Harvey, Brian Pearson, Sue Vernon, Paul Hilditch, Harry Tait, Ian Falconer, Archimandrite Ephrem, Eric Cross, Andrew Fairbairn, Richard Bailey, Peter Evans, Andrew Ballantyne, Jack Watt, Gerald Miller, Diana Crockford, Alexander Sawyer, Lindsay Sawyer, Claire Mac-Gregor, Margaret Fergusson, Ann Loades, Chris Rowland, Robert

Carroll, Philip Davies, David Clines, John Rogerson, Paul Morris, David Martin, John Andrews, Robert Hamilton, Gerard Byrne, Cyril Ashton, Myrtle Langley, Martin Molyneux, Marc Vervenne, Alexander Rofé, Raya Heller, Lauren Pfister, Alan Hauser, Lenore Erickson, Calum Carmichael and, in a class of her own, Deborah Sawyer.

Abbreviations

ABD	*Anchor Bible Dictionary*, ed. D. N. Freedman, 6 vols. (Doubleday, New York 1992)
APOT	*The Apocrypha and Pseudepigrapha of the Old Testament in English*, 2 vols. ed. R. H. Charles (Oxford 1913)
ASB	*The Alternative Service Book. Services Authorized for Use in the Church of England* (Oxford 1980)
AV	*Authorized Version of the Bible* (1611)
BP	*Biblia Pauperum. A Facsimile and Edition*. ed. A. Henry (Scolar Press, London 1987)
CCSL	*Corpus Christianorum. Series Latina* (Brepols, Turnholt 1953–)
CH	*The Church Hymnary* (revised edition, Oxford 1927)
CH³	*The Church Hymnary* (3rd edition, Oxford 1973)
CHB	*Cambridge History of the Bible*, 3 vols. (Cambridge 1969–70)
DBI	*Dictionary of Biblical Interpretation*, edd. R. J. Coggins and J. L. Houlden (SCM Press, London 1990)
DBTEL	*A Dictionary of Biblical Tradition in English Literature*, ed. D. L. Jeffrey, (Eerdmans, Grand Rapids, Michigan 1992)
EH	*English Hymnal* (Oxford 1906)
EJ	*Encyclopedia Judaica*, 16 vols. (Jerusalem 1971–2)
ELL	*Encyclopedia of Language and Linguistics*, ed. R. Asher (Pergamon Press, Oxford 1994)
FOC	*Fathers of the Church* (Washington 1947–)
HAM	*Hymns Ancient and Modern* (London 1916)
HAP	*Hymns and Psalms* (Methodist Publishing House, London 1983)
HON	*Hymns Old and New with Supplement*, ed. K. Mayhew (Bath Press, Avon 1989)
JAAR	*Journal of the American Academy of Religion*
JBL	*Journal of Biblical Literature*

JE	*Jewish Encyclopedia*, 10 vols. (Funk and Wagnall, New York 1904)
JJS	*Journal of Jewish Studies*
JSNT	*Journal for the Study of the New Testament*
JSOT	*Journal for the Study of the Old Testament*
JSS	*Journal of Semitic Studies*
JTS	*Journal of Theological Studies*
Lectionary	Order of Readings for use at Mass (Geoffrey Chapman, London 1970)
LW	*Luther's Works*, edd. J. Pelikan and others, 55 vols. (St Louis and Philadelphia 1955–)
MP	*Mission Praise* (London 1983)
New Sunday Missal	Texts approved for use in England and Wales, Ireland, Scotland and Africa (Geoffrey Chapman, London 1982)
NRSV	*New Oxford Annotated Bible* (*New Revised Standard Version*), edd. B. M. Metzger and R. E. Murphy (Oxford Unversity Press, Oxford 1991),
NTA	*New Testament Apocrypha*, 2 vols., edd. Hennecke, E., Schneemelcher, W., and R. McL. Wilson, London 1963–5
NTS	*New Testament Studies*
OBC	*Oxford Book of Carols*, edd. P. Dearmer, R. Vaughan Williams and M. Shaw (London 1928)
OCB	*Oxford Companion to the Bible*, edd. B. M. Metzger and M. D. Coogan (New York and Oxford 1993)
ODQ	*The Oxford Dictionary of Quotations* (2nd edition, Oxford 1953)
OTP	*The Old Testament Pseudepigrapha*, 2 vols., ed. J. H. Charlesworth (London 1985)
PG	*Patrologiae Cursus Completus. Series Graeca*, ed. J.-P. Migne (Paris 1857–)
PL	*Patrologiae Cursus Completus. Series Latina*, ed. J.-P. Migne (Paris 1844). *Supplementum* vol. 4, ed. A. Hamman (Paris 1967)
RB	*Revue Biblique*
REB	*Revised English Bible* (Oxford/Cambridge 1989)
RSV	*Revised Standard Version*, Ecumenical Edition (Collins, London 1973)
SBSA	*Song Book of the Salvation Army* (London 1986)

SNOBC	*Shorter New Oxford Book of Carols*, edd. H. Keyte and A. Parrott (Oxford 1993)
SOP	*Songs of Praise* (Oxford 1932)
TZ	*Theologische Zeitung*
VT	*Vetus Testamentum*
ZNW	*Zeitschrift für die Neutestamentliche Wissenschaft*

CHAPTER I

Introduction

Although one of the Prophets in what Christians call the 'Old Testament', Isaiah has been known in the Church from early times as 'more evangelist than prophet', and the Book of Isaiah as the 'Fifth Gospel'. This is because he has played a unique role in all kinds of context, from the cult of the Virgin Mary to anti-Jewish polemic, from mediaeval passion iconography to twentieth-century Christian feminism and liberation theology. Jerome (c.342–420), one of the most influential figures in the history of the Bible, introduces him as follows: '... he should be called an evangelist rather than a prophet because he describes all the mysteries[1] of Christ and the Church so clearly that you would think he is composing a history of what has already happened rather than prophesying about what is to come'.[2] He is obviously referring to passages like 9:6 where the birth of the Son of David is described as having already happened ('For to us a child has been born ...'), or chapter 53 where the events of the passion are not foretold as elsewhere in the prophets, but recounted in the past tense ('he was despised and rejected ...').

A much used early twelfth-century manuscript of Jerome's *Commentary on Isaiah* in Durham Cathedral Library has a miniature which nicely illustrates his perception of Isaiah (Plate 1). It shows Isaiah at the top with a scroll in each hand: one carries the verse associated with him more than any other in the mediaeval Church (*Ecce virgo concipiet* ... 'Behold a virgin will conceive ...' 7:14), while the other has some apocalyptic words from 24:16 (*secretum meum mihi, secretum meum mihi, vae mihi..!* 'my secret is with me, my secret is with me: woe is me!'). Jerome is looking up at him and saying, according to the

---

[1] Some manuscripts have *ministeria* 'functions, activities' instead of *mysteria*.
[2] Prologue to translation of Isaiah in *Biblia Sacra iuxta Vulgatam versionem*, 2nd ed. by R. Weber (Stuttgart 1975), Vol. II, p. 1096.

legend on his scroll: *Dic tu Isaias, dic testimonium Christi* 'Go on, Isaiah, tell them about Christ!'[3] But he goes further. He tells us we should also expect to find in the book of Isaiah instruction in physics, ethics and logic: 'whatever there is in Sacred Scripture, whatever the human tongue can express and the minds of mortals understand, is contained in that book'.[4]

Jerome's assessment of Isaiah is typical, and is echoed throughout Christian literature. Augustine (354–430), for example, once asked his bishop for advice on vacation reading, and the bishop (Ambrose) prescribed Isaiah 'because, I believe, he is more plainly a foreteller of the Gospel and of the calling of the Gentiles than are the others'.[5] Isidore of Seville (560–636)[6] and the influential thirteenth-century exegete Hugh of St Cher describe Isaiah in similar terms. Examples from Eastern Christianity include John Chrysostom (c.347–407), who called him 'the prophet with the loudest voice' (*megalophonotatos*),[7] and a seventh-century Syriac Bible manuscript in which Isaiah is introduced as 'the most highly praised of the Prophets'.[8]

In mediaeval mystery plays he regularly figures as the prophet who, more than any other, recognizes the Messiah. In a procession of foretellers of Christ in the York Cycle, for example, he is the only prophet, coming after Adam and Eve and before Symeon and John the Baptist. His function is to announce that his prophecy in 9:1–2 ('The people that walked in darkness have seen a great light') is fulfilled: 'Now I see this light …'[9] He plays a similar role in the corresponding sequence in the Chester Cycle.[10] In the prologue to Isaiah in the *Wycliffe Bible* (c. 1397) he is 'not oneli a profete, but more, a Gospellere', and a seventeenth-century commentator tells us he was known then as the 'fifth evangelist'.[11] An eighteenth-century Family Bible introduces Isaiah in very similar language: 'Isaiah is always called the Evangelical Prophet because he speaks more clearly of Christ and his Church than any of the others and describes

[3]   Cf. Sawyer, 'My secret is with me', pp. 308f.
[4]   Prologue to his *Commentary on Isaiah*: *CCSL* 73, pp. 1–2.
[5]   Conf.9,5 (1.276).
[6]   *Isaias formam evangelistarum et apostolorum expressit qui universa sacramenta Christi, non quasi futura, sed quam praesentia praedicavit*: *PL* 83, p. 114.
[7]   Diestel, *Geschichte*, p. 136.
[8]   *Vetus Testamentum Syriace* III,1 Liber Isaiae, p. 1.
[9]   *The York Plays*, ed. R. Beadle, London, 1982), pp. 332–3.
[10] *The Chester Mystery Plays*, ed. D. Mills, p. 304.
[11] Poole, *Commentary on the Holy Bible*, Vol. 2, p. 326.

the glories of the Gospel Dispensation in language so elevated that nothing can exceed it.'[12]

In the language of twentieth-century theological discourse, the contribution of scripture to Christian morality can be summarized in the list 'Moses, Isaiah, Jesus and Paul'.[13] The Catholic writer and journalist Paul Johnson puts it in terms not unlike those of some of his Christian predecessors: 'Isaiah was not only the most remarkable of the prophets, he was by far the greatest writer in the Old Testament. He was evidently a magnificent preacher ... and his words remained among the most popular of all the holy writings. The early Jews loved his sparkling prose with its brilliant images, many of which have since passed into the literature of all civilized nations. But more important than the language was the thought: Isaiah was pushing humanity towards new moral discoveries'.[14]

The pages devoted to Isaiah in the *Oxford Dictionary of Quotations*[15] further demonstrate the extent of his influence beyond his immediate Christian context within the Church, on English literature and western European culture in general. Messianic titles like 'Immanuel' (7:14), 'Prince of Peace' (9:6) and 'the Key of David' (22:22) that have become an integral part of Christian vocabulary, are Isaianic, as are such universally familiar expressions as 'swords into ploughshares' (2:4), 'the wolf dwelling with the lamb' (11:6–9), 'a voice crying in the wilderness' (40:3), 'a man of sorrows' (53:3), 'a light to the nations' (42:6; 49:6), 'good news to the poor' (61:1) and 'a new heaven and a new earth' (65:17). 'My house shall be called a house of prayer for all peoples' (56:7) is inscribed over the entrance to churches,[16] and Isaiah also gave us proverbs like 'There is no peace for the wicked' (48:22; 57:21).

John Bunyan chose the name 'Beulah' from Isaiah 62:4 for 'the land beyond the valley of the Shadow of Death' from which pilgrims could see the Heavenly City,[17] and Milton's description of Satan's fall from heaven in Book 1 of *Paradise Lost* was inspired by the mocking lament over the death of the King of Babylon in Isaiah 14.[18] Lilith, Adam's first wife and a literary model for radical feminists, also has her scriptural roots in Isaiah (cf. 34:1).[19] Handel's *Messiah* is largely

[12]   Ed. Benjamin Kennicott, Dublin 1793.
[13]   M. Wiles, *Faith and the Mystery of God*, p. 107.
[14]   Johnson, *History of the Jews*, p. 74.
[15]   Second edition (Oxford 1953), pp. 52–5.
[16]   The Priory Church in Lancaster is one example.
[17]   *Pilgrim's Progress*, Part 2.   [18]   See p. 160.   [19]   See pp. 216–19.

based on excerpts from chapters 9, 34, 40, 52, 53 and 60, while Mendelssohn's *Elijah* and Brahms' *German Requiem* contain some other memorable settings of Isaiah.[20] It has provided Christian artists with many of their favourite images, including the ox and the ass of the nativity scene (1:3), the six-winged seraphim (6:2–3), the 'Jesse tree' (11:1–2), the 'peaceable kingdom' (11:6–9), the 'good shepherd' (40:11), the 'man of sorrows' (53:3), and the 'winepress' (63:3). Significantly one of the few modern scholars to comment on the special role of Isaiah in the formation of Christian doctrine is an art historian.[21]

Possibly this special popularity of the book of Isaiah among Christians, and some of their distinctive interpretations of it, go back to Jesus himself, a view nicely expressed to me once by the late Brian Redhead. His answer to the question of why Isaiah had been so central to Christianity, was that he thought it was because Jesus had been 'brought up on Isaiah', in the same way that he himself had been 'brought up on *The Old Curiosity Shop*', because it was just about the only book in the house when he was a child. The seventeenth-century French artist Charles Le Brun (1619–1690) charmingly illustrates this possibility in *The Holy Family in Egypt*, where Jesus is being taught to read, by his mother incidentally, from a Hebrew scroll of Isaiah (Plate 2).[22] Ernest Renan in his *Vie de Jésus* (1863) also comments on the special role of Isaiah in Jesus' education.[23] There certainly are good arguments for the view that it was Jesus himself who found in Isaiah a special source of inspiration or enlightenment,[24] and laid the foundations for an Isaiah-based Christianity.

But another reason for the prominence of Isaiah in early Christianity is simply that Isaiah seems always to have had a peculiarly prominent place in Jewish Bible use too,[25] so that his popularity in a first-century Jewish sect is only to be expected. In our earliest reference to a Jewish 'canon' of scripture, Isaiah takes pride of place (Sir. Prologue; 49:17–25). He is noticeably prominent among the Dead Sea Scrolls, in both the scriptural and the sectarian texts.[26] In

---

[20] See pp. 171–175.

[21] Réau, *Iconographie*, Vol.II,1, p. 366; cf. M. Salmi, *La Pittura di Piero della Francesca* (Novara 1959), p. 68; Pickering, *Literature and Art*, pp. 274f, note 2; P. D. Hanson, 'Third Isaiah' (*Reading and Preaching the Book of Isaiah*, ed. C. R. Seitz), pp. 96f.: 'the Book of Isaiah, that book that is of such central importance to Christian faith from the time of the early disciples down to the present'.

[22] The Hebrew is clearly legible in the version in the Fitzwilliam Museum at Cambridge: Catalogue by J. W. Goodison and D. Sutton (1960), pp. 181–2, no. 339.

[23] E. Renan, *Vie de Jésus*, p. 28.

[24] See pp. 23–25.   [25] See also pp. 103–105.   [26] See below, p. 24

mediaeval Jewish lectionaries, which no doubt to a great extent reflect ancient practice, about half the *haftaroth* (readings from the Prophets) come from Isaiah, including the 'Consolation' readings from 40–61.[27]

This partly explains why Isaiah played such a disturbing role, especially during the Middle Ages, in anti-Jewish polemic.[28] Over and over again we find the Church choosing texts from Isaiah to prove how misguided the Jews are, and to authorize attitudes of arrogance and hostility towards them. It was precisely because Isaiah was such a popular text in both traditions that the Church's 'christification'[29] of Isaiah had such tragic consequences for the Jews.

A study of Isaiah in the history of Judaism would probably be just as revealing as the present study. Since the nineteenth century, for example, Zionists have made much use of Isaiah, as can be seen from the number of works of modern Jewish literature and music based on Isaianic themes, and also from the names given to many of the Jewish settlements in Israel, including one of the first, called Rishon le-Tzion 'first to Zion' (Isa.41:27).[30] Several monuments erected since the Second World War bear inscriptions from Isaiah, including the Holocaust Memorial in Jerusalem, Yad va-Shem (Isa.56:5).[31] More recently the Israeli Prime Minister Yitzhak Rabin chose words from Isaiah 57:19 to express his commitment to peace at the historic meeting with Yasser Arafat, Chairman of the Palestine Liberation Organization in Washington on 14 September 1993: 'Peace, peace to the far and the near, says the Lord'. It would be interesting to examine this more thoroughly.

But 'Isaiah in Judaism' would have to be a study in its own right, quite separate from 'Isaiah in the Church'.[32] For one thing, unlike traditional Christian uses of Isaiah which are based for the most part on Greek or Syriac or Latin or German or English translations, Jewish traditions are almost all much more closely related to the original Hebrew text or its ancient Jewish Aramaic translation, the Targum. A study of Jewish interpretations of Isaiah, like that of A. Neubauer and S.R. Driver, *The Fifty-Third Chapter of Isaiah*

---

[27] See *JE*, vol.6, pp. 136–7; Elbogen, *Jewish Liturgy*, pp. 143–9.
[28] See chapter 6.
[29] Cf. Diestel, *Geschichte*, p. 369: 'Christologisierung der Prophetie'.
[30] See also pp.103–5.   [31] See pp. 104–5.
[32] See most recently the superb article on 'Jewish Exegesis' by Raphael Loewe in *DBI*, pp. 346–54.

According to the Jewish Interpreters, begins and ends in a totally different world from a study of Isaiah in the Church.

Another point at which the study of the Bible in Judaism and the study, like the present one, of the Bible in the Church, would diverge, and one that cannot be stressed too much, is that, since the very beginning, Isaiah has been as much part of Christian scripture as the Gospels and Paul. The original anti-Jewish distinction between one part of scripture, the 'Jewish part', invidiously labelled the 'Old Testament', and another, labelled the 'New Testament', has led to misunderstandings and prejudices both about Judaism and about scripture, and, like other racist and sexist language, would be better dropped from the vocabulary of the Church.[33] The 'Prophets', including Isaiah, are in no way more 'Jewish' than the Gospels. The Gospels are Jewish through and through and the Prophets, especially in their ancient Greek version, were from the beginning at least as much part of Christian scripture as of the Jewish Bible.

It is important, although something that is rarely practised, to keep the study of Christian scripture, in which Isaiah is a 'Fifth Gospel', separate from the study of the Hebrew Bible in Jewish tradition. Christianity and Judaism are separate religions.[34] As soon as our attention shifts away from ancient Israel, where the roots of both Judaism and Christianity are equally to be found, and into the Common Era, then it is confusing to try to study both religious traditions at the same time. This practice, which has been widespread in institutions where Christian theology and Biblical studies are taught, has the inevitable result that Judaism suffers twice over, by, on the one hand, being identified with the 'religion of the Hebrew Bible' or 'ancient Israelite religion' (with supersessionist implications), and, on the other, being treated as 'background to the New Testament'.[35] The focus throughout then is on 'Isaiah in the Church'. Jewish responses to what Christians have done with Isaiah will be considered, and a chapter is devoted to the ugly story of Isaiah and Christian antisemitism. But a study of Isaiah's role in the history of Judaism must be kept separate, and awaits the undivided scholarly attention of someone better qualified than the present writer.

[33] Cf. Sawyer, 'Combating prejudices', pp. 269–78.
[34] Cf. Neusner, *Jews and Christians. The Myth of a Common Tradition.*
[35] Cf. Levenson, *The Hebrew Bible, the Old Testament and Historical Criticism. Jews and Christians in Biblical Study*; K. Stendahl, 'Antisemitism'; Sawyer, 'Combating prejudices about the Bible and Judaism', pp. 269f.

'Isaiah in Islam' is also a separate story. It too would require specialist treatment. The Arabic form of his name is Sha'ya, and Muslim writers from Tabari (died 923) on, were familiar with his role in the stories of Sennacherib's invasion and Hezekiah's illness.[36] In both Jewish and Muslim tradition, incidentally, Isaiah is remembered as an intensely unpopular prophet, not afraid to speak out against his own people, who suffered martyrdom at the hands of his enemies. There is a hint in al-Baydawi's influential thirteenth-century commentary on the Qur'an, that he may have had some special significance in Islamic tradition as well, which the other prophets did not have. In a comment on Sura 17:4 Baydawi states that the two sins committed by the Israelites were (1) the murder of Sha'ya ibn Amaṣya (=Isaiah) and (2) the murder of Zechariah and John the Baptist, and the intention to kill Jesus.[37] In a similar way in Christian tradition Isaiah keeps company with Moses, David, Jesus and Paul, rather than the other 'Old Testament prophets'.

Our concern here is the story of Isaiah in the history of Christianity. It is one part of the story of how Christians down the ages have used the Bible: in popular hymns and preaching, in art and music and literature, in the attitudes and assumptions of ordinary people and in official pronouncements and scholarly commentaries. There have been many studies of this from Ludwig Diestel's nineteenth-century work on 'the Old Testament in the Christian Church' to more recent titles such as *The Bible in the Sixteenth Century*,[38] *The Bible in Scottish Life and Literature*[39] and *The Bible and its Readers*.[40] Christopher Hill's *The English Bible and the Seventeenth-Century Revolution* dramatically records how central a role scripture can play, as self-help manual, oracle, source of courage, alternative law-book and the like, in major social and political developments.[41] 'The ancient and mediaeval career' of a particular biblical text (Genesis 1:28) is the subject of another recent example.[42] On the particular question of the influence of the Bible on English literature, two new publications have just appeared, an invaluable reference work entitled *A Dictionary of Biblical Tradition in English Literature*,[43] and a fascinating anthology with the title *Chapters*

---

[36] Cf. *EJ*, Vol. 9, cols. 67–8.
[37] *Encyclopedia of Islam*, Vol. 4 (London 1934), p. 343.
[38] Ed. Steinmetz, 1990.   [39] Ed. Wright, 1988.
[40] Edd. Beuken, Freyne and Weiler, 1991.
[41] Hill, *The English Bible and the Seventeenth-Century Revolution* (1993).
[42] Cohen, *'Be Fertile and Increase; Fill the Earth and Master It'* (1989).
[43] *DBTEL*.

into Verse. Poetry in English Inspired by the Bible.[44] From these and other
publications it is obvious that many of the examples investigated here
in relation to one book can be paralleled in the history of the
interpretation of other books of the Bible.

But the unique contribution of Isaiah to the life and work of the
Church, in all these different spheres of activity, is something that
has not been fully investigated until now. Whatever the reason for its
early prominence, the popularity of the Book of Isaiah and the
special role which it has played in the history of the Church and
western culture, make it an ideal case study for a history of biblical
interpretation. The story is all the more fascinating because it has
been so much neglected. A study of the use made of texts from Isaiah
by theologians like Augustine and Luther, composers like Byrd,
Bach, Handel and Brahms, artists, hymn-writers, preachers and
politicians, as well as in official pronouncements of the Church such
as the documents of the Second Vatican Council (1962–5), reveals a
great deal both about the meaning of scripture and about the history
of Christianity.

Most of the commentaries on Isaiah written over the last 200 or
300 years – and there are hundreds of them – have little or nothing
to say about the uses made of him by Christians down the centuries.
With a few notable exceptions, P.-E. Bonnard, *Le Second Isaie* (1972),
for example, who gives some space to popular and influential
Christian uses of Isaiah, and Brevard Childs' *Exodus* (London 1974),
commentaries are reluctant to include the history of interpretation
systematically. What the 'experts', with their overarching concern for
historical critical material, have been doing with Isaiah in their
commentaries, often has little or nothing to do with what the rest of
the world has been doing with him, and still does, in literature, art,
music, worship and politics. For most modern biblical experts,
including the majority of those who have written commentaries on
Isaiah, I think it is true to say, the role of Isaiah in Christian tradition
is of marginal interest, and scarcely worthy of serious scholarly
attention. Their sole concern has been with the original meaning of
the original text: anything later than that is rejected as at best
unimportant, at worst pious rubbish. If anything, they want their
main contribution to the study of the Bible to be a corrective one,
explicitly rejecting what people believe about it: 'Ah, but that is not

[44]   Atwan and Wieder, *Chapters into Verse* (1993).

what the original Hebrew meant!' The almost universally held perception of Isaiah, with which we began, as unique among the Prophets in the history of western culture, means nothing to them.

The introduction to Isaiah in the prestigious *New Jerome Biblical Commentary*[45] is typical. There are none of the superlatives of the older commentaries: instead the bulk of the introduction centres on historical and literary critical issues which read very much like the introduction to any other book of the Bible. Nor does the introduction to Isaiah in the *New Revised Standard Version* of the Bible make any mention of his special role in the Church,[46] despite its confessional format and its claim to be acceptable to all the major Christian Churches, Protestant, Anglican, Roman Catholic and Eastern Orthodox.[47] Even in a brief 'history of interpretation' of Isaiah by a leading British scholar, mention is made of its status as 'one of the foremost writings of the OT for the early Christian Church', but the highest praise is reserved for 'the brilliant philological and linguistic insights of W. Gesenius in his commentary of 1829' and 'the pioneering work of B.Duhm published in 1892'.[48]

The last fifteen or twenty years, however, have seen a distinct change in this situation. There are signs of a new interest among biblical experts in the history of interpretation.[49] This is evident, for example, in recent publications and research projects on the Second Temple Period, in particular on what was happening to scripture in that period, such as M. Fishbane, *Biblical Interpretation in Ancient Israel* and J. Barton, *Oracles of God. Perceptions of Ancient Prophecy in Israel after the Exile*. There is also the impetus given to the study of ancient sectarian uses of scripture by the Dead Sea Scrolls and the Nag Hammadi texts.

We may note also how the Greek Septuagint, the Aramaic Targumim, the Syriac Peshitta, the Latin Vulgate and other ancient versions of the Bible, are now more than ever before being studied as literature in their own right: not only as sources for reconstructing the original Hebrew text but also as evidence for how scripture was interpreted in various ancient contexts.[50] These constitute, for

---

[45] R. E. Brown, SS, J. A. Fitzmyer, SJ and R. E. Murphy, OCarm, edd. (London 1990), pp. 229–30, 329–32.

[46] *New Oxford Annotated Bible*, edd. B. M. Metzger and R. E. Murphy (Oxford University Press, 1991), p. 866.

[47] *New Oxford Annotated Bible*, p. x.   [48] *DBI*, p. 328.

[49] Sawyer, 'History of Interpretation', *DBI*, pp. 316–20.

[50] Cf. Muraoka, 'Bible translation: the ancient versions', p. 350.

biblical experts, something of an intermediate stage in the history of interpretation, bridging the gap between the ancient near east and later mediaeval and modern contexts. So we find a senior Biblical scholar moving from a critical commentary on Jeremiah, whose exclusive aim is to get as close as possible to the original words of the prophet,[51] to a study of five *Selected Christian Hebraists*, from Andrew of St Victor (died 1175) to the nineteenth-century Scotsman Alexander Geddes.[52]

Recent developments in what are loosely termed 'literary approaches' to the Bible have also been influential. Rhetorical criticism, canonical criticism, *Redaktionsgeschichte* and structuralism share with 'pre-critical' commentators like Jerome and Rashi an interest in the text as it stands, so that questions about the meaning of the text may come before questions about who wrote it and when, and what were their sources. For that kind of question, the centuries of Jewish and Christian exegetical tradition are a treasure-house of useful insights because these are the questions asked in the pre-critical age as well.[53]

The literary critics' concept of 'intratextuality' to a significant extent overlaps one of the main hermeneutical principles of earlier religious interpreters, namely, to work within the text as a closed corpus and use one passage of scripture to interpret another.[54] This type of semantic activity was highly developed in the pre-critical age, especially where readers knew the whole text of the Bible well, if not by heart. One of the most remarkable developments of recent years is the matching up of modern literary and semantic analysis of the biblical text with more amateurish ancient and mediaeval interpretations. Occasionally a modern interpreter discovers that he or she has come to the same conclusion as Jerome or Isidore of Seville. The reason why this does not happen more often is of course that few biblical experts are really familiar with, or interested in, the Christian exegetical tradition. It happens more often in Jewish Studies because Jewish scholars tend to be better acquainted with their (rabbinic and mediaeval) sources than Christians are with theirs. My own experience is that just as much light is often thrown on our texts, if not

[51] McKane, *Jeremiah. Vol. 1* (1986).
[52] McKane, *Selected Christian Hebraists* (1989).
[53] Sawyer, 'A change of emphasis in the study of the Prophets' (1982).
[54] Cf. Brett, 'Intratextuality', *DBI*, pp. 320–1.

more, by the post-biblical data as by the ancient parallels and other archaeological evidence usually quoted.[55]

The influence of modern literary criticism is evident also in the current interest in reader-response.[56] Given that we are never going to be in a position to get very near to the original intention of authors about whom we know almost nothing, and whose words have in any case passed through extremely complex scribal and editorial processes, this shift of emphasis has been a fruitful one within Biblical Studies. In the case of a sacred text like the Bible, the reader-response critics' dictum that 'the bare text is mute' has particular significance, since without the Church, the canonical text would not exist. For present purposes its significance is that it focusses on the history of interpretation for what may be called primary source material, in preference to archaeology and ancient near eastern parallels. A history of interpretation is then understood as the history of how readers (or listeners or exegetes) respond to the text. It is to be hoped that eventually the *Rezeptionsgeschichte* of a text like the Bible, that is to say, the history of how it has been 'received, handled, used' by readers, will regularly take its place in our commentaries as a normal part of biblical research, however numerous and complex the practical and theoretical problems involved may be.[57]

Another development, which has affected scholarly attitudes to the history of interpretation, is the heightened awareness, particularly since Bultmann,[58] of the role of presuppositions in biblical interpretation. This immediately switches attention away from the analysis of the text itself, to questions about who is doing the analysing, from the sources and methods of interpretation to the social, political and even psychological background of the interpreter. At the individual level we can ask what it was in Isaiah 40:8 that appealed to Luther so much,[59] or examine the situation in which Handel found himself when he set parts of the same chapter to music, to see whether this influenced his understanding of the text.[60] Collectively there are interesting questions about why certain interpretations became popular or influential at particular periods

---

[55] Cf. Sawyer, 'The role of Jewish studies in biblical semantics' (1986).
[56] Meyer, 'The challenges of text and reader to the historical–critical method', in *The Bible and its Readers* edd. W. Beuken, S. Freyne and A. Weiler, pp. 3–12.
[57] Carroll, 'Revisionings', especially pp. 226–8.
[58] Bultmann, 'Is exegesis without presuppositions possible?'.
[59] See below, pp. 128–131.   [60] See below pp. 171–173.

or in particular communities: Isaiah 7:9 and 53:8 in the patristic period, 7:14, 11:1, 16:1 and 45:8 in most of the cathedrals of mediaeval Europe, and 2:4 and 11:6–9 in the late twentieth century. How and why readers and interpreters come to their conclusions about what the text means – these consitute the basic subject matter of a history of interpretation.

Another factor in the new situation is the recognition that what a text does can often be as important as what it means. *Wirkungsgeschichte*[61] joins *Formgeschichte, Redaktionsgeschichte*, etc. as an integral part of Biblical Studies. The effect (*Wirkung*) of the text on those who have used it, recited it, preached on it, studied it and been influenced by it in different ways and in different contexts down the centuries, is part of the Biblical scholars' data. The Bible has been used to keep slaves in their place (Eph.6:5ff), to marginalize women (1 Timothy 2:8–15), to insult Jews (Isaiah 65:2–3) and to condemn the poor (Proverbs 10:4). It is against this background that we have to view the scholarly attention now being given to black Christian interpretation, feminist interpretation, materialist interpretation and the like wherever the Bible is studied.[62]

Finally, the Bible is now increasingly being taught and studied in the context of the study of religion where doctrinal, ethical, sociological and political considerations have their place alongside traditional textual linguistic skills. My own experience of teaching and studying the Bible in a university Department of Religious Studies has taught me to respect the beliefs and opinions of people who use it, and to keep them in mind as we study the text. Biblical Studies is seen as part of the study of Christianity or Judaism, in the same way that the study of the Qur'an is one part of Islamic Studies and the Vedas one part of the study of Hinduism.

One of the topics at a recent conference on 'The Sociology of Sacred Texts' held at Newcastle University was the problem of finding out who had a say in selecting the scriptural texts carved on stone monuments, such as war-memorials – the local vicar or minister? widows? mothers? local council officials? architects? artists? – and what people actually believed the inscriptions

---

[61] The term is Gadamer's (*Wahrheit und Methode*, p. xix), although his original definition of the term was concerned only with the 'effect' of historical tradition on the interpreter's consciousness (*das wirkungsgeschichtliche Bewußtsein*), rather than with a method.

[62] Cf. Küng and Moltmann, edd., *Conflicting Ways of Interpreting the Bible*; and see also the bibliography in Sawyer, 'The original meaning of the text' (revised edition, Leuven 1990), pp. 210–13.

meant.[63] This aspect of the study of sacred texts such as the Bible, in addition to the much more familiar historical critical questions about form, date, authorship and original meaning, has in our view been too long neglected. It is one of the chief aims of the present study to redress the balance, and focus on what has happened to the sacred text in the long history of its use by Christians.

It seems that the gap that has existed for over 200 years between the study of the Bible and the study of Church History and Christian theology, between experts in semitic languages and biblical archaeology, on the one hand, and theologians and Church historians, on the other, is at last being bridged. Interdisciplinary studies like Jeremy Cohen's monograph referred to above[64] and collections of essays like *A Walk in the Garden. Biblical, Iconographical and Literary Images of Eden*[65] and *Ritual and Remembrance. Responses to Death in Human Societies*,[66] are opening the way up for a new type of biblical research. The present work is intended as a contribution to this growing field of interest.

The study of this type of material need be no less historical or critical. There is just as much evidence, indeed usually far more, for what people believe the text means, or what they are told to believe it means, as there is for what the original author intended, and this can be treated with just the same degree of sensitivity and scientific rigour as a reconstructed original Hebrew text or any other ancient near eastern text. It also quickly becomes evident that what people believe a text means has often been far more interesting and important, theologically, politically, morally and aesthetically, in the history of the Church, than what it originally meant. This raises the question of criteria for evaluating diverse interpretations of the same text. Various answers to this question will emerge as we proceed, and we shall draw some conclusions at the end. For the moment we may simply note that there seems to be mounting dissatisfaction with the traditional view that the nearest to the original must necessarily be preferred: that chronological priority is some kind of guarantee of truth.

As this is something of a pilot project, designed to persuade future

---

[63] Davies, 'Lapidary Texts. A Liturgy Fit for Heroes?' in Davies and Wollaston, edd., *Sociology of Sacred Texts*, pp. 26–36.
[64] See note. 42.   [65] Edd. Morris and Sawyer (1992).
[66] Ed. J. G. Davies (1994).

writers of biblical commentaries to look at the texts they are working on from a wider perspective, some preliminary remarks on method are important. Diestel, mentioned above, is concerned with the whole of the 'Old Testament', not just one book. More recent works like Denis Nineham, *The Uses and Abuses of the Bible* (1976), R.M. Grant and D. Tracy, *A Short History of the Interpretation of the Bible* (1984) and J.W. Rogerson, C.C. Rowland and B. Lindars, *The Study and Use of the Bible* (1988), also have wider terms of reference and concentrate for the most part on the history of exegetical theory and method, without any real concern for the empirical data with which we shall be working. Rogerson's long entry on 'History of interpretation' in the new *Anchor Bible Dictionary* is another case in point.

Childs' commentary on Exodus provides a closer parallel. Every section concludes with a brief systematic history of how the text was interpreted in later Jewish and Christian tradition. But it differs from the present study in two ways. First, the history of interpretation in Childs is unashamedly appended to what is understood to be the main part of the commentary, whereas our aim here is to reverse the balance. The other difference, shared with all the other studies mentioned so far, emerges from a glance at the bibliographies given by Childs for each section. These are mainly references to scholarly commentaries and the like, and there is very little interest evident in sermons, poetry, the arts, and political or ethical literature. Our aim is to shift the balance away from the standard commentaries and what we might call the official academic history of exegesis, towards popular uses of Isaiah and the interaction between Isaiah and the Church and society at large. This is not another history aimed at scrutinizing the exegetical aims and methods of Origen, Jerome, Andrew of St Victor, Luther, Lowth, Duhm, Cheyne, Westermann, Clements and the like. For present purposes Handel's *Messiah* is as important a witness to what Isaiah meant in the eighteenth century as Lowth, and, for late twentieth-century Catholicism, post-Vatican II lectionaries and hymnbooks will be as valuable as the *New Jerome Biblical Commentary*.

So how are we to tackle what looks like an impossible task? Twenty centuries of theological treatises, commentaries, sermons, political speeches, hymns, oratorios, paintings, sculptures, novels and poems, in countless different languages, present the historian of interpretation with a bewildering task, and there are no exactly parallel models to follow. First, it was decided to follow the example of Diestel and the rest in dividing the material up broadly into *historical* periods. A purely thematic approach was considered: Isaiah in Christology, Isaiah and the Cult of the Virgin Mary, Isaiah and Social Justice, Women and Female Imagery in Isaiah, Isaiah and Antisemitism, and so on. This would have had certain advantages: it would certainly have highlighted the very different uses to which the book has been put, and at the same time enabled the reader to focus on one set of texts at a time. Another possible method with distinct advantages would have been to approach the material from the perspective of one academic discipline at a time: Isaiah in theology, hymnology, music, art history, literature, politics and the like.

But it soon became clear that in many cases a correlation between interpretation and historical context could be established which was sufficiently close to make it possible to build the material into a broadly historical framework, while retaining, as Jaroslav Pelikan has done in *Jesus through the Centuries*, the advantages of a thematic approach. Thus there are good reasons for devoting a large section of one chapter on the Mediaeval Period to the cult of the Virgin Mary, and another to Passion Iconography. Similarly much of chapter 12 on the contemporary situation is concerned with 'Justice and Peace'. But this does not mean that discussion of these topics is limited to those three chapters.

In some cases it is appropriate to carry the story of a particular image or interpretation through to its conclusion even though it means breaking out of the historical sequence. For example, although the roots of antisemitism go back to the early Church and erupt catastrophically during the Reformation and in the twentieth century, it was elements in the mediaeval Church that drove the antisemitic interpretation of Isaiah just about as far as it would go, and therefore that is the context in which it is given extended coverage. Similarly it is possible to trace the beginnings of historical criticism to Andrew of St Victor (died 1175) as Beryl Smalley does in her magisterial *Study of the Bible in the Middle Ages*, but chapter 10 on modern scholarship is clearly where it belongs. The condemnation of idolatry and the emphasis on scripture as the 'Word of God' can obviously be documented in many different periods, but they are undoubtedly special features of the reformers' interpretations of Isaiah and are accordingly treated there. Conversely, a few early uses of the 'peaceable kingdom' image and 'swords into ploughshares' are referred to in the discussion of contemporary Christianity in chapter 12.

The one apparent exception is chapter 9 on 'Isaiah in Literature and Music'. This is due to the fact that from the eighteenth century on 'Isaiah outside the Church', in literature and music, becomes as interesting as 'Isaiah in the Church'. Compositions inspired by passages from Isaiah are read, studied, recited, performed and appreciated, whatever the Christian convictions or affiliations the writers and composers may have had, by people who have few or none. This separates Milton's use of chapter 14 in *Paradise Lost*, Byron's *Sennacherib*, Handel's *Messiah*, Brahms' *German Requiem* and other literary and musical compositions that are part of modern secular culture, from strictly religious literature. Thus some examples from mediaeval Church music are discussed in chapter 4 in connection with the cult of the Virgin Mary, Luther's hymns in chapter 7 on the Reformation period, and the remarkable outburst of vernacular compositions based on Isaiah since the Second Vatican Council, in chapter 12. But this still leaves enough material to warrant a special chapter on the less exclusively religious uses of Isaiah in music and literature. Again there are plenty of cross-references which it is hoped will make for coherence and continuity.

Secondly, the approach is '*text-led*'. By focussing on a single book, we can get some idea of the sheer variety of interpretations documented for the same text, and the complex political, social, intellectual and theological factors involved. The primary questions throughout are 'How is the text of Isaiah used in such and such a context?', 'How was this word or phrase understood?' and 'What are the texts that were of particular significance – theological, aesthetic, political, ethical – to this or that writer or preacher or composer or artist?' The text in question, as has been pointed out already, is often the text of the Latin Vulgate or Luther's German Bible or the various official English versions, rather than the original Hebrew (which has seldom had a direct influence upon the Church), although, as we shall see, its relationship to the 'original text' is frequently interesting and relevant, and has to be discussed. But the text is always central to the discussion, and not merely referred to in the footnotes.

A third methodological decision was to omit, for the most part, any extended treatment of the theoretical question as to how a particular meaning was arrived at, whether by typology or allegory or other traditional exegetical method, or by some far-fetched play on words or even free association. Clearly this is an important issue in some cases, as for example where a text is deliberately altered to obtain a particular meaning. A blatant case of this will be discussed in connexion with antisemitic uses of Isaiah, where the personal pronouns are changed to make the application of a piece of prophetic invective to a particular audience, the Jews in this instance, more personal and confrontational. But more often than not, the technicalities of how a particular meaning was arrived at can be relegated to a footnote or simply ignored. The emphasis here will always be on how people have understood a text, and on when and where it has been used in the history of the Church.

This brings us to another guiding principle which distinguishes the present project from most other general studies in the history of interpretation. It is to have an *empirical* dimension. They devote a good deal of space to theoretical questions concerning the aims and methods of interpretation used in each period, and tend to measure 'progress' in exegetical method against the yardstick of modern historical criticism. For many this is what 'the history of interpretation' consists of. One of the most recent extended studies of the subject, the article on 'History of Interpretation' in the new *Anchor Bible Dictionary*, is almost exclusively concerned with the scholars and the theoretical.[67] The approach adopted here, by contrast, is more empirical insofar as we shall always keep the text and the people using it at the centre of attention. We shall throughout be motivated by the question of what people actually do with this text in the various Christian communities and contexts, past and present, where it has operated, and space will be made for what the social scientists call 'anecdotal material'.

It was a Baptist minister, for example, that first told me that Isaiah is known as 'the Fifth Gospel'. He had been brought up on this perception of Isaiah: 'if the other four ever get lost,' he said, 'it would not matter so long as we still have Isaiah.' Another evangelical Christian described the influence of Isaiah on his life, in terms of having had a 'special relationship with the prophet' since his student days. Chapter 8 on 'the Evangelical Tradition' owes much to comments like these, both written and oral. The same chapter focusses on the popularity among missionaries to India of Isaiah 60:9 with its reference to great ships bringing 'your sons from afar, their silver and gold with them', and of 49:12 ('... and these from the land

---

[67] Rogerson, 'Interpretation, History of'.

of Sinim') in the writings of nineteenth-century missionaries to China.

A Catholic student expressed her amazement when she found out that so many of her favourite hymns are taken almost word for word from the *Revised Standard Version* of Isaiah 40–66. Her impression is confirmed by the statistical fact, to be discussed in chapter 12, that a disproportionate number of scriptural references at the end of a popular collection of hymns, much used by English-speaking Catholics today, come from Isaiah, and that many of the hymns based on Isaiah were composed by Catholic priests in the 1970s and 1980s, in the aftermath of the Second Vatican Council. One of the most striking examples discussed in chapter 6 on 'Isaiah and the Jews' was given to me by an Israeli who told me how hurt and offended he had been by the antisemitic use of Isaiah 65:2–3, inscribed in Hebrew on the façade of a church in Rome.

This is a study that sets out to be primarily *descriptive*. We must first collect as much of the data as we can and familiarize ourselves with them, before 'comparative interpretation' (to use Clines' term[68]) can begin and value-judgements be introduced. What modern scholars say a text means, what the Church's official interpretation is, what it means to Milton or Handel or Blake or Brahms or Barth or Martin Luther or José Porfirio Miranda, and how ordinary people use it or understand it, these are all part of the data, and all, theoretically at least, of equal interest and importance to the historian of interpretation.

The task of locating and identifying representative examples in all the relevant literature would seem at first sight to be an insuperable problem. Maximum use can be made of the increasing number of studies and reference works specifically devoted to the history of interpretation, some already referred to, such as Pelikan, *Jesus through the Centuries*, Frerichs, ed., *The Bible and Bibles in America* (1988), Steinmetz, ed., *The Bible in the Sixteenth Century* (1990), Beuken and others, edd. *The Bible and its Readers* (1991), Sugirtharajah, ed., *Voices from the Margin: Interpreting the Bible in the Third World* (1991), Jeffrey, *A Dictionary of Biblical Tradition in English Literature* (1992) and Atwan and Wieder, edd., *Chapters into Verse. Poetry in English Inspired by the Bible* (1993). These can be useful both bibliographically and methodologically. Careful use can be made of the indexes of biblical references

---

[68]   Clines, *What does Eve do to Help?*, pp. 20–1.

appended to much of the relevant literature, especially older publications. Editions of Jerome, Augustine, Luther, Milton and the like come into this category, as do collections of survey essays such as those just listed and countless other significant or representative works such as H. Maccoby, *Judaism on Trial. Jewish-Christian Disputations in the Middle Ages* and J.P. Miranda, *Marx and the Bible*. Many of the major reference works like the *Cambridge History of the Bible* and G. Schiller, *Iconography of Christian Art* have indexes of scriptural references too, as well as valuable bibliographies. Some lectionaries and hymnbooks also have indexes of scriptural references. Part of the history of how a particular verse or passage is used can be traced quite easily in this way, while in many cases it becomes statistically very clear from even a cursory glance at such indexes which verses have been important in which contexts. It is a very rough and ready method, and little help at all in the case of much of the literature, not to mention the special problems involved in identifying Isaiah's influence in popular religion, the media, place-names and the like. But it is a start.

We have had to be *selective*. For each context – funeral orations, cathedral architecture, hymn-books, peace and war, party politics and the like – a few representative examples have been selected for detailed analysis, while as many other similar cases as I have been able to collect are referred to more briefly either in the main discussion or in the notes. Often there are also cross-references to other chapters where the same text is used in a different way, or where under similar conditions other texts have been used in the same way. Fuller discussion of this important issue must remain till the end. For the moment we shall work on the assumption that our main criterion is historical importance, although, since the author is human, other principles of selection inevitably operate as well. My own enthusiasms, prejudices and preferences as between one interpretation and another will no doubt occasionally surface. It will already have become obvious, for instance, that I do not share the bias which exists among many biblical scholars towards discovering – or, if that proves impossible, reconstructing – the original meaning of a text, and claiming for it something close to divine authority. In the long history of biblical interpretation this bias must take its place alongside the beliefs and presuppositions of the patristic period, the mediaeval Church, the Reformation, rationalism, feminism, Marxism and so on. It seems to me that, provided no special authority is claimed for another, later meaning, one which is manifestly not the original one or one that is clearly influenced by the bias of its author, we are entirely free to declare that this later meaning is more effective in its context, or more beautiful, or more historically significant, or indeed ethically more acceptable than the original.[69] In the light of what we discover, we are at liberty to challenge received tradition as to what the text can or should mean, applying the same theological, ethical and aesthetic criteria as are used to evaluate any other religious texts.

[69] Cf. Fiorenza, 'Ethical presuppositions'. See further, pp. 247–250.

CHAPTER 2

Isaiah and Christian origins

Isaiah's unique position in the Church goes right back to the beginning. He is far more often quoted or alluded to in the Gospels, Acts, Paul and Revelation than any other part of scripture (with the possible exception of Psalms). One estimate gives the total number of passages in which Isaiah 'seems obviously referred to' as 250.[1] Nor is it simply a matter of numbers: several of the Isaiah quotations, such as those concerning a mission to the gentiles (e.g. 9:1–2; 11:10; 42:6; 49:6) and a suffering messiah (53), seem to have played a decisive part in the formulation of early Christian tradition.[2] The range of contexts and subjects for which the earliest Christian writers found a relevant quotation from Isaiah is astonishing: they include the nativity, John the Baptist, the healing miracles, the parables, the passion, the resurrection, prayer, preaching, mission, salvation, forgiveness, the temple, faith and the last judgement.

He is frequently mentioned by name, a fact which strikingly distinguishes him from Jeremiah and the other 'writing prophets' and puts him in the company of Moses, Elijah and David. His name occurs over twenty times, including thirteen in the Gospels (six of them in Matthew) and five in Paul.[3] As a further example of how he was held in special reverence by the earliest Christian writers and preachers, Paul introduces two of his quotations from Isaiah in such a way as to make us think of the prophet's feelings as he spoke: 'Isaiah cried out ...' (Rom.9:27); 'Isaiah is so bold as to say ...' (10:20).[4]

[1] 'General remarks on Isaiah' in *The Holy Bible with ... Analytical Notes appended to each Book* (*The Analytical Bible*), Thomas Arnold, London, 1845, p. 474.
[2] Cf. Lindars, *New Testament Apologetic*, p. 77; Moo, *Old Testament in the Gospel Passion Narratives*, pp. 79–172; Dodd, *According to the Scriptures*, pp. 88–105.
[3] Matth.3:3; 4:14; 8:17; 12:17; 13:14; 15:7; Mark 7:6; Luke 3:4; 4:17; John 1:23; 12:38, 39, 41; Rom.9:27,29; 10:16,20; 15:41. His name appears three times in Acts as well (8:28,30; 28:25).
[4] Cf. Barrett, 'The interpretation of the Old Testament in the New', p. 391.

A glance at works like C.H. Dodd, *According to the Scriptures* (1952), B. Lindars, *New Testament Apologetic* (1961), R. Longenecker, *Biblical Exegesis in the Apostolic Period* (1975), A.T. Hanson, *The Living Utterances of God. The New Testament Exegesis of the Old* (1983) and Douglas Moo, *The Old Testament in the Gospel Passion Narratives* (1983), will show very clearly just how prominent Isaiah is in every part of the discussion of 'New Testament exegesis of the Old'. In a study of early Christian uses of the Old Testament, John Rogerson points out that, in the earliest Christian accounts of the life of Jesus, 'at almost every point his life had fulfilled one scripture or another'. Of his nine examples, all from Matthew, six are from Isaiah.[5] Not infrequently writers comment on this in passing,[6] but little attention has been paid to the specific question of whether Isaiah can be said to have had any special role to play at the earliest stage in the origin and development of Christian tradition, and if so what precisely it was.

This is partly because modern scholars have a tendency to concentrate on form and method to the exclusion of content. Longenecker's method, for instance, is to list the quotations, and then discuss such questions as the variety of introductory formulae, whether the quotations are from the Hebrew original or a Greek or Aramaic version, whether the treatment of the scriptural quotation is 'literalist' or 'midrashic', and the like. He does not even note in passing that over half of the quotations from the Prophets which he attributes to Jesus himself come from Isaiah.[7] The same applies to his examination of Christian uses of the Prophets in Acts[8] and to the evangelists' use of scripture,[9] where once again Isaiah takes pride of place. In the case of Paul, no less than twenty-seven of his thirty-seven quotations from the Prophets are from Isaiah.[10] A significantly high proportion of Dodd's 'primary sources of testimonies' used by the early Church come from Isaiah.[11] But like Longenecker, he makes no comment on this.

We must also remember that throughout the history of Christian uses of Isaiah down to the nineteenth century, there was only one

[5]   Rogerson and others, edd., *Study and Use of the Bible*, p. 5.
[6]   E.g. R. B. Y. Scott, 'Isaiah, Book of', p. 654; Hanson, *Living Utterances*, p. 23; cf. p.34; Moo, *Old Testament in the Gospel Passion Narratives*, p. 356; Seccombe, 'Luke and Isaiah'; Young, 'Isaiah and the Fourth Gospel'.
[7]   *Biblical Exegesis*, pp. 57–9.
[8]   *Biblical Exegesis*, pp. 86f.
[9]   *Biblical Exegesis*, pp. 134f.
[10] *Biblical Exegesis*, pp. 108–11.
[11] Dodd, *According to the Scriptures*, pp. 60–110.

Isaiah, and that it can be misleading to talk, as many modern writers do, about Paul's use of 'Deutero-Isaiah' or 'the Servant Songs' or the 'Isaiah Apocalypse' or the like. On the contrary, if we have good evidence that an ancient author or preacher was fundamentally influenced by a particular chapter or passage, Jesus by 53, Paul by 49:1–13 or the like, this means that anything else Isaiah said – in the whole book that bears his name – was probably read or remembered or interpreted in that light, and given special significance.

It could be that it was Jesus himself who was responsible for the prominence of Isaiah in early Christianity. Of course it is impossible to know for sure how many of the Isaiah quotations and allusions in the Gospels belong to the *ipsissima verba* of Jesus, especially in the case of such widely used passages as Isaiah 53. Longenecker lists eleven.[12] Douglas Moo attributes twelve of the eighteen references to Isaiah in the Gospel Passion texts to Jesus himself.[13] But it does seem highly probable, as has sometimes been suggested, that Chapter 53 in particular had a significant influence on his mind, and that he believed 'it was his destiny to fulfil the deep insights of this prophecy'.[14] The frequency of quotations from or allusions to the Book of Isaiah in the Gospels and elsewhere in the earliest Christian writings makes it likely that much of the rest of the book was familiar to Jesus too.

Bruce Chilton's detailed comparison of Jesus' sayings and the influential Jewish Aramaic translation of Isaiah known as the Targum concludes that both Jesus and the Targum draw on the same exegetical tradition,[15] and that the same 'vital, biblically based faith ... fed both primitive Christianity and rabbinic Judaism'.[16] When Jesus invokes passages like Isaiah 6:9–10 (Mark 4:12), 50:11 (Matth. 26:52) and 66:24 (Mark 9:47f.), he 'plays on the familiarity of his semi-literate hearers with such traditions ...'.[17] Isaiah seems always to have had a prominent place in Jewish Bible use, in all varieties of Judaism, so that Jews then as now, including Jesus, would be familiar with most of the quotations used by the early Christian writers and preachers. He takes pride of place among the Prophets in

---

[12] *Biblical Exegesis*, pp.57–9.
[13] *The Old Testament in the Gospel Passion Narratives*, pp. 162–4.
[14] Lindars, *New Testament Apologetic*, pp. 77–8; cf. Hanson, *Living Utterances*, pp. 27–32. Others believe the evidence for this is not strong enough: Hooker, *Jesus and the Servant*, p. 149.
[15] Cf. Chilton, *A Galilean Rabbi* (1984).
[16] Chilton, *A Galilean Rabbi*, p. 56.
[17] Chilton, *A Galilean Rabbi*, pp. 142–3.

the earliest reference to a 'canon' of scripture in the Book of Ecclesiasticus (Sirach) (c.180 BCE). In the long hymn 'in praise of famous men' (44–50), Isaiah receives more extended treatment than any other prophet except Elijah (49:17–25). His role in the destruction of Sennacherib, and the miracles he performed in the days of Hezekiah, are dramatically recounted: 'in his days the sun went backward and he lengthened the life of the king. By the spirit of might he saw the last things, and he comforted those who mourned in Zion. He revealed what was to occur in the end of time, and the hidden things before they came to pass.' Jeremiah, Ezekiel and the Twelve are allotted only one verse apiece. Isaiah is acclaimed as the one who 'was great and faithful in his vision' (44:22).

The Book of Isaiah is also prominent among the Dead Sea Scrolls.[18] The scriptural texts from Qumran contain a very high proportion from the Book of Isaiah, including the two famous Isaiah scrolls. One of these, the beautiful Isaiah Scroll A, familiar to visitors to the Shrine of the Book in Jerusalem, consists of seventeen strips of leather stitched together into a scroll almost seven-and-a-half metres long, and is the oldest complete biblical manuscript in existence.[19] There are fragments of four Isaiah commentaries,[20] an eschatological midrash on 61:1 ('to proclaim liberty to the captives ...') known to modern scholars as 'The heavenly prince Melchizedek',[21] and a work entitled *Tanḥumim* 'Consolations' beginning with a quotation from Isaiah 40 ('Comfort, comfort my people ...').[22] Other texts from Isaiah which were important for the Qumran sect include 40:3 ('Prepare in the wilderness ...') and 7:17, given highly distinctive sectarian interpretations in the Community Rule and the Damascus Rule respectively.[23]

In synagogue worship, throughout the ancient world, Isaiah was almost certainly much used. Although we know virtually nothing about synagogue lectionaries current in the time of Jesus, it is probable that Isaiah furnished many of the *haftaroth* or weekly readings from the Prophets that accompanied the Torah readings in

---

[18] Cf. Vermes, *The Dead Sea Scrolls*, pp. 201–2; Scott, *EB* 12 p. 654 'a favourite of the Qumran sect'.

[19] *The Dead Sea Scrolls of St Mark's Monastery*, ed. M. Burrows with the assistance of J. C. Trever and W. H. Brownlee (New Haven 1950), pp. xiii–xviii.

[20] 4QpIsaᵃ; 4QpIsaᵇ; 4QpIsaᶜ; 4QpIsaᵈ: cf. Vermes, *Dead Sea Scrolls in English*, pp. 267–70.

[21] 11Q Melch: see Vermes, *Dead Sea Scrolls in English*, pp. 300–1.

[22] 4Q 176: see Vermes, *Dead Sea Scrolls in English*, p. 302.

[23] 1QS VIII.12–16; CD VII,10–13; XIII.24–XIV.1: see Vermes, *Dead Sea Scrolls in English*, pp. 73, 88 and 98.

sabbath worship. According to Luke 4:17, it was a reading from Isaiah that Jesus preached on in the synagogue at Nazareth, although of course that does not prove whether it was the prescribed *haftarah* for the day or not.[24] What we do know is that in most extant Jewish lectionaries, which date from the early Middle Ages down to the present day, a very large proportion of the *haftaroth* (often about half) come from Isaiah.[25] They include the 'Consolation' readings from chapters 40–61, which were prescribed to be read on the seven sabbaths following the Fast of the Ninth of Ab. This series was almost certainly compiled in ancient times and reflects a situation that obtained many centuries earlier than our earliest evidence.[26] We can therefore be reasonably sure that, like most Jews then and now, Jesus and his followers would be specially familiar with the Book of Isaiah.

We can perhaps go further and suggest that, like most Jews then and now, they would also be specially familiar with those sections of Isaiah that were in the lectionary. With the well-known exception of chapter 52:13–53:12, which is rarely cited in the rabbinic literature and may at some stage have been deliberately omitted from the Jewish lectionary because of its christological asociations,[27] there is a remarkably close match between the Isaiah quotations in Table 1. and the list of *haftaroth* given, for example, in the *Jewish Encyclopedia*.[28] It may also be significant that well over two thirds of the Isaiah quotations in the Gospels, Paul's letters and Revelation come from chapters 40–61, 'the consolation chapters', which are so well represented in the lectionary (see table 1).

However that may be, it seems clear that Isaiah was there from the start and also that many of the Isaiah passages which are so familiar in the Christian context acquired their importance and popularity, not directly from the Book of Isaiah itself, but from the use made of them by Jesus himself or the first Christian writers and preachers. This is particularly true in the case of the Book of Revelation, which is heavily dependent on Isaiah for its language and imagery. Among the twenty or so Isaiah quotations, that found their way, in one form or another, into mainstream Christian tradition by way of the Book

24   Elbogen, *Jewish Liturgy*, p. 144.
25   Cf. Luke 4:17 and Acts 13:15: A. Buechler, 'Haftarah' in *JE* VI, pp. 135–7; Schürer, *History*, II, pp. 450–2.
26   See Elbogen, *Jewish Liturgy*, pp. 145, 425–6.
27   Cf. Montefiore and Loewe, *Rabbinic Anthology*, p. 544.
28   *JE* Vol. 6, pp. 136f.

Table 1. *Isaiah in the Gospels, Acts and Letters*

Isaiah	Matth.	Mark	Luke	John	Acts	Rom.	1Cor.	Eph.	Heb.	1P
1:9						Rom. 9				
5:1	Matth. 21*	Mark 12*	Luke 20*							
6:9–10	Matth. 13	Mark 4	Luke 8	John 12	Acts 28					
7:14	Matth. 1									
8:12–13										1P 3*
8:14			Luke *			Rom. 9*				1P 2*
8:17–18									Heb. 2	
9:1–2	Matth. 4									
9:7			Luke 1*							
10:22–3				John 12*		Rom. 9				
11:1	Matth. 2*					Rom. 15				
11:2										1P 4
11:5								Eph. 6		
11:10						Rom. 15				
12:3				John 7*						
13:10	Matth. 24*	Mark 13*								
22:13							1Cor. 15			
25:8							1Cor. 15			
27:13	Matth. 24*									
28:11							1Cor. 14			
28:12							1Cor. 14			
28:16						Rom. 9; 10				1P 2
29:10						Rom. 11				
29:13	Matth. 15	Mark 7								
29:14							1Cor. 1			
29:18	Matth. 11*									
35:3									Heb. 12	
35:5f.	Matth. 11*		Luke 7*							

	Matth.	Mark	Luke	John	Acts	Rom.	1Cor.	2Cor.	Phil.	1P
40:3	Matth. 3	Mark 1	Luke 3	John 1						
40:4—5			Luke 3							
40:6—8										1P 1
40:8		Mark 13								
40:9				John 12*						
40:13						Rom. 11	1Cor. 2			
41:8—9			Luke 1*							
42:1—4	Matth. 12									
42:6	Matth. 4		Luke 2*							
42:7										
43:19				John 7*						
44:3				John 7*						
45:9						Rom. 9*				
45:23						Rom. 14			Phil. 2*	
49:6					Acts 13					
49:8								2Cor. 6		
50:6	Matth. 26*									
51:6	Matth. 24*									
52:5						Rom. 2				
52:7						Rom. 10				
52:10			Luke 2*							
52:11								2Cor. 6		
52:15						Rom. 15				
53:1				John 12		Rom. 10				
53:3	Matth. 2*		Luke 24*							
53:4	Matth. 8									
53:5										1P 2
53:7—8					Acts 8					
53:9										1P 2
53:12		Mark 15	Luke 22							

Table 1 (*contd*)

	Matth.	Mark	Luke	John	Acts	Rom.	1Cor.	Eph.	Gal.	2P
54:1									Gal. 4	
54:13			Luke 23*							
55:1										
55:3				John 6						
56:7	Matth. 21	Mark 11	Luke 19	John 7*	Acts 13					
57:15	Matth. 5*									
58:6			Luke 4							
58:11										
59:7–8				John 7*		Rom. 3				
59:17	Matth. 8*							Eph. 6*		
59:19			Luke 13*							
59:20–21						Rom. 11				
60:6	Matth. 2*									
61:1–2	Matth. 11*		Luke 4							
62:11	Matth. 21									
64:4							1Cor. 2*			
65:1–2						Rom. 10				
65:17					Acts 7					
66:1–2	Matth. 5*									
66:22										2P 3
66:24		Mark 9								2P 3

of Revelation, the following is a selection of the most familiar: 'Holy, Holy, Holy, is the Lord of hosts' (6:3; cf. Rev.4:8); 'The key of the house of David' (22:22; cf. Rev.3:7); 'The skies shall roll up like a scroll' (34:4; cf. Rev.6:14); 'I am the first and the last' (44:6; cf. Rev.1:17; 22:13); 'Ho, every one that thirsts' (55:1; cf. Rev.21:6; 22:17); 'Your gates shall be open continually' (60:11; cf. Rev.21:25); 'The sun shall be no more your light by day' (60:19; cf. Rev.21:23; 22:5); 'I have trodden the winepress alone' (63:3; cf. Rev.19:15); 'Behold, I create new heavens and a new earth' (65:17; cf. Rev.21:1).

A recent study of the subject finds fifty 'certain and probable' allusions to Isaiah in Revelation, and concludes that the author appears to have been especially influenced by Isaiah in the key areas of 'visionary experience and language' (Isa.6:1–4), christological titles and descriptions (11:4,10; 22:22; 44:6; 65:15), and eschatology (e.g. 34:4; 55:1; 60:1–3, 5, 11, 19).[29] The use of Isaiah in Revelation requires special treatment beyond the scope of the present study. This brief mention merely serves to illustrate further the ubiquity of Isaiah at this early stage in the history of Christianity, and to underline the fact that many of the most familiar themes and quotations from the 'Fifth Gospel' owe that familiarity to their appearance already in early Christian scripture as much as to the Church's use of the original Book of Isaiah. They had already received their Christian meaning, in other words, almost before the Church came into existence.

So our story of 'Isaiah in the Church' begins with its unique prominence among the scriptural quotations in the Gospels, Paul and Acts, and we shall leave to the specialists the questions involved in unravelling the obscure processes which lie behind this phenomenon. The problem of identifying scriptural quotations and allusions is a notoriously difficult one, not least because of the uncertainty about what languages are involved. In many cases we simply do not know whether the writer is conversant with the original Hebrew, or relying on a Greek or Aramaic version. We also do not always know whether the Aramaic, Greek or Hebrew text being used is the same as the one to which we have access today. For present purposes I have simply used the cross-references given in many Bibles, especially the Common Bible (*RSV*) and the Nestlé-Aland edition of the Greek New Testament, compared with Longenecker's lists and Hanson's

---

[29] Fekkes, *Isaiah and Prophetic Traditions in the Book of Revelation*, pp. 279–82.

more recent discussion. It is also impossible to know whether the
evangelists had copies of Isaiah before them as they wrote, or
whether they worked from memory. 'The book of the prophet Isaiah'
is twice mentioned specifically in Luke's Gospel (3:4; 4:17ff.), and it
has been argued that Luke had a copy of Isaiah of his own or readily
available.[30] Alternatively it may be that first-century writers made
use of collections of *testimonia* or *florilegia*, 'anthologies' like those
discovered at Qumran, containing in convenient form scriptural
quotations on particular topics such as the Messiah or the Temple.
Another theory, which stresses awareness of the context from which
the quotations were taken, is that they made use of selected blocks of
scripture, considered to be of special significance.[31]

In the case of Isaiah, these would obviously have to include at least
chapters 6–9, 28–29, 42–44 and 52–53.[32] But the first thing that
strikes one is the sheer number and variety of texts from the whole
book of Isaiah that appear to be familiar to early Christian writers.
Around one hundred verses from forty-five of the sixty-six chapters of
Isaiah are either quoted directly or clearly alluded to, mainly in the
Gospels (forty-six), Paul (thirty) and Revelation (thirty). They range
from single phrases or verses, such as 7:14 in Matthew 1:23, to longer
passages such as 42:1–4 in Matthew 12 or 40:3–5 in Luke 3, and cover
all manner of topics from healing miracles (53:4 in Matth. 8:17) and
preaching good news to the poor (61:1 in Luke 4), to hypocrisy (29:13
in Matth.15:8–9) and hell-fire (66:24 in Mark 9:48). When we consider
that eight of the twenty-one chapters not quoted or alluded to at all
are 'Oracles against the foreign nations' (14–21), passages little used
throughout the history of interpretation of Isaiah, and four are in
narrative prose recounting stories about Sennacherib and Hezekiah
(36–39), whose relevance to Christian origins is equally tenuous, then
we must surely acknowledge that virtually the whole book as
interpreted by Christians down to the present, not just selections,
already played a part in the emergence of the new religion.

The number of passages informed or inspired by Isaiah is thus so
great that it should be possible to deduce something about the beliefs
of early Christian preachers and writers from their selection and
interpretation. First, let us consider which passages of Isaiah, promi-

---

[30]   Holtz, *Untersuchungen*, p. 41; cf. Seccombe, 'Luke and Isaiah', p. 252.
[31]   Dodd, *According to the Scriptures*, pp. 126ff; cf. Longenecker, *Biblical Exegesis*, p.89–92;
       Seccombe, 'Luke and Isaiah', p. 259.
[32]   Cf. Dodd, *According to the Scriptures*, pp. 107f. and Table 1.

nent in later periods in the history of Christianity, are conspicuous by their absence or barely represented in this earliest list. Two of the most popular – 7:14 ('A virgin will conceive ...') and 11:1 ('a rod out of the stem of Jesse ...') – occur only once, the latter in a somewhat veiled allusion (Matt.1:23; 2:23[33]), while other passages used in later times in connection with the ancestry of Christ (e.g. 16:1) and the virginity of his Mother (e.g. 45:8; 53:3) do not appear at all.[34] This nicely reflects the situation at an early stage in the development of Christian doctrine, before the patristic and mediaeval preoccupation with the nativity and the Virgin Birth. The same applies to the lack of interest in several other familiar texts, associated with the sophisticated christology of later times (e.g.9:6; 53:8), the doctrine of the Trinity (40:12), monotheism (45:5, 6, 14, 21,22) and the eucharist (6:7).[35]

Several of what we would today consider to be among the best-known quotations from Isaiah do not appear at all. These include the 'swords into ploughshares' passage (2:1–4), the 'wolf and the lamb' (11:6–9 and 65:25) and other future visions of peace and justice (e.g. 32:1ff.,16f).[36] This is also true, as one would expect, of those passages given prominence in recent times by feminist interpreters, such as those where female images are used of God (e.g. 42:14; 49:15; 66:13) and Lilith is mentioned (34:14).[37]

More striking is the absence of some of the passages which soon led to the view widely held from the patristic period on, that Isaiah was 'more evangelist than a prophet',[38] passages eventually to become, through liturgical use, especially in Advent – and in some cases through Handel's *Messiah* as well – widely used in the Church. The absence of 11:1–2 has already been remarked upon. 'Comfort ye, comfort ye my people' (40:1) is not there, nor is 'Arise, shine; for thy light is come' from 60:1. The 'good shepherd' in 40:11 is not there, and 'the ox and the ass' of 1:3 have not yet taken up their positions in the nativity scene either.

But undoubtedly the most surprising absentee from such a huge selection of Isaianic material cited or alluded to in the earliest Christian scriptures, is 9:1–7 (Hebrew 8:23–9:6), which contains the verse announcing the birth of the Messiah, in the past tense, as if he

---

[33] 'Nazarene' may refer to the word 'branch' (Hebrew *netzer*), the second part of Isaiah 11:1: see below pp. 76ff.
[34] See below, pp. 69–82. [35] See below, pp.51f. [36] See below, pp. 231ff.
[37] See below, pp. 206–219. [38] See below, pp.49f.

had already come: 'for to us a child is born ...' (verse 6). The first
two verses of the passage which give the geographical location of the
places around Galilee where 'the people who walked in darkness'
first saw the light, are quoted verbatim in Matthew 4:15–16, but as
we shall see below this is an exception for apologetic reasons. The
absence of the subsequent verses – 'For to us a child is born ... he
shall be called Wonderful Counsellor, Mighty God, Everlasting
Father, Prince of Peace' – from such a huge sample of Isaiah
quotations, is surprising. Is it merely an accident? Or does the
omission of this familiar messianic passage tell us something about
the exegetical, theological or political aims and interests of early
Christians?

When we look at what *is* there, we can perhaps gain some idea as
to why such passages so familiar from later Christian tradition had
no part to play in the beginning. Isaiah does play an important part
in the story of Christ's life and work in the Gospels, but there is a
distinctive emphasis in the selection of texts which is different from
that of later periods. In place of the later concern to root details of
the life, death and resurrection of Christ in Isaiah, and especially of
his person and his claim to be the Messiah,[39] it is clear that the
earliest Christian interpreters of Isaiah used him first and foremost to
authorize their mission to the gentiles. The positive side of this
focusses on 'universalistic' passages like 42:6 and 49:6, where the
phrase 'a light to the Gentiles' first appears. A darker, negative side
finds in Isaiah's recurring condemnation of his people's blindness (cf.
6:9–10; 29:13) scriptural authority for what was to develop into the
demonizing antisemitism of later Church history. Let us look at these
two aspects of early Christian uses of Isaiah in turn.

We begin with Paul's use of two verses, both more familiar from
other contexts, in a discussion of his mission to the gentiles in
Romans 15. The 'root of Jesse' image is cited from 11:10, rather than
11:1, and has nothing to do with the ancestry of Jesus or the sevenfold
gifts of the spirit which were to be so prominent in mediaeval
Christian iconography:[40]

For I tell you that Christ became a servant to the circumcised to show
God's truthfulness ... in order that the gentiles might glorify God for his
mercy. As it is written, Therefore I will praise thee among the gentiles, and

[39] See chapter 3   [40] See below, pp. 74–80.

sing to thy name (Ps.18:49) ... and further Isaiah says, The root of Jesse shall come, he who rises to rule the gentiles; in him shall the gentiles hope.

Later in the same context he quotes from the beginning of the fourth 'Servant Song' (52:15), but again he is not concerned with what was later to become the main theme of this passage for Christian interpreters, namely the Suffering Messiah: 'They shall see who have never been told of him, and they shall understand who have never heard of him'. Paul is thinking here instead of his journeys 'from Jerusalem to Illyricum' (v.19) and his plans to visit Rome and Spain (v.24), to tell people who have never heard of the Jewish Messiah about Christ.

His use of 45:23 ('To me every knee shall bow ...') in the previous chapter (Rom.14:11; cf. Phil. 2:10f.), and of 65:1–2 ('I have been found by those who did not seek me ...') in 10:20–21, are two more examples of Paul's use of Isaiah's missionary concerns. Isaiah 57:19 was probably in the author's mind in Ephesians 2:12 and 17 (cf. Acts 2:39). Elsewhere Paul uses two passages from Isaiah about foreigners (28:1f.; 45:23) in a discussion of the effect glossolalia might have upon 'outsiders or unbelievers' (1 Cor.14:25).

Three of the Gospels refer to 56:6f ('my house of prayer'), in the context of Christ's assault on the money-changers and pigeon-sellers (Matt.21:13; Mk.11:17; Lk 19.46). This is a remarkable passage about how one day foreigners will come to worship in the Temple at Jerusalem, 'to love the name of the Lord and to be his servants'. Mark in particular, by continuing the quotation to include the words 'for all the nations', seems to show that he at least was aware of its original context in Isaiah.

The much-used phrase 'a light to the gentiles' from Isaiah 49:6 has already been mentioned. 'A light to lighten the gentiles' in the last line of the aged Simeon's hymn (Luke 2:29–32), which as the *Nunc Dimittis* became one of the best-loved Christian hymns, was no doubt inspired by it. There are several indications that Isaiah 49 as a whole was fundamental to the thought of Paul.[41] Like the 'servant of the Lord' in Isaiah 49, he was called 'from the womb', that is to say, 'set apart before he was born' (Gal.1:15; cf. Isa.49:1). 'I have laboured in vain ...' from Isaiah 49:4 lies behind one of Paul's favourite phrases (cf. Gal.2:2; 4:11; 1 Cor.15:58; Phil.2:16; 1 Thess.3:5). He cites 49:8 in 2 Cor.6:2. Verse 6 then, we can be sure, had special resonances for

---

[41] Cf. Lindars, *New Testament Apologetic*, pp. 223f.

Paul, with its 'light to the gentiles' theme and its implied criticism of a wholly inward-looking mission. According to Acts 13:47, the verse was used, with a polemical slant to which we shall return later, by Paul and Barnabas in the synagogue at Pisidian Antioch: 'I have set you to be a light for the gentiles, that you may bring salvation to the uttermost parts of the earth'. The phrase also occurs in Isaiah 42:6, and according to Acts 26:17–23 Paul uses both 'the light to the gentiles' from this verse and the mission to 'open the eyes that are blind and to bring out from the prison those who sit in darkness' from verse 7 in his speech before Agrippa. The link in Isaiah 42:6–7 and Acts 26 between the idea of evangelizing the gentiles, on the one hand, and bringing sight to the blind and liberty to the oppressed, on the other, proves that Luke's best-known quotation from Isaiah, 61:1–2, used by Jesus in the synagogue at Nazareth, should be interpreted in this way as well (Luke 4:16–30). The two illustrations cited by Jesus in his sermon on the text are both foreigners, a Phoenician widow and a Syrian leper, and it is clear from the context that he is speaking about the rejection of the Jews, as well as the liberation of the oppressed.

In the light of all this evidence, we may add one of the best-known examples, 9:1–2 (Heb.8:23–9:1), cited in Matthew 4:12–16 and possibly alluded to in Luke 1:79: 'Now when he heard that John had been arrested, he withdrew into Galilee ... that what was spoken by the prophet Isaiah might be fulfilled: The land of Zebulun and the land of Naphtali, toward the sea across the Jordan, Galilee of the Gentiles -the people who sat in darkness have seen a great light ...' 'Galilee of the Gentiles' gives us the clue to why only the first verse of the messianic hymn is quoted, and why it was important to associate it with the preceding, geographical verse. Isaiah is used by Matthew to prove that it was right for Jesus to begin his ministry among the 'gentiles', rather than among the Jews in Jerusalem. This Isaianic theme appears in three other places in Matthew as well. The gifts of the wise men from the east (2:11) recall those brought to Zion from Midian, Ephah and Sheba in Isaiah 60:6,[42] and perhaps 59:19 lies behind Jesus' prophecy that 'many will come from east and west and sit at the table with Abraham, Isaac and Jacob in the kingdom of heaven' (8:11; cf. Luke 13:29).

Matthew's longest quotation from Isaiah is a kind of 'set-piece',

---

[42] Cf. pp. 49–50.

somewhat detached from its immediate context and seemingly intended as a comprehensive commentary on Jesus' Messiahship (Matth. 12:18–21; cf. Isaiah 42:1–4). It begins: 'Behold, my servant whom I have chosen, my beloved with whom my soul is pleased. I will put my spirit upon him, and he will proclaim justice to the gentiles'. The first half of this verse is probably alluded to in the account of the baptism story (Matth.3:17; Mark 1:11; Luke 3:22; cf. Luke 9:35). But in view of what we have seen of other early Christian uses of Isaiah, we can have little doubt of the importance attached to the second half in this context. Jonah may have acquired the title 'prophet to the gentiles' from his mission to Nineveh and the Assyrians (cf. Luke 11). But, for the earliest Christian writers and preachers, this was clearly a major theme, if not the dominant one, in their perception of Isaiah too.

Finally it is remarkable how many modern scholars refer to the influence on Paul and the early Church of one of the most famous Isaiah passages of all, although it is not in fact ever explicitly cited. Isaiah 2:2–3 ('in the latter days the mountain of the Lord's house shall be established ... all nations shall stream to it ...') is used to give scriptural background for the belief that in the new age gentiles will convert to Judaism without being required to accept circumcision, the dietary laws and all the other parts of Mosaic legislation.[43] It is also cited as scriptural authority for beliefs about the rebuilding of the temple at Jerusalem.[44]

The other theme to which Isaiah had a significant contribution to make, from the earliest times, is the negative corollary to the 'light to the gentiles' theme, namely, condemnation of those who reject the Gospel, especially the Jews. As we shall see in subsequent chapters, this has been a sinister thread running through interpretations of Isaiah, in commentaries, sermons and tracts, as well as Christian art and architecture, throughout the history of the Church. A book that has brought comfort and hope to Jews in exile in all ages, down to and including the present century, has often been used by Christians as a vicious weapon to wound and damage them, and this is a use of Isaiah which can be documented right back to the Gospels and Acts.

In this context Isaiah 6:9–10 takes pride of place. It is a frightening

---

[43] E.g. Davies, *Paul and Rabbinic Judaism*, p. 60; Munck, *Christ and Israel*, pp. 11f.; Rowland, *Christian Origins*, pp. 119, 150; Sanders, *Jesus and Judaism*, p. 214; Sanders, *Paul*, p. 50; Ziesler, *Pauline Christianity*, pp. 143–4.

[44] E.g. Rowland, *Christian Origins*, p. 163; Sanders, *Jesus and Judaism*, p. 87.

passage, reminiscent of the story of how God repeatedly 'hardened Pharaoh's heart' (Exod.4:21; 7:3; 14:4; cf. 14:17). Isaiah's mission to his people is one of unmitigating rejection: 'Go, and say to this people: "Hear and hear, but do not understand; See and see, but do not perceive." Make the heart of this people fat and their ears heavy, and shut their eyes; lest they see with their eyes and hear with their ears and understand with their hearts, and turn and be healed.' Rejection is signalled by the dismissive phrase 'this people', repeated twice, in preference to the more usual 'my people' or 'your people' or 'Israel'. There is to be no hope of forgiveness, no opportunity to repent. The theological implication is that the obduracy which Isaiah will encounter among his people, is not directly their fault, but like Pharaoh's the result of divine intervention. The passage thus contains a truly terrible comment on the nature and character of God.

Early Jewish and Christian interpretations of this passage have been the subject of a recent monograph by Craig Evans.[45] It is quoted in all four Gospels as well as in Acts, and was probably in Paul's mind in Romans 11, 2 Corinthians 3 and elsewhere.[46] It had an important role to play in the evolution of early Christian theology, and Evans suggests that Jesus himself used it 'as a way of summarizing and explaining the negative response of many of his contemporaries toward his ministry'.[47] Evans' main concern throughout, however, is academic and theological, as his brief conclusion makes clear, and he does not in my view take seriously enough the effect which the use of this passage by early Christian writers and preachers must have had on their audiences and on Jewish-gentile relations, both at the time and in the subsequent history of Europe. He even devotes a short section to arguing that its use in Luke-Acts is not 'antisemitic', in the strictest use of the term.[48] He does admit that it is 'anti-Judaic' and 'offensive to modern people of faith'.[49] But if that is the case, then surely more attention should be given to this aspect of his subject.

It is well-known that in most of the early Jewish and Christian interpretations of Isaiah 6:9–10, including the Greek, Aramaic and Syriac translations of the passage on which they are often based, the

[45] Evans, *To See and Not Perceive* (1989).
[46] Barrett, *Commentary on 2 Corinthians*, p. 120; Lindars, *New Testament Apologetic*, pp. 159–63; Evans, *To See and Not Perceive*, p. 83.
[47] *To See and Not Perceive*, p. 106; others disagree: see Hanson, *Living Utterances*, p. 68.
[48] *To See and Not Perceive*, pp. 123–6.
[49] *To See and Not Perceive*, p. 126.

stern idea that God was responsible for his own people's obduracy, as he was for Pharaoh's, is softened. The Greek version (Septuagint), which is the one used in Matthew, Mark, Luke and Acts, is typical: 'Go and say to this people, 'You shall certainly hear, but never understand; and you shall certainly see, but never perceive.' For the heart of this people has grown dull, and their ears are heavy of hearing, and they have closed their eyes, so as not to see with their eyes, or hear with their ears, or understand with their heart, or repent that I may heal them.' In contrast to what is in the Hebrew text, given in translation above, the unreceptiveness of the people is their own fault entirely, not due to any divine 'hardening of the heart'. The prophet's message to them in verse 9 is a prediction, not a command, and verse 10 is a description of how things are and what the consequence will be, not an instruction to Isaiah to do everything he can to ensure that his people will have no chance to repent or be healed. This is how the passage is used in Matthew 13:10–17, where it 'explains' why some people are able to understand the meaning of Jesus' teaching while others are not. It is simply a fulfilment of prophecy, and the prophet Isaiah is mentioned by name.

In Mark and Luke the passage is briefly alluded to in a similar context, although without the specific mention of the prophet and with the added dimension of the secrecy theme: 'To you has been given the secret of the kingdom of God, but for those outside everything is in parables.' (Mark 4:11; cf. Luke 8:10) But the passage is still a fiercely judgemental one, even with the mitigating modifications present in the Septuagint. Jesus' opponents have been rejected, they are beyond redemption. It is not merely a question of whose fault it is, their own or God's, or a discussion of the purpose of parables or 'the secrets of the kingdom'. Isaiah's words are used to divide the sheep from the goats, those whose eyes are blessed for they see and whose ears are blessed for they hear (Matt. 13:16), from 'this people' whose blindness and obduracy have placed them beyond the pale. Evans and others do not give enough weight to Isaiah's highly charged and twice-repeated phrase 'this people', picked up by Matthew (cf. Acts 28:26f.). The passage inevitably drives a wedge between the followers of Jesus and the rest of the Jewish people.

In John 12:37–43, a passage in which Isaiah is mentioned by name three times, the original, unmitigated meaning of the prophet is preserved and even heightened. Again the question is why so many people, including the Pharisees (v.42) are not convinced by all the signs: how can they be so blind? The answer is that, as 'Isaiah again said', 'He has blinded their eyes and hardened their heart, lest they should see with their eyes and perceive with their heart, and turn for me to heal them'. It is significant that Isaiah's vision of the 'Lord sitting upon a throne, high and lifted up' (Isa.6:1) is referred to in the next verse to give special authority to this damning attack on the Pharisees. The same passage probably lies behind John 9:39 as well where the blindness of the Pharisees is contrasted with the new-found sight of a blind man.[50]

But it is at the end of the book of Acts that the passage is used in one of the bitterest scriptural attacks on the Jewish people (Acts 28:25–28). At the end of a debate with the Jewish community in Rome, in which some were convinced by his teaching and some were not, Paul quotes Isaiah 6:9–10 in full, in which 'this people' are rejected without hope of healing, and concludes: 'Let it be known to you therefore that this salvation of God has been sent to the gentiles: they will listen'. It is often suggested that Psalm 67:2 was the scriptural basis for this final statement; but in view of the evidence discussed above for early Christian uses of the 'light to the gentiles' theme in Isaiah 42:6 and 49:6 (cf. also their use of passages like 9:1–2; 11:10; 42:1; 45:14,23; 52:10; 56:6f.; 60:6; etc.), it could be that it too derives, albeit indirectly, from Isaiah. Isaiah 49:6 is actually used in a very similar context in Acts 13:44–52, as we saw. However that may be, the juxtaposition of 'this people' who are blind and deaf and beyond redemption, and 'the gentiles' who are from now on to be the chief recipients of divine salvation, is obvious and deliberate. The same contrast appears in the Pisidian Antioch story (Acts 13), 'a major turning point' in Acts,[51] where the Jews are represented as jealous, abusive and threatening (as well as blind and deaf), while the gentiles 'were glad and glorified the word of the Lord' (v.48) and 'the disciples were filled with joy and with the Holy Spirit' (v.52). The story which began in Jerusalem ends in Rome, and Isaiah is used to explain, but more important to authorize, both the turning point in chapter 13 and the climax in 28.

Another passage from Isaiah used in this aspect of early Christian apologetic, is the song of the vineyard in chapter 5. Again this is a very hard-hitting attack on 'the house of Israel and the men of Judah' (v.7), and is dramatically applied by Jesus, shortly before his death, to the rejection of the Jews: 'Therefore I tell you, the kingdom

[50] Evans, *To See and Not Perceive*, pp. 129ff.
[51] Evans, *To See and Not Perceive*, p. 127.

of God will be taken away from you and given to a nation producing fruit.' (Matth.21:43; cf. Mark 12:1–12; Luke 20:9–19). It is connected in the Lucan version of the story (and some manuscripts of Matthew 21:44) with another passage from Isaiah, which also had an important part to play in early Christian apologetic: 'And he will become a sanctuary and a stone of offence and a rock of stumbling to both houses of Israel, a trap and a snare to the inhabitants of Jerusalem. And many shall stumble thereon; they shall fall and be broken; they shall be snared and taken' (Isaiah 8:14–15; cf. Luke 20:18; Rom.9:32f; 1 Pet.2:8). This twist given by Luke to the vineyard parable brings us finally to Paul's use of Isaiah, in particular, those passages in which Isaiah attacks the Jewish people for their arrogance, unbelief and blindness. But here Paul's own writing is quite unlike the stories told about him in Acts 13 and 28: Jewish unbelief is a cause for 'great sorrow and unceasing anguish' (Rom.9:2) to him in his letters. In his letter to the Romans, where he discusses at length what for him was a heart-rending and perplexing tragedy, he quotes Isaiah, or alludes to him, no less than seventeen times. He mentions him by name three times, but not in the stern, gloating manner of Acts: 'The Holy Spirit was right when he said to your fathers through Isaiah the prophet ...' (Acts 28:25). Instead Isaiah '*cries out* (*krazo*) concerning Israel ...' (Rom.9:27; cf. 8:15; Gal.4:6)[52] and 'is even more daring when he says ...' (Rom.10:20 *REB*).

Nor is there the same emphasis on the joyful response of the gentiles at the words of Isaiah (Acts 13:48). In both Acts and the Letters, Isaiah is central to Paul's preaching, not so much to provide scriptural authority for its content, concerning, for example, the messiahship of Jesus, but to explain the aim and direction of his evangelism.[53] It is significant, incidentally, that Paul is the first of many famous Christians, from Jerome to Handel, to make use of Isaiah 52:7: 'How beautiful are the feet of those who preach good news!' (Rom.10:15; cf. Eph.6:15). We shall discuss Paul's use of 53:1 and 65:1 in Romans 10 in a moment, in connexion with his mission to the gentiles.

We come now to the Isaiah quotations which speak of the negative side of that mission. First there are two of Isaiah's 'remnant' passages, used in Romans 9:27–28 to describe the tragedy of the fate of 'the sons of Israel' as dramatically as possible: 'though the number

---

[52] The word *krazo* can be used of 'angry shouting' but in Paul it is associated with 'pleading'.
[53] Cf. Lindars, *New Testament Apologetic*, p. 247.

of the sons of Israel be as the sand of the sea, only a remnant of them
will be saved; for the Lord will execute his sentence upon them with
rigour and dispatch' (Isaiah 10:22–3). If the Lord of hosts had not left
us children, we would have fared like Sodom and been made like
Gomorrah (1:9). 'The stone of stumbling' passage in Isaiah 8:14, used
by Luke as a comment on the parable of the vineyard, as we saw, is
also quoted by Paul. But he combines it with another 'stone' passage
in Isaiah 28:16, in order to introduce another Isaianic theme, crucial
to his argument, redemption by faith: 'They have stumbled over the
stumbling stone, as it is written, Behold I am laying in Zion a stone
that will make people stumble, a rock that will make them fall; and
whoever believes in him will not be put to shame' (Rom.9:32–3). The
last part of Isaiah 28:16, the positive part, is repeated again in the
next chapter (10:10).

In the same context, 53:1 is quoted to describe the enigmatic
phenomenon that some people do not believe the Gospel when they
hear it preached to them, and this leads into what Paul seems to
believe is Isaiah's most daring prophecy of all (65:1–2): 'I have been
found by those who did not seek me; I have shown myself to those
who did not ask for me … But of Israel he says, All day long I have
held out my hands to a disobedient and contrary people.'
(Rom.10:20–21). He describes the obduracy of Israel by paraphrasing
another text from Isaiah 29:10 that is even more unrelenting than
6:9–10: 'God gave them a spirit of stupor, eyes that should not see
and ears that should not hear, down to this very day.' (Rom.11:7).

But finally, on the basis of Isaiah 59:20–21, he argues that all Israel
will eventually be saved, when 'the full number of the gentiles come
in' (Rom.11:25–7). His people, despite their disobedience and disbelief, are not rejected: they are still loved by God 'for the sake of their
forefathers' (Rom.11:28). He concludes with a kind of doxology on
'the depths of the riches and wisdom and knowledge of God',
quoting Isaiah, along with Job, to describe the unsearchable judge-
ments and inscrutable ways of God: 'For who has known the mind of
the Lord, or who has been his counsellor.' (cf. Isaiah 40:13–14). Paul,
heavily dependent on Isaiah, does not conclude with the rejection of
the Jews, however blind and stubborn they may be, but with faith in
a God who remains true to his covenant and who will in the end
show mercy to his people: 'as it is written (cf. Isaiah 59:20–21; 27:9),
the Deliverer will come from Zion, he will banish ungodliness from
Jacob; and this will be my covenant with them when I take away

their sins.' (Rom.11:26f.). For Paul, as for all Jews down the ages, the Book of Isaiah, especially the 'consolation readings' from 40–61, was a source of strength and hope, not unmitigated judgement and condemnation. Like every biblical text, Isaiah can be used in many ways. For Paul the Jew, it was a book about ultimate salvation, the salvation of Israel as well as the salvation of the gentiles.[54] It is a tragedy that in the history of Christianity Isaiah has more often than not been used to criticize and condemn the Jews, and Paul seen as the founder of antisemitism.[55]

[54] Cf. Williamson and Allen, *Interpreting Difficult Texts*, pp. 34–9; Segal, *Paul the Convert*, pp. 276–84.
[55] Cf. Maccoby, *Paul and Hellenism*, p. 182; cf. p. 100.

CHAPTER 3

The Early Church

From the relative simplicity of studying uses of Isaiah in a closed corpus, written in one language over a period of less than a century, we move to the vast area of the patristic writings, which are in several languages and span a period of about six centuries, roughly from the death of Paul in Rome in c.64 or the destruction of Jerusalem in 70, to the rise of Islam in the middle of the seventh century. The volume of extant patristic writings is enormous, most of it saturated with scriptural quotations, including many from Isaiah. The period also sees the beginnings of Christian iconography where Isaiah figures quite prominently.

Many of the developments of this period, in liturgy and doctrine especially, gave Christianity the form and character which in some parts of the Church have remained virtually unchanged down to the present century. It was in this period that 'the ox and the ass' first made their appearance in nativity scenes, for example, and the *Sanctus* became part of the eucharistic prayer. Most of the central areas of Christian belief such as the doctrines of the Incarnation, the Trinity and the Church took more or less their final shape in the creeds and councils of the fourth and fifth centuries. Christian attitudes towards the Jews were hardened in this early period of Church history as well. Isaiah had a significant role to play in all these developments.

Another aspect of the period which set the course of Church history for many centuries was the development and refinement of a particular approach to biblical interpretation. We are not primarily concerned here, as so many other studies in the history of interpretation are, with the technicalities of exegetical method, inevitably judged against the yardstick of modern critical scholarship,[1] but with

---

[1]   Cf. Young, 'Allegory and the ethics of reading'.

42

how people, ordinary members of Christian communities as well as bishops, scholars and leaders of the Church, actually understood and used Isaiah in practice. A few general comments on the aims and interests of patristic exegesis as they affect our main theme, however, are necessary.

First, it was during this period that the canon of Christian scripture was fixed. For the earliest writers such as Clement, Bishop of Rome around the end of the first century, it is clear that 'scripture' means the Five Books of Moses, the Prophets, especially Isaiah, and the Writings, especially Psalms and Job. Quotations from these texts, introduced by the formula 'it is written' or 'scripture says' or 'the Holy Spirit says', far outnumber the occasional references to the words of Jesus.[2] In Christian tradition the canonical status of the 'Fifth Gospel', in other words, antedated that of the other four.

By the end of the second century, at the latest, the Gospels, the Pauline Epistles and other apostolic writings were being raised to the status of canonical scripture, so that Isaiah and the other books of the Hebrew Bible were finally removed from their original context, where they had been shared with the Jews, and relocated in a larger Christian Bible. In this context, the unity of the Bible, from Genesis to Revelation, becomes an article of faith.[3] The relationship between the earlier books of scripture and the more recent – with or without the tendentious labels of 'Old Testament' and 'New Testament' – is not merely a matter of promise and fulfilment. In principle every part of scripture is now believed to be equally inspired and to contain truth about the theology, ethics, liturgy and political structures of the Church. Isaiah then ceases to be primarily a prophet whose words were fulfilled in the Gospels, and who gave meaning to the events and beliefs of the apostolic age. In terms of truth and authority, he now stands on the same level as the Gospels and Paul.

The Bible in its new Christian context also ceases by and large to be read, studied and quoted in Hebrew. It is likely that one of the main reasons why the Greek of Isaiah diverges so widely from the original Hebrew[4] was its popularity among Christians, since they knew it only in Greek (or Latin versions of the Greek), and had little

2   See the index of Biblical references at the end of T. Chevallier, *A Translation of the Epistles of Clement of Rome, Polycarp and Ignatius and of the Apologies of Justin Martyr and Tertullian* (London 1851).
3   Cf. 2 Tim.3:16, cited by Cyril of Alexandria (Lett.41:3; *FOC* 76, p. 170).
4   Cf. Burkitt, 'The debt of Christianity to Judaism', p. 84: 'Worst of all is Isaiah, the Greek of which is very often unintelligible'.

or no knowledge either of the Hebrew original or of any of the exegetical traditions that were based on it. By the time Jerome sought to recover something of the *hebraica veritas* in his Latin translation, which was to win the official approval of Augustine and eventually of the whole Western Church, Christian Greek versions of many key words and phrases, like 'virgin' in Isaiah 7:14, had after nearly 400 years become too widely accepted into the Church's tradition for them to be rejected in favour of an ancient Hebrew original.

Lines of continuity in the way scripture was interpreted can readily be traced from the apostolic writings discussed in the previous chapter, into the writings of the Church Fathers. Chief among these was the belief that the Prophets could only be properly understood when viewed from the perspective of the age of fulfilment which had now dawned in the life, death and resurrection of Christ. As the Church established itself, interpretations already present in the Gospels and Paul, such as the identification of Christ with the Suffering Servant in Isaiah 53, for example, and the application of Isaiah's call to preach the good news to the gentiles, were confirmed and disseminated throughout the rapidly expanding Christian world. Jesus' own use of Isaiah 61:1–2 in the synagogue at Nazareth (Luke 4) could be cited to give dominical authority to this view of scripture.

Thirdly, in the scholarly writings of the Church Fathers on the meaning of scripture, the realization that it was possible, indeed essential, to look beyond the 'literal sense' of scripture to its 'spiritual sense', became official doctrine. The 'spiritual' sense was derived from the text by various ingenious methods such as allegory, typology and gematria which had been elaborately worked out by Alexandrian Jewish scholars, and had two main attractions for the founders of Christianity. On the one hand, it meant that the Bible provided a virtually infinite source of delight and inspiration for the communities that regarded it as their sacred text. They could go on almost indefinitely finding new meanings in it, relevant to their circumstances.

On the other hand, this method of interpreting scripture was ideal for distinguishing between the official interpretations of the Church and the heretical interpretations of other communities claiming scriptural authority from the same scripture, in particular the Jews. The 'blindness' of the Jews (cf. Isa.6:9–11) in effect means their inability or unwillingness to accept the particular interpretations put upon scripture by Christians. While some agreement on the literal meaning of the Hebrew original could theoretically be achieved, agreement on the spiritual sense was by definition impossible, as Justin Martyr's *Dialogue with Trypho the Jew* illustrates. We shall see later just how powerful a weapon the 'Fifth Gospel' became in the hands of a Church dedicated to the punishment of heresy and the persecution of the Jews.

With these few introductory remarks, we turn now to our task of conveying some idea of the sheer range of contexts where Isaiah is used. We shall first try to gain some idea of popular Christian perceptions of Isaiah, as 'more evangelist than prophet', and consider in fairly general terms how he was used in early formulations of Christian doctrine. Then, in a very brief survey of a selection of passages from letters and sermons, we will attempt to give some idea of uses to which Isaiah was put by bishops and leaders in the general life of the Church. A final section will be devoted to the use of Isaiah in the liturgy and especially to the history and influences of probably the most widely used verse in the book, from the period of the early Church right down to the present.

As we have seen, the assessment of Isaiah as 'more evangelist than prophet' appears by implication at the beginning of our period where he takes pride of place among the Prophets of Christian scripture. From the same period comes an even more impressive witness to his central role in Christianity. In the non-canonical Christian work known as the 'Martyrdom and Ascension of Isaiah', which is roughly contemporary with the Epistles of Clement and Barnabas, the prophet recounts a vision in which he sees the whole life of Christ. In an explanation to his audience, addressed several times as Hezekiah the king and Isaiah's son Shear Jashub, he says: 'And the rest of the vision of the Lord, behold, it is recorded in parables in my words which are written in the book which I openly proclaimed. Moreover the descent of the Beloved into the realm of the dead is recorded in the section where the Lord says "Behold my servant is prudent".' (52:13).[5] In other words, for the author of this work, the Book of Isaiah contains details of the birth, life, death and resurrection of Christ 'in parables', that is to say, for those who have eyes to see and ears to hear. By the end of the fifth century Jerome's hyperboles[6] about Isaiah had become official Church doctrine.

The earliest representation of him in Christian art suggests that

[5]   Ascension 4:19: see *NTA*, 2, 650.
[6]   See above, pp. 1–2.

already it was as the prophet of the Virgin Birth that he was best known on account of 7:14 (cf. Matth.1:23). In a second-century fresco in the catacomb of St Priscilla in Rome he is shown standing opposite the seated Virgin and Child (Plate 3).[7] The star which the prophet points to almost certainly comes from Isaiah 11:1 and 10 (cf. Rom.15:12), combined with another famous messianic prophecy from Numbers 24:17, as it is in the roughly contemporary writings of Justin Martyr (c.100–c.165): 'Isaiah said, "A star shall rise out of Jacob, and a flower shall spring from the root of Jesse and in his arm shall the nations trust" '.[8]

'The Martyrdom and Ascension of Isaiah' also portrays the prophet as having a particular interest in the Virgin Birth. By far the longest section focusses on Mary (11:1–16), concluding in the following way: '. . . But the story about the infant was spread abroad in Bethlehem. Some said, "The virgin Mary has given birth before she has been married two months." But many said, "She did not give birth; the midwife did not go up (to her), and we did not hear any cries of pain."

Incidentally, the popular early Christian 'good shepherd' motif appears on an adjacent fresco in the same catacomb, and certainly owes its inspiration, partly at least, to the details of Isaiah 40:11: 'He will feed his flock like a shepherd, he will gather the lambs in his arms, He will carry them in his bosom, and gently lead those that are with young'.[9]

It is also probable that the much-used 'Suffering Servant' passage in chapter 53, cited in full by both Clement and Justin, influenced early Christian perceptions of the prophet. The 'Martyrdom' makes special reference to 52:13, and there are some other verbal links with the Suffering Servant passages.[10] Although it is not until later that he is represented as primarily prophet of the passion,[11] early Christian interest in traditions about his martyrdom, suggests that a link was made between Isaiah's suffering and Christ's. The source of the

---

[7] See Bertelli, *Roma Sottoterranea*, Plate 8, entitled 'Il buon pastore e la Madonna di Isaia'.

[8] *1 Apol.*32, 12–13. The third part of the quotation alludes to 11:10. Cf. Daniélou, *Symboles*, p. 113. See also below, pp. 74ff.; *BP*, p. 54.

[9] *CHB* 2, 283.

[10] A phrase from 52:13 (applied to 'the Beloved' = Christ) occurs in 4:21, and the Hebrew original of expressions like 'tormented in body' (1:7: cf. 53:5), 'sent and seized' (3:12; cf. 53:8), 'he did not cry out' (5:14: cf. 53:7), 'for me alone' (5:14: cf. 63:5), and 'the Lord has mixed the cup' (5:14: cf. 51:17,22) may also be derived from Isaiah.

[11] See below, chapter 5. It is not until mediaeval times that he is represented with a saw, symbol of his passion and martyrdom.

tradition that he was sawn in half by the wicked king Manasseh is not known. It is not mentioned in the Bible, although sawing in half as an excruciating mode of execution does appear in 2 Sam.12:31 (MT; cf. Vulgate), 1 Chron. 20:3, Susanna 59 (Daniel 13:59) and Hebrews 11:37. Although Iranian and other non-Israelite parallels are sometimes adduced as possible sources,[12] the tradition is probably ancient and Jewish.[13] However that may be, Isaiah is the only prophet remembered as having been killed and buried, like Jesus, in Jerusalem, and he was already most probably the chief example in the author's mind in passages about the death of the prophets before Christ, such as Matthew 23:28–39 and especially Luke 13:33–4. The same applies to the servants beaten and killed by the tenants in the Parable of the Vineyard (Matth.21:33–41), as well as to the explicit reference in Hebrews to martyrs who were 'sawn in two' (11:37).[14] Although not yet represented with the saw as a symbol of his martyrdom, as he is throughout mediaeval Europe,[15] he was undoubtedly already perceived as a prophet with much to say on the suffering and martyrdom of Christ. For Justin, 'Isaiah sawn asunder' meant more than Plato's philosophy.[16]

Finally, as we saw in the previous chapter, a major aspect of popular early Christian perceptions of Isaiah was undoubtedly his role as a prophet to the gentiles. In the patristic period the Book of Isaiah was much used in debates about one of the most intriguing gentile 'messianic prophecies', namely, the fourth *Eclogue* of Virgil, known as the 'Pollio'. In language and imagery often strikingly close to Latin versions of Isaiah, this first-century BC poem, written in honour of the emperor Augustus, foretells the coming of an age of peace, a new heaven and a new earth, heralded by the appearance of a virgin (*iam redit et virgo*) and the birth of a boy (*nascenti puero*), where mountains burst into song, trees and flowers grow up in wild places, and goats and lions live together in peace.

Constantine the Great and Augustine both claimed the fourth *Eclogue* as a gentile prophecy of Christ, using Isaiah as the

---

[12] See Knibb, 'Martyrdom', p. 151.
[13] The question of the relationship between the 'Martyrdom' and the Book of Isaiah is not discussed by Charles, 'Martyrdom of Isaiah', pp. 155–8, or Knibb, 'Martyrdom', pp. 143–55. The 'Martyrdom and Ascension' in its present form is strongly influenced by Christian tradition and some of the possible connections with Isaiah, such as the 'cup' reference (cf. Matth.20:22), may have been mediated through the Gospels.
[14] See chapter 5.   [15] See pp. 98f.
[16] Frend, *The Rise of Christianity*, p. 239.

proof,[17] and there grew up a mediaeval legend that Paul visited Virgil's grave and wept because he had not lived long enough for Paul to meet him.[18] According to Dante, it was because of Virgil that the Roman poet Statius (c. AD 45–96) converted to Christianity. When they meet in Purgatory, Statius hails Virgil both as the reason for his success as a poet and as the one who brought him to baptism, quoting from the fourth *Eclogue*.[19] Ancient writers picked up Virgil's reference to the Cumaean Sibyl, a Graeco-Roman (woman) prophet, whose words are reputedly preserved in another gentile text much used in the patristic period, the *Sibylline Oracles*. She too foretold the coming of Christ in language similar to Isaiah's, and was for this reason occasionally paired with Isaiah in Christian iconography.[20]

The most remarkable fact about patristic perceptions of Isaiah is the way in which, to use Jerome's words again, the book of Isaiah contains 'all the mysteries of Christ ... born of a virgin, worker of famous deeds and signs, who died and was buried and rose again from hell, the Saviour of all nations'.[21] The process of relating the Gospel stories to Isaiah and the prophets which was begun in the Gospels, is now carried much farther. On the one hand, new texts are discovered to describe events already recounted in the Gospels, while, on the other, new details in the story, not found in the Gospels themselves, are added on the authority of scripture. When we see the extent of this process in terms of the range of text used and the ingenuity of the interpreters, the conclusion that authors turned with special enthusiasm and expectation to the Fifth Gospel, seems inescapable. In the words of one modern authority on the period, 'Jesus Christ was interpreted less in terms of the Gospels than in those of the messianic prophecies of Isaiah'.[22] The author of the Epistle of Barnabas, for example, quotes Isaiah (not Paul or Jesus) to prove the error of Jewish understanding of texts on circumcision, sabbath and the like, and Justin Martyr, in arguing the case for the

---

[17] Constantine, *Oration to the Saints*, 19–21; Augustine, *City of God*, 10:27: cf. Pelikan, *Jesus through the Centuries*, pp. 35ff.

[18] Cf. Royds, *Virgil and Isaiah*. On Pope's use of the *Pollio*, see pp. 161f.

[19] *Purgatorio*, 22:66–73.

[20] Cf. Schiller, *Iconography*, I, p. 19, Fig. 33; Pelikan, *Jesus through the Centuries*, pp. 37–8. She is mentioned alongside David in the 'Dies Irae', a thirteenth-century hymn sung at requiem masses (*teste David cum sibylla*), and figures prominently beside Isaiah in Michelangelo's Sistine Chapel ceiling.

[21] CCSL 73, p. 1 *Comm. Es.*, Prologue.

[22] Frend, *The Rise of Christianity*, p. 136.

truth of scripture, in effect tells the whole Gospel story in the language of the prophets, mainly Isaiah.

To illustrate this the following 'Gospel narrative' has been constructed entirely from quotations from the 'Fifth Gospel', selected from the countless Isaiah passages that are regularly applied in ancient and mediaeval Christian literature to the story of the life, death and resurrection of Jesus.[23] The process was already well developed in the first century, as we have seen, but it gathers momentum over the centuries, fuelled by patristic commentaries such as those of St Jerome (c.342–420), completed between the years 408–10,[24] in the West and St Cyril of Alexandria (died 444)[25] in the East. It reaches its climax in such works as the remarkable *Ysaye Testimonia de Christo Domino*, attributed to the influential Isidore of Seville (c.560–636),[26] and the mediaeval *Biblia Pauperum*.[27] Isidore's polemical *De Fide Catholica ex Veteri et Novo Testamento Contra Judaeos*, which we shall discuss more fully in another context,[28] is also dependent more on Isaiah than on any other part of scripture.

Behold a virgin shall conceive and bring forth a son (7:14 LXX, Vg), a rod out of the stem of Jesse (11:1). His name shall be called 'Immanuel' (7:14), 'Wonderful counsellor, the mighty God, the everlasting Father, the Prince of Peace' (9:6), Key of David (22:22), the Christ (45:1 LXX, Vg). To us a child is born (9:6). The ox knows its owner and the ass its master's crib (1:3). The gentiles will come to your light and the kings to your rising ... they shall bring gold and incense (60:6). The idols of Egypt shall be moved at his presence (19:1).[29] Behold my servant ... in whom my soul delights (42:1). The spirit of the Lord will rest upon him, the spirit of wisdom and understanding ... (11:2). By the way of the sea, beyond Jordan and Galilee of the nations (9:1), the Lord has anointed me to preach good news to the poor ... (61:1). Surely he has taken our infirmities and borne our sicknesses (53:4). Then the eyes of the blind shall be opened ... then shall the lame man leap like a hart (35:5–6). The glory of the Lord is risen upon you (60.1). He shall be a precious cornerstone, a sure foundation (28.16), but also a stone of offence and a rock of stumbling to both the houses of Israel (8:14).

[23] References to the patristic literature are not normally given for each text but examples may be located at the relevant point in one or other of the two Isaiah commentaries, the Isidore works or the *Biblia Pauperum*.

[24] *CCSL* 73; *PL* 24; cf. Abel, 'Le commentaire de St-Jérôme sur Isaie', pp. 200–25; Kelly, *Jerome*, pp. 299–302.

[25] *PG* 70, ; cf. Kerrigan, *St Cyril of Alexandria*.

[26] *PL Suppl.* 4, cols. 1821–39.

[27] Cf. Engelhardt, *Der theologische Gehalt der Biblia Pauperum*, pp. 138f.

[28] See pp. 113–15.

[29] A detail of the story not in the Gospels but familiar to Christians from the ninth century on: cf. Schiller, *Iconography*, 1, pp. 117f.; *BP* p. 59.

He said, 'Go and tell this people, Hear indeed, but understand not ...'
(6:9).

I will weep bitterly ... because of the destruction of the daughter of my
people (that is, Jerusalem 22:4). Say to the daughter of Zion, Your saviour
comes (62:11 LXX, Vg). My house will be called a house of prayer for all
people (56:7). My servants shall eat but you shall be hungry, my servants
shall drink but you shall be thirsty ... (65:13). Ho everyone that thirsts,
come to the waters ... (55:1). He was brought as a lamb to the slaughter
(53:7). The government (that is, the cross bearing the inscription 'King of
the Jews' on it) shall be upon his shoulder (9:6), and there shall come up
briars and thorns (5:6). I gave my back to the smiters and my cheeks to
those that pluck out the hair; I hid not my face from shame and spitting
(50:6). He was wounded for our transgressions, and bruised for our
iniquities (53:5). From the sole of the foot even to the head there is no
soundness, but bruises and sores and bleeding wounds (1:6). He was
numbered between the transgressors ... and made intercession for the
transgressors (53:12). They made his grave ... with a rich man (53:9). His
tomb will be glorious (11:10 Vg). Now I will arise, says the Lord, now I will
lift myself up, now I will be exalted (33.10). Then shall your light break forth
like the dawn (58:8). Seek the Lord while he may be found (55:6). Behold
my servant shall understand, he shall be exalted and lifted up (52:13 LXX,
Vg); he shall be high and lifted up (6:1). I will set a sign among them ... I
will send survivors to the nations, to the sea, to Africa and Lydia, to Italy
and Greece, to islands afar off, to those who have not heard about me and
have not seen my glory; and they will proclaim my glory to the nations
(66:19).

It is really quite extraordinary how complete the story of the life of
Christ, told almost entirely in the words of Isaiah, can be. The 'Fifth
Gospel' version of the story actually contains virtually all the details
that are in the other four, as well as some like the ox and the ass in
the nativity scene, the shattering of the idols in Egypt and some of
the more lurid details of the passion narrative,[30] which are not.
Some of them are more far-fetched than others, some obviously
depend on the Latin or Greek versions rather than the original
Hebrew. There are many more, omitted from the above anthology
only because they would not fit verbatim into the narrative sequence.
They include references to the treachery of Judas in 3:8–11 ('it shall
be ill with him, for what his hands have done will be done to him'),
the agony in Gethsemane (33:7), and the well-known winepress
imagery from 63:1–3 which will be discussed later in relation to
mediaeval passion iconography.

[30]   Cf pp. 87–90.

Though our sources have been for the most part the writings of scholars, we may assume that this was how Isaiah was perceived by ordinary people as well, as 'more evangelist than prophet'. We turn now to the more rarefied and erudite world of early Christian doctrine. This was the period of the great councils of Nicaea, Constantinople and Chalcedon where heresies were identified and ruthlessly rejected, and orthodox Church doctrine was crystallized in the creeds. In this process too, Isaiah provides frequently cited scriptural authority for almost every argument. We shall look at a few examples.

The doctrine of the Trinity is supported by a number of texts from Isaiah. The best known of these, 'Holy, holy, holy' from 6:3, is the subject of a special study later.[31] Another comes from the famous creation hymn in Isaiah 40:12–26. The Hebrew word translated 'measure' in English versions of verse 12, is derived from the numeral 'three', and, translated into Latin as *tribus digitis* 'with three fingers' (verse 12), was taken as a scriptural witness to the Trinity. Passages like 48:16 were also cited in this context as they apparently describe the activity of the three persons of the Trinity: 'And now the Lord God has sent me and his Spirit' (cf. 42:1). The relationship between the second and third persons of the Trinity is described in passages like 42:1 and 61:1 ('The Spirit of the Lord God is upon me'), which were used to authorize the addition of the *filioque* clause ('and from the son') in western creeds. The sevenfold gifts of the spirit, represented by doves in Christian art[32] and celebrated in the famous Latin hymn, attributed to Rabanus Maurus (776–856), *Veni creator spiritus* ('Come, O Creator Spirit')[33] appear in 11:2:

> Thou the anointing Spirit art
> who dost thy sevenfold gifts impart.[34]

This particular contribution of Isaiah to Christian theology features in a mediaeval sculpture of the prophet in the south porch of Lausanne Cathedral, where he is represented as carrying in his hand, in place of his more usual attributes, a round disk with the seven doves on it.[35]

We have already discussed the use of Isaiah in the context of the

---

[31] See pp. 59–64. [32] See below, p. 74. [33] *HON* 580.
[34] *EH* 153 (*CH* 182), in a translation by Bishop Cosin (1594–1672). Other English versions of *Veni Creator Spiritus* include those of John Dryden (1631–1701) (*EH* 156; *SOP* 181 *CH* 184) and Robert Bridges (1844–1930) (*SOP* 179).
[35] Réau, *Iconographie*, ii.i, p. 366; Kirschbaum, *Lexikon*, ii, p. 355.

story of the life, death and resurrection of Jesus Christ. His role in
the evolution of traditional christology is no less prominent. 9:6 ('for
to us a child is born . . .') is naturally much used in relation to the
doctrine of the incarnation. The first part proves he was both 'born
. . . (of the Father and therefore divine)', and 'given . . . (by the Virgin
and therefore human)'.[36] Alternatively the first part describes him as
both a 'child', that is to say a 'human child', and a 'son', that is to say
'the son of God'.[37] The title 'Mighty God' in the second part of the
verse proclaims his divine nature. The iconography of a painting by
Andrea Mantegna (c.1430–1506) of the Infant Christ as 'Imperator
Mundi' was inspired by Isaiah 9:6 too.[38]

66:7 is used to prove Christ's pre-existence. It is a difficult verse in
any case, and by assuming that the two clauses in each half-verse
have different subjects, the following interpretation is achieved:
'before she (Mary was in labour, he (God) gave birth (to his Son
. . .'); and before her (Mary's) time came to have a child, he (God the
Father) had given birth to a son (in heaven outside of time).' 53:9
refers to his sinlessness,[39] and the ineffable mystery of the incarnation
is often expressed in the words of 53:8: *Generationem eius quis enarrabit?*
Who will be able to explain his generation (that is, how he was
'generated')? Human language cannot describe how both 'sub-
stances' or 'natures', divine and human, came together in one
person: it is a matter of faith.[40] The Arians used the verse to argue
that the terms 'of one substance with the Father' should be removed
from the creeds.[41] Several passages, including 2:4,[42] 11:3f. and 32:1,
describe the Second Coming: 'he shall judge between the nations . . .
(2:4); with righteousness he shall judge the poor . . . and with the
breath of his lips he shall slay the wicked' (11:4).

In both Jewish and Christian tradition the book of Isaiah ends
with a reference to the resurrection of the dead (66:22[43]), and a
much quoted description of the eternal punishment that awaits the
wicked after death: 'their worm shall not die, their fire shall not be
quenched, and they shall be a sight for all flesh' (66:24).[44] Isaiah

---

[36]   *FOC* 22. 166.

[37]   *PL* Supplement 4, 1831.

[38]   Lightbrown, *Mantegna*, p. 148, plate 138.

[39]   E.g. *PG* 14,720 (Origen); *PG* 62, 194 (John Chrysostom).

[40]   E.g. Eusebius, *History*, 2:2; *PL* 54, 226 (Leo the Great).

[41]   Cf. Bettenson, *Documents*, p. 43.

[42]   Cf. *BP*, p. 122.

[43]   *PG* 7, 1222 (Irenaeus).

[44]   E.g. *PG* 331, 1264 (Basil); *PG* 36, 409 (Gregory of Nazianzen).

66:24 is quoted by Jesus in Mark 9:14 and from there becomes one of the Church's main scriptural proof texts for the notion of hell-fire.[45] So gruesome is this conclusion to Isaiah, that Jewish liturgical practice is to end the reading of this portion of scripture by repeating a previous verse.[46] Another passage from Isaiah that plays an important role in Christian concepts of hell is 33:14 ('Who among us can dwell with the everlasting burnings?').[47] There is also the celebrated description of the fate of the king of Babylon in chapter 14, containing not only the reference to Lucifer's fall from heaven, but also a unique description of the reception awaiting a newcomer to the abode of the dead: 'Sheol beneath is stirred up to meet you when you come. It rouses the shades to greet you, all who were leaders of the earth ... "You too have become as weak as we are! You have become like us!"' (verses 9–10). These images of hell from Isaiah appear throughout Christian literature from Luke 10:18 and 2 Cor.11:14,[48] to Milton's *Paradise Lost*[49] and Hobbes *Leviathan*.[50]

We shall follow the example of Jewish tradition, and end this discussion of Isaiah in the context of early Christian doctrine, by recalling one of his more pleasant contributions to Christian language and images of the after-life. It occurs in chapter 26, a passage much quoted in the context of funerals and epitaphs: 'The dead will rise up, and those who are in their graves will awake, and those who are on the earth will rejoice. For the dew from you is healing to them, but the land of the wicked will perish.' (LXX).[51]

There were few aspects of the life of the Church in the patristic period to which Isaiah did not have a significant contribution to make. The Fathers found important references to the sacraments of baptism and the eucharist in Isaiah. Baptism appears in verses like Isaiah 1:16 ('Wash and be clean'),[52] 12:3 ('with joy you shall draw water from the wells of salvation')[53] and 55:1 ('All who thirst come to

---

[45]   Cf. Bernstein, *The Formation of Hell, passim.* No other verse of scripture is referred to more often (Index of Biblical References, p. 390).

[46]   A. Cohen, ed., *The Soncino Humash* (1947), p. 1188.

[47]   Cf. Wheeler, *Death and the Future Life in Victorian Literature and Theology*, p. 11.

[48]   Bernstein, *The Formation of Hell*, p. 250.

[49]   See below, p. 160.

[50]   Part III, chapter 38: ed. C. B. MacPherson (Penguin, Harmondsworth 1968), pp. 486–9.

[51]   Cf. Sawyer, 'Isaiah as a source-book for scriptural texts about death and mourning', pp. 86–102.

[52]   *CCSL* 73, p. 18 (Jerome); *PL* 83, 531 (Isidore).

[53]   *PL* 83, 530 (Isidore); *BP*, p. 66.

the waters').[54] Isaiah refers to the eucharist in 65:13 ('My servants shall eat ... drink ... rejoice ... sing ...'),[55] although undoubtedly his most important contribution to the eucharist appears in chapter 6 in the *Sanctus*.[56] The sign of the cross is given a scriptural origin too, not only in Ezekiel 9:4, but also in Isaiah 66:18 (cf. 5:26; 55:13).[57]

The institution of bishops and deacons was authorized by reference to 60:17, and their powers further strengthened by the symbol of the 'key of David' from 22:22. An early Bishop of Rome used the first of these texts in such a way as to make it clear that, for him, it constituted older and more reliable scriptural evidence than 1 Timothy 3:1 and Titus 1:7: 'This was not a new thing, since it was written long ago concerning bishops and deacons. Scripture says somewhere: "I will appoint their overseers (*episkopous*) in righteousness, and their ministers (*diakonous*) in faith"'.[58] Irenaeus, Bishop of Lyons from 178 to about 200, used the same verse in a similar context.[59] Jerome uses 3:12 to castigate Church leaders for allowing women too much influence in ecclesiastical appointments.[60] Basil the Great (c.330–379) used the Preface to his *Commentary on Isaiah* as an opportunity to condemn Montanism, holding up Isaiah as an example of a true prophet, quite distinct from those who are 'caught up outside themselves (*extra se raptos*), their mind being swallowed up by the Spirit'. Basil's *Preface*, which has been described as a standard anti-montanist work, was used by Jerome and translated into Latin by Erasmus (c.1467–1536).[61]

Elsewhere Clement cites Isaiah 66:2 and the whole of chapter 53 in a recommendation of the virtue of humility (1 Cor.13:16). Ambrose, Bishop of Milan (c.339–97), whose special fondness for Isaiah has been mentioned already, uses the same verse in his funeral oration on the death of the Emperor Theodosius, an example which we may take as typical of patristic handling of scripture. As well as applying familiar, comforting passages like 35:10 to the situation ('sorrow and sighing shall flee away'), he selects two powerful and memorable passages from Isaiah to build his peroration on. Of all his many achievements, none brought Theodosius more credit than the famous act of public penance Ambrose persuaded him to perform to

---

[54] *PL* 83, 530 (Isidore).   [55] *PL* 83, 536 (Isidore).
[56] See below, pp. 59–64.   [57] *PL* 83, 534 (Isidore).
[58] 1 Clem.42:5; cf. *CHB*, 2, p. 164.
[59] *CHB*, 2, p. 428.
[60] *CCSL* 73, p. 52; cf. Kelly, *Jerome*, pp. 301–2.
[61] Cf. Screech, *Erasmus*, pp. 206–10.

make amends for a massacre in Thessalonica. So Ambrose begins his peroration with Isaiah 66:2. There are other passages in scripture about humility and contrition (Ps.51, for example, and Mic.6:8), but none is more appropriate to the occasion than this verse, coming as it does amid the visions of a new heaven and new earth, with the Lord enthroned above it all, and just before one of the most radical attacks in the whole Bible upon earthly institutions and human efforts ('the sacrifice of an ox is like murder . . . ' Isa.66:3).

Ambrose then chooses 60:3 for his climax: 'Kings shall walk in your light: this means, they shall walk openly, especially Gratian and Theodosius before other princes, no longer protected by the weapons of their soldiers, but by their own merits; clothed not in purple garments but in the mantle of glory.' The keyword in this passage, one of the best known 'kings' texts, employed in accounts of the adoration of the magi and elsewhere,[62] is 'your light', and the contrast between this-worldly light and the glory of heaven. Later in the same chapter comes the eschatological passage, familiar to Christians from the Apocalypse of St John: 'The sun shall be no more your light by day, Nor for brightness shall the moon give light to you by night; but the Lord will be your everlasting light, and your God will be your glory.' (60:19; cf. Rev.21:23; 22:5).

The fluent manner in which a preacher like Ambrose uses Isaiah verbatim confirms his familiarity with the text. But it also seems clear from these and other examples that, far from expatiating at length on a verse out of context, he has the whole chapter or section of the book in mind and is thus able to appreciate the full effect of the language and imagery of Isaiah.

Augustine, advised to read Isaiah by his bishop,[63] tells us he had to put it aside at first reading because he could not understand it, but eventually, like all his contemporaries, he turned to it to find scriptural authority for all kinds of argument and was clearly much influenced by it. Like Jerome and many others, he describes Isaiah as an evangelist rather than a prophet.[64] A particularly apt example of Augustine's use of Isaiah is his citing, more than once, of the famous proverb in 7:9, in the context of a discussion of the relationship between faith and reason. The Greek version, quoted with approval by Jerome (although not in the Vulgate), Cyril of Alexandria and

[62] See p. 49.   [63] See p. 2.
[64] *City of God*, 18, 29 (ed. Wand, p. 296).

others, has 'If you do not believe, you will not understand', and this provides Augustine with the perfect proof-text for his views on the matter. In one place he calls in the prophet Isaiah in person to adjudicate between those who say you must understand before you can believe, and those who, like Augustine himself, say *Crede ut intelligas* 'believe so that you may understand': Let the prophet adjudicate, or rather let God Himself adjudicate through the prophet. Let us both be silent ... let the prophet answer: 'If you do not believe, you will not understand' (Isa.7:14).[65] So the issue is settled – to Augustine's satisfaction at least.

Isaiah also played a not unimportant role in the origins and development of the monastic movement. On the one hand, the concept of the wilderness blossoming like the rose is developed in Isaiah as nowhere else: 'The wilderness and the dry land shall be glad, the desert shall rejoice and blossom; like the crocus it shall blossom abundantly ... (35:1–2). For the Lord will comfort Zion; he will comfort all her waste places, and will make her wilderness like Eden, her desert like the garden of the Lord ...' (51:3). A recent study of desert spirituality prints Isaiah 35:1–2 on the title page, and shows how the theme is most developed in Isaiah.[66] On the other hand, there is the momentous description of John the Baptist, a model for every ascetic Christian, as 'the voice of one crying in the wilderness', a phrase taken from a Greek version of Isaiah 40:3 (cf. Matth. 4:3; Mark 1:3; Luke 3:4).[67]

We come now to Isaiah's role in the origins and development of Christian liturgy, beginning with the prominent place in Advent and Christmas liturgies which Isaiah still holds today. Of the seven 'O Antiphons' or 'Greater antiphons' to be sung on the seven days up to Christmas, so-called because they all begin with one of Christ's titles prefaced by the vocative 'O', three are from Isaiah: *O radix Jesse* (11:10), *O Clavis David* (22:22), and *O Emmanuel* (7:14 and 59:20).[68] A mediaeval Latin hymn, beginning *Veni Immanuel*, is based on five of these antiphons, including all the Isaiah ones, and is the origin of the nineteenth-century English Advent hymn 'O come, O come, Immanuel'.[69] The continuing influence of this Isaianic composition can be heard in James

---

[65] *PL* 38, 257 (Augustine); cf. *PL* 33, 453; *PL* 37, 1552; 40,181ff.
[66] Cf. Lowth, *The Wilderness of God*, pp. 35ff.
[67] Lowth, p. 36f.   [68] *EH* 734.
[69] *EH* 8; *CH* 109; *HON* 384; cf Moffatt, *Handbook*, pp. 56f.

Macmillan's concerto for percussion and orchestra entitled 'Veni, Veni, Emmanuel', first performed in 1992.[70]

In addition to the 'O Antiphons', many other texts from Isaiah figure in the Advent and Christmas liturgies.[71] Lectionaries include a vast selection of passages: visions of the future such as 2:1–5, 4:2–6, 26:1–6, 35:1–10, 40:1–11 and 62:1–5, hymnic celebrations such as 52:7–10, 54:1–10 and 60:1–6, and most of the traditional christological passages like 9:1–6, 11:1–10 and 49:1–6. Single verses are frequently used as antiphons: the best known of these are probably 'A boy is born' (*Puer natus est* 9:6), 'Behold a virgin' (*Ecce Virgo* 7:14),[72] 'Prepare the way of the Lord ...' (40:3) and the *Rorate coeli* (45:8).[73]

Isaiah's prominence in the mediaeval monastic liturgy may also be mentioned here, as this too no doubt had its origins in a much earlier period. Of the twenty-one 'Lesser Canticles' sung at Mattins, no less than eleven are from the Book of Isaiah.[74] Predictably they include three for Advent (40:10–17; 42:10–16; 49:8–13) and three for Christmas (9:2–7; 66:10–16; 26:1–12). Most of these passages will figure again later in our survey, for example, in the context of our discussion of Handel's *Messiah* (9:2–7; 40:11), Brahms' *Requiem* (66:13), funerals (26:3; 66:13) and female images of God (42:14; 66:13). The hymnic style of much of Isaiah, especially chapters 40–66, has often been noted, and the appropriateness of several of them to be sung as canticles in public worship can be seen in the specific references in most of them to singing (e.g. 'Sing to the Lord a new song' in 42:10; 'Sing for joy, O heavens' in 49:13), or rejoicing (e.g. 'Rejoice with Jerusalem' in 66:10). Two of the others (Isaiah 33:2–10; 13–18) are sung on Sundays *per annum*, that is to say, every Sunday throughout the liturgical year, outside of the seasons of Advent, Christmas, Lent and Easter.

Special mention may be made of Isaiah 61:6–9 which was used on feasts of the apostles, martyrs and confessors, and in the most recent Catholic lectionary appears as one of the readings at masses for priestly or religious vocations: 'You shall be called the priests of the Lord, people shall speak of you as ministers of our God; you shall eat the wealth of the nations, and in their riches you shall glory ...' (61:6). The appropriateness of this verse, in particular the economic

---

[70] See p. 175.
[71] *ASB*, pp. 417–86; *New Sunday Missal*, pp. 1–60; *Lectionary*, pp. 1–75.
[72] See below, pp. 66–69.   [73] See pp. 69–72.
[74] Harper, *Forms and Orders*, pp. 256f.

relevance of the second half to mediaeval monastic life, scarcely requires comment. It is omitted when the passage is read in modern times at Confirmation. The remaining two Lesser Canticles from Isaiah (61:10–62:3; 62:4–7) are sung at the Feast of Virgins.[75] We shall return to this popular passage later when we come to discuss the role of Isaiah in the cult of the Virgin Mary, and again in our chapter on female imagery in Isaiah.

The most important canticles from Isaiah, however, are the two that are included in many psalters, such as the famous ninth-century Utrecht Psalter, the St Alban's Psalter and the Canterbury Psalter,[76] both of the twelfth century, and the fourteenth-century Queen Mary's Psalter in the British Museum, where they are accompanied by colourful and exegetically interesting illuminations. They are known as the Isaiah Canticle (12:1–6) and the Hezekiah Canticle (38:10–20).

The first of these, *Confitebor tibi domine* (Isaiah 12), described by modern literary critics as a hymn of thanksgiving, is readily applied to a variety of Christian contexts. The Vulgate contains an important variation from the Hebrew. In place of the word 'salvation' (Hebrew *yeshu'a*) in verses 2 and 3, the Latin has *salvator* 'saviour', thus identifying 'salvation' with Christ and making the christological application more explicit.[77] The ninth-century Utrecht Psalter for instance, relates it to the transfiguration (Plate 7).[78] It depicts Christ at the top, in a mandorla, flanked by Moses and Elijah, with Peter standing looking up and James and John prostrate. Beneath is the eucharistic 'well of the saviour' (Isaiah 12:3) from which streams flow out and through the gate of a city wall. Two men are drinking from the well directly, while farther away groups of men and women, both inside and outside the city, are bringing cups and jars to it and singing praises.

The illuminated initial *C* in the twelfth-century St Alban's Psalter, in a rich tapestry of Isaiah allusions, shows the kneeling prophet looking up towards God who is enthroned above him (Plate 8).[79] With his right hand he points towards a well at the foot of the cross from which two people are drinking. The cross has leaves and

[75] Harper, *Forms and Orders*, p. 257.
[76] Trinity Coll.Cambridge, R17:1 fol.262vo.
[77] The Vulgate makes the same change elsewhere: 62:11 has already been listed; 45:8 will be discussed below, pp. 81ff.
[78] De Wald, *Illustrations of the Utrecht Psalter*, pp. 65–6.
[79] Dodwell, *St Alban's Psalter*, p. 268.

branches sprouting from it (cf. 11:1) and the figure of a lamb on the crosspiece (53:7). In a painting of Isaiah in the Uffizi Gallery in Florence, the Dominican artist Bartolommeo (1472–1517) chose four words from the Isaiah canticle as the text to sum up Isaiah's prophecy: ECCE DEUS SALVATOR MEUS 'Behold, God is my saviour' (v.2). The grammar of this rhyming epigram permits two interpretations: not only that God is the source of salvation, but also 'My Saviour is God'. In Bartolommeo's painting, in which Isaiah is pointing urgently towards Christ, the second interpretation is clearly intended, and the words provide another Isaianic proof text for the divinity of Christ. The English poet Michael Drayton (1563–1631) included a metrical rendering of the passage in his *Harmonie of the Church*.[80]

The other major Isaiah canticle, Hezekiah's prayer on recovery from a near-death experience (Isaiah 38), contains some vivid images of death, which inspired the illuminator of the St Alban's Psalter to show death as a monster lurking beside Hezekiah's feet.[81] He also singled out a reference to Hezekiah's failing eyesight ('my eyes are weary with looking upward' v.14) as having some special significance in this context. An eighth-century fresco in the Church of Santa Maria Antica in Rome shows the prophet at the dying king's bedside, addressing the words of Isaiah 38:1 to him: 'Set your house in order because you are about to die'. Poems inspired by Hezekiah's prayer include one by the English poet William Habington (1605–64), beginning 'Time! where didst thou those years inter/which I have seen decease?' (cf. Isa.38:10) and 'The Song of Esechia' by Joseph Hall (1574–1656) in which every image is vividly and faithfully rendered.[82]

Where, when and why the song of the seraphim in Isaiah's vision beginning 'Holy, holy, holy', came to be included as the *Sanctus* or *Trisagion* in the eucharistic prayer remains an enigma.[83] It is not associated with the Last Supper in the Gospels, or in any Jewish meal prayers. It is conspicuous by its absence in Paul's account of the Last Supper, as also in the Didache and Justin Martyr. It does appear in Revelation 4:8 and is discussed in 1 Clement 34:6–7, but neither is a eucharistic context. Yet by the fourth century it has become a central

[80]   Atwan and Wieder, edd., *Chapters into Verse*, p. 390.
[81]   Dodwell, *St Alban's Psalter*, Plate 92a.
[82]   Atwan and Wieder, edd., *Chapters into Verse*, pp 396–400.
[83]   Spinks, *Sanctus*, pp. 1–7.

part of the eucharistic prayer in virtually every variety of Christianity, East and West, where it has remained until today.

It figures in the *Te Deum*, an ancient Latin hymn traditionally (though almost certainly wrongly) attributed to St Ambrose, and since mediaeval times prescribed to be used daily at Mattins. Isaiah's vision is the inspiration for several other popular hymns,[84] including Bishop Heber's famous one for Trinity Sunday, discussed below, and another nineteenth-century one beginning 'Bright the vision that delighted/ Once the sight of Judah's seer'.[85] Rudolph Otto wrote of the *Sanctus*: 'In whatever language they resound, these most sublime words that have come from human lips always grip one in the depths of the soul, with a mighty shudder, exciting and calling into play the mystery of the otherworldly latent therein'.[86] Outside the context of Christian worship, the *Sanctus* is familiar to a wide audience of secular music-lovers too, from public performances of the great masses by Bach, Mozart, Haydn, Beethoven, Verdi, Britten and many others.

The Sanctus probably originated in Syria and Palestine, influenced by Jewish liturgical practice and, perhaps more significantly, by Jewish Merkavah mysticism. It is generally agreed that the prominence of the *Sanctus* (Hebrew *qĕdushah*) in Jewish daily prayer goes back many centuries before the earliest prayer-books, which are mediaeval. There is plenty of evidence that by the time of Christ it was also much used in mystical descriptions of heaven, both Jewish and Christian. Revelation 4:8 is an early Jewish example, where, as in synagogue worship, Isaiah 6:3, Ezekiel 3:12 and Daniel 7:10 are brought together. According to both Jewish and Christian tradition reflected in many early post-biblical texts, it is the central act of heavenly worship,[87] and in singing it, worshippers and mystics expressed their longing to join with the angels in singing the *Sanctus* before God in heaven.[88] Tertullian appears to believe that in reciting 'Hallowed be thy name' in the Lord's Prayer, Christians are almost doing this here on earth already.[89] This interpretation figures also,

---

[84]   E.g. *HON*, 213, 214, 215, 457, 599. On 215, see below.

[85]   *EH* 372; *HAP* 445. Some versions omit the first verse and begin 'Round the Lord in glory seated/Cherubim and Seraphim' (*CH* 2); cf. Moffatt, *Handbook*, pp. 1–2.

[86]   Quoted by Spinks, *Sanctus*, p. 8.

[87]   See Alexander, '3 (Hebrew Apocalypse of) Enoch', p. 245: cf. 3 Enoch 1:12; 22B:7; 48B:2.

[88]   E.g. 3 Enoch 35–40; Testament of Adam 4:8; 4 Baruch 9:3; the belief appears also in the Hekhalot literature, 1 Clement, and Aphrahat's *Demonstration* XIV; see Spinks, *Sanctus*, pp. 48ff; *OTP* 1, pp. 993f.; Vol.2, pp. 169, 424f. The *Sanctus* is referred to in the Ascension of Isaiah 8:17–18.

[89]   Cf. Spinks, *Sanctus*, p. 52.

incidentally, in the Anglican 1662 Book of Common Prayer (and all modern versions of it) which introduces the *Sanctus* in the eucharistic prayer as follows: 'Therefore with angels and archangels and the whole company of heaven, we laud and magnify thy glorious name, evermore praising thee and saying . . .'

There is no need to trace in detail the history of Christian uses of Isaiah 6:3 in the *Sanctus* down to the present time, as Spinks has already covered the ground with egregious thoroughness, expertise and imagination. But it will be interesting to survey the sheer breadth of interpretation and variety of function documented down the ages for this extraordinarily fertile passage. The elements in Isaiah 6 which have captured the imagination and made this passage so memorable and popular, include (1) the striking threefold repetition of the word 'Holy', (2) the dramatic account of a man's vision of God and the angels (including unique details of what they looked like), and (3) the theme of a man's sense of sinfulness in the presence of God, followed by an equally dramatic act of divine forgiveness involving touching his lips with a burning coal. The relevance and easy applicability of all these elements to Christian theology and in particular to the theology of the eucharist, made it almost inevitable that the passage would play an important role in the history of Christianity.

According to Revelation 4:8, and parallels in the Jewish Targums, the threefold repetition of the word 'Holy' was apparently understood to refer to three aspects of God's creative energy, past, present and future: 'Holy, holy, holy is the Lord God almighty, who was and is and is to come'.[90] The Targum of Isaiah 6:3 gives a different explanation of the threefold repetition: 'And they were crying one to another and saying, Holy in the highest heavens, the house of his *Shekinah*; holy upon earth, the work of his might; holy for endless ages is the Lord of hosts: the whole earth is full of the brightness of his glory'.[91]

Christian interpreters predictably found references here to the doctrine of the Trinity, as we noted above. Some believed there were only two seraphim and that these represented the Son and the Holy Spirit, a view ridiculed, incidentally, by St Jerome in his commentary on this passage. Monteverdi's beautiful *Duo seraphim clamabant* in his *Vespers of the Blessed Virgin* (1610), continues the tradition, although a

---

[90] Cf. Deut.32:39 in Targum Pseudo-Jonathan: Spinks, *Sanctus*, p. 48.
[91] Stenning, *Targum*, p. 20.

third voice, a bass, joins the two tenors for the second, explicitly trinitarian part beginning *Tres sunt qui testimonium dant in coelo* ('They are three who give testimony in heaven'). A far commoner trinitarian view, documented in Christian literature from the patristic period down to the present, is that the threefold repetition points to the three Persons in the one Godhead. Bishop Reginald Heber's famous hymn, beginning 'Holy, Holy, Holy, Lord God Almighty', based on Isaiah 6 and Revelation 4, celebrates the doctrine of the Trinity and has traditionally been sung on Trinity Sunday. The first and last verses begin with the song of the 'cherubim and seraphim' and end with the refrain: 'God in three persons, blessed Trinity'. The hymn, one of Tennyson's favourites apparently,[92] contains three other 'trinities', inspired by the threefold repetition. The first is in verse 2 where there is an echo of Revelation 4:8: 'which wert, and art and evermore shalt be'. A second comes at the end of verse 3 where God is described as 'perfect in power and love and purity', and a third in verse 4 which puts an elegant tripartite gloss on Isaiah's original 'the whole earth is full of his glory': 'All thy works shall praise thy name in earth and sky and sea'.

By contrast some modern variations avoid the trinitarian interpretation entirely, no doubt on the grounds that this is not what the original text of Isaiah 6:3 actually meant. The threefold repetition instead is interpreted by reference to three attributes of God, as in Revelation 4 and the Targum of Isaiah. The following example apppears in a modern version of the eucharistic prayer from New Zealand: 'Holy God, Holy and merciful, Holy and just, glory and goodness come from you. Glory to you most high and gracious God'.[93] The ancient *Liturgy of St John Chrysostom*, still used by the Orthodox Church at normal eucharists on Sundays and weekdays, similarly preserves the earliest tradition by avoiding any trinitarian ideas: 'Holy God, Holy and Strong, Holy and Immortal, have mercy on us.'

The second theme that has echoed down the ages from Isaiah 6 in Christian worship is its angelology, much elaborated in Revelation and all the other ancient Jewish and Christian descriptions of the heavenly court referred to above. One indication of the extent of the influence of Isaiah 6 on western Christian culture, is the ubiquitous representation of angels throughout Christian art, ancient and

---

[92] *EH* 162; *CH* 1; *HAM* 160; *SOP* 187; *HON* 215; Moffatt, *Handbook to the Church Hymnary*, p. 1.
[93] Spinks, *Sanctus*, p. 187.

modern, as having six wings. Twentieth-century examples include the seraph on the tower of the YMCA building in Jerusalem, built in 1928, and a pair of stained glass windows designed in 1979 for a Church in Newcastle upon Tyne,[94] one showing a six-winged angel with a smoking, burning coal in his hand (Plate 21), the other being a simple representation of the eucharistic chalice and wafer.

Christian versions of the *Sanctus* often add human participants to Isaiah's six-winged seraphim and Ezekiel's 'living creatures' (cf. Rev.4:6–8). The *Te Deum*, for example, adds 'the glorious company of apostles ... the noble fellowship of prophets ... the white-robed army of martyrs'. The second verse of Bishop Heber's hymn discussed above is a typical example from the nineteenth century: 'Holy, holy, holy! All the saints adore thee, casting down their golden crowns around the glassy sea; Cherubim and seraphim falling down before thee.'

Others consider such ancient angelology outdated and irrelevant, and play it down by introducing the Sanctus with no mention of the seraphim in Isaiah's vision at all, as in a recent Dutch Catholic example cited by Spinks:[95] 'Together with Him and with His Church from the whole world we want to thank you, and praise you, and sing to you ...' Against this rationalist modern view, it may be argued, as Spinks does, that the mention of angels and the heavenly host in the introduction to the *Sanctus* serves to emphasize the unity of the earthly and the heavenly Church, especially in worship at the moment of the eucharistic prayer, rather than merely perpetuating ancient mythology.[96] In the words of an eighth-century Patriarch of Constantinople, 'the Church is the earthly heaven in which the heavenly God dwells and moves'.[97] It is interesting, though irrelevant for our purposes and those of Christian worshippers, that the retention of a traditional angelological preface preserves more of 'the original biblical setting (and temple cultic setting?) of the *Sanctus*.'[98]

The third element in the *Sanctus* which has played a central role in Christian worship since the Reformation, the sense of sins forgiven, also goes back to its original context in Isaiah 6. This is uppermost in the liturgy of the eastern Church where the live coal that touches

[94] L. C. Evetts, St Silas Church, Byker, Newcastle.
[95] Spinks, *Sanctus*, p. 179.
[96] Spinks, *Sanctus* p. 199.
[97] Germanus (died 733): cited by T.Ware, *The Orthodox Church*, p. 269.
[98] Spinks, *Sanctus*, p. 199.

Isaiah's lips and takes away his sins, is one of the commonest images of the body of Christ in the eucharist. St John Chrysostom comments on the relation of the eucharist to Isaiah's vision: 'that altar is a type and image of this altar, that fire of this spiritual fire. But the seraphim did not dare touch it with their hands, but only with the tongs; you take it in your hands.' Greek Orthodox priests use the words of Isaiah as they kiss the chalice, and the 'spoon' by which the people receive communion is called *labis* in Greek, the word used in Greek versions of Isaiah 6 for the 'tongs' with which the seraph took the live coal from the altar. In orthodox Christian art this 'spoon' containing a burning coal is commonly associated with Isaiah, in preference to the saw or a branch of the Jesse tree which are more frequent in western art.[99]

This interpretation of the *Sanctus* is not restricted to eastern Christianity, however. Martin Luther also used Isaiah 6 to express his belief that the mass is primarily a declaration of sins forgiven. With typical hermeneutical boldness, he cuts through the trinitarian doctrine and angelology that had occupied previous interpreters of the passage, and focusses instead on the experience of the prophet, first made aware of his sinfulness in God's presence and then receiving divine forgiveness at the touch of a burning coal on his lips. For Luther therefore the *Sanctus* should come at the end of the eucharistic prayer. The threefold repetition of the word 'Holy' sums up the experience of meeting God face to face in the mass, and should be used to inspire the people receiving forgiveness in the Sacrament to say, with Isaiah, 'Here am I! Send me.' A celebrated Scottish preacher similarly uses the imagery of chapter 6 to illustrate the 'miracle' of how an unworthy human being can 'mediate the word of God to men'.[100] Bach's *Cantata no. 94* (*Höchst erwünschtes Freudenfest*) for Trinity Sunday interprets the vision in this way too, as does the dramatic Benjamin West painting *The Call of Isaiah* (1782).[101]

[99] Réau, *Iconographie*, II.1, p. 366.
[100] Stewart, *Preaching*, pp. 180f; see below, pp. 146f.
[101] Von Erffa and Staley, *The Paintings of Benjamin West*, Plate 283.

CHAPTER 4

The Cult of the Virgin Mary

It was in mediaeval Europe that the cult of the Virgin Mary reached its zenith.[1] Countless cathedrals, churches and colleges were dedicated to the Virgin Mary, Our Lady – Notre Dame in France, Santa Maria in Italy and Spain. There are numerous representations of the Virgin, including some of the world's best-known paintings like Piero della Francesca's *Madonna della misericordia*, Leonardo's *Virgin of the Rocks*, and Titian's *The Assumption*. New and important feasts in her honour were introduced; popular compositions like the *Salve Regina* were produced; the *Ave Maria* became part of the liturgy; and pilgrimages, the veneration of relics and other traditions associated with Our Lady were instituted. In all this Isaiah played a central role both in providing scriptural authority for widely held beliefs about Mary, and in inspiring writers, composers, architects and artists with images that were to become integral to her worship all over the world.

This does not mean of course that the roots of the cult do not go back much earlier, or that it does not continue to flourish right down to the present day. Isaiah figures prominently already in biblical and patristic traditions about Mary, as we saw.[2] Traditions connecting Isaiah with the annunciation and the nativity go right back to the beginning (Matth.1:22–3) and remained popular throughout the patristic literature.[3] It is alongside Mary that he first appears in Christian art (Plate 3). In modern times Isaiah 61:10 was prescribed as the entrance antiphon at mass on the Feast of the Immaculate Conception, instituted by Pius IX in 1854, and 66:10–14 designated as one of the readings for the Feast of Our Lady of Lourdes,[4] instituted as a local feast in 1891 and as a universal feast in 1907. The first of these texts, which sees Mary and/or the Church in the figure

---

[1]   Cf. Warner, *Alone of All Her Sex.*
[2]   See above, pp. 45f.   [3]   See above, pp. 49f.   [4]   See chapter 10.

65

of a 'bride adorned with a crown', figures in mediaeval Christian representations of the resurrection[5] or the eternal blessedness of the righteous in the world to come.[6] The second, in which God is represented as a mother nursing her children, also appears in the mediaeval literature,[7] and has been given fresh theological significance in recent feminist exegesis.[8] But it is to the mediaeval period that most of our attention in this chapter must be directed.

Isaiah's special association with the Virgin is in the first instance due to the fact that in the Greek and Latin versions of 7:14, he alone among the prophets seems to refer to her explicitly: *Ecce virgo concipiet et pariet filium* ... ('Behold a virgin will conceive and bring forth a son...'). In mediaeval and Renaissance art this is easily the commonest text with which he is associated.[9] Other texts appear with him in both eastern and western Christian iconography. In the eleventh-century mosaic of Christ Pantocrator in the dome of the monastery Church of Daphni near Athens, for example, he bears a scroll with part of the Greek version of Isaiah 4:2 ('On that day God will shine in the council with glory'). The Dominican artist Bartolommeo (1472–1517) chose a pithy theological phrase from the Latin version of chapter 12 (*Ecce deus salvator meus* 'Behold my God and saviour') for Isaiah's text,[10] and an *Isaiah* by Pietro Perugino (1447–1523) has a banderol with the words of 66:1 ('heaven is my throne, but the earth is my footstool').[11] But these are exceptions. Most frequently he is accompanied by a scroll with 7:14 on it as in paintings by Taddeo Gaddi (c.1300–66) and Duccio di Buoninsegna (c.1260–c.1320), as well a stained glass figure of Isaiah in the Michaeliskirche in Hildesheim and the splendid twelfth-century Italian painting of the prophet in the Church of Santa Croce in Florence. Numerous illuminated manuscripts portray Isaiah in this way too, including the Exeter Gospel Book in the Bodleian, and the Durham manuscript of Jerome's *Commentary on Isaiah* (Plate 1). Statues of the prophet, such as the one on the west doorway of the Cathedral

[5] Enghelhardt, *Der theologische Gehalt der Biblia Pauperum*, p. 139.
[6] *BP*, p. 127.
[7] E.g. *BP*, p. 126; on *ecclesia lactans*, see also below, pp. 72–73.
[8] See chapter 10.
[9] Cf. Réau, *Iconographie* II.1, p. 366; Kirschbaum, *Lexikon* II, p. 355. The words of the famous 'Jesse tree' verse (11:1, on which see below, pp. 74ff.), the richly allusive messianic verse 9:6, and others such as 63:3 and 66:1 also appear on Isaiah's scroll, but not nearly so frequently.
[10] See chapter 3.
[11] *L'opera completa del Perugino*, ed. C. Castellaneta (Milan 1969), Plate 56.

at Cremona (Plate 9) and the one on the south doorway of St Peter's Church at Moissac, carry this scroll as well. No doubt the now illegible inscription on the famous relief at Souillac was 7:14 (Plate 10), and perhaps Michelangelo's youthful Isaiah on the ceiling of the Sistine Chapel is also keeping that place with his finger.

Isaiah, with or without his *Ecce virgo* scroll, often accompanies representations of the Annunciation. In an early example by Simone Martini (c.1284–1344), now in the Uffizi Gallery, Isaiah is depicted in the top right hand corner, with the words of 7:14 on his scroll, opposite Ezekiel who has 44:2 ('This gate shall remain shut')[12] on his. Rafaellino del Garbo's *Annunciation* in the Convent of San Francesco in Fiesole shows Isaiah pointing excitedly towards the Virgin, placing the emphasis on the two opening words of our text ECCE VIRGO 'Behold the Virgin!' and the fulfilment of his prophecy. The verse appears in Hebrew in Giambattista Cima's *Annunciation* (1495) in the Hermitage, St Petersburg, where it is carved on a wooden canopy above the head of the Virgin,[13] and also in the seventeenth-century French artist Charles Le Brun's *Holy Family in Egypt* already referred to, which portrays Mary reading the text and thus charmingly suggests that the book played a part in preparing Mary for her role as Virgin Mother of God (Plate 2). In Matthias Grünewald's version of the Annunciation on the famous Isenheimer Altar executed in 1512–15 and now in the Colmar Museum, the point is made even more clearly: Mary has been reading the relevant chapter of Isaiah (in Latin) at the very moment when the archangel Gabriel arrives.[14] Isaiah, with what is clearly intended to be the Hebrew original in his hand, floats about in the background (Plate 11).[15]

The tradition continues down into the nineteenth century as can be seen on a column, standing in front of the little Piazza Mignanelli near the Spanish Steps in Rome. This was put up in 1857, three years after the proclamation of the dogma of the Immaculate Conception referred to above, and shows Isaiah, along with three other prophets, again with ECCE VIRGO CONCIPIET ... on his scroll. Another nineteenth-century example is a Bible illustration by Alfred Rethel (1816–59), dated about 1852, showing Isaiah with a

[12] On this reference to Mary's virginity, see p. 73.

[13] *The Hermitage, Leningrad: Medieval & Renaissance*, ed. V. F. Levinson-Lessing (Paul Hamlyn, London, 1967), Plate 26; P. Humfrey, *Cima da Conegliano* (Cambridge 1983), Plate 43, pp. 106–9.

[14] *Grünewald*, Plates 18, 24.

[15] *Grünewald*, Plate 22; Huysmans, 'The Grünewalds in the Colmar Museum', p. 5.

scroll on which he has apparently been writing the words *Emmanuel Godt mit uns* ('God with us') from the second part of 7:14, and pointing eagerly to, among other things, a nativity scene above him.[16] Of several examples from twentieth-century Holland, one in the Catholic Church of St Martin in Giesbeck, dated 1916, shows Isaiah before a sullen-faced King Ahaz, pointing upwards to an inset nativity scene at the top of the window, while beneath in Dutch are the words of verse 14 in full.[17]

One of the best illustrations of Isaiah's role in mediaeval cathedral architecture is to be found in the Cathedral at Chartres, built in the thirteenth century. We shall look in detail at the famous Jesse window, based on Isaiah 11:1–2, below, and at the statue of Isaiah at the main entrance. For the moment we shall look at his appearance in one of the four famous lancet windows beneath the south rose window. These portray the four major prophets, bearing on their shoulders the four evangelists: Jeremiah with St Luke on his back, Isaiah with St Matthew, Ezekiel with St John, and Daniel with St Mark.[18] In this remarkable convention, found in Notre Dame in Paris as well, the prophets are depicted as giants from the past supporting the evangelists and providing them, so to speak, with a spiritual vantage point from which they have a wider view of events in the life of Christ.[19] Matthew sits on Isaiah's shoulders (Plate 12) because it is only in his Gospel (1:23) that the key text 7:14 is cited.[20] Matthew is also the only Gospel that contains an allusion (2:23) to the other major verse from Isaiah which left its mark on mediaeval Church architecture, namely 11:1 ('a rod (*virga*) will come forth from the root of Jesse'). We shall return to the 'Jesse window' at Chartres later.

Jeremiah figures in the cult of the Virgin Mary too, mainly on account of 31:22: *creavit Dominus novum super terram: femina circumdabit virum* ('The Lord has created a new thing upon the earth: a woman will embrace (or enclose) a man'). In the context of Christian

---

[16] C. G. Boerner, *Nachgelassene Zeichnungen von Alfred Rethel (1816–1859). Neue Lagerliste* (Düsseldorf 1968), no.49.

[17] The Stichting Kerkelijk Kunstbezit in Nederland (Utrecht) lists one painting and three stained glass windows representing Isaiah before King Ahaz, that is to say, the occasion on which Isaiah uttered the words of 7:14.

[18] Cowan, *Rose Windows*, pp. 14–15, Plates 35–37.

[19] Cf. R. Klibansky, 'Standing on the shoulders of giants'; Smalley, *The Study of the Bible in the Middle Ages*, pp. 123f; Mâle, *L'art religieux du XIII siècle en France*, p. 10. Katzenellenbogen, *The Sculptural Programs of Chartres Cathedral*, p. 102.

[20] Matthew cites Isaiah by name six times: see above, p. 21.

theology, this perplexing verse was understood to refer to the doctrine of the Virgin Birth. In art the verse appears sometimes with Isaiah 7:14,[21] and adaptations of other verses from Jeremiah (e.g.18:20; 2:32) are as prominent in masses of the Virgin as the Isaiah texts. This explains no doubt why in the Chartres window he is associated with St Luke, the other Gospel which starts with the nativity stories. Ezekiel too appears alongside Isaiah sometimes, as in the Biblia Pauperum and Simone Martini's painting already referred to. But no other prophet has had so significant and so influential a role to play in mediaeval perceptions of the Virgin as Isaiah. It is as though 7:14 is at the centre of an ever-widening circle of texts adduced in all kinds of contexts – liturgical, doctrinal, artistic, sociopolitical and ethical – in which the Virgin Mary is venerated.

It is not necessary to go over texts again that are already familiar from our earlier discussion of the nativity (1:3; 9:1–6), the visit of the magi (60:1–6), and the flight into Egypt (19:1).[22] Nor shall we spend time on very general texts used to describe the coronation of the Virgin (35:2; 61:10; cf.also 11:1).[23] Of special interest is the way in which a number of texts from Isaiah are used in this context, as Warner noted, to promote a particular view of women. First, a theme which recurs in several much-used texts from Isaiah associated with the Virgin, is the notion that a woman's body is like a field or a piece of earth in which men sow their seed. It was not until the nineteenth century that scientists discovered the ovum, and before then such a notion of women as the totally passive recipients of a male action in conception was the dominant one. Several Isaiah texts were used to express it.

One of the most popular was the Latin version of 45:8: *Rorate coeli desuper, et nubes pluant justum; aperiatur terra, et germinet Salvatorem.*[24] English has no word for 'to send down dew' (corresponding to verbs for 'to rain', 'to snow', etc.) and thus English translations of this verse are less beautiful (and less accurate) than the Latin: 'Drop down, ye heavens, from above';[25] or 'Shower, O heavens, from above, and let the skies rain down righteousness; let the earth open, that salvation may spring up' (*NRSV*). One reason for the popularity and liturgical success of the Latin version is thus the first word *Rorate* 'send down

21 E.g. *BP*, p. 50.   22 See above, pp. 49f.
23 Cf. *BP*, p. 119; on her appearance among the kings in the Jesse tree, see pp. 74f.
24 See Sawyer, 'Christian interpretations of Isaiah 45:8'.
25 Cf. *EH*, 735.

dew' which is more euphonious than any of the English versions. The Latin also replaces the word 'salvation' (*NRSV*; Hebrew *yesha'*) with the word *Salvatorem* 'saviour', as is done elsewhere, making it even more amenable to christological interpretations ('Let the earth open up and bring forth a Saviour').[26] The verse is then a prayer that the Holy Spirit should come down upon the Virgin Mary like dew, so that she will conceive and bear a saviour. The same notion appears also in traditional christological interpretations of Isaiah 53:2, understood as a reference to Christ born of a virgin 'like a root out of dry ground',[27] and in the image of Gideon's fleece miraculously moistened by dew when the rest of the ground was dry (Judges 6:36–8). The first page of the *Biblia Pauperum*, illustrating the Annunciation, contains a good example of this, in which the Judges passage is accompanied by Isaiah 7:14 and Psalm 72:6: '. . . may he be like showers that water the earth'.[28] The well-known fifteenth-century meditation on the Incarnation beginning 'I sing of a maiden' also makes use of this image:

> . . . He came all so still
> Where his mother was,
> As dew in April
> That falleth on the grass.
> He came all so still
> To his mother's bowr,
> As dew in April
> That falleth on the flower.
> He came all so still
> Where his mother lay,
> As dew in April
> That falleth on the spray . . .[29]

There is another mediaeval example in the York Cycle of mystery plays where *Rorate coeli desuper* is one of several Latin quotations from Isaiah, lavishly expounded by the 'Doctour' at the beginning of the Spicers' contribution on the 'Annunciation and Visitation' (the others are 7:14, 9:6 and 11:1).[30] John Bale (1495–1563) also develops the 'dew' image in his religious drama *God's Promises*,[31] while a

---

[26]   Cf. pp. 58–9.   [27]   *CCSL* 73.2,1, 588 (Jerome).

[28]   *BP*, p. 50. Henry cites Ambrose, Bernard of Clairvaux and others as authorities for the image. For the liturgical addition of *Dominus* in Psalm 72:6, see pp. 80–82 on *Emitte agnum*.

[29]   *OBC*, 183; cf. Duffy, *Stripping the Altars*, pp. 256–7.

[30]   Beadle, ed., *The York Plays*, pp. 112f.

[31]   J. Bale, *God's Promises*, p. 115. See also p. 82.

better-known example is the macaronic poem by William Dunbar (1460–1520). It is written in Scots, but the first verse begins with words from the Latin liturgy *Rorate coeli desuper*, corresponding to *Gloria in excelsis* in the last verse, and all seven verses end with an equally familiar Latin refrain from Isaiah 9:6.

> *Rorate coeli desuper.*
> Hevins distill your balmy schouris,
> For now is rissin the bricht day ster
> Fro the ros Mary, flour of flouris;
> The cleir sone quhome no clud devouris,
> Surmunting Phebus in the est,
> Is cummin of his hevinly touris
> *Et nobis Puer natus est.*

The reference to 'the bright day-star from the rose Mary' in verse 1 also comes from Isaiah.[32] It is interesting that in this celebration of the nativity, the poet says nothing about the Annunciation, or the baby in a manger or the wise men from the east. Instead he uses the *Rorate* to introduce a hymn of praise, more like the *Te Deum* or the *Benedicite* than a Christmas carol.[33]

The *Rorate*, combining Isaiah 45:8 with 64:6–7, 9–12, 16:1 and 40:1, became one of the most familiar passages from Isaiah in the Latin mass. An English version is printed in full in the *English Hymnal* for use in Anglican churches.[34] As an introit it was sung at the beginning of Advent masses and masses of the Virgin Mary. 'Rorate Masses' in Advent were popular from the fifteenth century, and this is where the *Collegium Rorantistarum* ('College of Rorate-singers'), a chapel choir established in Krakow in 1543, got its name.[35]

It still has a place in the vernacular mass as the introit on the fourth Sunday of Advent, where it is associated with Isaiah 7:14 and the doctrine of the Virgin Birth,[36] and there are modern settings of the *Rorate* by the South African born John Joubert, formerly Professor of Music at Birmingham, and the Scottish composer Thea Musgrave. The image of the Virgin, and of women in general, as parcels of land, however, has mercifully little or no appeal today, and a quite different interpretation of 45:8 has developed, severing its association with the Virgin Mary. Martin Luther had already

---

[32] Combined with Numbers 24:16: see above, p. 46.
[33] S. Carpenter, 'The Bible in Mediaeval Verse and Drama', pp. 74f.
[34] *EH*, 735.　[35]　J. Mráček, 'Rorate chants', p. 185.
[36] *New Sunday Missal*, p. 15.

attacked the 'papistic preachers' of his day who 'twisted the passage and applied it to the blessed Virgin'.[37] In contemporary Christianity it has become a prayer for justice and freedom, and as such inspired the refrain for a hymn composed in 1967, which no longer has any connection with the cult of the Virgin:

> Rain down justice,
> you heavens, from above;
> let the earth bring forth for us
> the one who is to come.[38]

This contrasts with the official modern translation of the verse, as used in the liturgy.[39] Here both the 'justice' and the 'salvation' of the original Hebrew have disappeared in favour of 'the Just One' and 'the Saviour', so that the verse remains a celebration of the miraculous conception of Christ, rather than a prayer for justice, and the mediaeval view of the role of women in child-bearing implicitly retained.

Isaiah has an important role to play in another part of the cult of the Virgin, namely, in the celebration of her marriage, as symbol of the Church, to Christ.[40] On the last two pages of the *Biblia Pauperum*, Isaiah 66:10 is applied to the beatific vision of Christ gathering the souls of the faithful into the New Jerusalem, and 61:10 is used to describe how, like a bridegroom, he adorns her with the crown of eternal life. The climax of the book of Revelation uses similar imagery, equally dependent on Isaiah. But Isaiah has a further contribution to make to this image, recently analysed in grim detail by Caroline Walker Bynum in her *Holy Feast and Holy Fast. The Religious Significance of Food to Medieval Women* (1987). In a chapter on 'Woman's body as food' she discusses the close relationship, in mediaeval iconography as well as literature, between the image of the lactating Virgin, nourishing her Church, and the image of Christ – like the more familiar pelican symbol – feeding his people with the blood that flows from his breast: 'both men and women ... saw the body on the cross, which in dying fed the world, as in some sense female'.[41] She notes the frequent parallelism in mediaeval art between the image of the Virgin presenting her breast and the figure of Christ exposing his wound, between the Nursing Virgin and the

---

[37]   *LW* 17, p. 125.   [38]   *HON*, 459.   [39]   *New Sunday Missal*, p. 15.
[40]   Cf. *BP*, p. 127; Warner, *Alone of all her Sex*, pp. 121–33.
[41]   Bynum, *Holy Feast and Holy Fast*, p. 270.

Man of Sorrows, a parallelism known to art-historians as the 'Double Intercession'.[42]

What interests us here is that the very same parallelism occurs already in the imagery of Isaiah.[43] On the one hand, 66:11–12 describes the 'consoling breasts' of the Church, the New Jerusalem, at which the faithful suck and are satisfied, while, on the other, in 49:15 the image is applied to God or Christ: 'Can a woman forget her baby, that she should have no compassion on the son of her womb? Even these may forget, yet I will not forget you'. Similarly, in 54 (cf. Gal.4:27) the mother image refers to the Church, and God is her husband,[44] while in 42:14 and 66:13 it is God who is once again compared to a mother. As the *ne plus ultra* of this development, Walker Bynum refers to 'a picture of a stunning reversal, in which Mary drinks from the breast of Christ while holding him in her arms'.[45] When we take seriously the imagery of Isaiah 42, 49 and 66, it is almost as 'stunning'.[46]

The famous relief of the prophet Isaiah which stands at what was once the main entrance to the Cathedral of Notre Dame at Souillac on the river Lot in South West France, may serve to illustrate another aspect of mediaeval attitudes towards women (Plate 10). Opposite Isaiah there is a relief of Joseph, not the Joseph one might perhaps expect in a church dedicated to Mary, but the Joseph from the Genesis story.[47] This gives us the key to Isaiah's role here. The common theme linking Joseph and Isaiah is virginity or chastity. From the story of his chaste rejection of Potiphar's wife (Gen.39), Joseph came to be used as a symbol of chastity, foreshadowing, like Isaiah 7:14, the virginity of Mary. The Virgin Mary's role as patroness or guardian of a celibate priesthood is well known.[48] What is interesting for our purposes is the way in which our prophet is here apparently being used to promote the Church's teaching on chastity and celibacy, dominated as it has been by suspicion of women and sex in general.

[42] Bynum, *Holy Feast and Holy Fast*, p. 272.
[43] Bynum lists Isaiah 49:1, 49:15 and 66:11–13 among 'the most important biblical roots' of this, but does not point out that 49:15 and 66:11–13 are the most specific on her list. She might have added Psalm 131:2. See also pp. 205–211.
[44] See Sawyer, 'Daughter of Zion', pp. 93–6.
[45] Bynum, *Holy Feast and Holy Fast*, p. 272; cf. also Bynum, *Fragmentation and Redemption*, pp. 93–108.
[46] Cf. Sawyer, 'Radical images of Yahweh in Isaiah'.
[47] Cf. Schapiro, *Romanesque Art*, pp. 104–9.
[48] Warner, *Alone of All Her Sex*, pp. 158f.

One of the most influential Isaianic images in mediaeval Christian art and literature is that of the Jesse tree from 11:1–2:

> *Et egredietur virga de radice Jesse*
> *et flos de radice eius ascendet.*
> *Et requiescet super eum spiritus Domini:*
> *spiritus sapientiae, et intellectus,*
> *spiritus consilii, et fortitudinis,*
> *spiritus scientiae, et pietatis.*
> *Et replebit eum spiritus timoris Domini.*

> A rod will come forth from the root of Jesse,
>   and a flower will arise from its root.
> And the spirit of the Lord will rest upon him,
>   the spirit of wisdom, and of understanding,
>   the spirit of counsel, and of fortitude,
>   the spirit of knowledge, and of piety;
> And the spirit of the fear of the Lord will fill him.

The magnificent lancet window of Chartres Cathedral, where one of the earliest and most beautiful stained glass representations of the Jesse tree is to be found, actually keeps quite close to the text (Plate 13). At the bottom Jesse, the father of David and thus ancestor of the Messiah, lies sleeping. From his loins (or perhaps from his side like Eve emerging from Adam's side), a stylized family tree is depicted with four kings, the Virgin Mary ('the Second Eve') and Christ enthroned at the top. Seven doves surround Christ, symbolizing the seven gifts of the spirit listed in the second part of the passage, and on each side of the tree Christ's spiritual ancestors are represented as well, in the form of the prophets with Isaiah as always located close to the Virgin.[49] In the words of one modern commentary on the 'visual music' of this exquisite work of art, 'the theme or "melody" of the branches ascends in beautiful arabesques to explode in the seven gifts of the spirit'.[50]

There are 'Jesse windows' in many of the great French cathedrals, Le Mans, Angers, Troyes and Soissons, for example, and also in the Sainte-Chapelle in Paris. English examples include the remains of one in York Minster[51] and a huge fourteenth-century stone fragment

---

[49]   Mâle, *L'Art religieux du douzième siècle en France*, pp. 168–70; Watson, *The Early Iconography of the Tree of Jesse* (1934); Schiller, *Iconography*, I, pp. 15–22.
[50]   Lee, Sedden and Stephen, edd., *Stained Glass*, p. 37.
[51]   Lee, Sedden and Stephen, edd., *Stained Glass*, p. 71.

in Abergavenny Priory in Wales,[52] as well as a fine fifteenth-century example in the Abbey Church of St Mary at Dorchester in Oxfordshire.[53] In the magnificent central doorway of the thirteenth-century north porch at Chartres, Isaiah takes his place among the heralds of Christ, waiting like the aged Symeon 'for the consolation of Israel'. From the left, in chronological order, each carrying a symbol of Christ, stand Isaiah with a branch from the tree of Jesse, Jeremiah with a cross, Symeon with the Christ child, John the Baptist with the lamb, and Peter with the chalice. On the other side of the door, in perfect symmetry, stand five other heralds of Christ: Melchizedek with a chalice like Peter, Abraham with his son Isaac, corresponding to Symeon with the child Jesus, Moses with the bronze serpent, corresponding to Jeremiah with the cross, Samuel with a sacrificial lamb like John the Baptist's, and, corresponding to the branch from the tree of Jesse in Isaiah's hand, stands King David, the chief descendant of that tree. Above them in four of the great archivolts is an impressive Jesse Tree, made up of two rows of kings, accompanied, as in the Jesse window, by two rows of prophets.[54]

The west front of the Cathedral of Notre Dame at Reims is another example.[55] The central doorway is again flanked by various heralds of Christ, including Isaiah, the 'Fifth Evangelist', grouped with John the Baptist, the aged Symeon and other figures from the Gospels rather than with the Prophets. Above them in the arch over the doorway are the ancestors of Christ, arranged in the shape of another tree of Jesse. The family tree of David emerges from Jesse's body and leads upwards to David, Solomon, Rehoboam and the rest till we reach the top of the tree, in this case, the Virgin Mary to whom the cathedral is dedicated. Amiens Cathedral has a similar façade, where the main entrance is flanked by prophets and saints, angels and martyrs, and the ancestors of the Messiah each symbolically clutching a branch of the tree.[56] Two other striking examples worth mentioning are to be found on the marvellous central marble column of the twelfth-century Portico de la Gloria in the Cathedral of Santiago de Compostela, and on the ceiling of the Church of St

---

[52] Thorold, *Collins Guide to Cathedrals*, p. 317.

[53] Thorold, *Collins Guide to Cathedrals*, p. 186; Lee, Sedden and Stephen, edd., *Stained Glass*, p. 37.

[54] Katzenellenbogen, *Sculptural Programs of Chartres Cathedral*, p. 34.

[55] Bony, *French Cathedrals*, p. 160.

[56] Bony, *French Cathedrals*, p. 97.

Michael in Hildesheim.[57] Other examples will be discussed later as they appear in other contexts.

In one of the earliest examples, an eleventh-century Bible manuscript in Dijon, it is the subject of the illuminated initial letter at the beginning of the book of Isaiah, the only illustration, presumably selected for this purpose as the most typical or memorable or influential verse in the book.[58] A well-known example from the twelfth-century Lambeth Bible will be discussed below (Plate 14).[59] In another, from Prague, Isaiah is depicted as seated beside Jesse, embracing him as it were, with the words of 11:1–2 on a banderol encircling them both.[60] A clear indication of the central role played by this verse in mediaeval perceptions of Isaiah is the frequency with which he is represented as holding a branch of the Jesse tree in his hand.[61] In the fourteenth-century Dublin Bible, a Jesse tree appears at the beginning of the Psalter, now with a life of its own unattached to Isaiah, showing David and Solomon as well as Christ and the Virgin Mary, thus highlighting both the Davidic authorship of the Psalms and their christological application.[62]

In earlier periods the first verse had been much quoted in messianic contexts, both Jewish and Christian. The Jewish Targum has 'And the king shall come forth from the sons of Jesse, and the Messiah from his sons' sons'.[63] Paul applies it to Christ in Romans 15:12. In Latin tradition it is sometimes combined with Balaam's 'star prophecy' in Numbers 24:17, where the word *virga* 'rod, sceptre' also occurs.[64] The catacomb painting referred to above as the earliest representation of Isaiah is one example of this; another appears on page 3 of the *Biblia Pauperum*, where it is linked to the visit of the magi and the appearance of 'a star in the east' (Matth.2:9). Possibly the prophecy referred to in Matthew 2:23 that the Messiah would be called 'the Nazarene' (Hebrew *notzri*) was derived from the use of the term *netzer* 'branch' (Vg *flos* 'flower') here, as early Christian commentators, including Jerome, believed.

---

[57]   Watson, *Early Iconography*, pp. 106ff, 125ff; Plates XXI and XXVII; Schiller, *Iconography* I, p. 18; fig. 29.

[58]   Watson, *Early Iconography*, p. 87, Plate III; Schiller, *Iconography* I, p. 16; fig. 23.

[59]   See p. 121.

[60]   Vyšehrad Ms XIV. A.13, fol. 4v: see Watson, *Early Iconography*, Plate I; Schiller, *Iconography* I, p. 16, fig. 22.

[61]   Réau, *Iconographie*, II, 1, p. 366; Kirschbaum, *Lexikon*,II , p. 355.

[62]   Trinity College (Dublin) Library Ms. A.1.2.

[63]   Chilton, *Glory of Israel*, p. 88.

[64]   E.g. *BP*, p. 54. The star-prophecy lies behind the story of the magi as well.

The rest of the passage, interpreted in the light of Isaiah 42:1f., 61:1f. and the baptism narrative in the Gospels, similarly focusses on the Messiah, the descent of the Holy Spirit upon him 'like a dove', and the new age of justice and peace which he will inaugurate.

What was the appeal of this imagery from Isaiah 11 which appears all over mediaeval Europe? What happened to this passage in the Middle Ages can be explained by reference to two developments in its exegetical history, both involving a shift of emphasis away from an exclusive focus on the person, character and achievements of the Messiah himself. On the one hand, in the context of the cult of the Virgin Mary, the similarity of the Latin words for 'rod' (*virga*) and 'virgin' (*virgo*) took on an extra significance, and 11:1 was interpreted in two parts. The first part of the verse about 'a *virga* from the root of Jesse', following on from 7:14 (*ecce virgo concipiet filium*), is then applied to the Virgin, while the second part about a 'flower' continues to refer to the Messiah himself. As scriptural authority for this connection, Jerome and others cite the famous words of Solomon, given a messianic interpretation, like the rest of the Song of Solomon: *Ego flos campi et lilium convallium* ('I am a rose of Sharon, a lily of the valleys') (Song of Solomon 2:1). Thus, while the second half of the verse stays firmly within the Jewish messianic tradition, the first half turns the spotlight on the Blessed Virgin Mary and provides both the inspiration and the scriptural authority for her inclusion in the branches of the Jesse tree. The *Bible Moralisée* shows a simple tree emerging from Jesse and at the top a bird symbolizing the Holy Spirit from verse 2. In an anonymous sixteenth-century Italian *Jesse Tree* in the National Gallery, the Madonna even takes the place of the Messiah at the top, sitting with the Christ child on her knee.[65]

Before turning to the second reason for the popularity of this verse in the mediaeval Church, a well-known fifteenth-century German hymn to Mary, still sung at Christmas time all over the world, provides us with a summary, in the vernacular, of mediaeval Christian interpretations:

> Es ist ein Ros' entsprungen
> Aus einer Wurzel zart,
> Als uns die Alten sungen
> Aus Jesse kam die Art;

---

[65] Warner, *Alone of All Her Sex*, fig. 13.

Und hat ein Blümlein bracht,
Mitten im kalten Winter
Wohl zu der halben Nacht.

Das Röslein das ich meine,
    Davon Jesaias sagt,
Ist Maria die reine,
    Die uns dies Blümlein bracht.
        Aus Gottes ew'gem Rat
        Hat sie ein Kindlein g'boren,
        Ist blieb'n ein' reine Magd.

Wir bitten dich vom Herzen,
    Maria, Rose zart,
Durch dieses Blümleins Schmerzen,
    Die er empfunden hat,
        Wollst uns behülflich sein,
        Daß wir ihm mögen machen,
        Ein' Wohnung hübsch und fein.

The Virgin is the 'rose' from the stem of Jesse, 'foretold by Isaiah' (verse 2). The 'rod' (*virga*) in 11:1 is associated in the liturgy with Numbers 17:8 (the blossoming of Aaron's rod)[66] and the 'roses' in Ecclesiasticus 24:14 (cf.39:13; 50:8).[67] Jesus is there too in the image of 'the little flower' (*das Blümlein*) 'that Mary brought to us', whose advent and nativity are celebrated in the first two stanzas and whose sufferings feature in the third.

Several English versions of this exist, most of them twentieth-century compositions, but none of these has gained much popularity.[68] The imagery survives in the more ancient and much more widely-used Advent hymn 'O come, O come, Immanuel', discussed above:[69]

O come, thou rod of Jesse, free
Thine own from Satan's tyranny;
From depths of hell thy people save,
And give them victory o'er the grave.

But notice how here the 'rod of Jesse' is not Mary, but Jesus, and the

[66] *Virga Jesse floruit: Virgo Deum et hominem genuit: pacem Deus reddidit, in se reconcilians imma summis*: this variation on the theme, bringing together Numbers 17:8 and Isaiah 11:1, was one of the Gospel acclamations recited at masses of the Virgin Mary until modern times.
[67] A reading from Sirach 24 was also prescribed for several of the Marian masses.
[68] Compare *SNOBC* pp. 100–4. *OBC* 76 gives only the original German.
[69] See pp. 56f.

image comes as much from 11:4 ('he shall smite the earth with the rod of his mouth') as from the genealogical Jesse tree in verse 1.[70] Quite apart from the changed role of Mary in the Reformed tradition, like many of the mediaeval interpretations of Isaiah, the verbal association between the 'rod' in verse 1 and the Virgin Mary is an exclusively Latin one (*virga/virgo*) and disappears in translation.

The other main reason why the Jesse tree imagery played so prominent a role in the mediaeval Church is a socio-political one. Clearly the ancestry of Jesus held a particular fascination for mediaeval artists, living as they did in a society where kings and knights set great store by their lineage. In earlier interpretations of this passage, there is no particular interest evident in this aspect of messianism. Jerome, for example, makes no mention of it. But in mediaeval stained glass and sculpture the family tree of Christ with which the Gospel of St Matthew begins, looms very large as we have seen. Matthew's genealogy spans twenty-eight generations, fourteen from David to the exile and fourteen from the exile to Christ (Matthew 1:17), and so there are often precisely twenty-eight kings in the Jesse trees such as those we looked at above. Matthew 1:1–17 provides the content for the tree, while Isaiah 11:1 provides its structure and imagery. This cannot be dissociated from mediaeval preoccupation with lineage and ancestry. It is significant that for mediaeval commentators like Andrew of St Victor, nobility and royal connections constitute such an important part of their brief introductory biographies of Isaiah.[71]

We must also remember that in mediaeval times it was believed that human kings received their authority from the same divinely appointed source as the ancestors of Christ. Thus, for example, when David and Solomon are represented in the tree, as the spiritual ancestors of Christ, they are understood to be at the same time the spiritual ancestors of the Kings of France.[72] The image of a tree no doubt appealed to artists and those who commissioned them simply because of its artistic potential. It readily fits the demands of window architecture, as well as providing endless scope for elaborate variation on the manuscript page. But it is at the same time the symbol of a hierarchy, and its ideological function in the Middle Ages cannot be ignored. It stands for the fixed order of a social and political

[70] See below, p. 228
[71] Cf. Smalley, *The Study of the Bible in the Middle Ages*, pp. 135–6.
[72] Katzenellenbogen, *Sculptural Programs*, p. 34.

system controlled by the king, who is perceived as having supreme
authority at the top. The Coronation of the Virgin is another
popular image which is obviously politically motivated too. It first
appears in the twelfth century and was perhaps invented by the Abbé
Suger of St Denis, a staunch supporter of the French monarchy, who
greatly influenced the evolution of mediaeval iconography, including
the Jesse tree with both Jesus and the Virgin Mary depicted as
reigning monarchs.[73]

A later, rather less lovely example from a sixteenth-century
window in the Church of St Etienne in Beauvais adds further
evidence for the contemporary political dimension of the Jesse tree
image.[74] In it some of the ancestors are suspiciously like sixteenth-
century French personalities: Solomon is an ugly, toothless, wizened
old man, and one of the others is actually the artist himself, Engrand,
with an armband bearing his initials. At the top of the tree sprouts a
lily, emblem of France, of course, as well as of the Virgin. It is not
hard to recognize here a decline in the earlier popularity of this
motif: in place of former splendour and political confidence are
disenchantment and not very subtle irony.

It rarely appears again as a productive motif, although it remains
familiar in surviving mediaeval art, literature and music as we have
seen. This was due in part at least to the fact that at the Reformation
the centrality of both the cult of the Virgin Mary and the Roman
hierarchy was challenged. Without those two pillars of the mediaeval
Church, the imagery of Isaiah 11:1–2 became less widely used. The
passage remains in Advent lectionaries to this day, but the emphasis
is more on the gifts of the spirit in verse 2 or the actions of the
Messiah as described in subsequent verses, than on his ancestry.[75]
The merging of the Jesse tree image with images of the crucifixion
will be discussed in a later chapter.[76]

Another verse, whose popularity in the Middle Ages was no doubt
also due largely to a peculiar interest in the ancestry of Jesus, is
Isaiah 16:1: *Emitte agnum, dominatorem terrae, de petra deserti ad montem filiae
Sion.* The passage is part of a prophecy against Moab, which begins
in the previous chapter: 'An oracle concerning Moab. Because Ar is

[73]   Warner, *Alone of all her Sex*, pp. 113–14.
[74]   Lee, Sedden and Stephen, edd., *Stained Glass*, p. 139.
[75]   Along with 42:1–4 and 61:1–3, it is prescribed for Confirmation services in the latest
       Catholic lectionary. *Lectionary*, p. 889.
[76]   See below, pp. 94ff.

laid waste in a night, Moab is undone; because Kir is laid waste in a night, Moab is undone ...' (15:1). Within a Christian context this is not a very illuminating passage, one has to admit, and at first sight Chapter 16 does not seem to be much better. The *NRSV* and most modern versions find the Hebrew problematical and follow the Jewish Targum: 'Send (*or* They have sent *RSV*) lambs to the ruler of the land, from Sela by way of the desert, to the mountain of the daughter of Zion.' The Hebrew text, however, is followed quite closely by Christian tradition as for example in the Latin version given above, and may be translated as follows: 'Send forth a lamb, who will conquer the earth, from a rock in the desert, to the mountain of the daughter of Zion'. It does not require much imagination to recognize here, as Christian tradition has done from ancient times, an allusion to Ruth the Moabitess, the grandmother of Jesse and thus the rock from which the ancestors of Christ were hewn (cf. Isaiah 51:1). In an illustration of the verse from a thirteenth-century *Bible Moralisée*, Isaiah points to the Virgin Mary who stands in the rocky wilderness tenderly holding the Lamb in her arms.[77] Maybe the familiar Catholic image of 'Our Lady of the Rocks' owes something to this passage, and perhaps also Leonardo da Vinci's *Virgin of the Rocks* in the Louvre.

The passage beginning *Emitte agnum* became a regular part of western Christian language about the Lamb of God,[78] his ancestry, his coming to Jerusalem and his victory over the world. In at least one monastic order Isaiah 16 was prescribed to be read in the second week of Advent,[79] and the verse beginning *Emitte Agnum* sung as an antiphon.[80] Since the sixteenth century at the latest, the vocative *Domine* 'O Lord' was inserted after *Emitte Agnum*,[81] an improvement felt to be justified, no doubt, by its similarity to the beginning of the next word *dominatorem*: 'Send forth the lamb, O Lord, who will conquer the earth ...' The rest of the passage contains prayers for good counsel, justice and the protection of refugees, not unlike the sequel to 11:1. It ends with a statement of faith in the throne of David 'on which will sit one who judges and seeks justice and is swift to do what is right.' In its Latin version, followed incidentally by the

---

[77] Laborde, *Bible Moralisée*, folio 111v.
[78] The suffering of Christ is compared to that of a lamb before its shearers in a more familiar passage in Chapter 53 to which we shall return later: see pp. 87–91.
[79] *Breviarium Monasticum*, p. 220.   [80] *Ibid*, p. 32.
[81] *Biblia Sacra iuxta Vulgatam Versionem*, 11, p. 1112.

Geneva Bible translators and the Reims Douay version,[82] this is a
fine messianic passage, similar to 9:1–6, 11:1–5, 42:1–4 and the like,
but less familiar nowadays. A rare English example occurs in Act VI
of John Bale's religious play, *God's Promises* referred to above. In a
remarkable dialogue between God 'the heavenly Father' (*Pater
caelestis*) and Isaiah, in which passages from Isaiah are alternately
allocated to the two speakers, Isaiah utters the following prayer,
based on *Emitte agnum* (16:1), *Rorate* (45:8) and 64:1:

> Open thou the heavens, and let the lamb come hither
> Which will deliver thy people altogether.
> Ye planets and clouds! Cast down your dews and rain,
> That the earth may bear our healthful savour plain.[83]

It does figure in a modern Catholic hymn, and parts of the passage
are cited by the liberation theologians.[84] But it is not in the Sunday
lectionaries any more, nor is its mediaeval interpretation even
referred to in most modern commentaries. This is a case where we
might well ask which interpretation, within the context of the
Christian Church, is more effective or more important: the obscure
reconstructed original meaning of a prophecy against a country that
no longer exists, or a richly allusive expression of Christian belief
about Christ, his Davidic ancestry, his triumph in Jerusalem and
the establishment of justice and peace? It is certainly a fine
illustration of our thesis that the later career of a passage in the
context of Christian tradition at the very least deserves a mention in
a serious commentary.

[82] Cf. Rashkow, *Upon the Dark Places*, p. 121.
[83] Bale, *God's Promises*, p. 115.
[84] See below, pp. 227f.

CHAPTER 5

The Man of Sorrows

In the later Middle Ages we can detect a clear change of emphasis in perceptions and representations of Isaiah, marked by the appearance of different verses on his scroll and new interpretations of even the most familiar Isaianic texts and images. The poem about the 'Suffering Servant' in Chapter 53 had always been one of the main passages which earned for Isaiah the title 'evangelist' among Christians, but from the twelfth century on texts from this chapter were given special prominence and provided the inspiration for a number of influential new images. Particularly significant were the first person plurals in this passage, by which the Church was able to relate the suffering of Christ to the lives of the faithful: 'he was wounded for *our* transgressions ... all *we* like sheep have gone astray ... the Lord laid on him the iniquity of *us* all'.

One of the earliest examples in art is a twelfth-century enamel plaque in the British Museum, showing the head of Isaiah. In place of the far commoner inscriptions discussed above in the context of the cult of the Virgin Mary,[1] we find the first words of 53:4: *Vere langores nos(tros ipse tulit)* ('truly (he bore) our weaknesses') (Plate 4). By the time of Chaucer (c.1343–1400), this had become the normal perception of Isaiah: from being primarily a 'Prophet of the Annunciation', with the spotlight on 7:14 and 11:1–2, he had become a 'Prophet of the Passion'. In the *Parson's Tale*, Isaiah 53:5 is quoted to remind people of their responsibility for Christ's agony.[2] The Parson also quotes Isaiah incidentally to remind them of the fear of death (Isaiah 14:11)[3] and hell-fire (66:24).[4] Claus Sluter's famous statue of Isaiah, which we shall look at shortly, is another example

---

[1] See pp. 66ff.
[2] *The Parson's Tale*, line 280; Blake, p. 607.
[3] *The Parson's Tale*, line 198; Blake, p. 603.
[4] *The Parson's Tale*, line 210; Blake, p. 603.

from the late fourteenth century. From a later period Lukas Cranach the Younger (1515–86) includes in his representation of the 'Call of Isaiah' (Isaiah 6) scenes of Gethsemane, the carrying of the cross and the crucifixion, as examples of Isaiah's prophecies being fulfilled (Plate 20). The Wittenberg Bible of 1534 also selects the Passion as one of two prophecies depicted in the same scene: the other is the parable of the vineyard from chapter 5, a passage interpreted already by St Matthew (Matt.21:33–46) as referring to the passion.[5]

A clear illustration of the change in Christian perceptions of the 'fifth evangelist' can also be seen in the use made of the symbol of the lamb. In earlier centuries (following Rev.5:6ff.;, 14:1ff.; 21:23) the 'Lamb of God' was represented as a symbol of Christ's victory. This was the context in which Isaiah 16:1, for example, came into Christian tradition: *Emitte agnum, Domine, dominatorem terrae.*[6] From the tenth century, however, in line with developments discussed above, the suffering of the Lamb is more poignantly depicted, and as we shall see, for instance, in Sluter's use of Isaiah 53:7, grouped with other passages of scripture describing or lamenting the betrayal, humiliation and suffering of Christ.[7] Finally it is also a sign of the times that texts from Isaiah figure on no less than seven of the eight pages devoted to the Passion in the *Biblia Pauperum*, a work which was popular from the fourteenth century on.[8]

According to Emile Mâle, the fourteenth and fifteenth centuries were the age when 'the Passion became the chief concern of the Christian soul'.[9] We have seen how the popularity of the Jesse tree motif waned towards the end of the Middle Ages as the power of the ecclesiastical hierarchy was challenged all over Europe. Later we shall discuss the influence of the Reformers' *sola scriptura* doctrine and their rejection of some of the most widespread beliefs and practices of the mediaeval Church, including the cult of the Virgin Mary. It is highly likely that these were already among the factors that contributed to the new emphasis on the suffering of Christ. Gertrud Schiller

[5]   Schmidt, *Die Illustration der Lutherbibel 1522–1700*, p. 200.
[6]   See above, pp. 8off.
[7]   See Schiller, *Iconography* II, pp. 117–21.
[8]   Three predictably come from Isaiah 53 (2–3, 7, 11). The others are 3:11 (Judas' kiss), 5:20 (Jews unjustly condemn Christ), 1:4 (Christ is mocked) and 11:10 (Entombment). See *BP*, pp. 87–102; cf. Marrow, *Passion Iconography*, fig. 94; Pickering, *Literature and Art*, p. 269; Plate 29a.
[9]   Mâle, *Religious Art in France. The Late Middle Ages* (1986), p. 83. Cf. Duffy, *Stripping the Altars*, p. 234.

gives theological and ecclesiastical reasons for the change.[10] A new view of Christ's Passion, stressing the humility of Christ and the redemptive function of his death, first began to influence the iconography of the Church in the Carolingian art of the ninth century. Later, through the Church's teaching, represented by St Bernard of Clairvaux (1090–1153), for example, and St Francis of Assisi (?1189–1226), the faithful were led to believe that the sufferings and death of Christ were actually caused by their sins, and that redemption was possible only by means of the sacraments of the Church. The affirmation of the doctrine of transubstantiation at the Fourth Lateran Council in 1215 and the institution of the Feast of Corpus Christi in 1264 were expressions of these major changes in the theology of the Western Church. The sufferings of the Virgin Mary (cf. Luke 2:35) came to be an important element in liturgical and theological tradition too, and early 'Legends of the Cross' were given new significance.

In such a context the visualization of Christ's Passion and death on the cross assumed central importance for individual believers both in their private devotion or meditation and in the public celebration of the eucharist. From the thirteenth century or so the dominant image of Christ throughout Europe changed from that of Christ in his glory, an image in which, as we saw, the vision of Isaiah frequently had a significant role to play,[11] to that of Christ Crucified or 'the Man of Sorrows', characterized by a new artistic realism unknown in earlier iconography.[12]

In his *Passion Iconography in Northern European Art of the Late Middle Ages and Early Renaissance*, James Marrow fills out this general picture by a close study of fourteenth- and fifteenth-century representations of passion scenes from Germany and, especially, the Netherlands. He detects a 'sadomasochistic and erotic element' in the new spirituality, manifested in a preoccupation with the specifics of Christ's torments and his tormentors, and in the expansion of the Passion narrative with all manner of gruesome details and apocryphal anecdotes not mentioned in the Gospels.[13] Most significant for present purposes is Marrow's contention, following Kurt Ruh[14] and F.P. Pickering,[15] that

---

[10] Schiller, *Iconography*, II, pp. 9–12.
[11] See above, chapter 3.
[12] Schiller, *Iconography*, II, pp. 151–8.
[13] Marrow, *Passion Iconography*, pp. 13–17; cf. Pickering, *Literature and Art*, pp. 283f.
[14] Ruh, 'Zur Theologie des mittelalterlichen Passionstraktats'.
[15] Pickering, *Literature and Art in the Middle Ages*.

the brutal figures, cruel anecdotes and new incidents of torment not mentioned in the Gospel narratives, are derived from the Psalms and the Prophets, especially Isaiah.[16] It is not just a question of 'the spirit of the times' or 'late mediaeval realism'. The source of virtually all the gruesome new details in the Passion plays, in pictorial representations of the Passion, in the 'Passion tracts', 'Lives of Christ' and other literature of the time, is the Bible. The new descriptive detail with which episodes from the Gospel narratives like the arrest, the flagellation and the crowning with thorns are filled out, comes directly from biblical texts, such as Psalm 22, Isaiah 53 and Job.[17]

There are many lurid passages in Isaiah, like the description of a diseased body in Isaiah 1:6, which in other contexts are interpreted as metaphors and often attract little attention. But in late mediaeval European Christendom, there emerged a distinctly unhealthy, rather ghoulish interest in such texts, which then played a not insignificant role in the life of the Church. Marrow correctly identifies the source of the vivid new language used to describe Christ's passion in this period, and his numerous examples of how biblical metaphor is transformed into descriptive narrative are extremely useful for a history of interpretation. We shall have many opportunities to refer to his work in the following pages. It is interesting to note, however, that he does not comment on the special significance of Isaiah's role in the process, in spite of the fact that Isaiah figures so prominently in his discussion. In a general comment on Christian uses of Old Testament metaphors and symbols, he notes that Isaiah was referred to as 'a fifth Evangelist' by Jerome, Augustine and Isidore of Seville.[18] But nowhere does he recognize the truly remarkable contribution of Isaiah to the material he is studying. With Psalms, Isaiah is easily the most often quoted biblical text (pp. 351–3). Four of the eight key texts in his chapter on 'The Suffering Christ' are from Isaiah (1:6; 63:1–2; 53:4; 53:2),[19] and three in 'Recurring Torments' (50:6; 53:7; 63:3),[20] while his long chapter on the 'Secret Passion' tracts, so-called for their preoccupation with 'sensational, non-Gospel narrative', is peppered with references to Isaiah (e.g. 1:6; 5:6; 5:11–12; 7:23–7; 53:4; 53:7).[21] The uses to which Isaiah is put in

[16]   Marrow, *Passion Iconography*, pp. 2–5.
[17]   Marrow, *Passion Iconography*, pp. 190–8.
[18]   Marrow, *Passion Iconography*, p. 191.
[19]   Marrow, *Passion Iconography*, pp. 44–67.
[20]   Marrow, *Passion Iconography*, pp. 68–94.
[21]   Marrow, *Passion Iconography*, pp. 94–170.

the vernacular passion literature of Germany and the Low Countries, and the 'simplistic connections' perceived there between Isaiah and the passion story, surely cannot be fully appreciated without taking account of the close relationship that existed in the minds of Christian clergy and laity between the 'Fifth Gospel' and the other four.

Our discussion of this vast subject begins with a famous statue of Isaiah by the French sculptor Claus Sluter, completed between 1380 and 1400. On the hexagonal base of what was probably once a large crucifix over a fountain in Dijon visited by pilgrims, are represented six prophets, each holding a scroll with a verse about Christ's suffering. Moses carries a quotation from Exodus about the afternoon sacrifice of a lamb, a reference to the crucifixion between the sixth and the ninth hour (Exod.29:39). David's is from Psalm 22: 'they pierced my hands and feet ...' (22:16). Jeremiah, who has an angel weeping above him, has *O vos omnes* from Lamentations 1:12: 'O you who pass by, look and see if there is any sorrow like unto my sorrow'. Zechariah's verse is 'They weighed out thirty pieces of silver' (11:12), and Daniel's 'After sixty-two weeks the anointed one will be put to death' (9:26).

Isaiah stands out from the rest as older and more thoughtful and seems to be in conversation with Daniel. He is also different from the others in being bare-headed and in the amazing detail of the contemplative, tight-lipped expression on his face (Plate 17). The verse on his scroll comes from Chapter 53: 'Like a lamb before its shearer he is dumb, and he will not open his mouth'. This is a very different Isaiah from the youthful, energetic prophet at the door of Notre Dame de Souillac.[22] It looks almost as if Sluter is following a tradition that the author of chapter 53 was an older, more solemn Isaiah than the author of the messianic prophecies in the earlier chapters. He alone of all the prophets is young and beardless in some manuscripts of the *Biblia Pauperum* too, as are Bartolommeo's in the Uffizi, Michelangelo's famous *Isaiah* on the ceiling of the Sistine Chapel,[23] and one by Piero della Francesca.[24] Such examples are hardly enough to

---

[22] See pp. 67, 73. Plate 10.
[23] The youthful appearance of Michaelangelo's *Isaiah* perhaps has less significance than the other examples, as some of his other prophets are youthful too: namely *Daniel*, *Joel* and *Jonah*.
[24] Salmi, *La Pittura di Piero della Francesca*, p. 68, Plate XVIII.

prove that there was an early awareness of differences in the authorship of the Book of Isaiah, in anticipation of more recent scholarship.[25] But the contrast is there, not only between youth and old age, but also between the joyful expectancy of verses 7:14 and 11:1, and the grim solemnity of 53. By the fourteenth century a new era had begun, marked both by a new artistic realism[26] and by theological and spiritual developments which dramatically changed Christian perceptions of scripture. Both are illustrated by Sluter's *Isaiah*.

53:7, which was already applied to Christ by Philip in Acts 8:31–5 and is read at mass on the Wednesday of Holy Week, provided writers and artists of the late Middle Ages with scriptural authority for three distinct details in their representations of the Passion. First, it describes the victim as 'dumb before its shearers'. This not only points to Christ's silence before Caiaphas the High Priest (cf. Matth.26:63), but also underlies the stark contrast, frequent in late mediaeval depictions of the Passion, between the calm mute face of Christ and the open mouths and glaring eyes of his jeering tormentors.[27] There are two particularly horrifying examples by Hieronymus Bosch, the *Carrying of the Cross* and *Ecce Homo*.[28]

Black American slaves found comfort and inspiration in this image from Isaiah 53 too:

De blood came twinklin' down
An' He never said a mumblin' word.
De blood came twinklin' down
An' He never said a mumblin' word.
Not a word – not a word – not a word.[29]

They identified their sufferings with those of Christ, whipped, spat upon and humiliated, but unlike many of their mediaeval Christian forebears, some found the motivation to accept their lot without protest and even forgive their tormentors.[30]

Secondly, there is the reference to the shearing of the victim, yet one more detail which can be horribly elaborated if the will is there to do so. The tradition that Jesus' beard was pulled by his persecutors

---

[25] Not according to Kirschbaum, *Lexikon*, II, p. 355.
[26] See pp. 83ff.
[27] Marrow, *Passion Iconography*, pp. 96–7.
[28] Marrow, *Passion Iconography*, Fig. 28, 130; Schiller, *Iconography*, II, p. 75, fig. 264.
[29] Johnson and Johnson, *Negro Spirituals*, p. 41; cited in Wills, *Under God*, p. 202.
[30] On Christian anti-Jewish uses of these images and texts, see below, pp. 102f.

had long been familiar from Isaiah 50:6, read at mass on the Monday of Holy Week. But the idea present in many late mediaeval texts, that his hair and beard were completely pulled out so that he looked as if he had been shorn like a sheep, comes from the reference to shearers in 53:7. The following quotation from a Dutch Passion tract is typical: 'And those who could not reach him stuck their lances and spears into his blessed hair and pulled him from afar so that his holy hair lay strewn in the way'.[31] The 'shearing' is also sometimes incorporated into descriptions of the crowning of Christ with a crown of thorns.[32] In Christian literature and art since Augustine and Isidore we find a play on words connecting the mocking *Calve, calve* 'baldhead!' from the Elisha story (2 Kings 2:23), with *Calvary*, the hill where Jesus was stripped bare and jeered at by his persecutors.[33] But the lurid variations on this theme, involving Isaiah 50:6 and 53:7, do not appear until they are required by late mediaeval spirituality.

Finally, Isaiah 53:7 is a verse about 'leading' the victim to its death, cited in countless mediaeval sources, along with Jeremiah 11:19, in relation to Christ carrying the cross. In earlier traditions Christ is depicted as walking independently while now, thanks largely to Isaiah 53:7, the scene is transformed: 'And the savage dogs cast nooses and ropes about the sweet lamb, and an iron chain around his shoulders, and led him out to be crucified'.[34] Grünewald's version connects this with a vernacular variation of 53:5, which is inscribed on a building overlooking the scene: *Isaiah: Er ist um unserer sünden willen geschlagen* 'he is beaten for our sins' (Plate 18).[35]

It also comes to be applied with gruesome originality to the leading of Christ back to Jerusalem after his arrest in Gethsemane. In this 'new, richly orchestrated event known from contemporary sources as the *ductio Christi*',[36] Christ is shown on all fours like an animal, being kicked and struck and dragged along by ropes, as his tormentors take him down the stony path from the Mount of Olives and up into Jerusalem: 'He was led or dragged through thistles and thorns, and over hard sharp stones, leaving remnants of his holy

---

[31] Marrow, *Passion Iconography*, p. 75.
[32] Marrow, *Passion Iconography*, p. 72.
[33] Marrow, *Passion Iconography*, p. 69; cf. *BP*, pp. 92,94.
[34] Cf. Marrow, *Passion Iconography*, pp. 163–4; *BP*, pp. 93, 95.
[35] Cf. *Grünewald*, p. 16.
[36] Marrow, *Passion Iconography*, p. 96.

flesh and blood sticking along the way'.[37] 'The thorns and thistles' come from Isaiah too (5:6 and 7:23–4; cf. Gen.3:18).[38]

Before we leave this part of the story, we must consider another verse which plays a significant part in the development of late mediaeval passion iconography, namely Isaiah 1:6: *A planta pedis usque ad verticem non est in eo sanitas; vulnus et livor et plaga tumens* – 'From the sole of the foot even to the top of the head, there is no soundness in it, but wounds and bruises and swelling sores'. Although it does not appear in lectionaries for Holy Week, this verse is cited in mediaeval discussions of the significance of the blood of Christ,[39] and used, sometimes with Job 1:7 ('loathsome sores from the sole of his foot to the crown of his head'), to justify various gruesome details in representations of the flagellation.[40] First, it refers to the fact that no part of his precious body was spared. In some traditions, there is even the added detail that he was turned round so that people could see that there were wounds everywhere. Second, the verse suggests that, in scourging him, they started from the bottom and worked up: 'they started from the bottom upwards ... because if they had begun from the head down, His body would have been covered with blood, and they would not have been able to determine if it were thoroughly wounded'.[41] Finally the verse is used to describe Christ's appearance after the flagellation, the list of 'wounds and bruises and swelling sores' providing further inspiration for the artistic imagination. Earlier commentators often link the language and imagery of this description of suffering and disease with Isaiah 53, but the next stage in which it figures so graphically in passion accounts, in its own right, is a late mediaeval development.

One final comment on the image of the lamb in Isaiah 53 concerns its use (via John 1:29) in the *Agnus Dei*, a prayer which has been an integral part of the mass in the Western Church since the seventh century: *Agnus Dei, qui tollis peccata mundi, miserere nobis* ('Lamb of God, who takest away the sins of the world, have mercy on us'). According to the late mediaeval theology represented by Sluter's use of Isaiah 53, Christ is not so much the 'Lamb of God that *takes away*

---

37 Marrow, *Passion Iconography*, pp. 99–104.
38 Elsewhere the verse is cited in connection with the crown of thorns: Marrow, *Passion Iconography*, pp. 100–1.
39 E.g. in the Bull *Unigenitus* of Clement VI, 1343: Bettenson, *Documents of the Christian Church*, p. 183.
40 Marrow, *Passion Iconography*, pp. 47–50.
41 Marrow, *Passion Iconography*, p. 48.

the sins of the world' as the 'Lamb of God that *bears* the sins of the world', weighed down by them and taken away to be slaughtered because of them. The phrase comes from Isaiah 53:4,[42] but it is interesting to compare the original Isaiah reference (in both the Latin and the Greek versions), where the emphasis is on the suffering of the Servant ('our pain he endured . . .' *REB*), to its use in Matthew 8:17 where it is applied to Jesus' healing miracles ('carried away our diseases . . .' *REB*). The word *tollis* in the *Agnus Dei* is ambiguous, and, although it is customary to translate it as 'take away', following Matthew 8:17 and John 1:29, there is no doubt that the original Isaianic image of the suffering servant 'bearing our sins', like the scapegoat in Leviticus 16, has been dominant in the Church from the late mediaeval period till today.

As artists became bolder in their representation of Christ's physical and psychological suffering, other words and phrases from Isaiah 53 took on new significance.[43] Matthias Grünewald's crucified Christ of the Isenheim Altar is a case in point. It seems to refer to verse 4, where the condition of the suffering servant is compared to that of a leper (Vulgate *quasi leprosus*).[44] Before treatment at the Isenheim monastery hospital, patients suffering from blood and skin diseases, who must have resembled Grünewald's crucified Christ, were brought to the altar to be assured of the possibility of participating in his resurrection.[45] The disfigurement and unrecognizability that appear in many descriptions of the passion are influenced by chapter 53 too.[46]

An intriguing modern example of the application of Isaiah 53 to the passion is recorded from the Church of SS Nicolas and Barbara in Amsterdam (now demolished), where three of the Stations of the Cross, executed by the ceramic artist J. van Hulst of Harlingen in 1886–9, are accompanied by the prophet Isaiah with verses in Latin from chapter 53. The third station (Christ falls for the first time) is accompanied by verse 8: 'I was struck because of the crime of my people (53:8)'. 'My people' here is usually interpreted as referring to the Jews and thus to their responsibility for Christ's suffering, a

---

[42] Cf. also v.12, and the scapegoat ritual in Lev.16, especially 16:22. See Schiller, *Iconography*, II, p. 117.

[43] Schiller, *Iconography*, II, p. 71.

[44] Cf. Pickering, *Literature and Art*, p. 111; Marrow, *Passion Iconography*, p. 54; cf. *Grünewald*, plates 6–8.

[45] *Grünewald*, p. 14.

[46] Marrow, *Passion Iconography*, p. 54–7.

feature of nineteenth-century Church art and architecture we shall come across again.[47] The mention of the disfigured 'countenance' (Latin *aspectus*) explains the choice of 53:2 as Isaiah's comment on the sixth station (Veronica wipes Christ's face) (Plate 19), and beside the twelfth station (the crucifixion) the prophet carries a banderol with the words of Isaiah 53:12 (cited in Luke 22:37): 'he was numbered with the sinners . . .'

Isaiah 53 also provided the title for a representation of the Suffering Christ that has been described as 'the most precise visual expression of the piety of the Late Middle Ages',[48] namely, 'the Man of Sorrows'.[49] This 'unambiguously devotional image' first appears in the Western Church in the twelfth century, and thereafter for many centuries became one of the most popular themes in the history of Christian art. Those of Bellini (c.1470–1500),[50] Mantegna (1431–1506)[51] and Dürer (1494–1522)[52] are among the best-known. 'The Man of Sorrows' or *imago pietatis* (*Erbärmdebild* in German) is distinguished from all other pictures of the Passion and Crucifixion, by the absence of temporal or spatial detail. Artists dwell on the physical and mental details of an individual's suffering, without placing it in any context, whether that of ancient Jerusalem or, as was frequently the custom in mediaeval and Renaissance art, that of their own day. Nor is there any direct allusion to the divinity of Christ. Nothing distracts from the human face of the Suffering Christ. The image is designed to make it easy for the devout to identify their own plight with the suffering of Christ, in a type of mysticism familiar to us from the experience of St Francis of Assisi, who suffered the wounds of Christ, the stigmata, in his own body. Albrecht Dürer (1471–1528) expresses the same notion in his *Self-portrait as the Man of Sorrows* of 1522, in which he actually gives Christ his own features .[53] The influence of the 'Man of Sorrows' can be seen in countless subsequent representations of the 'Solitary Christ Crucified', including those of Titian (c.1565), Rubens (c.1615), and Rembrandt (1631).[54]

---

[47] See chapter 6.
[48] Schiller, *Iconography*, II, pp. 197–223; cf. Pickering, *Literature and Art*, pp. 99–102.
[49] The actual phrase *vir dolorum* rarely accompanies the depiction of the image in art.
[50] Schiller, *Iconography*, II, figs. 724, 739, 748.
[51] Schiller, *Iconography*, II, fig. 751.
[52] Schiller, *Iconography*, II, figs. 723, 726–9.
[53] Schiller, *Iconography*, II, fig. 729.
[54] Schiller, *Iconography*, II, figs. 813–16.

There can be little doubt as to the connection between this image and Isaiah 53. In the first place, although in fact the verse is seldom directly associated with the *imago pietatis*, the term itself, 'Man of Sorrows' (Vulgate *Vir dolorum*) is derived from verse 3: 'He was despised and rejected by men; a man of sorrows (*vir dolorum*) and acquainted with grief'. Secondly, there are the obvious parallels between the content of Isaiah 53 and the 'Man of Sorrows' motif. The Isaiah passage is characterized by the same absence of spatial and temporal detail as the 'Man of Sorrows'. There is nothing at all in it about when or where the events took place. There is not even any indication in the text as to the identity of the 'Man of Sorrows' himself (or the 'Suffering Servant', as he is referred to nowadays). It is thus, as we shall see later in our discussion of modern scholarly commentaries on the passage, immediately applicable to all kinds of individuals and situations, and remains so in the Church even when it is applied to the sufferings of Christ. The open-endedness of Isaiah 53, like the lack of spatial and temporal detail in the 'Man of Sorrows' image, makes it an ideal expression of the belief that Christ's suffering incorporates the suffering of all humanity.

Thus even where precise verbal links are not present, commentators on crucifixion imagery in general often assume a connection with Isaiah 53. Schiller, for example, cites the chapter to give some kind of scriptural basis for the way in which a fifteenth-century *Pietà* 'does not depict any scene from the story of the Passion', but rather presents 'the sacrificed Christ in every particular'.[55] In the same way, hymnologists assume that Isaiah 53 was the inspiration for the hymn *O Haupt voll Blut und Wunden* by Paul Gerhardt (1607–1676), 'the greatest German hymn-writer of the seventeenth century'[56] which appears in various English versions in most hymn-books (*O Sacred Head sore wounded* by Robert Bridges is one).[57]

A third explanation of the recurring connection between Isaiah 53 and the 'Man of Sorrows' is the sheer familiarity of the biblical passage in the Church. It is one of the readings for Good Friday in the Anglican Book of Common Prayer, whence one of the best-loved arias and three of the choruses in Handel's *Messiah* were derived.[58] In the Roman Missal it appears, with the 'Wine-press'

---

[55] Schiller, *Iconography* II, p. 219.
[56] Andrews, *Study of German Hymns*, p. 58.
[57] Cf. Moffat, *Handbook*, pp. 41 and 571.
[58] See pp. 171ff.

passage (Isa.63:1–7) and the Luke Passion narrative, in the mass for the Wednesday of Holy Week. English editions give it the title 'Jesus, the Man of Sorrows'.[59] In the most recent Catholic lectionary it is prescribed to be read out on Good Friday with part of Hebrews 4–5, Philippians 2:8–9 and the Passion according to St John,[60] as well as at masses for the sick and the mass of the Mystery of the Holy Cross. Several recently composed hymns are based on Isaiah 53 too.[61]

Like the 'Man of Sorrows' image, it speaks to all sufferers, including the marginalized (vv.2–3), people in mental or physical pain (vv.3–5) and the innocent victims of injustice (vv.7–9). It also contains a scriptural basis for all the main Christian soteriologies: individual salvation through mystical union with Christ, as in the above examples; salvation according to the traditional doctrine of expiation in which Christ takes away the sins of the world like a sacrificial lamb (cf. John 1:29);[62] and salvation through acts of divine intervention when the Messiah comes (cf. Matth.8:17).[63]

In addition to focussing on different passages in Isaiah such as those we have been considering so far, the Church in the later Middle Ages also interpreted some familiar ones in a new way. Even the 'Jesse tree' motif was adapted to fit the new Passion iconography. This had been one of the most popular images in the mediaeval Church, as we saw, associated, on the one hand, with the cult of the Virgin Mary and, on the other, with notions of the divine right of kings. In the 'Jesse windows' at Chartres and elsewhere, Mary is a central figure among the royal ancestors in the family tree of Christ. Both she and Christ are depicted in the topmost branches of the tree as monarchs enthroned in glory. But it can be turned into an image of suffering too. An early example of this merging of the images of the tree of Jesse and the tree of the cross is to be found in a fourteenth-century manuscript of the *Speculum Humanae Vitae*.[64] Jesse lies at the foot of the picture and the exalted Christ is at the top, surrounded by the seven doves that represent the gifts of the Spirit,

---

[59] *St John's Missal for Every Day*, revised J. Rea, Salford 1961.

[60] *Lectionary*, pp. 161f.; 994; 1002.

[61] *HON*, 223, 370, 427.

[62] See above.

[63] See Flesseman-van Leer, 'Die Interpretation der Passionsgeschichte vom Alten Testament aus', pp. 89–90; Stenning, *The Targum of Isaiah*, pp. 178–81; Schürer, Vol. 2, pp. 547ff.

[64] See Schiller, *Iconography*, II, pp. 135–6, fig. 442. On a parallel 'merging' of the Tree of the Cross with the Tree of Life and the Tree of Knowledge in mediaeval Christian iconography, see O'Reilly in Morris and Sawyer, edd., *A Walk in the Garden*, pp. 167–204.

as in the Jesse windows discussed above.[65] Mary is there too, together with the traditional figures of prophets, evangelists and others. But between Mary and the exalted Christ, as part of the wooden trunk of the tree of Jesse, is the tree of the cross on which Christ is crucified. Also incorporated into the tree of Jesse here is the Lamb, a detail recalling the *Emitte Agnum* from Isaiah 16:1, which, as we saw, speaks of a lamb coming triumphantly from Moab, homeland of Jesse's ancestor Ruth,[66] but also associated with Christ's sacrifice on the Cross.

The Brougham Triptych, a carved wooden altarpiece, made in Antwerp at the beginning of the sixteenth century and located now in Carlisle Cathedral,[67] is another fine example (Plate 15). A central motif is the Jesse tree, emerging from the side of the standing figure of Jesse at the foot. Around him stand several prophets carrying scrolls, one of whom is obviously Isaiah, although the texts on their faded scrolls are no longer legible. But the most striking feature is the figure of the crucified Christ at the top, in place of Christ the King or his Virgin Mother. The French author Victor Hugo (1802–85) interprets the Jesse tree in this way too in his poem *Booz endormi*.[68] Another modern example can be seen in the Church of St Martin in Cuyck, Holland.[69] Here the central part of the neogothic style altarpiece, made around 1900 by H.van der Geld, again shows the crucifixion and the Jesse Tree combined.

Another way in which the Jesse Tree is brought into the context of Passion iconography can be seen in a seventeenth-century stained glass window in Troyes Cathedral, inspired by another verse from Isaiah. The inscription reads: *torcular calcavi solus* 'I trod the winepress alone' (63:3). The image of the winepress comes originally from Isaiah 63:1–7, which was recited, along with chapter 53, at mass on the Wednesday of Holy Week. In many contexts the red garments of the wine-treader are cited as a prefiguration of the sufferings of Christ drenched with his own blood, especially in late mediaeval depictions of the Flagellation.[70] In others the image was incorporated

---

[65] See pp. 74ff.

[66] See above, pp. 8off.

[67] The 'Brougham Triptych' was brought to England in the early nineteenth century by Lord Brougham and Vaux to be placed in Brougham Chapel by his home near Penrith. It is currently on loan to Carlisle Cathedral.

[68] See p. 164.

[69] I am grateful to the Stichting Kerkelijk Kunstbezit, Utrecht, for this reference.

[70] Marrow, *Passion Iconography*, pp. 83–94; Schiller, *Iconography*, pp. 228–9; cf. Duffy, *Stripping the Altars*, p. 252.

into descriptions of Christ's tormentors literally treading him under-
foot as he fell to the ground under the weight of the cross. Other
verses from Isaiah fill in the details, especially 50:6 ('I gave my back
to the smiters') and 51:23 ('Bow down that we may pass over ...').[71]

The Troyes Cathedral window, however, follows a bizarre but
popular interpretation of the verse, which goes back to the Church
Fathers. According to this, Christ, the True Vine (John 15:1), is
imagined as 'the first cluster pressed in the winepress' (*primus botrus in
torculari pressus*).[72] In art Christ is then depicted as being crushed in
the winepress, his blood flowing out into a chalice. This grotesque
image appeared in the Holy Week liturgy as well: 'When they
pressed thy blessyd body as a ripe clustre upon the pressure of the
cros'.[73] In the Troyes window and elsewhere, the allusion to the Jesse
tree image still remains as well. Christ lies like Jesse at the bottom of
the picture, and from his breast rises a new family tree, the true vine.
In its branches is the 'family' of the Twelve Apostles (John 15:5),
related to one another by the wine of the Holy Sacrament, that is,
the blood of the crucified Christ, not the blood of Jesse. Like the
crucifix at the top of the Jesse tree on the Brougham Triptych, this
astonishing transformation of the Jesse tree illustrates just how
powerful the new preoccupation with Christ's suffering was.

The winepress in chapter 63 appears in other contexts as well,
such as the 'grapes of wrath' imagery, used by the American John
Steinbeck (1902–68) in the title of his greatest novel, published in
1939, and descriptions of the fate of the wicked on Judgement Day
(cf. Rev.19:13–15). The engraving on the title page of a Bible printed
in Germany in 1641, for instance, shows Christ in the winepress
wielding the pennon of the resurrection as he conquers death and the
devil.[74] But it is also 'one of the most important metaphorical images
in mediaeval passion lore ... best known as a metaphor for the
Crucifixion'.[75] St Bernard of Clairvaux, for example, in a paraphrase
of Philippians 2:8, describes Christ as 'obedient to the Father, even
unto the press of the cross which he trod alone' (*usque ad torcular crucis
quod utique solus calcavit*).[76] In art this notion can be represented in

[71]   Marrow, *Passion Iconography*, p. 80; Ruh, 'Zur Theologie des mittelalterlichen Passionstrak-
       tats', p. 24.
[72]   Cf. Marrow, *Passion Iconography*, p. 80.
[73]   Duffy, *Stripping the Altars*, p. 253.
[74]   Schiller, *Iconography*, ii, p. 229, fig. 812.
[75]   Marrow, *Passion Iconography* p. 83; cf. Schiller, *Iconography*, ii, pp. 228f.
[76]   Cf.Marrow, *Passion Iconography*, p. 83.

many different ways. In some, like a sixteenth-century example in a stained glass window in a Church in Conches, the primary image is the winepress (Plate 16). But it is designed to make us think of a cross, and the crowd of bystanders is more reminiscent of a crucifixion scene than one of wine-pressing. Christ stands alone, naked except for a scanty cloak of bright red cloth hanging over one shoulder. Above there is a scroll with the text from Isaiah 63 already quoted. Even though he also bears in his hand the rod with which he ultimately punishes the wicked (cf. v.5), the emphasis is on the loneliness of the suffering Christ.

Alternatively the primary image may be the cross as in a Bavarian painting of *Christ in the Winepress* from about 1500.[77] This shows Christ carrying the cross, but, following Isaiah 63:1–3 rather than the Gospel narrative, he is alone, the 'cross' is in fact attached at one end to the giant wooden screw of a winepress, and Christ's bleeding feet are trampling on a great wooden vat of grapes, not the stones of the *via dolorosa*. In the foreground, in a lively vintage scene, half a dozen figures are collecting and processing the juice of the grapes in a variety of wooden containers. Another early sixteenth-century example, by the French artist Jean Bellegambe, has a fairly conventional representation of the crucifixion at the top, except that the inscription above Christ's head reads *torcular calcavi solus* ... ('I trod the winepress alone ...') from Isaiah 63, and below the faithful can be seen eagerly bathing in the holy water and blood that flow from the *fons pietatis*.[78]

It may seem odd that a passage more familiar from its use in the context of Judgement Day (cf. Rev.19:15) and the *Battle Hymn of the Republic*[79] can also be associated with the Passion. As we saw, the idea of Christ as the true vine was no doubt one factor that led to this development, and the mediaeval preoccupation with scriptural accounts of suffering and death was certainly another. But it may also be worth pointing out that there are other references to suffering in chapter 63: it is not all about Judgement Day and the triumphant defeat of the wicked. In verse 1, the Hebrew translated 'striding' (*REB*) or 'marching' (*RSV*; *NEB* 'stooping') is used elsewhere only of captives, prostitutes, gypsies and travellers,[80] although this is rarely

---

[77] Schiller, *Iconography*, II, p. 229, fig. 810.
[78] Marrow, *Passion Iconography*, p. 84, Plate v (opposite p. 58); on the *fons pietatis*, see Wadell, *Fons pietatis* (1969).
[79] *CH* 155; *SOP* 578; *HON* 349.
[80] Cf. Sawyer, 'Radical images', pp. 76–7; see pp. 208f.

reflected in Christian versions and commentaries. Verse 9 as it stands is certainly about a suffering God: 'in all their affliction he was afflicted': *RSV*).[81]

A tree figures prominently in another Isaianic tradition. In an earlier chapter we argued that the pre-eminent role of Isaiah among the Prophets, even at the very beginning of the history of the Church, springs not only from his prophecies about Christ and the Virgin Mary, but also from traditions about his martyrdom.[82] Direct links between the apocryphal 'Martyrdom of Isaiah' and the Biblical Isaiah (especially Chapter 53), as also between the 'Martyrdom' and the Passion narratives, are hard to prove.[83] But the Church Fathers certainly made the connection,[84] and so provided the basis for a development in the history of the iconography of the Passion which reached its apogee in the art of the later Middle Ages.

From early mediaeval times Isaiah had been represented either carrying a saw as the symbol of his martyrdom, or in the process of being sawn in half.[85] An interesting example from pre-Norman Britain, in which Isaiah is suspended upside down during the sawing, has recently been identified on part of a stone cross in Winwick Parish Church[86] (Plate 5). In early thirteenth-century editions of the Bible, produced in Paris and widely distributed throughout Europe, for example, the Book of Isaiah was invariably introduced by a miniature representing the prophet kneeling before his executioners who are equipped with a large saw. The influence of the Parisian stationers can be traced in countless thirteenth- and fourteenth-century German and Italian examples. There are numerous variations on the theme. In many Isaiah is tied to a branch cross in a manner consciously reminiscent of the crucifixion. From the late fourteenth and fifteenth century onwards, his martyrdom is increasingly pictured from the viewpoint of the hangman, as it were, with the focus on the wood, nails and ropes of the gallows, and in this form it serves as one of the three fixed antitypes of the erection of the cross in most of the extant manuscripts of the *Speculum Humanae Salvationis*.[87] Occasionally Isaiah even appears alongside Abel, Isaac,

---

[81] Sawyer, 'Radical images' , p. 80.
[82] See chapter 3, pp. 46f.   [83] See p. 47.
[84] E.g. Justin Martyr, *Contra Tryphonem*, 110; Origen, *Comm. on Matth.*23:37; *PL* 15, 1800 (Ambrose).
[85] Réau, *Iconographie*, II.1, p. 369.
[86] Bailey, *Viking Age Sculpture*, pp. 159–61, Fig. 39.
[87] Bernheimer, 'The Martyrdom of Isaiah', pp. 20–21.

the three youths in the fiery furnace and other prefigurations of martyrdom and the death of Christ.[88]

A tree figures prominently in many of these mediaeval representations of the martyrdom, the tree of Isaiah's 'crucifixion' corresponding to the tree on which Christ was crucified. This goes back to an ancient Jewish legend, preserved in the Talmud and elsewhere, according to which Isaiah tried to escape from his executioners by pronouncing the forbidden Name of God. He was instantly swallowed up by a cedar tree, but this was then sawn in half and Isaiah killed. The tree on which – or in which – Isaiah was slain was visited by mediaeval pilgrims to Jerusalem such as the somewhat sceptical Dominican brother Felix in the fifteenth century, and was still being showed to pilgrims in the 1920s.[89] A Victorian traveller and writer describes it as 'an old, old tree, supported by props of piled stones, still standing near the waters of Siloam ... a hoary and venerable tree like an old man in the last decrepitude of age'.[90] It is Isaiah's words that the same writer chooses for her final view of the city, still 'in the possession of the wild Ishmaelite ... The prophet on this very hill may have stood and gazed and pondered what manner of man that should be whom he himself had described so minutely, He who was to come as a lamb to the slaughter, the rejected and despised of men'.[91]

All three Isaianic images of the Cross – the tree of Jesse, the wooden wine-press and the tree of Isaiah's martyrdom – derive from a book which has much to say about suffering, from the sores and wounds of suffering Israel in chapter 1 to the 'Man of Sorrows' in 53 and hell-fire in 66:24. As a modern scholar recently puts it, 'that book that is of such central importance to Christian faith from the time of the early disciples down to the present, ends on a dark note – 66:24'.[92] In that context the 'leap of faith' from the original text to the Church's uses of it down the ages may seem less bizarre or unjustified. It depends on one's starting point.

[88] Clemen, *Romanische Monumentmalerei*, plates 22, 23; cf. Bernheimer, 'Maryrdom of Isaiah', pp. 33–4.
[89] Meistermann, *Guide to the Holy Land*, p. 245. Cf. Bernheimer, 'Martyrdom of Isaiah', pp. 26–7.
[90] Mrs Oliphant, *Jerusalem. Its History and Hope* (1891), p. 240.
[91] *Id.*, p. 508.
[92] P. D. Hanson, 'Third Isaiah' (*Reading and Preaching the Book of Isaiah*, ed. C. R. Seitz), pp. 96f.

CHAPTER 6

Isaiah and the Jews

An inscription over the door of the Church of San Gregorio a Ponte Quattro Capi, in the centre of Rome, provides us with an ugly example of our next topic: Isaiah in the context of Christian antisemitism (Plate 30). The text from chapter 65 is cited by Paul (Rom.10:21) and may have suggested the words, but what is striking is that the inscription runs on into the next verse, in such a way as to ensure that it becomes a piece of much more personal, more direct, more contemporary verbal abuse: 'All day long I have stretched out my hands to a rebellious people, who walk in a way that is not good, following their own devices; a people who provoke me to my face continually' (65:2–3a). The text, which is given in Hebrew as well as Latin, now refers to people who are there all the time, that is to say, Jews going in and out of the ghetto, and implies in strong biblical language that the Christians' God hates them. What is still more sinister is that the inscription accompanies a fresco depicting the crucified Christ, whose hands 'stretched out' on the cross clearly imply that it is Christ himself who is addressing the chilling words of Isaiah to the Jews.

The church, originally built in 1729 under Pope Benedict XIII, was refurbished in 1858 on the instructions of Pope Pius IX.[1] It was then that the inscription was added. Today visitors to the church are given a leaflet explaining, somewhat disingenuously, that the words are addressed to all humanity. But why in that case it should be in Hebrew as well as Latin is not explained. The façade remains unchanged, a menacing example of nineteenth-century Christian antisemitism, with its Hebrew inscription for every Jewish visitor to the centre of Rome to read.

Another striking example from a very different, and less public,

---

[1]   Blunt, *Guide to Baroque Rome*, p. 63.

context, will help to set the scene. It appears as the frontispiece in a work by an imperial physician and writer in sixteenth-century Vienna (Plate 23).[2] The thirty-four–year-old author, a converted Jew, is depicted as standing with his wife and four children at the foot of the cross, pointing to the crucified Christ and applying to him the words of Isaiah 33:22, printed in Hebrew and Latin: 'For the Lord is our Judge, the Lord is our Lawgiver, the Lord is our King, the Lord will save us.' Just how hurtful and distasteful the Christian use of texts from the Hebrew Bible must be to a Jew, is hard for gentiles to appreciate. But it has been without a doubt a major factor in the tragic history of Jewish-Christian relations from the beginning.

A fundamental theme running through the Gospels (including the 'Fifth Gospel') and the liturgy in virtually every part of the Christian Church, is the blindness and stubbornness of the Jews in failing to accept Jesus as the Messiah, and their guilt in humiliating him and putting him to death on the cross. This perception of the Jews as blind, ignorant, obdurate and wilfully guilty of deicide appears in Christian art and literature, in scholarship and in popular belief, right down to the present.

One of the reasons for the Church's persistent targeting of Jews, especially in the Middle Ages, is the historical circumstance that, unlike other heretics and infidels, Muslims for example, Jewish communities were actually present for all to see in many of the major cities of Christian Europe. Thus when Pope Innocent III (1198–1216) and his immediate successors instilled new zeal into the Church, reflected especially in the founding of the two most influential orders of mendicant friars, the Dominicans and the Franciscans, and orchestrated a fresh assault on heresy, the Jews were inevitably in the firing line. With few exceptions 'the predominant attitude of the friars toward the Jews was marked by an aggressive missionary spirit and often violent animosity'.[3] It has been argued that, building on existing anti-Jewish feeling, which had been stirred up in the eleventh and twelfth centuries by the Crusades, it was the friars who eventually developed a new Christian ideology according to which the Jews had no right to exist in Christian Europe, and that it was they who were to a large extent responsible for the systematic expulsion of the Jews from every country in Europe, starting with England in 1290.[4] There

---

[2]   P. Weidner von Billeburg, *Loca praecipua fidei Christianae collecta et explicata* (Vienna 1559).
[3]   Cohen, *The Friars and the Jews*, p. 43.
[4]   Cohen, *The Friars and the Jews*, p. 14.

were certainly other factors involved in the expulsions, and in the increase of systematic persecution of the Jews after the thirteenth century, especially political and socio-economic ones, but what is absolutely clear is that, from the Jewish viewpoint, it was the Dominicans and Franciscans who were their most hated and feared enemies in mediaeval Europe.[5]

A study of the uses of Isaiah in this context mirrors the grim story of Christian antisemitism. It is no coincidence that Jerome's commentary on Isaiah is characterized by fiercer animosity than usual against the Jews, exulting in their present humiliation and making frequent reference to their blindness, immorality and greed.[6] The reasons for Isaiah's prominence in this area are not hard to find. In the first place, the 'Fifth Gospel' contained, as we have seen, so many popular Christian proof-texts, concerning central points of Christian orthodoxy such as the Virgin Birth, the divinity of Christ, redemptive suffering and the eucharist, that it was always in the forefront of the Church's fight against heresy, particularly, for reasons which we shall consider later, the Jews. In the earliest example of extended anti-Jewish polemic, the *Dialogue with Trypho the Jew* by the second-century philosopher Justin Martyr, Isaiah is quoted far more frequently and at greater length than any other part of scripture, including the Psalms and Gospels.[7] The same applies to the polemical writings of Tertullian, John Chrysostom, Isidore of Seville and many others.

One of the main 'characters' in Isaiah, according to the Church's christological interpretations, is the 'Messiah'. There is a great deal in the book about him – his divine origin, his birth and lineage, his miracles, his passion, death and resurrection[8] – and this inevitably puts him right at the centre of what in every period must be considered the main source of disagreement between Jews and Christians. Not only do the Jews challenge the Church's interpretation of texts like Isaiah 7:14 and chapter 53: they reject the fundamental Christian belief that Jesus is the Messiah. We might add that, as we saw, according to the Church's teaching, there is a particular emphasis in Isaiah on the intense suffering of Christ, and this was there waiting to be used as ammunition against those responsible, that is to say, the Jews. The more violent the Jewish crimes against Christ, as recounted by Isaiah, the more violent the anti-Jewish invective.

5 Cohen, *The Friars and the Jews*, p. 13.
6 Cf. Kelly, *Jerome*, pp. 300–1.
7 See below.
8 See pp. 48ff.

In a previous chapter we saw how representations of the passion became increasingly more concerned to depict Christ's suffering in a wealth of detail, much of it derived from Isaiah. When we remember that, to the artists of these paintings as well as to their pious viewers, the jeering crowds and fiendish tormentors were Jews, and that the harsher the suffering, the greater their guilt, then we must include a whole host of other images in our collection of horrific mediaeval representations of Jews (Plate 18). We need only list the texts which accompany five out of the six scenes from the Passion in the *Biblia Pauperum* to see that this is so: Judas betrays Christ with a kiss (Isa.3:11); Jews condemn Christ (5:20); Christ is mocked (1:5); Christ carries the Cross (53:7); the Crucifixion (53:11).[9] In all these, Isaiah is unmistakably associated with antisemitic propaganda.

Another very important reason why Isaiah in Christian hands became such a thorn in the flesh for the Jews was the fact that it was so popular in their tradition as well. As we saw in our discussion of reasons why Isaiah played such an important role in the life of Jesus and his earliest followers, Isaiah seems always to have had a special place in Jewish Bible use down the ages.[10] Thus by using Isaiah to prove the truth of their own claims, Christians could hope to make their challenge to Judaism and the Jews all the more powerful. This is not the place to enter into a full-scale study of 'Isaiah in the history of Judaism', but there is no doubt such a study would be as rewarding as the present survey of 'Isaiah in the history of Christianity', and a brief discussion of this subject is required to explain the intensity of the clash between Jews and Christians on the battlefield of Isaiah interpretation.

Isaiah's role in the Zionist movement has not, to my knowledge, been noted, let alone investigated, but would probably illustrate how Isaiah can be caught in the crossfire, as it were, between Judaism and Christianity. The early Zionist organization 'Bilu', for example, took its name from the initials of the four Hebrew words *bet yaʿăkov lĕku vĕnelĕka* ('House of Jacob, go and we will go') in chapter 2, and chose words from 60:22 as its motto: 'A little one shall become a thousand, and a small one a strong nation.'[11] In Christian tradition, as

---

[9]   *BP*, pp. 90–9. On Isaiah's role in the Passion story, see also pp. 86–90.
[10] See above, pp. 4f.
[11] Vilnay, *Guide to Israel* (19th edition), p. 256. One might compare the application of 2:3 to the thriving Jewish communities of twelfth-century southern Italy ('Out of Bari shall go forth the Torah ...') – before they were wiped out by the Dominican Inquisition in the thirteenth century: Cohen, *The Friars and the Jews*, p. 85.

represented by the influential twelfth-century illustrated *Bible Moralisée*, this verse is applied to Isaiah's unsuccessful attempt to lead the Jews to Christ.

No doubt the rise of Zionism was one reason for the huge success of Abraham Mapu's novel about Isaiah entitled *Ahavat Tziyyon* ('The love of Zion'), which was published in 1853 and translated into several European languages, including no less than three English versions. Since the establishment of the State of Israel in 1948, a significant number of oratorios and cantatas on Isaianic themes and visions, by Jewish composers, have appeared,[12] and a picture of the famous Isaiah Scroll from Qumran appeared on the Israeli 10 Lira note in the 1950s.[13]

A disproportionate number of place-names in the modern State of Israel are derived from Isaiah. One of the first Jewish settlements in Palestine, established by immigrants from Russia in 1882, was called Rishon le-Tzion ('first to Zion') from 41:27. Others include Shear Jashub ('a remnant will return' 7:3), Nes Harim ('A banner on the mountains' 18.3), Ariel (29:1), Mevasseret Tzion ('O thou that tellest good tidings to Zion' 40:9), Mevasseret Yerushalayim ('O thou that tellest good tidings to Jerusalem' 40:9), Morag ('threshing sledge' 41:15), Mesillat Tzion ('highway to Zion' cf. 11:16; 40:3; 49:11; 62:10) and Or Tal ('the light of dew' cf. 26:19).[14] Chapter 35, which begins with the image of the 'desert blossoming like a rose', and ends with the return of the ransomed to Zion, provided the settlers in the North West Negev with another five: Tiphrah ('blossom'), Gilat ('joy') and Rannen ('singing') from verse 2, Maslul (another word for 'highway') from verse 8 and Peduyim ('ransomed') from verse 10 (cf. 51:11).[15] Another wilderness scene from Isaiah 32 provided the name of one of the first two Jewish neighbourhoods in Jaffa, Neveh Shalom ('a habitation of peace' 32:18).[16] Finally to these may be added another group of three settlements in the same area, Berosh, Tidhar and Te'ashur, which were named after some of the trees in 41:19: 'I will put in the wilderness cedars, acacias, myrtles and olive trees; I will set in the

---

[12] *JE* 9, cols.69–70.
[13] Vilnay, *Guide to Israel* (3rd edition), p. 72.
[14] *EJ*, Decennial Volume 1973–1982, pp. 352–60.
[15] Vilnay, *Guide to Israel* (19th ed., Jerusalem 1977), pp. 305–6.
[16] The other was Neveh Tzedek ('habitation of righteousness') from Jeremiah 31:22 (Engl.31:23). Neveh Shalom was also chosen, incidentally, as the name for a more recent international, ecumenical kibbutz founded by a Dominican priest in 1979. See p. 222.

desert *berosh, tidhar* and *te'ashur*.' The fact that there is considerable doubt as to the precise species of tree referred to by these three biblical words, as some of the modern English versions clearly demonstrate – 'fir ... pine ... box' (*AV*), 'cypress ... plane ... pine' (*RSV*), 'juniper ... plane ... cypress' (*JB*) – gives them an aura of biblical mystery not present in the four other much commoner words in the first half of the verse.

It is said that during the British Mandate, Isaiah 43:1–3a ('When you pass through the waters, I will be with you ...') was selected as a Bible reading in a clandestine broadcast by the Haganah and interpreted as a reference to the ships of illegal immigrants.[17] 43:2 is still the motto of the Tel Aviv harbour authority.[18] Another verse from Isaiah provides the motto for parts of the Reali College in Haifa and the Herzliya College in Tel Aviv, which house students intending to take up a military career: 'In quietness and confidence shall be your strength' (Isaiah 30:15).[19] The 'Davidka' monument to the defenders of Jerusalem in 1948 bears an inscription taken from the Sennacherib story ('I will defend this city to save it' 37:35).[20] Isaiah 2:4 ('swords into ploughshares') appears on a 'Monument of Peace' set up after the Six Day War in 1967.[21] The name of the national Holocaust Memorial in Jerusalem, Yad va-Shem ('a monument and a name'), from Isaiah 56:5, and the Israeli Prime Minister's use of Isaiah 57:19 after his meeting with Yasser Arafat, were referred to in chapter 1. The words of 26:2 ('Open the gates that the righteous nation may enter ...') appear in shining gold letters on the façade of the new synagogue building in Berlin.

This brief digression must suffice to show how popular the Book of Isaiah can be among Jews as well as Christians and how full of emotive images and phrases. Inevitably it was all the more satisfying for the enemies of the Jews if they could quote Isaiah to prove them wrong. At the same time it becomes clear just how vastly different their application and interpretation of Isaiah have been from the Church's use of the same text. An inscription on the gates of the Russian Compound on Jaffa Road, in the centre of Jerusalem, sums up this awkwardness caused by the fact that two quite separate communities,

[17] I am grateful to Professor Alex Rofé for this information.
[18] Vilnay, *Guide to Israel* (19th ed.) p. 228.
[19] Vilnay, *Guide to Israel* (19th ed.), p. 61.
[20] Vilnay, *Guide to Israel* (19th ed.), p. 108.
[21] See below, p. 232.

especially in Israel, so proudly and lovingly, claim the same text as a source of inspiration and authority. The Compound, in which the green-domed Russian Orthodox Cathedral stands, was built in the 1880s at a time when Russian Christians were travelling in large numbers to the Holy Land as pilgrims. But of course so were Russian Jews at the time, fleeing from persecution under the Tzars, and, under the aegis of the newly formed Zionist organizations, seeking refuge in Palestine. Ominously the Russian Church leaders chose for the inscription on their church in Jerusalem, a text filled with overtones and resonances among Jewish Zionists as well: 'For Zion's sake I will not hold my peace, and for Jerusalem's sake I will not rest' (Isa.62:1).[22]

Another example appears on the tower of the very prominent YMCA (Young Men's Christian Association) building in Jerusalem. Here the words of the *Shĕma* (Deut.6:4), the fundamental confession of the Jewish faith, are carved in Hebrew beside the words of Isaiah 9:5 (English 9:6): 'His name shall be called Wonderful counsellor ... Prince of Peace'. This use of the *Shĕma* in a conspicuously Christian context epitomizes the problem. Isaiah has been so thoroughly 'christianized' in European culture that Jewish minority uses and interpretations have had little chance of being heard. Jewish translators of Isaiah have difficulty in finding English words that do not 'exude christology'.[23] In the 1917 Jewish Publication Society version, for example, they had to banish the 'Prince of Peace' from 9:6 (Hebrew 9:5) altogether, substituting 'the Ruler of Peace'. The 1978 version has 'a peaceable ruler'.

But there was a third reason why Isaiah had this special role in anti-Jewish polemic. We have mentioned more than once the repeated attacks on 'Israel' and the Jewish people that run through the book, many of them in unforgettably vehement and vivid language.[24] This is not a matter of interpretation on which there might be disagreement between Jews and Christians. As we saw, this is an aspect of the prophet already seized upon by some of the earliest Christian writers and preachers, who were themselves Jews.[25] Ironically Jewish tradition itself singles him out as the prophet most

[22]   Vilnay, *Guide to Israel* (19th ed.), pp. 88–9.
[23]   J. D. Sarna & N. M. Sarna, 'Jewish bible scholarship and translations' in *The Bible and Bibles in America*, ed., E. Frerichs, p. 100.
[24]   Cf. Ruether, *Faith and Fratricide*, p. 128, and p. 273, note 56.
[25]   See pp. 35ff.

guilty of having maligned his own people. According to a well-known ancient Jewish midrash on the story of Isaiah's vision (6:6–7), what happened was that he was punished (by having his mouth scorched) for presuming to call his own people 'unclean': 'The Holy One, blessed be He, said to him, You are permitted to say, 'I am a man of unclean lips', since you are your own master. But are you also the master of my children that you refer to them as a people of unclean lips?'[26] Another midrash tells how, when the time for his martyrdom came, his whole body became like marble and the saw of his persecutors could not hurt him. Only his mouth was vulnerable, because of what he had said about the people of God, and when the saw reached his lips he died.[27]

From a critical exegetical point of view, of course, these vehement attacks in the Book of Isaiah are not directed at the Jews of Christian Europe but at people living in Jerusalem and elsewhere two-and-a-half thousand years ago, just as some of the all too familiar statements in the Gospels blaming 'the Jews' for the death of Christ were originally addressed to people living in the first century AD. But that has not prevented the Christian Church from using such language to give scriptural authority to their repeated assaults on the Jews down the ages.

We shall look in this chapter at examples of the Church's use of Isaiah as a weapon in anti-Jewish polemic, first as a major source of scriptural evidence to prove they are in error on such fundamental matters as the doctrine of the Trinity, the coming of the Messiah, the 'true Israel' and the 'Law', and second, when textual and exegetical arguments proved incapable of settling the issues, as a source of much of the language and imagery of rejection and persecution.[28]

Controversies and debates between Jews and Christians go right back to the beginnings of Christianity. We may distinguish three stages in the early history of Jewish-Christian debate. Jesus' arguments with the 'Scribes and Pharisees' started the process, although we must remember that those arguments were originally internal disputes within Judaism, and in that respect not something entirely new.[29] Some of the themes in early Jewish-Christian dialogue, such as questions about the covenant, the law, the role of the gentiles, the

---

26   Ginzberg, *Legends of the Jews*, Vol.4, p. 263.
27   Talmud *Yebamoth* 49b; *EJ* 9, col. 67. On Muslim tradition, see p. 7.
28   Cf. Gager, *Origins of Anti-Semitism*, p. 159.
29   Gager, *Origins*, pp. 134–59.

interpretation of scripture and even messianic claims about Jesus of Nazareth, were certainly seen by some in this way. It is in that context that we have to view Jewish arguments that Jesus could not be the Messiah (e.g. because of the manner of his death), and that Christian interpretations of some biblical texts, such as Isaiah 7:14 and 11:1, based on inaccurate Greek translations from the original Hebrew, were frankly impossible.[30]

Secondly, it soon became clear, as Christian missionaries began to make their presence felt throughout the Roman Empire (cf. Acts 17:6; 18:13), that there was more at stake than theological and religious truth. Since Christian claims that they were the 'true Israel' would inevitably affect the social and political standing of the Jews in relation to the Roman authorities, the issue of who was right became a matter of life and death. It is in that context that we have to understand why so many polemical works were produced on both sides.

Thirdly, it was little more than a century before many communities had Christian bishops with a degree of political status and power which the Jewish communities in Europe and the Near East never again possessed. Many Christian apologists then had nothing to fear from the Jews, and their motive in writing was sometimes more theological than political or polemical, and addressed as much to Christians as to Jews. The effect of this upon Christian beliefs about and attitudes towards the Jews, however, was appalling, and left its mark on the history of Christianity to this day.

Our task is to consider Isaiah's part in Christian anti-Jewish writings, both theological treatises like Isidore's *De Fide Catholica adversus Judaeos*, by authors who may never have met a real Jew in their lives, and those in which real Jews are present, either in the mind and experience of the writer, as in the case of John Chrysostom in Antioch towards the end of the fourth century, or physically, on stage, as it were, as in the mediaeval disputations.

One of the earliest examples of anti-Jewish writing is Justin Martyr's *Dialogue with Trypho the Jew*, written around 160 AD. It purports to be the account of a dialogue that took place in Ephesus shortly after the end of the war led by Bar Kochba against the Romans (130–5). Although the account presents a veneer of moderation and politeness throughout, and concludes with both participants

---

[30] Gager, *Origins*, pp. 158f.

parting amicably and promising to pray for each other, there is a great deal of bitterness in what is actually said. The Christian does most of the talking, and most of what he says is spiced with some of Isaiah's most virulent invective. Near the beginning he accuses the Jews of blindness, citing Isaiah 6:10.[31] He hurls at his Jewish audience the menacing words with which we began this discussion of Christian antisemitism (65:1–3). In his summing up at the end, he argues that Jews who cling to their old erroneous beliefs have been rejected, quoting Isaiah 29:13[32] as well as two really horrifying passages, one beginning 'You rulers of Sodom ...' from the first chapter (1:9), and the description of hell-fire from the last: 'They shall look upon the carcasses of people that have transgressed against me. Their worm shall not cease, and their fire shall not be extinguished; and they shall be a loathsome sight to all flesh' (66:24). Christians, as the 'New Israel' and the children and co-heirs of Christ, will be saved, while the 'Old Israel' ('people that have transgressed against me') will become 'like Sodom and Gomorrah' and 'a loathsome sight to all flesh'.

It is also in this very long and influential work that they are unambiguously accused, for the first time in the history of Jewish-Christian relations, of deicide.[33] Justin tells them straight out: 'You have murdered the Just One and His prophets before him.' Moreover, they feel no remorse for having 'crucified the only just and sinless Man'. They are also guilty of cursing in their synagogues all those who believe in Christ and spreading malicious rumours about them 'in every land'. Any trials and tribulations that befall the Jews, says Justin in a horrifying observation frequent all through the history of Christianity, are therefore justly deserved: 'For this reason God cries out to you through Isaiah, Behold how the just perish and no-one notices ... But draw near, you wicked sons, seed of the adulterers and children of the harlot. Upon whom have you jested, and upon whom have you been opening your mouth and putting out your tongue? (57:1–4). With good reason, therefore, does Isaiah cry out: Because of you my name is blasphemed among the Gentiles (52:5) ... Woe unto their soul for they have taken evil counsel against themselves, saying let us bind the Just One for he is useless to us. Therefore they eat the fruit of their deeds .... (3.9ff) ... Woe unto them that draw iniquity as with a long cord ... Woe unto them that

---

[31] Chapter 12. Cf. Evans, *To See and Not Perceive*, p. 154; see pp. 36ff.
[32] A favourite of Justin, and of other Christian polemicists: see below.
[33] *Dialogue*, 16 and 17.

call evil good and good evil; that put light for darkness and darkness for light ... (5:18–20)'. This is the kind of abusive language running through Justin's *Dialogue with Trypho*, considered acceptable, no doubt, because most of it is in Isaiah, but well beyond the bounds of polite discourse.

Isaiah is without a doubt Justin's favourite source of scriptural proof-texts, for his theological arguments as well as his invective. Lengthy texts central to Christian teaching are cited in full, often with minimal comments, including 39:8–40:17, 52:10–54:6 and 63:15–64:12, while other texts like 29:13 (on the rejection of the Jews) and 53:8 (which proves the divine origin of Christ), are cited repeatedly. Such texts from Isaiah were so fundamental to Christian belief, and the christological interpretation of them so self-evident, that often all Justin has to do to dismiss the Jewish challenge is to quote another similar text, or to repeat the same text again (one can imagine, in a louder voice).

We shall restrict ourselves to a few comments on the use of Isaiah in this early polemical context. In a brief introductory section, devoid of biblical references, incidentally, Justin gives some account of his personal background, his disillusionment with Greek philosophy and his conversion to Christianity, and it is agreed that biblical authority is superior to Plato. The dialogue then focusses on the matter of religious observances. In answer to Trypho's comment that Christians do not observe the Mosaic law, which he argues (on the basis of Genesis 17:9–14) applies to strangers and purchased slaves alike, Justin quotes two familiar passages from Isaiah (51:4–5; 55:3–5), and an even more popular Christian text from Jeremiah (31:31–2) about a new law and a new covenant which supersede the old ones.

His use of the 'Suffering Servant' passage (52:13–52:12), which he quotes in full in this part of the discussion, is interesting. In the first place, he begins the quotation at 52:10 ('The lord shall bare his holy arm in the sight of the gentiles ...'), and continues it into chapter 54 ('Sing, O barren woman ...'). This has the effect of putting the story of the atoning suffering and death of Christ (as recounted in Isaiah's words) into a gentile, missionary context. We shall see later how eighteenth- and nineteenth-century missionaries picked out phrases from these same texts such as 'Sprinkle many nations' (52:15) and 'Stretch out the guy ropes ...' in a similar way.[34]

---

[34]	See pp. 155ff.

The wider context which he cites also contains the call to 'Depart ... touch nothing unclean ... sanctify yourselves ...' (52:11), and this provides Justin with scriptural authority for a discussion of the Christian sacrament of baptism 'which was instituted for the sins of the people of God, as Isaiah testifies',[35] in contrast to circumcision which, according to Justin, was a divine punishment on the Jews, marking them off from all other people for a special degree of suffering. When Isaiah cries to his people, 'Wash yourselves, be clean, take away the evil from your souls!' (1:16), he is calling for Christian baptism, which is 'the true circumcision'. In the same way, on the subject of fasting, he quotes Isaiah 58:1–12 in full with the comment, 'therefore be circumcised rather in your heart, as the above quoted words of God demand' (cf. Deut.10:16–17).[36]

Trypho the Jew naturally challenges most of Justin's statements, and in particular accuses Justin of being selective in his choice of quotations; but that in no way cramps his style. He goes on to use Jewish scripture, especially Isaiah, to prove the messiahship of Jesus, the Virgin Birth, the divine origin of Jesus, the doctrine of the Trinity and virtually every other Christian belief. But we shall leave him there, and move on now to look at the role of Isaiah in other even more influential examples of anti-Jewish polemic.

The frequent use made of Isaiah 6:9–10 by Tertullian (c.160–c.225) has recently been discussed elsewhere.[37] We shall move on to John Chrysostom (c.347–407), whose eight *Discourses against the Jews* have been described as 'the most violent and tasteless of the anti-Judaic literature of the period'.[38] Preached around the time of the Jewish festivals in the years 386–7, they were aimed at Jews living in Antioch and at Jewish converts in the Church whom he accuses of 'Judaizing'.[39] One reason why the language is so extreme is that the Church in Antioch could not tolerate 'judaizers', many of them new and insecure converts to Christianity who were tempted to return to their former Jewish practices – especially at the time of the festivals. The Jews in Antioch were seen as a threat and John Chrysostom saw it as his duty to tell his flock Sunday after Sunday what evil, demonic, immoral, debauched people they were. The effect of such

---

[35] *Dialogue*, 14.   [36] *Dialogue*, 15.
[37] Evans, *To See and Not Perceive*, pp. 154–6.
[38] Ruether, *Faith and Fratricide*, p. 173.
[39] A recent translator prefers the title *Discourses against Judaizing Christians*: P. W. Harkins, *FOC* 68 (1979).

rhetoric, by one of the Church's greatest preachers, upon Christian perceptions of the Jews, was devastating, especially now that Christianity had the full authority of the Roman Empire behind it as the official religion, and Judaism had not. In the fifth and sixth centuries communal violence continually erupted against the Jews in Antioch, until they were finally expelled from the city altogether.[40]

Chrysostom found in Isaiah plenty of ammunition for this assault on the Jews. With Isaiah's authority he calls them 'dogs' (56:10),[41] stubborn and shamefaced ('your forehead is bronze': that is to say, incapable of blushing).[42] He tells them they behave like drunkards (29:9);[43] they resemble the citizens of Sodom and Gomorrah (1:10).[44] He quotes 1:15 at them: 'your hands are full of blood',[45] and brings in Isaiah as his chief witness when he is explaining that their present troubles are due to their own crimes against Christ: 'And I shall give the ungodly for his burial, and the rich for his death' (53:8–9). He (Isaiah) did not simply say 'the Jews', but 'the ungodly'. What could be more ungodly than those who first received so many good things and then slew the author of those blessings?'.[46]

Augustine's sermon *Adversus Judaeos*, written probably some time after *De Civitate Dei* (425),[47] cites two of the familiar verses from Isaiah about the Jews' blindness (6:10) and disbelief (65:2), and, like John Chrysostom, just quoted, uses chapter 53 to accuse them of deicide. But his main theme here is the Church's mission to the gentiles, summed up in 49:6 ('I have given you to be a light to the gentiles'). The famous Zion passage in 2:2–5, a passage that has always been of special significance to the Jews,[48] provides him with scriptural authority for the main part of his argument. He points out that the prophet envisages all the nations of the world saying, 'Come let us go up to the mountain of the Lord', not just the Jews, and repeatedly quotes verse 5 ('O house of Jacob, come let us walk in the light of the Lord'), taunting them with the Christian claim that it is no longer addressed to them. Sarcastically and with blatant disregard for the context, he paraphrases the next verse to prove it: 'For the Lord has

---

[40]   Ruether, *Faith and Fratricide*, p. 180; cf. C. Kraeling, 'The Jewish Commmunity in Antioch', *JBL* 51 (1932), pp. 130ff.

[41]   4.6.3.   [42]   5.4.5.   [43]   8.1.1.

[44]   4.6.2.   [45]   7.3.5.   [46]   6.5.4.

[47]   For a list of scholars who view this work as a sermon rather than a treatise, see bibliography in *Adversus Judaeos* ('In Answer to the Jews') (translated by Sister Marie Liguori), *FOC*,15, pp. 387f.

[48]   See p. 103.

cast off his people, the house of Israel'.[49] Once again the tone is hardly one of 'persuasive firmness and kindness',[50] and one has to take with a pinch of salt his concluding appeal to Christians to show great love, kindness and humility towards the Jews.

Isidore of Seville's *De fide Catholica adversus Judaeos* was written in the early seventh century, right at the end of the patristic period and just before the spread of Islam. He was not a very original scholar, but extremely well versed in the writings of the fathers so that his work therefore often provided later generations with a convenient digest of what had by his day become received Christian doctrine. He was much used for this purpose in the mediaeval Church and his influence on the development of Christian tradition was profound. *De fide Catholica* was written, according to the author's dedicatory letter, to strengthen the Christian faith by means of Old Testament texts, and at the same time to expose the 'ignorance of the faithless Jews' (*infidelium Judaeorum imperitiam*). It is in two parts. Book I, as we saw in an earlier chapter,[51] contains proof-texts from the Old Testament (*veteris testamenti signacula*), especially Isaiah, for virtually every aspect of the person, life, death, resurrection and ascension of Christ. Here we need only note that special attention is devoted to the part the Jews played in the crucifixion. A short paragraph on the 'Jews shouting, Crucify him!' uses three texts from Isaiah including one of the verses which attributes the destruction of Jerusalem in 70 AD to this crime: *ruit Jerusalem, et Judas concidit, quia lingua eorum contra Dominum* (3:8; cf. 57:4; 5:7).[52]

In the next paragraph Isidore also uses part of Isaiah's taunt against Babylon to fill out the infamous verse from Matthew 27: 'For because the Jews who sinned against Christ condemned their posterity too, saying, "His blood be upon us and upon our children" (Matt.27:25), Isaiah once preached the following rebuke to them: *Semen pessimum, praeparate filios vestros occisioni in iniquitate patrum vestrorum*) ('O most evil seed, prepare your sons for slaughter because of the crime of your parents') (14:20).[53] Third person pronouns ('his sons ... their fathers') of the original Hebrew are regularly changed to second person pronouns ('your sons ... your fathers') to make the application of Isaiah's invective to the contemporary situation more personal and more biting. At the end he explains, with Isaianic

---

[49] *Adversus Judaeos* 8, 11.   [50] Liguori, *FOC* 15, p. 389.
[51] See p. 49.   [52] *De Fide*, 27.2.
[53] *De Fide*, 27–28.

sarcasm, that the texts are listed to show that 'all these things are contained in the books of the Hebrews, read by the Jews, but not understood by them, as the prophet testifies: "The words of this book will be like the words of a book that is sealed: if you give it to someone who cannot read, saying, Read this, they will say, I cannot read; but if you give it to someone who can read, saying Read this, they too will say, I cannot, the book is sealed" ' (Isaiah 29:11–12).

Book II targets the Jews even more directly. The first two chapters focus on the universality of the Gospel, making full use of some of the texts from Isaiah which we will discuss below in the context of the Church's eighteenth- and nineteenth-century foreign missionary work (e.g. 9:2; 11:10; 42:5–8; 45:20, 23; 51:4; 52:15; 54:1–3).[54] But already the ominous appearance of 65:1–2 among these texts prepares the way for more systematic and explicit anti-Jewish polemic. Texts like 40:9 ('O thou that tellest good tidings to Zion ...') and 65:2 ('I held out my hands to them every day') are used to prove that the Jews, no less than the gentiles, were offered the chance to follow Christ; and passages about the obduracy and blindness of the Jews (especially 6:9–11, 29:9–13 and 65:1–3) repeatedly quoted to explain why they have not. He turns the 'first to Zion' (*rishon le-tzion*) passage used by Jewish settlers (41:27)[55] against them by quoting the next verse ('But there was nobody there to respond').

Isidore then proceeds, like Justin Martyr and many Christian writers down the ages, to enumerate the sufferings of the Jews, the catastrophes that have befallen them and the end of their religion, as the just and inevitable results of their disbelief. Isaiah foretold that the Jews in their blindness would be expelled from Jerusalem (43:8) and the gates opened for the righteous gentiles to enter instead (26:2). They were also guilty of deicide ('because of the crimes of my people' 53:8), and for this 'the Lord poured out upon them the heat of his anger and the might of battle' (42:25 Vg). The destruction of Jerusalem was 'because their speech and their deeds were against the Lord' (3:8; cf. 1:7; 25:1–5; 32:13). Isaiah provides ample scriptural authority for the belief that the old covenant is abrogated (43:18, 22: 'remember not the former things'; cf. 42:9), and with it the Jewish Sabbath (1.13), circumcision of the flesh (cf. 43.18), and animal sacrifice (1:11; 66:3). In their place are baptism for the remission of sins (1:14; 12:3; 55:1), the sign of the cross (5:26; 55:13; 66:18) and the

---

[54]   See pp. 152–157.
[55]   See above, p. 104.

sacrament of the eucharist (65:13). This last text from Isaiah provides Isidore with the arrogant, gloating, belligerent language and imagery for his final crushing blow against the Jews:

Thus says the Lord God: Behold my servants will eat while you go hungry; my servants will drink while you thirst. My servants will rejoice while you are humiliated; my servants will rejoice with joyful heart, while you cry out with aching heart and wail with contrite spirit; You will give up your name to my chosen ones to be a curse; the Lord God will slay you, but his servants he will call by another name, so that those who bless themselves in the land will be blessed by God.

Isidore inserts *id est, Christianos* after 'servants' in the last sentence, and then actually spells out the horrific application of these verses to the Jewish people:

So Israel is slain, and a people from among the gentiles takes their place. The Old Testament is taken away from them and the New is handed to us. We are given the grace of the food of salvation and the cup of Christ's blood, while they faint from hunger and thirst. Another name, 'Christian', is given to a new people; and everything that happens now resounds with the newness of grace ... O the lamentable folly of the luckless Jews! (*O infelicium Judaeorum deflenda dementia*).

Again and again in the long and shameful history of Christian antisemitism we find the last word goes to Isaiah.

This extended example from Isidore sets the scene for our brief look at some of the mediaeval disputations between Jews and Christians. In the summer of 1263 King James I of Aragon summoned Rabbi Moses ben Nahman (Nahmanides) of Gerona to a disputation with the Dominican Friar Pablo Christiani before the royal court in Barcelona. Nahmanides was one of the most respected Jewish scholars of the time, and it was no doubt the king's aim, by discrediting him, to undermine the faith and confidence of the whole of Spanish Jewry. Pablo was a convert from Judaism and an energetic proselytizer among the Jews of Spain and France. He was thus the ideal Christian protagonist in the debate, able to offer his Jewish opponent a challenge which was both informed by his Jewish education and sharpened by his passionate commitment to the cause of converting his former co-religionists to Christianity.

We have both a Christian account of the debate, which is a brief official document in Latin drawn up by the Dominicans, and a very much more extended Hebrew version purporting to be by

Nahmanides himself. Both are clearly motivated by factors other than the aim to record precisely what happened, although the official Christian account is manifestly more biassed than the more careful and detailed Jewish version. But both agree on the basic agenda of the debate, and provide us with sufficient evidence for our present purpose, which is to examine Isaiah's role in the arguments of Nahmanides and Friar Pablo. Pablo intended to prove four propositions about the Messiah and the messianic age: (1) that the Messiah had come in the person of Jesus Christ; (2) that the Messiah was both divine and human; (3) that the Messiah had suffered and died for the salvation of the human race; and (4) that the legal requirements of the Mosaic law were no longer valid now that the Messiah had come.[56] The first three of these do not touch the heart of the Jewish faith as they do the Christian, as Nahmanides himself says.[57] But the last, if Nahmanides could be forced to give way on it, would undermine the whole *raison d'être* of Judaism.

All four propositions recur as major topics of debate elsewhere in Jewish-Christian dialogue and anti-Jewish polemic, and, although much attention is always given to other Jewish texts as well, that is to say, the 'oral tradition' as contained in the Talmud, Midrash and Targumim, both sides make constant use of texts from scripture, especially Isaiah. As one would expect, the 'Suffering Servant' passage (52:13–53:12) is again at the centre, a passage always more familiar and more important to Christians than Jews. But now we hear the Jewish reply to Christian claims that it, more than any other passage in the Prophets, describes the life, death and resurrection of Christ. In Barcelona Nahmanides argues that, according to the 'plain meaning' of the text, this passage speaks of the suffering of the people of Israel in general, citing passages elsewhere in Isaiah where 'the servant of the Lord' is identified with 'Israel' (41:8) and 'Jacob' (44:1). Pablo has no difficulty in showing that there are Jewish texts in which the servant in this passage is identified with the Messiah, and that there are Jewish traditions about a suffering Messiah. Nahmanides knows all this perfectly well and offers to give 'an excellent and detailed explanation of the passage', but is not allowed to – 'they did not want to hear it'.[58]

[56]   Christian account: cf. Maccoby, *Judaism on Trial*, pp. 147f; J. Cohen, *The Friars and the Jews*, p. 111.
[57]   Maccoby, *Judaism on Trial*, p. 119.
[58]   Maccoby, *Judaism on Trial*, p. 113.

The debate does not go all Pablo's way by any means, according to Nahmanides' account at any rate. In fact he was so successful in defending Jewish belief against Pablo that his friends pleaded with him to restrain himself for fear of reprisals from the host community. At one point Pablo returns to the 'Suffering Servant' passage and reminds Nahmanides that the servant, according to a Jewish commentary on 52:13, was 'exalted above Abraham, lifted up above Moses and higher than the ministering angels'.[59] This proves it must refer to Jesus since only he is both Messiah and God himself. But Nahmanides has no trouble proving from other texts that 'higher than the angels' is a common hyperbole applied to other righteous humans. He later has the opportunity to point out too that Jesus does not fit Isaiah 53 in every detail: for example, his grave was not 'with the wicked' (53:9). Elsewhere he uses another of the Church's favourite verses against them, arguing from 11:1, which tells of the human ancestry of Jesus,[60] that the Messiah cannot be divine.

In perhaps his most powerful speech of the debate, Nahmanides declares that he cannot believe the Messiah has come yet because, quoting a text much used by modern Christian writers, artists and preachers, and now inscribed on a sculpture at the entrance to the United Nations building in New York (Isaiah 2:4; cf. Micah 4:3),[61] the messianic age is to be characterized by global peace. He says: 'Yet from the days of Jesus until now, the whole world has been full of violence and plundering, and the Christians are greater spillers of blood than all the rest ... and how hard it would be for you, my lord king, and for your knights if they were not to learn war any more!'[62] In spite of the Jew's impressive showing at Barcelona, his devious Dominican opponent put it about that he was discredited, even among his own people.[63] In particular his admission that he did not believe that some of the Jewish scriptures, namely the homiletical parts of the Talmud, were authoritative, undermined his credibility as a rabbi. In fact Nahmanides did leave Spain a few years after Barcelona, but no doubt this was as much because of the king's intensified onslaught on the Jewish community at large following the disputation, led by Pablo Christiani himself, as because of any

[59]   Yalkut, Isaiah, 476; cf. Maccoby, *Judaism on Trial*, p. 122.
[60]   See pp. 74–80.   [61]   See pp. 231ff.
[62]   Maccoby, *Judaism on Trial*, p. 121.
[63]   Cf. Cohen, *The Friars and the Jews*, pp. 118ff.

personal failure on the part of Nahmanides. He is remembered and
respected as one of the great mediaeval rabbinic authorities.

Before leaving the subject of Isaiah's role in Jewish-Christian
debate, we shall look briefly at the Tortosa Disputation of 1413–14.[64]
Isaiah provides the chilling words with which the Christian
spokesman, a converted Jew called Geronimo, opened the debate:
'Come now and let us reason together, saith the Lord ... but if you
refuse and rebel, ye shall be devoured by the sword' (Isa.1:18, 20).
The Disputation was chaired by the Pope himself,[65] who, in order to
assert his supreme authority, uses God's words from Isaiah, as if they
were his own : 'It has gone forth from my mouth and I shall not go
back from it' (Isa.45:23). It was attended by seventy cardinals and
bishops, and was blatantly set up with the aim of converting all the
Jews in Aragon and Catalonia, by proving, from the Jews' own texts,
particularly the Talmud, that the Messiah had come. The atmo-
sphere was far from relaxed. Twenty years earlier, the Jewish
communities of that part of Spain had been decimated by a ferocious
campaign of persecution and massacre, stirred up by Christian
fanatics; and immediately after it the Pope publicly indicted the
Talmud for heresy and ordered its confiscation from all Jews who
possessed a copy.[66] Moreover, the leader of the Jewish delegation,
Don Vidal, was converted and appointed to a high office in the
Church. The Jews in fifteenth-century Spain lived in constant fear of
their Christian neighbours, and those threatening words of Isaiah, on
the lips of a man who represented Christian power over them, must
have struck terror into their hearts as the twenty-one months of
debate began.

French religious drama provides some telling examples of the
use of Isaiah as the champion of Christianity against the Jews. The
twelfth-century *Mystère d'Adam* is a case in point.[67] Based on a
pseudo-Augustinian sermon written in the sixth century, the play
begins with the words *vos, inquam, convenio, O Judei!* ('You, I say, do
I challenge, O Jews!'). Isaiah is the last and most important of the
prophets who file in one after the other, proclaiming the truth of
Christian claims that Jesus is the Messiah. The others all have one

[64] Maccoby, *Judaism on Trial*, pp. 168–215.
[65] Strictly he was one of three claimants to the office of Pope: Maccoby, *Judaism on Trial*, p. 94.
[66] Cohen, *The Friars and the Jews*, p. 168.
[67] Talmage, *Disputation and Dialogue*, pp. 90,100–108.

proof-text each: Abraham cites Genesis 22:17f., Moses Deuteronomy 18:15, Balaam Numbers 24:17, Daniel 9:24, 26, Habbakuk
3:2 and so on. Isaiah has two: 11:1 ('the root of Jesse') and 7:14 ('A
virgin shall conceive'). After his exposition of the first of these, he is
challenged by the Jew who asks if he had made it up or dreamt it,
or was it a joke? Isaiah is an old man: perhaps he has lost his
mind:

> *Jew*: 'Thou seem'st to me a dotard grey,
> Thy mind and sense all gone astray!
> A soothsayer thou seem'st indeed,
> Skilled in the glass, perchance to read;
> Come, read me now this hand and tell
> whether my heart is sick or well.'

> *Isaiah*: 'Thou hast sin's murrain in thy soul,
> Ne'er in thy life shalt thou be whole!'

Isaiah then silences the Jew with the other verse from Isaiah (7:14)
and his commentary on it. Finally, to shame the disbelieving Jew, a
token gentile appears on the scene, the Babylonian king Nebuchad-
nezzar, who boasts that he recognized the Son of God in the burning
fiery furnace (Dan.3:25). In another very different example, Christian
prejudice against the 'Old Testament' so outweighs traditional
respect for the 'Fifth Gospel', that Isaiah is actually rebuked for not
telling the truth: 'Isaiah you who know what is true,/why do you not
tell the truth?' After giving his christological testimony he is escorted
back to hell with the other prophets as if he cannot really be
trusted.[68]

We end with a look at some examples of the influence of Isaianic
images upon mediaeval Christian representations of Jews and the
Synagogue. The ox and ass that always appear in the earliest nativity
scenes (even in some cases where Mary and the shepherds are
absent[69]), come from Isaiah 1:3, sometimes also connected with an
ancient Greek version of Habbakuk 3:2 ('between two animals you
will be known'). Some commentators like Gregory of Nazianzus
(c.329–90)[70] interpret the ox as a symbol of the Jews and the ass as
the gentiles loaded with the sins of idolatry, so that Isaiah's prophecy
implies that all humanity will be free when the Messiah comes.

---

[68] Cf. Roston, *Biblical Drama in England*, p. 30.
[69] Schiller, *Iconography*, I, pp. 59–61, figs.143, 144, 150.
[70] *PG* 45, 1138.

Others, including Origen and Jerome, found in the invidious, taunting contrast between dumb animals who recognize their master in the manger, and Israel who 'does not know, my people do not understand', a proof-text about the blindness and obduracy of the Jews who reject Christ. Jerome uses the image of the ox and the ass in Isaiah 1:3 to score another point over the Jews as well. In his commentary on 1:3, he notes that there is another passage in Isaiah where these two animals are mentioned together, one of Isaiah's visions of a new age, ending with the words: 'Happy are you who sow beside all waters, who let the feet of the ox and the ass range free' (32:20). Quoting the law in Deuteronomy that 'you shall not plough with an ox and an ass together' (22:10), he concludes that in the new age people will no longer be bound by the law, a further argument for the rejection of the Jews and Judaism.

In mediaeval and Renaissance art, the ox who knows his owner is frequently depicted as behaving more respectfully towards the infant Jesus, than the ass who only 'knows his master's stall'. This is so, for example, in Botticelli's *Mystic Nativity*, in the National Gallery in London. The ox symbolizes true faith while the ass embodies materialism and the inability to appreciate the miracle of Christ's birth. It is not difficult to see how this distinction between the two animals can be given an antisemitic interpretation too. Finally in a rather bizarre fifteenth-century representation of the nativity scene on a roof boss in a Church in Nantwich, this tendentious interpretation of the ox and ass motif is developed to the point where the two animals, representing respectively the Gentiles and the Jews, are engaging in a most unseemly tug of war over the infant Christ's swaddling clothes. Even this innocent motif, so familiar from pictures of the nativity scene right down to the Christmas cards of the present day, has been pressed into the service of antisemitic polemic.

One of the commonest mediaeval Christian representations of the Jewish people portrays them in the allegorical image of a downcast, blindfolded woman, holding in one hand a broken piece of one of the tables of stone on which the Ten Commandments were written, and trying to support herself with a broken staff in the other. Opposite her stands the confident disapproving figure of another woman representing the Church, with a crown on her head, a chalice in one hand and a banner firmly placed on the ground in the

other.[71] One example can be seen in a twelfth-century Bible manuscript in Lambeth Palace (Plate 14).[72] This time it is in the explicitly
Isaianic context of a Jesse tree.[73] The two women representing
Ecclesia and Synagoga appear at the top of the tree, on either side of
the figures of Christ and the Virgin Mary. Isaiah is depicted twice,
first at the foot of the tree where he holds a scroll with the words of
11:1 on it, and again at the top beside Synagoga. Synagoga is a limp
dejected figure, her head turned away from Christ and covered in a
veil which is being held there by God's hand. She is accompanied on
either side by two male figures, Moses and Isaiah. Moses is behind
her, trying to persuade her to turn round and face Christ. Isaiah has
her by the wrist, and is clearly also trying to draw her towards Christ
on whom his eyes are firmly fixed. The allegory is clear: the Jews,
despite the efforts of Moses and Isaiah, are blind and obdurate.

This degrading image of the veiled Synagogue is derived from 2
Corinthians 3:14–16: 'But their minds were hardened; for to this day,
when they read the old covenant, that same veil remains unlifted,
because only through Christ is it taken away. Yes, to this day,
whenever Moses is read a veil lies over their minds; but when one
turns to the Lord, the veil is removed.' Clearly Paul's mention of
Moses here explains his appearance beside Synagoga. But the phrase
'their minds were hardened', especially in a context where 'hardening' is achieved by veiling and includes blindness, is no less obvious
an allusion to Isaiah 6:9–11[74] or possibly 29:10,[75] and explains his
presence in the scene as well.

For general descriptions of the blindness of the Jews, as well as
their deafness, obduracy and stupidity, Christian writers and
preachers have made constant reference to the book of Isaiah,
especially those two passages from chapters 6 and 29, but also 1:3,
42:18–19 and 65:1–2. We have already discussed 6:9–10, as a much-
used text in the Gospels and Acts.[76] In almost every period of
Church history this passage is repeatedly applied to the Jewish
rejection of Christ. For the Church Fathers, as Craig Evans shows, it
was used to explain why the Jews had rejected, and continue to

[71]   Cf. Schlauch, 'The allegory of Church and Synagogue' pp. 448–64; Seifert, *Synagogue and Church in the Middle Ages*, pp. 95–109.
[72]   For a useful discussion see *Legacy of Israel*, edd. Bevan and Singer, pp. xxiv–xxv.
[73]   See pp. 74ff.
[74]   Cf. Barrett, *A Commentary on the Second Epistle to the Corinthians*, p. 120.
[75]   Evans, *To See and Not Perceive*, p. 83.
[76]   See above, pp. 36ff.

reject, Christ. He identifies three ways in which Isaiah 6:9–10 and related texts were used to explain what he calls this 'embarrassment' for the Church: (1) it was to fulfil the prophecy of Isaiah (e.g. Justin Martyr, Origen, Athanasius, Ambrose, Chrysostom); (2) the text proves that the Jews are habitually obdurate so that their rejection of Christ was only to be expected (e.g. Eusebius, Jerome); (3) the text proves that they were predestined to reject Christ and therefore actually prevented by God from believing in him (e.g. Tertullian, Augustine).[77]

As noted above,[78] Evans is less interested in the appalling consequences for the Jews of the Church's persistent citation of such texts, than in their place in the development of Christian doctrine. His survey of the patristic period concludes that 'Isaiah 6:9–10 is still understood as a major witness to God's absolute sovereignty',[79] and the worst examples of blatant antisemitic uses of the verse, and others like it, are for the most part kept to the footnotes at the end of the book.[80] Nowhere does he take seriously the insidious, cumulative effect which the constant repetition of statements about the blindness and obduracy of the Jews, often in the violent and vehement language of Isaiah, was bound to have upon the perceptions and attitudes that Christians have had in regard to some of their fellow-citizens.

The roots of what is later known as 'the demonization of the Jews' are to be found in the Fathers. John Chrysostom (c.347–407), for example, commenting on Isaiah 53:1 and 6:10, quoted in John 12:34–41, says that Jewish obduracy is due to the fact that 'demons dwell in their souls'.[81] According to Cassiodorus (c.485–c.580) too 'the Jews are obdurate and sons of the devil'.[82] This is the kind of language that led to those mediaeval representations of *Synagoga caeca* ('blind Synagoga') and the Friars' concerted assault on the Jews from the thirteenth century on. In the late mediaeval *Biblia Pauperum*, a description of the fall of Lucifer in Isaiah 14:12–15 is applied to the Jews: 'The proud devils signify the Jews, who were afraid of losing their position and land, and so crucified and killed the good and

[77] Evans, *To See and Not Perceive*, pp. 153–62.
[78] See p. 36.
[79] Evans, *To See and Not Perceive*, p. 162.
[80] Evans, *To See and Not Perceive*, pp. 222–4.
[81] *Against the Jews*, 1.6; cf. Evans, *To See and Not Perceive*, p. 22, note 60.
[82] *Expositions on the Psalms*, 17.46 (on Ps.18:44–5). Cf. Evans, *To See and Not Perceive*, pp. 159 and 222, note 71.

humble Jesus; and they themselves fell into the pit they had themselves made, that is to say, they are alive in Hell'.[83]

The very distinguished Franciscan scholar Nicholas of Lyra (c.1270–1340) applied Isaiah 29:12 to the stubbornness of the Jews with just the same confidence as earlier, less sophisticated commentators.[84] On 29:9 Luther says 'the prophet speaks about that most wretched blindness of the Jews who could not read in spite of open books'.[85] Elsewhere he uses Isaiah 29 to express his views on a more specific failing of the Jews, namely the uselessness of their rabbis when it comes to translating the Bible, despite their knowledge of Hebrew.[86] Calvin also applies both 6:9–10 and 29:9–10 to the Jews, though in a less polemical tone.[87]

Another example from the Reformation period appears in a semi-humorous emblem inspired by Isaiah 6.9–10.[88] In one half it depicts a group of Jews continuing in their old ways, rejecting the truth of Christian interpretations of scripture, while the other, in a bizarre scene perhaps reminiscent of the seraph taking a burning coal from the altar, shows a hand with a pair of spectacles in it, emerging from the clouds around an open Bible. The truth of scripture can only be perceived through spectacles designed and provided by God.

Before we leave the image of 'blind Synagoga', there is another verse of Isaiah frequently associated with her. The broken staff in her right hand, symbol of the humiliation, powerlessness and poverty of the Jews, seems to be derived from Isaiah 3:1: 'For behold the Lord, the Lord of hosts, is taking away from Jerusalem and from Judah stay and staff'.[89] Isidore of Seville cites this verse in the same context as 6:9, 29:11 and a reference to 'the veil placed over the heart of the Jews'.[90] A poignant example of this image is to be found in a painting by the fifteenth-century artist Konrad Witz (Plate 22). The image has also been used, incidentally, as the title of a recent study of 'Judaism through Christian Eyes'.[91]

The broken tablet of the law in her left hand in some examples may also have an Isaianic connection.[92] 2:3 ('out of Zion shall go

[83] *BP*, p. 87.
[84] Cohen, *The Friars and the Jews*, p. 178.
[85] *LW*, vol. 16, p. 242.   [86] *LW*, vol. 54; p. 408.
[87] *Commentary on Isaiah*; cf. Evans, *To See and Not Perceive*, p. 224, note 74.
[88] *Emblemata*, ed. Henkel-Schöne, p. 1841.
[89] Cf. *Legacy of Israel*, edd. Bevan and Singer, p. xiii.
[90] *De Fide Catholica contra Judaeos*, 2.21 (*PL* 83, p. 528).
[91] Manuel, *The Broken Staff. Judaism through Christian Eyes* (1992).
[92] See p. 35.

forth the law') is cited in support of the Christian contention that, when the Messiah comes, the old Mosaic law would be removed and a new law take its place. Other passages frequently used in the same context include 43:18–19 which implies that the old law is to be forgotten, and 51:4: 'a (new) law will go forth from me and my justice for a light to the peoples'.[93] We saw already how the ox and the ass motif from Isaiah 1:3 and 32:20 provided Jerome with scriptural authority to make the same point about the abrogation of the Jewish law in the messianic age.[94]

Such uses of Isaiah in the context of Jewish-Christian relations continue right down to the present. There are still Christian evangelical organizations which find scriptural support in Isaiah for their attitudes and activities in relation to the Jews. 'Jews for Jesus' is a modern example, which, like the mediaeval friars,[95] makes much use of Isaiah, especially chapter 53, in its attempts to convert Jews to Christianity.[96] They even sell 'Isaiah 53 baseball shirts'. Like so many Christian writers from earlier eras,[97] they also cite Isaiah 6, somewhat ironically, to explain why the Jews did not accept Christ and why salvation was offered instead to the gentiles.[98]

It is only in the second half of the twentieth century that the Church has begun to make efforts to rectify this situation by removing blatantly anti-Jewish phrases from hymns and prayers, and issuing official statements exonerating Jews from the charge of deicide. Before the 'reformation' brought about by the Second Vatican Council in 1962–5, prayers were still offered in Catholic churches throughout the world on Good Friday 'for the faithless Jews' (*pro perfidis Judaeis*) and 'for the blindness of that people' (*pro illius populi obcaecatione*).[99] Since then, in the light of the Vatican II 'Declaration on the Relation of the Church to Non-Christian Religions' (*Nostra Aetate*, 28 October, 1965), and other official pronouncements, some of these offensive traditions have been removed from the liturgy. It is interesting that, at this most recent stage of the process, all the polemical texts we have been considering are conspicuous by their absence: the only text from Isaiah referred to in

---

[93]   Justin Martyr, Dialogue 11; Isidore of Seville, *De Fide Catholica contra Judaeos*, 2.14.1,6 (*PL* 83, 520–1).
[94]   See above, p. 120.   [95]   See above, pp. 101f.
[96]   E.g. Rosen with Proctor, *Jews for Jesus*, pp. 47–8.
[97]   Cf. pp. 36ff.
[98]   Rosen with Proctor, *Jews for Jesus*, p. 113.
[99]   *Missale Romanum*, p. 267.

Nostra Aetate is 66:23: 'From, new moon to new moon, and from sabbath to sabbath, all flesh shall come to worship before me, says the Lord'.[100] The situation in the Church of England is less clearcut. The notorious Good Friday prayer for 'Jews, Turks and Infidels' remains in the 1662 prayerbook, which is still used in some Churches (and stoutly championed by the Prayerbook Society). Some of the patronizing and insulting language about the Jews has been removed from the more recent *Alternative Service Books*, but there is still mention of their 'ignorance, hardness of heart and contempt for your word'.

[100] *Vatican II Documents*, ed. A. Flannery, p. 741.

CHAPTER 7

The Reformation

In the sixteenth century, the Reformers' radical challenge to traditional authority, and consequent divisions in the Church, affected Christian uses and perceptions of the Bible, and of Isaiah in particular, in many ways. The majority of the innovations that took place at that time in the theology, liturgy and structure of the Church remain characteristics of Reformed Christianity to this day, and for that reason we shall not restrict ourselves in this chapter and the next to sixteenth-century sources alone. We shall try to identify the earliest examples we can find of particular uses, in the sixteenth century or earlier, but we also propose to draw on material from four-and-a-half centuries of Protestant Christianity, right down to the present time.

We begin with some general remarks on the Bible in the sixteenth century, and some examples of innovations in the reformers' use and interpretation of Isaiah, and then, as ever ruthlessly selective, we will focus in this chapter and the next on texts, which may be said to epitomize three new emphases in the history of Christianity: scripture and especially the 'Word of God' passage *par excellence,* 40:6–8; polemic against idolatry with reference to passages like 41:7 and 44:9–20; and education beginning with 54:13, a favourite of Martin Luther's ('all thy children will be taught of the Lord)'.

We must first take account of fundamental changes in the role of the Bible in the Church. For the Reformers the Bible was the sole authority, above that of the Church's current leaders as well as that of sixteen centuries of accumulated Christian tradition, and it was therefore given a central position in every aspect of Church life. Not that this was entirely new in the history of Christianity, as we have seen, but what was new was the emergence of Protestant Churches that claimed to have recovered the true meaning of scripture, buried under centuries of official Church doctrine, much of it hard, if not impossible, to defend on scriptural grounds. They found support for their new understanding of scripture in the pioneering work of such biblical scholars as Andrew of St Victor and Nicholas of Lyra, and, more recently, in that of the humanists Reuchlin and Erasmus. These and others shifted the emphasis away from the study of the Latin Vulgate, which remained for Catholics the official version of the Bible until the present century, and devoted their textual and linguistic expertise to the study of Hebrew, Aramaic and Greek. Like Jerome, they also appreciated the value of Jewish scholarship in their search for what the text means.

There were those who did not want a complete break with tradition while at the same time paying due regard to what the biblical experts said the text actually means. Luther's handling of Isaiah 7:14 is an excellent illustration of this. Having accepted that the Hebrew word *'almah*, traditionally represented, on the authority of Matthew 1:23, as *parthenos*, *virgo* in the Church's official Greek and Latin versions of the passage, does not in fact mean 'virgin' at all, but 'young woman', Luther is nonetheless sufficiently devoted to the mediaeval Latin use of this verse in the cult of the Virgin Mary, to argue that the 'young woman' must have been a virgin: otherwise, he says, the prophecy would not have been a 'sign' or 'miracle'.[1] Luther's respect for traditional perceptions of Isaiah is also reflected in his assessment of the importance of chapter 52:13–53:12: 'This is the foremost passage on the suffering and resurrection of Christ and there is hardly another like it ... "our", "us" and "for us" must be written in letters of gold'.[2]

For many reformers traditional views of Isaiah as an 'evangelist', based as they were in many respects on patristic methods of exegesis, lost their appeal. Commentaries like those of Oekolampadius (1525) and later Campegius Vitringa (1714–32) are typical.[3] John Calvin's use of Isaiah displays the same break with patristic and mediaeval tradition, though statements such as that of Luther just quoted are not uncommon. What is interesting is that now the reasons why the Reformers carried on the tradition that Isaiah is in some ways unique among the prophets are different from those of St Jerome. Even without the elaborate typologies and allegories of earlier generations, they find in the *sensus literalis* of the language and imagery of Isaiah

[1]   *LW* 16, p. 84.
[2]   *LW* 16, pp. 1–39; 17, pp. 40–66.
[3]   Diestel, *Geschichte*, pp. 273, 436–8.

all they need to make him relevant to the preaching of the Christian Gospel. Calvin's interpretation of Isaiah paid great attention to the task of determining the prophet's own intention and the original historical context, he meticulously avoided the language of allegory and typology, but at the same time believed that it was essential to ensure that every interpretation was both christocentric and relevant to the contemporary Church. By means of what has been termed 'kerygmatic analogy', he interprets 26:19 ('Thy dead men shall live'), for example, as referring to the believers' new life in Christ here and now, and the creation of a new heaven and new earth in 65:17 to 'the restoration of the Church after the return from Babylon', and the whole reign of Christ from the First to the Second Coming'.[4]

Perceptions of Isaiah change in the fifteenth and sixteenth centuries. He is no longer primarily the Prophet of the nativity or of the Virgin Mary or of the Suffering Messiah, or the scourge of the Jews. Different texts now capture the attention of Christian writers and artists. In a sixteenth-century Scottish satire, for example, he is the champion of truth in an unjust society.[5] Another sixteenth-century emphasis is on Isaiah as the scourge of idol-worshippers, focussing on the many famous passages in which Isaiah ridicules or condemns idol-worship.

These and other uses of scripture were possible and popular because of the parallels which the reformers saw between the abuses committed by Isaiah's audience in ancient times, and what was going on in their own day. What Isaiah said to them could therefore be applied, more or less unchanged, without recourse to typology or allegory or other types of patristic exegesis, to sixteenth-century Europe. This does not apply, paradoxically, to the first examples, which will therefore serve to illustrate how much of the Church's traditional methodology was preserved by some of the leading figures of Protestant Christianity, despite their outward rejection of all that it signified. It also illustrates one of the striking differences between Luther and Calvin.

If any verse from Isaiah can be identified as an 'axiom' for the early Reformers, as 7:14, 11:1, 6:3 and 53 were in other periods, then it must be 40:8: 'The word of our God abides for ever'. Already 1 Peter 1:23–25 interprets this verse as referring to 'the good news which was preached to you', an 'imperishable seed ... the living and

---

4   Cf. Muller, 'Calvin's exegesis of Old Testament prophecies', p. 74.
5   See below, p. 136.

abiding word of God'. Of course in the apostolic age, the 'good news of Christ' was not yet identified with scripture, even if, as we saw, the 'Fifth Gospel' already came near to fulfilling that role. But for Luther 'the word of God' in this passage was identified with the Bible, the ultimate authority in the Church, and through his influence the verse became one of the most popular and widely used expressions of their new Bible-centred faith.

We need hardly point out that, from a historical point of view, 'the word of God' (or the far more frequent 'word of the Lord') in the biblical prophets, originally meant something quite different, as in expressions like 'hear the word of the Lord' (Isa.1:10; 28:14; 39:5; 66:5). Consequently, the more critical or scientific exegetes of the Reformation period, including Calvin, found no reference in 40:8 to scripture. Although he said of the verse that it 'comprehends the whole Gospel in a few words', his more literal method of exegesis prevented him from using it as a direct reference to Christian scripture,[6] as Luther and others did. As early as 1526, on Luther's own recommendation,[7] his supporters were putting the words *Verbum Dei Manet In Aeternum* 'the Word of God abideth for ever' above the doors of their quarters and embroidering the initials *VDMIÆ* on their coatsleeves. The soldiers accompanying the Elector of Saxony and Philip of Hessen to the Reichstag of Spiers also had it inscribed on their cloaks.[8] Already the original or literal sense of the verse, and the wording, have been modified to make the verse into a Reformers' slogan.

By 1625 the truth of this maxim was so much taken for granted, that it could be used in the context of a poem addressed to a duke: *Scilicet ut VERBUM DOMINI manet omne per aevum/Sic nescit pietas, et tua fama mori* ('as the word of the lord abides to all eternity/so your faith and your reputation know not how to die').[9] The dedication is *Ad D.Christophorum, Duc. Wirtebergicum, et Tecc*, and the accompanying engraving of St Christopher carrying the Christ child through the water, bears the title *V.D.M.I.Æ.*(Plate 25).

No-one makes more use of the verse than Luther himself. Next to Psalms, Matthew and Romans, Isaiah is the most frequently cited book of scripture in Martin Luther's writings,[10] and 40:8 one of his

---

6   Calvin, *Commentary on Isaiah*, vol. 3 (Edinburgh 1852), p. 212.
7   *LW* 17, p. 13; *LW* 49, p. 155.
8   Augustijn, 'The Sixteenth-Century Reformers and the Bible', p. 59.
9   Henkel-Schöne, *Emblemata*, cols.1857–8.
10   *LW* 55, pp. 349–462.

most frequently cited verses. He describes it as an 'axiom',[11] and the rule one has to live by 'in this empire of the Church'.[12] In what amounts to a kind of doxology on the enduring power of scripture, he explains the meaning of the Hebrew verb *yaqum* in 40:8 as follows: 'it stands, that is, it is steadfast, it is certain, it does not give way, it does not quiver, it does not sink, it does not fall, it does not leave you in the lurch'.[13] In a note on Romans 6:17 he further glosses 40:8 with a reference to Psalm 119:89: 'For ever, O Lord, thy word is firmly fixed in the heavens'.[14]

In most cases the verse is used for blatantly polemical purposes. The Word of God 'stands for ever' over against papal authority: e.g. 'no-one would dare to change it except the Antichrist, that is, the papacy'.[15] He quotes it against the Anabaptists[16] and in a tract entitled 'That these words of Christ "This is my body", etc. still stand firm against the fanatics'.[17] When one considers that for Luther 'the word of God stands for ever' means in practice 'the word of God as preached by me and those like me (as opposed to the Pope or Eck or the Anabaptists) stands for ever',[18] one cannot help comparing this constant recourse to Isaiah 40:8 with his most famous axiom 'Here I stand (i.e. am steadfast, certain, do not give way, do not quiver, do not sink, do not fall, and will not leave you in the lurch)'. 40:8 expresses his passionate belief that God has revealed to him the true meaning of the Bible. 'The books of Emser, Eck, the snot-nose (Cochlaeus) and Wetzel ... have vanished and come to nothing,' he says, 'but the word of our God stands for ever'.[19] He does not of course claim for himself the credit for this new view of scripture: 'If it had been up to us, not a single word of the entire Holy Scripture or of the Gospel would have remained'.[20]

Isaiah 40:8 was the text of a sermon preached in Wittenberg on 31 October 1690 on the occasion of a service to celebrate the centenary of Luther's Reformation. The preacher, J. Deutschmann, finds in Isaiah 40:1–9 all the scriptural authority he needs to show that the 'Word', on which the reformers built a new Church, is 'the most divine, the most necessary (witness all the imperatives in these

---

[11]   *LW* 14 p. 381.   [12]   *LW* 41 p. 134.
[13]   *LW* 15 p. 272.   [14]   *LW* 25, p. 54.
[15]   *LW* 41, p. 212; cf. *LW* 40, p. 333.
[16]   *LW* 40, pp. 247,260.
[17]   *LW* 37, p. 19.
[18]   Cf. 'Are you the only one that is right?' *LW* 54, pp. 18f.
[19]   *LW* 41, p. 189.   [20]   *LW* 11, p. 381.

verses), the most pleasant (vv.1,2), the most evident (vv.1,9), the most perfect (combining law and Gospel), the most universal (vv.1,9), the most penetrating (vv.3–4), the most lasting (v.8) and the most glorious (v.5)'.[21]

Handel's famous setting of 40:1–11 in the *Messiah* omits verses 6–8, presumably because they do not appear in the Advent Lectionary used by his librettist,[22] but, in Luther's translation, they were the inspiration for one of the finest choruses in Brahms' *German Requiem*, composed 125 years later.[23] More recently verses 6–8 are printed in full, in King James' *Authorized Version*, at the end of a collection of essays on *The Bible in Scottish Life and Literature*.[24] They are used there by a Presbyterian author as a *cri de coeur* on the waning influence of the Bible on Scottish society: 'without the Bible its spirit is being starved and its imagination atrophied'. Finally, almost as a sign of the reformation in the Roman Catholic Church, 40:8 is used to put a final, scriptural seal on the Second Vatican Council's *Dogmatic Constitution on Divine Revelation* (*Dei Verbum*, 18 November 1965).[25] Verses 6–8 are still omitted, however, from the reading prescribed for the second Sunday in Advent,[26] and from the half a dozen or so new Catholic hymns based on the passage.[27]

Several other texts from Isaiah figure in the Reformers' rediscovery of scripture. Luther identifies 'the law and the testimony' in 8:20 respectively with scripture and 'oral preaching',[28] and elsewhere uses this verse in his description of the Bible as 'a kind of door or an opening through which the light of dawn appears'.[29] The same verse, along with verse 16, is cited more than once by John Wesley (1703–1801) who finds in it an expression of the Reformers' doctrine of scripture. In a sermon, he uses 8:16–20, with its reference to 'familiar spirits and wizards', to prove that the will of God must be sought, not 'by dreams and visions, particular impressions or sudden impulses', but in 'the law and the testimony', that is to say, in scripture.[30] A student at the University of Wittenberg, known

[21] J. Deutschmann's sermon can be read in Durham Cathedral Chapter Library.
[22] They are conspicuous by their absence from other lectionaries as well.
[23] See below, pp. 174f.
[24] Gibson, 'The Bible in Scotland today', p. 219.
[25] See below (chapter 12).
[26] *Lectionary*, pp. 12–13; Isaiah 40:1–11 is read in full, however, on Tuesday of the second week in Advent (*Lectionary*, p. 17).
[27] *HON* 127, 385, 459, 686, 698, 775,.
[28] *LW* 16, p. 95.   [29] *LW* 33, p. 92.
[30] Wesley, *Works* 3, *Sermons* 2, p. 54; cf. 1, p. 683.

officially since 1922 as Lutherstadt, wrote a doctoral dissertation on Isaiah 34:16 ('seek and read from the book of the Lord': cf. John 5:39), entitled *On the Legitimate Study of Sacred Scripture*.[31]

Another text from Isaiah used by Protestants to celebrate the power of the Bible as 'the Word of God' is 55:10–11. No doubt Bach's Cantata *Gleich wie der Regen und Schnee* ('As the rain and snow come down from heaven …') was also inspired by the Reformers' zeal for the Word of God. More recently a writer on the influence of vernacular translations of the Bible upon English culture in the Reformation period quotes the passage in full as his peroration: 'The English Reformation was the greatest religious revival in our history … .(It) left deep and immovable marks on our culture and therefore on the culture of lands beyond the seas which, for good or ill, Englishmen colonized and conquered … 'So shall my word be that goeth forth out of my mouth: it shall not return unto me void, but it shall accomplish that which I please, and it shall prosper in the thing whereto I sent it" (Isaiah 55:10–11).[32] A Festschrift in honour of a distinguished Protestant scholar, known especially for his work in the field of Biblical Studies, also gets its title from this passage: '*The word of the Lord shall go forth': Essays in Honour of David Noel Freedman in Celebration of his Sixtieth Birthday* (Eisenbrauns, Winona Lake, Indiana 1983).

This brings us to another source for the study of Reformation Christianity, namely funerals and epitaphs.[33] Here too Isaiah has had a not insignificant contribution to make, especially chapters 24–27 commonly known today as the 'Isaiah Apocalypse', which are always a particularly rich source for epitaphs. Luther recommended four passages from Isaiah among his 'biblical texts suitable for epitaphs'.[34] The first focusses on victory over death ('He will swallow up death for ever …' 25:7–9), a passage quoted by Paul in his discourse on resurrection in 1 Corinthians 15. The second provides him with scriptural authority for the belief that there are hidden chambers where the redeemed can hide safely until the Judgement is past – a notion expressed more graphically elsewhere in Isaiah (especially 2:19) and, incidentally, in a traditional folk-song based on

---

[31]   *De legitimo sanctae scripturae scrutinio*, Wittenberg, 1711 (Durham Cathedral Chapter Library).

[32]   Wilson, *The People and the Book*, p. 161; on other texts from Isaiah frequently used in the context of Christian foreign missions, see below, pp. 152ff.

[33]   See further Sawyer, 'Isaiah as a source-book for scriptural texts about death and mourning'.

[34]   *LW* 53, pp. 328–9.

the Isaiah passage: 'Oh sinner man, where you going to run to ... all on that day?'[35] His other two Isaianic epitaphs both come from Isaiah 26. The one refers to the resurrection of the dead ('Thy dead shall live ...' 26:19), and the other to hiding from the wrath of God (26:20).

Isaiah was a particular favourite of St Ambrose (c.339–97), as we saw in an earlier chapter.[36] A number of funeral orations delivered by Ambrose in Milan Cathedral at the end of the fourth century thus provide us with a useful case-study. He used Luther's first Isaianic epitaph from chapter 25 to good effect on the occasion of the funeral of his brother Satyrus in 378. In particular by stressing the second verse, he turns the listeners' attention to the faith that survives death: 'It will be said on that day, 'Lo, this is our God; we have waited for him that he might save us ...' [37] The passage is still widely used as one of the readings at masses for the dead,[38] and it provides the last words in the Jewish 'Prayer in the house of mourning', which we shall discuss later. Ambrose quotes Luther's other two recommended epitaphs as well, the first to speak of the divine dew that makes our bodies grow again after we die: 'Awake and sing for joy, you who dwell in the dust! Your dew is the dew of light ...'[39]

Another verse from chapter 26, containing the word 'peace' repeated twice and traditionally translated into English 'peace, perfect peace' (verse 3), figures in a collection of recommended epitaphs, published in 1897 by J. Braithwaite & Son, a firm of funeral undertakers in Derby. It was also the inspiration for a hymn once popular at funerals: 'Peace, perfect peace, in this dark world of sin'. The author, Dr Edward Bickersteth (1825–1906), is said to have written it, in a few minutes, as he sat at the bedside of a dying friend, and then recited it to him. It was also sung at the funeral of the Scottish theologian and orientalist, William Robertson Smith, in 1894.[40] It was not one of Luther's four Isaianic epitaphs, but his fourth does express a similar view of death: 'The righteous perish ... they are taken away from the evil to come. They shall enter into peace; they shall rest in their beds' (57:1–2). The Latin of this passage

35   *HON*, 429.
36   See pp. 2, 55.
37   *FOC* 22, pp. 224–5.
38   *New Sunday Missal*, p. 985; *Lectionary*, pp. 942, 960, 964, 1001; *ASB* 1980, pp. 331f.
39   *FOC* 22, pp. 226–7.
40   Moffatt, *Handbook*, p. 152.

contains the words *iustus perit, pax* and *requiescat*, all very common in funerary inscriptions.

The rest of Isaiah 26:3 appears as an epitaph in a fresco by Raphael (1483–1520). This was commissioned by the papal proto-notary and humanist Johannes Goritz in 1510 to overlook his tomb in the Church of Sant'Agostino in Rome.[41] It shows Isaiah displaying a scroll with the first part of 26:2–3: 'Open the gates that a righteous nation which keeps faith may enter'. Perhaps we can detect a whiff of self-righteousness on the part of the papal official, which gives the text a rather different slant. The inscription, which is in Hebrew letters, surprisingly stops just before the twice-repeated word *shalom* 'peace, perfect peace', which, as we have just seen, figures elsewhere in funeral traditions. The dedicatory inscription in Greek above Isaiah's head refers to a sculptural group by Andrea Sansovino, which stood beneath the fresco depicting St Anne, the Virgin Mary and the Christ-child, and reminds us of Isaiah's main role in Christian tradition: 'To Anne, the Mother of the Virgin, to the Virgin Mother of God, and to Christ the Redeemer'.

Another Isaianic epitaph appears in the Royal Mausoleum at Frogmore, designed by Queen Victoria for Prince Albert and herself. Isaiah is one of four statues presiding over the tomb and his text is from Isaiah 32:8: 'But the liberal deviseth liberal things, and by liberal things shall he stand' (Plate 29). Her choice of this verse at first sight seems odd. The imagery of the other three texts, David's on sunrise (2 Sam.23:4), Solomon's on wisdom (1 Kings 3:10) and Daniel's on the resurrection of the dead (12:3), is unproblematical. Did she know of a sermon preached on this text by John Donne in the presence of King Charles I in 1628: 'the very forme of the office of a king is Liberality, that is Providence, and Protection and Possession and Peace and Justice shed upon all'?[42] The Queen herself had a hand in choosing the texts and most likely it was intended to express both the love and respect she had for her husband, Prince Albert, whose short life (1819–61) (referred to in Solomon's text: cf.1 Kings 3:10) she perceived as characterized by philanthropy, progress and enlightenment, and the ideals to which she aspired herself in her own long reign.

The irreversible divisions that appeared in the Church in the sixteenth century, and the hatred and bitterness that flared up

[41] Ettlinger, *Raphael*, pp. 121–3, plates 117, 118.
[42] Simpson and Potter, edd., *The Sermons of John Donne*, p. 243.

between Christian and Christian, bring into play another set of texts from Isaiah, heavy with political overtones. One example is William Byrd's *Ne irascaris* which he composed soon after the martyrdom of Edmund Campion in 1581: 'Be not exceedingly angry, O Lord, and remember not iniquity for ever. Behold, consider, we are all thy people. Thy holy cities have become a wilderness, Jerusalem has become a desolation' (64:9–10).[43]

Three of Bach's six 'Isaianic' cantatas are for Advent, Christmas and Epiphany: *Bereitet die Wege* ('Prepare the way') from chapter 40, *Uns ist ein Kind geboren* ('Unto us a child is born') from chapter 9 and *Sie werden aus Saba alle kommen* ('They will all come from Saba') from chapter 60. In these he is following mediaeval tradition, except that the words are in the vernacular instead of Latin. But there is also a political one. Cantata No.39 *Brich den Hungrigen dein Brod*, based on Isaiah 58:7, was first performed in June 1726 on behalf of Protestant refugees from Salzburg who were seeking asylum in Leipzig: 'Share your bread with the hungry, and bring the homeless poor into your house …' These are powerful political imperatives in that context, typically Isaianic and typical of modern perceptions of the prophet too.[44]

Finally, to end on a more optimistic note, another political text from Isaiah, more familiar today than in earlier periods, is 2:4 ('swords into ploughshares'), a prophecy that 'comes up with pathetic frequency in our militant literature'.[45] In the preface to a new edition of a work originally published in 1376, Barbour's *Bruce*, dated 1616, the author states that now, that is to say, in the reign of James VI (= James I of England), that prophecy has been fulfilled.

As we saw, in many periods of the history of the Church the prime targets of the polemical language of the biblical prophets were the Jews. Now we see this language directed instead, or rather as well, at Catholics by Protestants and vice versa. Passages like Isaiah 5:13–14, cited in his *Babylonish Captivity of the Church*, provided Luther with suitably polemical language to attack the priests and clergy for depriving the laity, not only of the chalice, but also of proper education in the beliefs and practices of the Church: 'Therefore my people have gone into exile because they have no knowledge; their

---

[43] Kerman, *The Masses and Motets of William Byrd*, pp. 42ff.
[44] Whittaker, *Cantatas*, Vol. 1, p. 688; see also below, pp. 244ff.
[45] Moffatt, *The Bible in Scots Literature*, p. 131; see below, pp. 231ff.

nobles have died of hunger, and their multitude is parched with thirst' (5:13).[46]

A Scottish contemporary of Luther, the satirist David Lyndesay (1490–1555), likewise and for the same reasons, applied 56:10 to the Roman prelates: 'For Esayas in his work/calls them like dogs that cannot bark,/that called are priests and cannot preach,/nor Christ's law to the people teach'.[47] In his better known *Ane Satyre of the Thrie Estates*, first performed before King James V of Scotland at Linlithgow Palace in 1540, 'Truth', in the stocks because she is found to be carrying a copy of the New Testament in the vernacular, remembers Isaiah as the prophet who would understand her suffering in a corrupt society:

> The prophecy of the prophet Esay
> is practised Alas! on me this day,
> who said that veritie should be trampled down
> amid the street and put in strong prison.
> His five and fiftieth chapter, who list look,
> should find these words written within his book.[48]

The reference is incorrect. If any particular passage was in the author's mind, it may have been 59:14. But what is interesting is that Isaiah is here introduced as the champion of truth over against injustice and deceit, an aspect of the prophet central to modern Christianity, and frequently in the forefront of sixteenth-century preaching as well.

A famous sermon preached by John Knox before the Scottish king, Queen Mary's new husband Lord Darnley, in St Giles Cathedral in Edinburgh in August 1565, and for which he was severely reprimanded and briefly banned from preaching, was an extended exegesis of nine verses from Isaiah chapter 26 (13–21).[49] In the course of this mammoth declamation, the only one of Knox's sermons to have survived, written down by himself twelve days after he preached it and accounting for over fifty pages of his collected works, he makes it clear who he thinks verse 13 refers to ('other lords besides thee have ruled over us') and who 'that harlot Jezabel' is. Maybe he glanced down at the chubby face of the young Darnley seated in the royal pew beneath him, when he quoted another verse

[46] *LW* 36. pp. 116f.
[47] *Complaynt to the King's Grace*, lines 330f.
[48] *Four Morality Plays*, ed.P. Happé, p. 489.
[49] *The Works of John Knox*, ed. Laing, Vol. VI, pp. 221–73.

from Isaiah: 'Babes shall rule over them' (3:4).[50] No wonder Darnley was put off his food and had to go a-hawking to work off his anger.[51]

A somewhat bizarre illustration of the new order appears in a sixteenth-century woodcut of Isaiah 52:7 (Plate 24).[52] It has the legend QUAM DULCIS SEMITA PACIS – ESAI.LII.VII ('How lovely is the path of peace' Isa.52:7), and shows two legs, cut off below the knee, weighed down by three great pieces of timber, representing the duties of a parish minister. One of the legs is adorned with an olive branch, symbol of peace, while the other stands in an alms plate, representing the gifts due to him from his grateful flock.

Among the most popular verses in Isaiah in the context of anti-Catholic invective are the passages condemning idolatry. There are earlier representations of this aspect of Isaianic prophecy. Isaiah 19:1 prompted the apocryphal tradition that the 'Flight of the Holy Family into Egypt' was accompanied by the fall of the Egyptian idols.[53] This in turn came to signify the overthrow of pagan religion, disbelief and doctrinal error in general.[54] The thirteenth-century Gothic *Bible Moralisée* gives four illustrations of Isaiah's attitude towards idolatry. At 1:4 and 2:8 ('their land is filled with idols ...'), Isaiah is seen to be sternly rebuking a group of men with hands raised in reverence towards small idols in human form, while at chapter 44:13 he expresses scorn or even amusement at the scene of a craftsman, with axe in hand, kneeling in awe before a statue of a young man carrying a huge sword. At chapter 46 ('Bel bows down (Lat.*confractus est*), Nebo stoops') he looks grimly on as two angels hurl the Babylonian idols down from their pedestals.

From approximately the same period there are two stained glass versions of the subject in a lancet window in the apse of the Sainte-Chapelle in Paris.[55] They are part of a complete Isaiah window, which shows among other things Isaiah leading his people towards the light (2:5), the Annunciation (7:14), Isaiah carrying the Christ child (42:1 ?), the winepress (63:1–6), and the martyrdom of Isaiah. In the more elaborate of the two, which is at the bottom of the window and therefore among the most conspicuous scenes confronting a visitor to the chapel, one of the idolaters is explicitly labelled

[50] Cf. Percy, *John Knox*, p. 401.
[51] Cf. D. F. Wright, 'The Bible in the Scottish Reformation', pp. 174–5.
[52] Henkel-Schöne, *Emblemata*, cols.1024–5.
[53] See above, pp. 49–50.
[54] Cf. *BP*, p. 134.
[55] Aubert and others, *Les Vitraux de Notre Dame*, pp. 172–84; 6 plates.

MAHOMETA 'Muhammad'.[56] The other may well be intended to represent the Jews, who at that time, together with the Muslims, epitomized the heretic in the eyes of the Church militant. Idolatry in such a context was a matter of heresy within the Church, the idols being interpreted as erroneous doctrines and the prophet standing for the powerful orthodox preaching of the Church leaders. The contemporary relevance of this biblical theme for the authorities in twelfth-century Paris, especially in regard to the Jews, can be seen in its appearance not only in the Isaiah window of the Sainte-Chapelle, but also in windows devoted to Deuteronomy, Joshua, Ezekiel, Jeremiah and Kings, where it is invariably interpreted as referring to the idolatry of the Jews. Isaiah alone attacks also the Muslims.[57]

But in Protestant art of the sixteenth and seventeenth centuries, Isaiah appears as the scourge of Catholics as well as the scourge of heretics such as the Jews. In his representation of 'Isaiah's satire on the sculpting of idols' (44:15–17), the Dutch painter J. Jordaens, who converted to Calvinism in later life, puts in a good deal of detail from the passage itself, but the main idol, a nude female figure wearing what appears to be a crown, and surrounded by a crowd of men, women and children with outstretched hands praying desperately to her, looks very like a statue of the Virgin Mary, despite arguments to the contrary (Plate 26).[58] In the hands of a Protestant artist, the verse ironically becomes a thinly veiled attack on the very cult in which Isaiah had played so important a part in an earlier age. Idolatry seems to have been a topic of special interest to Jordaens as one might expect from an ex-Catholic. In another drawing he depicts the Golden Calf story from Exodus 32 on one side, corresponding to a scene of debauchery on the other, and adds the caption: 'Which is better, to make the image of a beast into God, or the image of God into a beast?'[59] Maybe the prophetic figure in the centre of the work is Isaiah.

Luther too uses some of the idolatry passages in Isaiah to good effect. In his commentary on 41:7, for instance, he makes a wicked pun on the name of one of his fiercest opponents: 'The craftsman, the goldsmith who beats with the hammer, encourages him who

[56]   Aubert and others, *Les Vitraux de Notre Dame*, p. 179; Dyer-Spencer, 'Les vitraux de la Sainte-Chapelle de Paris'.
[57]   See also pp. 154ff.
[58]   Cf. Benisovitch, 'Un dessin de Jacob Jordaens à la E. B. Crocker Gallery (Sacramento)'.
[59]   R. A. d'Hulst, *J. Jordaens*, Sotheby 1974.

strikes the anvil, saying, "That is well soldered"; and they fasten it with nails so that it cannot be moved'. He identifies the two idol-makers in the verse, the 'craftsman', that is to say, 'the one who beats with a hammer' (*malleus*), and the goldsmith, ridiculed by Isaiah. The first is obviously Johannes *Faber* (Latin for 'craftsman'), known as 'the hammer of the heretics' and author of a celebrated attack on the 'Lutheran heresy' entitled *Malleus in Haeresim Lutheranam* ('A Hammer for Lutheran Heresy') (1524), and the other Johannes Cochlaeus, another of Luther's vicious and unpopular opponents, elsewhere referred to as 'snot-nose'. Luther sees the Pope as the idol in the verse, and condemns the efforts of the 'craftsmen' to prop him up with their arguments and publications which are as misplaced and ineffectual as the hammer and nails and solder of pagan idol-makers.[60] Luther, in striking contrast to Calvin and other more sophisticated Reformation exegetes, is again continuing mediaeval exegetical methods.

One of the longest of the *Sermons or Homilies appointed to be read in Churches in the time of Queen Elizabeth of Famous Memory* (1562) is the one against idolatry.[61] In this another passage from Isaiah is cited twice: 'To whom then will ye liken God or what likeness will ye compare unto him? The workman melteth a graven image, and the goldsmith spreadeth it over with gold, and casteth silver chains. He that is so impoverished that he hath no oblation chooseth a tree that will not rot ...' (40:18–20). Elsewhere Isaiah 42:17 is used to good effect as well.

Idols, especially those associated in their minds with the Church of Rome, remained a preoccupation of Protestant writers. The following verses from a well-known eighteenth-century hymn beginning 'Arm of the Lord, awake, awake!', based on Isaiah 51:9 and surrounding passages, are typical:

> Say to the heathen from Thy throne,
> 'I am Jehovah, God alone';
> Thy voice their idols shall confound,
> And cast their altars to the ground.
>
> Arm of the Lord, Thy power extend;
> Let Mahomet's imposture end;
> Break papal superstition's chain,
> And the proud scoffer's rage restrain.

[60] *LW* 17, pp. 37–9.
[61] 4th ed., Oxford, 1816, pp. 144–225.

The second of these verses, reminiscent of the Sainte-Chapelle window, has been omitted from most modern versions, but reveals the association, in the mind of its author, a Protestant lay preacher, between the idol-worship condemned by Isaiah in ancient times and the 'papal superstition' of his own day.[62] The abhorrent application of such language and imagery to Muslims, Hindus and others will be discussed in the next chapter.[63]

We end by way of contrast with a less violent or polemical use that is sometimes made of the idolatry passages from Isaiah. A spiritual or moral interpretation of Isaiah 2:20 appears in a verse of William Cowper's famous hymn *O for a closer walk with God*:

> The dearest idol I have known,
> Whate'er that idol be,
> Help me to tear it from thy throne,
> And worship only Thee.[64]

[62] Moffatt, *Handbook*, pp. 123f.
[63] See below, pp. 154ff.
[64] *CH* 457; *EH* 445. Moffatt, *Handbook*, p. 156.

1. St Jerome urging Isaiah to 'tell them about Christ!'. From a twelfth-century manuscript of Jerome's *Isaiah Commentary*.

2. Jesus learning Hebrew from the Book of Isaiah, open at chapter 7. *The Holy Family in Egypt* by Charles Le Brun (1619–90).

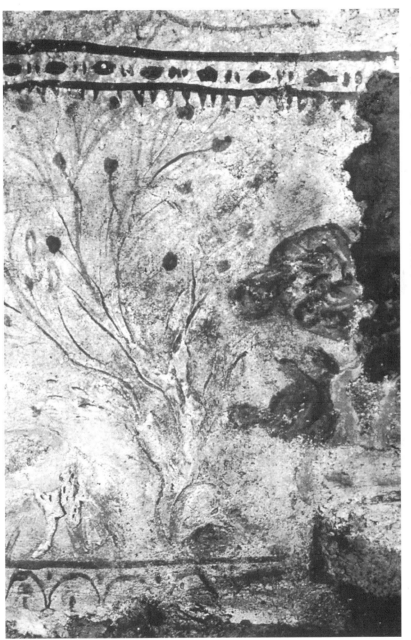

3. The earliest Christian representation of Isaiah, with Madonna and Child. Second-century catacomb painting in the Church of St Priscilla, Rome.

4. 'Truly (he bore) our weaknesses' (Isaiah 53:4). Twelfth-century enamel plaque.

5. Martyrdom of Isaiah. Pre-Norman Christian carving on part of a huge stone cross now in Winwick Parish Church, Cheshire.

6. Martyrdom of Isaiah. Illuminated initial of the Isaiah Canticle (Isaiah 12) from the thirteenth-century Arundel Psalter.

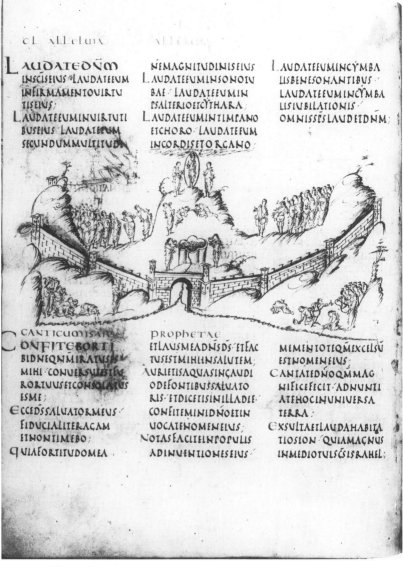

LAUDATEDN̅M̅
INSCIS EIUS·LAUDATEEUM
INFIRMAMENTOUIRTU
TISEIUS;
LAUDATEEUMINUIRTUTI
BUSEIUS·LAUDATEEUM
SECUNDUMMULTITUDI

NEMAGNITUDINISEIUS
LAUDATEEUMINSONOIU
BAE·LAUDATEEUMIN
PSALTERIOETCŶTHARA
LAUDATEEUMINTIMPANO
ETCHORO·LAUDATEEUM
INCORDISETORGANO·

LAUDATEEUMINCŶMBA
LISBENESONANTIBUS·
LAUDATEEUMINCŶMBA
LISIUBILATIONIS·
OMNISSP̅S̅LAUDETDN̅M̅;

CANTICUMISAI
CONFITEBORTI
BIDN̅EQ̅NMIRATUS
MIHI·CONUERSUSEST̅
RORTUUSETCONSOLATUS
ESME;
ECCEDS̅S̅ALUATORMEUS·
FIDUCIALITERAGAM
ETNONTIMEBO;
QUIAFORTITUDOMEA·

PROPHETAE
ETLAUSMEADN̅SD̅S̅·ETFAC
TUSESTMIHIINSALUTEM;
AURIETISAQUASINGAUDI
ODEFONTIBUSSALUATO
RIS·ETDICETISINILLADIE·
CONFITEMINIDN̅OETIN
UOCATENOMENEIUS;
NOTASFACITEINPOPULIS
ADINUENTIONESEIUS·

MEMENTOTEQ̅MEXCELSU̅
ESTNOMENEIUS;
CANTATEDN̅OQ̅MMAG
NIFICEFECIT·ADNUNTI
ATEHOCINUNIUERSA
TERRA·
EXSULTAETLAUDAHABITA
TIOSION·QUIAMAGNUS
INMEDIOTUIS̅C̅S̅ISRAHEL;

7. Illustration of the Isaiah canticle (Isaiah 12) from the ninth-century Utrecht Psalter, showing 'the wells of salvation' (12:3) and the Transfiguration (Matthew 17:1–8).

8. Illuminated initial of the Isaiah canticle (Isaiah 12) from the twelfth-century St Alban's Psalter, showing two figures, one drawing water, the other Isaiah himself at the foot of the Cross as a tree of life.

9.   Twelfth-century statue of Isaiah beside the west door of Cremona Cathedral. The words on his scroll read 'Behold a virgin will conceive and bring forth a son . . .' (7:14 Vg).

10. Twelfth-century stone relief of Isaiah which originally stood beside the entrance to the Cathedral of Notre Dame at Souillac.

11.   The Virgin with Isaiah 7:14 open in front of her, just as the angel Gabriel arrives. Isaiah is in the background. *The Annunciation* by Matthias Grünewald (1470–1528).

12. Lancet window in Chartres
Cathedral showing St Matthew on
Isaiah's shoulders.

13. 'A rod shall come forth from the
root of Jesse' (Isaiah 11:1). Twelfth-century
'Jesse tree' window in Chartres Cathedral
showing Christ enthroned at the top.

14.   Jesse tree (Isaiah 11:1–2) showing Isaiah trying to lead 'Blind Synagogue' (6:9–10) to Christ. Twelfth-century Lambeth Bible.

15. Central panel of Brougham Triptych in Carlisle Cathedral showing a Jesse tree with Christ crucified at the top. Antwerp, sixteenth century.

16. 'I trod the winepress alone' (Isaiah 63:3). Sixteenth-century stained glass illustration of 'Christ in the Wine-Press' in the Church of Sainte-Foi in Conches.

17. Claus Sluter's statue of Isaiah with the words of 53:7 on his scroll ('Like a lamb
before his shearers . . .'). Dijon, fourteenth century.

18.   'He is beaten for our sins': Isaiah 53 invoked to explain Christ's Passion. Painting by Matthias Grünewald (1526).

19. 'We looked on him and he had no face' (Isaiah 53:2 Vg): Veronica wiping Christ's face. Church of SS Nicholas and Barbara, Amsterdam 1886–9 (now demolished).

20. 'The vision of Isaiah' (Isaiah 6), including scenes of the Passion and Crucifixion of Christ (Isaiah 53). Bible illustration by the German artist Lukas Cranach (1515–1586).

21. Six-winged seraph with a burning coal (Isaiah 6:1–8). One of two stained glass windows (1979) by L. Evetts, St Silas Church, Byker, Newcastle upon Tyne.

22. 'Blind Synagogue' (Isaiah 6:9–10) with a 'broken staff' (Isaiah 3:1) in her hand. Painting by the Swiss artist Konrad Witz (c.1400–46).

I.N.R.I.

DOMINVS ENIM IV-
DEX NOSTER. DOMI-
NVS LEGIFER NOS-
TER. DOMINVS REX
NOSTER. IPSE SAL-
VABIT NOS.
ESAIÆ 33.

כִּי יְהוָה שֹׁפְטֵנוּ
יְהוָה מְחֹקְקֵנוּ יְה
וָה מַלְכֵּנוּ הוּא
יוֹשִׁיעֵנוּ
יְשַׁעְיָה לב

ÆTAS
EORVM

24
I
34

1559

23. 'The Lord is our Judge. The Lord is our Lawgiver . . .' (Isaiah 33:22). Frontispiece
of book by Paul Weidner, imperial physician and converted Jew. Vienna, 1559.

24. 'How beautiful are the feet of him that. . .publisheth peace!' (Isaiah 52:7). A comment on the duties and privileges of a parish minister. Woodcut, Frankfurt 1581.

25. 'The Word of the Lord abideth for ever' (Isaiah 40:8). Woodcut, Nuremberg, 1625.

26. *Isaiah's satire on the sculpting of idols* (Isaiah 44:15–17) by the Dutch painter Jakob Jordaens (1593–1678), a convert to Calvinism.

27. 'They shall beat their swords into ploughshares' (Isaiah 2:4). *The Preaching of Isaiah* by the Flemish painter Jan Brueghel the Elder (1569–1625).

"Which is the Way"
"The Right or the Left"

28. 'This is the way: walk ye in it, when ye turn to the right hand and when ye turn to the left' (Isaiah 30:21). William Blake's ambidextrous God from *The Book of Urizen*.

29. 'The liberal deviseth liberal things, and by liberal things shall he stand' (Isaiah 32:8). Statue of Isaiah presiding over the tombs of Prince Albert and Queen Victoria.

30. 'I have stretched out my hands all day long to a rebellious people . . .' (Isaiah 65:2–3). Inscription in Hebrew and Latin on a church overlooking the Jewish Ghetto. Rome, 1858.

31. 'As a mother comforts her children, so I will comfort you' (Isaiah 66:13). Illustration from fifteenth-century *Biblia Pauperum*.

32. 'Lilith' (Isaiah 34:14 *NRSV*), once symbol of 'serpentine feminine bestiality', nowadays of radical feminism. Painting by the American artist Kenyon Cox (1856–1919).

HAGAR

Egyptian Slave Woman

She was wounded for
our transgressions;
she was bruised for
our iniquities.

33. Part of Isaiah 53:5 in an illustration from Phyllis Trible, *Texts of Terror. Literary-Feminist Readings of Biblical Narratives* (1984).

34. 'Let us beat our swords into ploughshares'. Bronze sculpture presented to the United Nations Building, New York, in 1959 by the Soviet Union.

*'Poor Grigoriev. He tried to beat an
SS-20 into a ploughshare'*

35. Cartoon from the post-Cold War era. *The Independent*, 28 December 1991.

The lion with the fatling on did move,
A little child was leading them in love.

The leopard with the harmless kid laid down,
And not one savage beast was seen to frown.

The wolf did with the lambkin dwell in peace.
His grim carnivorous nature there did cease.

When the great PENN his famous treaty made
With indian chiefs beneath the elm tree's shade.

36. 'A little child shall lead them . . .' (Isaiah 11:6). An early version of 'The Peaceable Kingdom' by the American Quaker artist and preacher Edward Hicks (1780–1849).

37. '. . . and the lion shall eat straw like the ox . . .' (Isaiah 11:7). A later version of Edward Hicks' 'The Peaceable Kingdom' (1846–7).

38. 'New heavens and a new earth . . . the wolf and the lamb shall feed together . . .'
(Isaiah 65:17, 25). War memorial window in the Reformed Church in Spaarndam,
Holland.

CHAPTER 8

The Evangelical Tradition

One of the chief aims of the Reformers was to ensure that everyone, not just scholars and priests, had access to the whole of scripture, not just the Gospels and Psalms. Again this is not entirely a new phenomenon when we remember the efforts of the preaching orders in the late Middle Ages. But the Reformers went much further, laying far greater emphasis on the doctrine of the priesthood of all believers, and the teaching of the Bible to everyone became the hallmark of Reformed Christianity. For this Isaiah provided Luther with one of his favourite texts: 'All thy children shall be taught of the Lord' (54:13).[1] He uses it along with Isaiah's vision that 'the earth shall be filled with the knowledge of the Lord as the waters cover the sea' (11:9) to give scriptural authority to his teaching on the priesthood of all believers,[2] and more specifically to his passionate conviction that all members of the Church, young and old, must receive instruction in the Bible.[3] Isaiah 65:24 ('Before they call, I will answer ...') is another verse he cites in this context along with Jeremiah 31:34 and Psalm 149:9–10.[4] Luther's energetic contemporary Urbanus Rhegius also interpreted Isaiah 54:13 as referring to the 'common teaching of the Gospel by which everyone of the predestined is enlightened and saved',[5] and proved his commitment to this goal by writing a six hundred page anthology of biblical prophecies of Christ, beginning at Genesis 3, for his wife.[6]

The Reformers' defiant production and dissemination of vernacular translations of the Bible was a key factor in this area. Luther's German Bible, completed in 1534, William Tyndale's English translation, for which he was burnt at the stake in 1536, the influential

---

[1]   *LW* 55, p. 395.   [2]   *LW* 36, pp. 138f; *LW* 40, p. 21.
[3]   *LW* 17, pp. 243f; *LW* 54, p. 18.   [4]   *LW* 40, p. 21.
[5]   Cf. Hendrix, 'The use of scripture in establishing protestantism', p. 47.
[6]   Hendrix, 'The use of scripture in establishing protestantism', pp. 42f.

Geneva Bible of 1560, produced by Protestant refugees from Mary Tudor's England, and King James' *Authorized Version* of 1611, were among the most successful. William Tyndale used words from Isaiah in a preface to his English translation of the Bible: 'For who is so blind as to ask why light should be shown to them that walk in darkness, where they cannot but stumble, and where to stumble is the danger of eternal damnation ... that light destroyeth darkness and verity reproveth all manner of lying' (cf. 9:2).[7]

The influence of these sixteenth- and seventeenth-century translations on the language and culture of Europe, and of England in particular, is inestimable.[8] One writer argues that the English reformation was 'a revival inspired and sustained by the written word of God ...'.[9] Arguably the pages of quotations from Isaiah deemed worthy to be included in the *Oxford Dictionary of Quotations* would be considerably shorter were it not for the success of the *Authorized Version* in which they all appear. More space is devoted to the Book of Isaiah (in the *Authorized Version*) than to any other book of the Bible apart from the Book of Psalms and the Gospel of Matthew. One might add that Handel's *Messiah* would have been very different without the *AV* translation of Isaiah.[10]

Bible study was encouraged at all levels, and this became an enduring feature of Protestant Church life to this day from the 'Bible belt' of the United States to the Highlands of Scotland. Biblical education was introduced into English schools in the sixteenth century.[11] Religious education in British schools consisted for many years almost entirely of Bible Study and is still sometimes referred to, even where the syllabus has been widened to include other things, as 'scripture'. 'Bible classes' and 'Bible Study groups' were organized in every church. Texts were learnt by heart. As well as a 'Family Bible', households aspired to have editions of the Bible with cross-references and other 'Helps to the Study of the Bible'. Immensely popular concordances were produced, especially Alexander Cruden's *Complete Concordance to the Old and New Testaments, with Notes and Biblical Proper Names under one Alphabetical Arrangement*, first published in 1736 and still in print. Biblical anthologies were produced such as *Daily Light on the*

---

[7] Cited by Hammond, *The Making of the English Bible*, p. 16.
[8] Cf. Hill, *The English Bible and the Seventeenth-Century Revolution*.
[9] Wilson, *The People and the Book*, p. 161.
[10] See below, pp. 171ff.
[11] Wilson, *The People and the Book*, pp. 116–18.

Daily Path: A Devotional Text Book for Every Day of the Year in the Very Words of Scripture.[12] Here too quotations from Isaiah and Psalms top the list of the most popular devotional texts. The Bible became the world's best-seller, and within it Isaiah was one of the best-loved and most often quoted books.

Everyone, even beggars it seems, could quote scripture, or at any rate use apt proverbial sayings and aphorisms culled from the Bible. In Walter Scott's *The Antiquary*, for instance, the old beggar Edie Ochiltree applies the words of Isaiah 1:13 ('an abomination to me') to the 'grand parafle o' ceremonies' that filled churches in the old days. Musing on the ruins of an ancient abbey, he comments: 'I wonder whether this is mair pleasing to Heaven than when it was lighted wi' lamps, and candles nae doubt ... and wi' the mirth and the frankincent they speak of in the Holy Scripture'.[13]

Another example, from an earlier period, of the use of proverbial sayings from Isaiah can be found in *The Imitation of Christ*, a highly successful manual of spiritual devotion, first put into circulation anonymously in 1418 and later attributed to Thomas à Kempis (1379–1471). It is by no means saturated with scriptural quotations. Isaiah is cited only three times, and in all three cases the quotations are in the form of proverbial sayings, cited with total disregard for their original prophetic context. The fact that they are Isaianic or even scriptural is irrelevant: they have already become popular aphorisms with a life of their own. One had this independence already in the Book of Isaiah where it appears twice (Isa.48:22; 57:21), and is still in use today: *Non pax est impiis* 'There is no peace for the wicked'.[14] The second also remains popular in Christian devotional and theological writings: *Vere tu es Deus absconditus* 'Truly thou art a God that hidest thyself' (Isa.45:15).[15] It has been prominent in recent years in the context of Holocaust Theology, both Jewish and Christian. A recent paper on the subject cites Terrien, Balentine and Davidson as examples of Christian theologians who maintain that complaints about God's apparent absence can be confessions of faith in his presence, and the Orthodox Jewish theologian Eliezer Berkovits for whom the Isaiah verse is central to

[12] S. Bagster & Sons., London (no date); cf. *Morning Light; Or, Waking Thoughts for Every Day of the Year*, SPCK London (no date).
[13] *The Antiquary*, chapter 21; cf. Moffatt, *The Bible in Scots Literature*, p. 238.
[14] *Imitatio Christi*, 2.6.1. Cf *ODQ*, p. 54.
[15] *Imitatio Christi*, 4.13.2. Cf. *ODQ*, p. 54.

his thought.[16] Thomas à Kempis' third Isaianic aphorism does not seem to have caught on, in spite of the fact that it is, especially in the Latin, extremely colourful and effective: *erubesce Sidon, ait mare* 'blush, Sidon, says the sea' or more colloquially, 'You ought to be ashamed of yourself (as the sea said to Sidon)!'(23:4). Thomas à Kempis addresses it to anyone tempted by the blandishments of this world when there is the prospect of eternal life and lasting pleasure for those who follow the way of humility and obedience.[17]

All manner of biblical quizzes, competitions and crossword puzzles were devised to test knowledge of the Bible. In 1941 a Presbyterian minister in Pittsburg, Pennsylvania, organized a poll to discover 'the ten greatest men of the Bible', which revealed, somewhat surprisingly, that Isaiah was eighth. Since so little is known about his life, he was the only one of the ten to gain his place on the strength of a book rather than on account of his heroic or saintly deeds.[18] In communities where people knew the whole Bible, more or less from cover to cover, a variety of biblical jokes became popular and Isaiah naturally figures in several. The *AV* translation of 37:36 provided one well-known example: 'and when they arose early in the morning, behold they were all dead corpses'. Children used to enjoy singing about a bear-cub in William Cowper's famous paraphrase of 49:15: 'Can a woman's tender care/Cease towards the child she bare (she-bear)?' Another example of unintentional comedy is the gravestone in memory of one Obadiah Wilkinson and his wife Ruth, which bears the epitaph (cf. Isaiah 40:2): THEIR WARFARE IS ENDED. The word 'warfare' (*RSV* 'service') no doubt was intended to refer, as in the original Hebrew, to this life as time spent in the service of God. Rather thoughtlessly applied to the way a couple had spent their married life together, however, it suggests something rather different.[19]

Then there is the notorious pun, of unknown origin, on Isaiah's name: Who is the funniest-looking man in the Bible? Isaiah of course, because one *eye's 'igher* than the other. This pun of course only works in communities where the English or Anglican pronunciation of the prophet's name is used, and therefore not familiar to

---

[16]   C. M. Pilkington, 'The hidden face of God in Isaiah 45:15; a reflection from Holocaust Theology'. Paper read at the Winter Meeting of SOTS in London in January 1994.

[17]   *Imitatio Christi*, 3.3.3–4.

[18]   Macartney, *The Greatest Men of the Bible* (Abingdon, Atlanta, 1941).

[19]   Simpson, *Holy Wit*, p. 59.

Scots or Americans who pronounce *Isaiah* to rhyme with *Leah*. There is also a neatly worded poem, also of unknown origin, in which the biblical English of Isaiah 40:6 is used to comic effect:

> The steed bit his master:
> How came this to pass?
> He heard the good pastor
> Cry, 'All flesh is grass.'[20]

A comic epitaph on the same theme runs as follows:

> Beneath the gravel and these stones
> Lies poor Jack Tiffey's skin and bones.
> His flesh, I often heard him say
> He hoped in time would make good hay.
> Quoth I, 'How can this come to pass?'
> And he replied. 'All flesh is grass'.[21]

Hilaire Belloc (1870–1953) finds room in one of his epigrams for another play on words, based on a quotation from Isaiah (cf. 1:18):

> When I am dead, I hope it may be said:
> "His sins were scarlet", but his books were read.[22]

The anti-smoking lobby finds scriptural authority in Isaiah's vision in chapter 6, for a sarcastic comment on a room full of smokers: 'The whole house was filled with smoke and I said, "Woe is me!"' (Isaiah 6:4–5). 30:21 has been angrily addressed to unhelpful back-seat drivers: 'Thine ears shall hear a word behind thee, saying, "This is the way, walk ye in it", when ye turn to the right hand and when ye turn to the left.' William Blake seems to have seen something comic in this verse too. In a painting with the caption 'Which is the way, the right or the left?', he represents God as a bearded old man, crouching down in a very uncomfortable position and attempting to write at the same time with both hands, while looking straight in front (Plate 28).[23]

In a collection of essays *On Humour and the Comic in the Hebrew Bible*, Robert Carroll imagines the scene if the 'daughters of Zion', rebuked by Isaiah in chapter 3, were to meet their critic on the

---

[20] Atwan and Wieder, edd., *Chapters into Verse*, p. 400.
[21] Johnson, *Book of Proverbs and Epitaphs*, p. 100.
[22] *ODQ* (2nd ed.1953), p. 41.
[23] 'Book of Urizen' (1794), Plate 1; cf *The Complete Graphic Work of William Blake*, edd. D. Bindman and D. Toomey, Plates 289, 289a.

streets of Jerusalem, himself 'buttock-naked' as he was, according to
20:2–4, for three years: 'on one side of the street the half-naked
Isaiah ranting at the women for their obsession with sartorial styles,
and on the other side these formidable half-naked women glowering
at their critic (the text is silent on the matter of the women's
response to 3:16–23)'.[24]

The name of Isaiah's son Mahershalalhashbaz (8:1,3) has always
been a source of mild amusement in Bible-literate communities. A
rare occurrence of the name outside its original context appears in
an English graveyard, on the tombstone of one Mahershalalhashbaz
Tuck, who died on 15 September 1893 aged 54 years. His extraordinary name is explained as follows by the vicar of East Dereham
who married him on Christmas Day, 1867: his father wished to call
him by the shortest name in the Bible and chose 'Uz'. But he was
advised against this name for some reason by the clergyman, and in
pique gave him the longest.[25] One might also mention in this context
the following cautionary inscription on a house in Dunfermline.
Based on Isaiah 30:33, it is reminiscent of that earnest nineteenth-
century Scottish commentator on current events, McGonagle: 'Since
an hour's fire on 25 May 1624 with its fierce flames could work such
damage, O think of the fearful fires which the breath of Jehovah with
a torrent of brimstone, will kindle.'[26]

The Bible was now at the centre of public worship too. In many
Churches worship began with the ceremonial carrying in of the
Bible. It was placed in the pulpit, now located in the optical centre of
the building (where the altar in Catholic Churches had been), and
from which sermons saturated with the language and imagery of
scripture were delivered. The imagery of Isaiah's vision in chapter 6,
so influential in the history of the eucharist,[27] was now applied to
preaching: ' "Woe is me! for I am undone; because I am a man of
unclean lips: mine eyes have seen the King" ... Let the preacher ...
pause ere he mount the pulpit steps and breathe the secret prayer,
"God be merciful to me a sinner." There will be days when the sense
of personal unworthiness smites and shatters us until we cry, "My
God, my God, why hast thou forsaken me?" It is then, by some
miracle of divine loving kindness, at such a moment of desolation,

---

[24]   R. Carroll,'Is humour also among the prophets?', pp. 182–3.
[25]   *A Norfolk Diary*, ed H. B. J. Armstrong, p. 123.
[26]   Moffatt, *The Bible in Scots Literature*, p. 82.
[27]   See chapter 3, pp. 59ff.

that there comes the angel, touching a man's lips with a live coal from the altar of God'.[28]

At his ordination, the Revd Ian Paisley, militant politician and founder of the Free Presbyterian Church of Ulster, was armed by his mother with a suitably defiant text from Isaiah: 'No weapon that is formed against thee shall prosper; and every tongue that shall rise against thee in judgment thou shalt condemn' (Isa.54:17).[29] Equipped with vernacular translations of the Bible and confident that their congregations were becoming daily more and more conversant with the text, writers and preachers in all parts of society could use biblical texts even more fluently and pointedly than St Jerome and St Ambrose had done centuries before. Isaiah 52:7 ('How beautiful are the feet of *those* (Hebrew *him*) who …') is adapted to apply to preachers: this is how it is used in Handel's lovely aria in the *Messiah*, for example, and in the quaint sixteenth-century woodcut discussed in the previous chapter.[30]

Most of John Wesley's surviving sermons are on rather obvious texts from the Gospels and Paul. Only two are on texts from Isaiah, and one of these was never preached. The first is interesting because he identifies the vineyard in Isaiah's allegory (Isaiah 5:1–7) with the Methodist movement, rather than the whole Church (or the Jews) as other preachers and commentators before and since have done.[31] This gives him the opportunity to look back over more than half a century of Methodist revivalism, and to make some typically challenging criticisms of the present situation in England, in particular Oxfordshire where the sermon was preached in 1787.[32] The other (unpreached) sermon on Isaiah is a bitter attack on life in Oxford, entitled 'Hypocrisy in Oxford' and loosely based on Isaiah 1:21: 'How the faithful city has become a harlot …'.[33] There was an idea that he might submit it as part of the examination for the degree of BD (which incidentally he never achieved), and he certainly did not expect many dons or students to hear it as it was due to be preached on a Sunday in the summer vacation. In the event he was dissuaded from preaching the sermon but he obviously felt very strongly about its subject matter because he spent a great deal of time on it. Not

---

[28] Stewart, *Preaching*, pp 180–1.
[29] *The Independent* 18 September, 1994, p. 9.
[30] See p. 137.   [31] See above, pp. 38ff.
[32] *Works* III, Sermons 3, pp. 502–17.
[33] *Works* IV, Sermons 4, pp. 389–407.

only was it all very carefully prepared in English: he also wrote a version in Ciceronian Latin. It consists of numerous criticisms of the current state of the Church in Oxford, especially among students and dons. He begins with a rather tedious assault on doctrinal errors, especially Pelagianism, and then moves into a catalogue of the sins which he says are rampant among the clergy and divinity students of Oxford. These include not keeping the sabbath holy, wearing immodest clothing, frequenting taverns and gambling, but also the sin of not studying Hebrew and the other relevant languages: 'who (almost) is there that can be said to understand Hebrew? ... how few can readily read and understand so much as a page of Clemens Alexandrinus, St Chrysostom or Ephraem Syrus? ... How is the faithful city become an harlot!'

Unlike Wesley, Charles Spurgeon (1834–92) makes frequent use of Isaiah in his sermons, selecting texts from every part of the book which he makes relevant to the day to day situations of his congregation. He comforted the aged and infirm with the words of 46:4 ('Even to your old age I am He, and even to hoar hairs will I carry you').[34] In a sermon preached on the fifth of November he identified the 'weapon that is formed against thee' (54:17) as the gunpowder of Guy Fawkes.[35] He used the words of 65:5 to condemn 'holier than thou' self-righteousness,[36] and 47:14 to describe hell-fire ('there shall not be a coal to warm yourselves at or a fire to sit beside').[37] He chose 44:3–5 to comment on the success of recent exemplary revivalist meetings in Newcastle and Edinburgh ('I will pour water on him that is thirsty, and floods upon the dry ground'),[38] and 42:9 to attack modern 'sham Christian critics' of the Bible who have invented a 'second Isaiah'.[39] In an analysis of sin, guilt and forgiveness, built on 64:6–8, a passage often used by the mediaeval Church as well,[40] he makes much of the reference at the end to God as Father, recalling the parable of the Prodigal Son and Paul's use of the term Abba 'father' (Rom.8:15; Gal.4:6).[41] In a remarkable word by word exposition of 49:16 ('Behold, I have graven thee on the palms of my hands'), Spurgeon allows himself the exegetical license to identify this with the moment in Christ's

---

[34] *Sermons*, pp. 361ff.   [35] *Sermons*, pp. 152ff.
[36] *Metropolitan Tabernacle Pulpit, containing sermons preached and revised by C. H. Spurgeon*, Vol. xxv (London 1880), pp. 553ff.
[37] Vol. viii (1862) pp. 211ff.   [38] Vol. xx (1874), pp. 13f.
[39] Vol. xxv (1880), pp. 684f.   [40] See above, pp. 71ff.
[41] Vol. viii (1862), p. 131.

passion when 'the executioner with the hammer smote the tender hands of the loving Jesus ...'.[42]

He actually claims that it was a verse from Isaiah ('Look unto me and be ye saved, all the ends of the earth' 45:22) that converted him. This was the text of a sermon by a Methodist lay preacher in Colchester, after which Spurgeon declared: 'He had not much to say, thank God, and that compelled him to keep on repeating his text, and there was nothing needed – by me at any rate – except his text.'[43] Most of his many sermons (well over a thousand) were published in various formats and continued to exert his influence – and that of Isaiah – on Christians all over the English-speaking world, not by any means only within his own Baptist circles.

At first no hymns were sung in the Calvinist tradition as they were associated with the mediaeval Catholic tradition against which the Reformers were rebelling. Metrical versions of the Psalms, the first of which were composed in Geneva at the instigation of John Calvin, were much used instead. The earliest English versions of these were composed in Geneva by Protestant refugees from Mary Tudor's England. 'Paraphrases' of scriptural passages were added to the metrical psalms and by the end of the eighteenth century had been approved for use in Scottish churches.[44] A significant proportion (twelve out of sixty-six) of the paraphrases printed in the official Scottish Psalter of 1929, are paraphrases of passages from Isaiah. They comprise the following: 1:10–19; 2:2–6; 9:2–8; 26:1–7; 33:13–18; 40:27–end; 42:1–13; 49:13–17; 53; 55; 57:15–16; 58:5–9. Of these two found their way into hymn-books all over the world, and became popular throughout English-speaking Christendom: *Behold! the mountain of the Lord* (2:2–6) and *Hark the glad sound! the Saviour comes* (9:2–8). Although most of the other passages are well enough known in the original, especially 26:1–7 and the passages from 40–66, the eighteenth-century paraphrases were less successful. Three of the passages have staged something of a comeback in recent years, providing inspiration for both feminists (49:13–17)[45] and liberation theologians (1:10–19; 58:5–9).[46]

Without attempting a detailed study of the hymns written in English during the eighteenth and nineteenth centuries, it is clear

[42] Vol. IX (1892), p. 304.
[43] Cf. Stewart, *Preaching*, p. 138.
[44] Wright, ed., *The Bible in Scottish Life and Literature*, p. 147f.
[45] See below, pp. 206ff.   [46] See below, pp. 202ff., 228ff.

that they contain enough allusions to Isaiah for us to draw some broad conclusions about the kind of texts that were most popular and how they were interpreted. This in turn will tell us something about forms of Christian piety in that period. Let us look at two examples. There is first the recurring emphasis on 'peace', not so much freedom from war as freedom from personal worries, cares and trials. In several texts which we have not come across before, but which receive new attention in this period, this 'peace' actually comes quite close to the original Hebrew *shalom*, in the sense of 'wholeness, health, prosperity'. 66:12, for example, inspired a young English poet, Frances Ridley Havergal (1836–79), to compose the hymn 'Like a river glorious/Is God's perfect peace' which contains the following typical nineteenth-century definition of 'peace':

> Not a surge of worry
> Not a shade of care,
> Not a blast of hurry,
> Touch the spirit there.[47]

The 'perfect peace' in the second line of the first verse comes verbatim from 26:3 (*AV*), where the Hebrew has *shalom shalom*. This was the inspiration for another hymn, discussed above in relation to funerals and bereavement. Beginning with the words 'Peace, perfect peace, in this dark world of sin?' it defines peace as freedom from 'thronging duties', 'sorrows surging round', separation from 'loved ones far away' and the like.[48]

It is in this context that we have to understand the popularity of the image of Christ as 'Prince of Peace' (Isaiah 9:6),[49] and the famous vision of the 'Peaceable Kingdom' in 11:6–9. The American Quaker artist Edward Hicks, as we shall see, made it clear that in his famous painting of the subject, the animals represent more the warring elements within human nature, than anything political. In a beautiful verse which we might almost call a nineteenth-century version of the *Rorate*,[50] another American Quaker, John Greenleaf Whittier (1807–92), actually removes the 'justice' from Isaiah 45:8 and substitutes 'quietness':

> Drop Thy still dews of quietness,
> Till all our strivings cease,

---

[47] *CH* 443.
[48] *EH* 468; *CH* 444; there is a modern hymn beginning with the same words (*HON* 445). See above, pp. 133f.
[49] See above, p. 106.   [50] See pp. 71ff.

> Take from our souls the strain and stress,
> And let our ordered lives confess
> The beauty of Thy peace.[51]

It is not until modern times that the far more politically-minded 'Justice and Peace' Movement and the like have made other texts from Isaiah, and other interpretations of the same texts, more common.[52]

The other example of an Isaianic image which was very popular in eighteenth- and nineteenth-century piety comes from 40:11, a verse already formative, as we saw, in the earliest stages of the history of Christianity:[53] 'He shall feed his flock like a shepherd; he shall gather the lambs with his arm; and carry them in his bosom and shall gently lead those that are with young'. This verse fills out the 'good shepherd' image, more familiar from Psalm 23, with the phrases 'gather ... with his arm', 'carry ... in his bosom' and 'gently lead' which recur in many popular hymns from the period.[54] The imagery appears also in the first verse and refrain of *Safe in the arms of Jesus, safe on his gentle breast*, the best-known of nearly 8000 hymns by the blind hymn-writer Fanny Crosby (1820–1915), and said to have given 'more peace and satisfaction to mothers who had lost children than any other'.[55] It is no coincidence that this verse and 52:7 ('How beautiful are the feet ...'), are among the best-loved arias in Handel's *Messiah*, an eighteenth-century work which, as one writer puts it, 'sums up to perfection and with the greatest eloquence, the religious faith, ethical, congregational and utterly unmystical, of the average Englishman'.[56]

The extensive role of Isaiah in *The Song Book of the Salvation Army* (1986) – as frequent as the Gospels – provides an interesting case-study in revivalist Christianity. A verse we have not come across so far, for example, but one of the most frequently cited verses in this context, is 1:18. It appears in no less than 23 hymns,[57] and provides the refrain for three of them: e.g. 'I've washed my robes in Jesus blood,/and he has made them white as snow' (Hymn 359). The blood motif from the winepress image of 63:3 appears in several

---

[51] *Dear Lord and Father of mankind*: EH 383; CH 245; HON 116.
[52] See below, chapter 10.
[53] See p. 46.
[54] E.g. CH 310, 328, 569; cf. Moffatt, *Handbook*, p. 570.
[55] EH 580; CH 707; cf. Moffatt, *Handbook*, p. 239.
[56] Dean, *Handel's Dramatic Oratorios and Masques*, p. 315.
[57] *Concordance to SBSA* (ed. W. Metcalf, 1992), p. 208.

hymns as well,[58] as does the image of Christ having the names of the faithful written on his hands (49:16).[59] A related image, much used in this context, is the 'dross' of human sin, derived from the 'faithful city' poem in Isaiah 1:21–6. Its popularity no doubt influenced by the fact that it rhymes with 'Cross', 'dross' figures in ten hymns including the following, an English version by John Wesley of a hymn by the prolific eighteenth-century German-Moravian hymn-writer Count Nicholas Ludwig von Zinzendorf: 'Wash out its stain, refine its dross,/Nail my affections to the Cross'.[60]

Another much-used image derived from Isaiah 51:3 and 58:11 (cf. John 4:14) is that of the soul as a 'watered garden'. Charles Wesley's hymn beginnning 'Come thou all inspiring Spirit' contains the following example: 'Make our hearts a watered garden,/Fill our spotless souls with God'. Beulah from 62:4 is used in a similar way:

> Is not this the land of Beulah,
> blessed blessed land of light,
> where the flowers bloom forever,
> and the sun is always bright?[61]

Finally chapter 6 figures in several hymns. In an earlier chapter we considered some of the ways in which this familiar passage has been applied to the eucharist. In the far less sacramental context of Salvation Army worship, the same words are used in a very different way. In one hymn, for example, the original narrative style is converted into prayer, giving the refrain 'Touch me again …'.[62] In another the words are taken almost verbatim from Isaiah: Here am I, my Lord, send me (2x)./I surrender to obey thy call (2x).[63]

This leads us into the final part of this chapter, a look at the foreign missionary activities of the Churches, which found much of their inspiration in Isaiah. As we saw, the earliest Christian preachers found in Isaiah the authority for their mission to the gentiles.[64] There is an extended treatment of this aspect of Isaiah from our own century in a characteristically tendentious interpretation of some of the Ebed Yahweh passages (notably 42:1–4; 49:6, 8; 52:13–53:12) by the Protestant theologian Karl Barth (1886–1968).[65]

---

[58] *SBSA* 512, 532.
[59] Charles Wesley, *Arise my soul arise*: *SBSA* 106.
[60] The first line is 'O Thou to whose all searching sight'.
[61] *SBSA* 320.   [62] *SBSA* 610.
[63] *SBSA* 482.   [64] See above, pp. 32ff.
[65] *Church Dogmatics*, Vol. 4, Pt. 1, pp. 28–32.

Fifteenth- and sixteenth-century Spanish missionaries and explorers believed they were fulfilling some of the prophecies of Isaiah. Christopher Columbus (1451–1506) proclaimed himself to be the 'messenger of the new heaven and the new earth' (Isaiah 65:17), and his contemporaries, both Jewish and Christian, interpreted his name as meaning 'dove', a reference not only to Jonah (Hebrew *yonah* 'a dove'), who embarked for Tarshish in the distant west, but also to the doves in Isaiah 60:8–9: 'Who are these that fly like a cloud, and like doves to their windows. Surely the isles shall wait for me, and the ships of Tarshish ...'[66] But the heyday of new contacts between European Christians and the peoples of the rest of the world, the distinctive application of Isaiah to the massive overseas enterprises of the Church, and the discovery of new texts and new meanings, were above all a feature of the eighteenth and nineteenth centuries.

William Carey, who was the driving force behind the founding of the Baptist Missionary Society in 1792, is a conspicuous example. According to his sister, his revolutionary *Enquiry into the Obligations of Christians to Use Means for the Conversion of the Heathens* (1792) was inspired by the opening words of chapter 62 ('For Zion's sake I will not keep silent');[67] and one of the most important proposals he makes there, the idea of combining Christianity with commerce, in particular working with the East India Trading Company, is given scriptural authority by reference to 'the ships of Tarshish', cited 300 years earlier in relation to Christopher Columbus, in 60:9: 'Surely the isles shall wait for me, and the ships of Tarshish, to bring thy children from afar, their silver and their gold with them, unto the name of the Lord thy God ...'[68] Then in May 1792 he delivered his famous sermon in Nottingham, known by its title *Expect great things from God; Attempt great things for God.* His text came from Isaiah 54:2–3: 'Enlarge the place of thy tent, and let them stretch forth the curtains of thine inhabitations; spare not, lengthen thy cords, and strengthen thy stakes. For thou shalt break forth on the right hand and on the left; And thy seed shall inherit the gentiles, and make the desolate cities to be inhabited'.

His choice of text may have been influenced by the rather awkward use of the imagery of Isaiah 54:2 in one of William Cowper's hymns, written a few years earlier for the opening of 'the

[66] Boitano, *Shadow of Ulysses*, pp. 63–8.
[67] Smith, *The Life of William Carey*, p. 23.
[68] Smith, *The Life of William Carey*, p. 25.

great room in the Great House' at Olney where local prayer-meetings were to be held:

> Behold! at thy commanding word,
> We stretch the curtain and the cord;
> Come thou, and fill this wider space,
> And help us with a large increase.[69]

However that may, it caught the imagination of his Church, and within six months the first English missionary society was formed.

A reference to 'the land of Sinim', identified by many as China, in Isaiah 49:12 provided missionaries to China with the scriptural motto they needed. The Prussian missionary Karl Gützlaff wrote a series of articles with this title in 1844.[70] The flyleaf of a book by an American missionary has commentaries on the verse, dating from the second to the eighteenth centuries to prove it referred to China,[71] and a study of American Quaker missions to China, published in 1925, has the title *Ohio Friends in the Land of Sinim*.[72]

Another example of how Isaiah can be applied to a specific geographical region appeared recently in a leaflet printed by the Bible Society as part of a campaign to raise funds to help provide Bibles for Egyptian Christians. Under the title 'God's Word for Christians in Egypt', two verses from the 'Oracle concerning Egypt' in chapter 19 are cited, one of them in an Arabic translation: 'When the people there [in Egypt] are oppressed and call out to the Lord for help, he will send someone to rescue them. The Lord will reveal himself to the Egyptian people, and they will acknowledge and worship him' (19:20–21). The leaflet goes on: 'Imagine how thrilling it would be to read these words while sitting on the banks of the Nile – to be an Egyptian Christian, reading a prophecy about your own country in your own language – to be part of its fulfilment'.

A look at some of the hymns written to accompany the expansion of foreign missions confirms the significant role the often imperialistic language and imagery of Isaiah had to play in what is now looked back upon as a rather less than wholesome chapter in the history of Christianity. We have already seen how Isaiah's attacks on the idol

---

[69] *The Poetical Works of William Cowper*, ed. H. S. Milford, p. 450. The verse is omitted from the version in the *English Hymnal*, No. 422 and the Scottish *Church Hymnary* (revised edition), No.247. Cf. Moffatt, *Handbook*, p. 88.

[70] *The Chinese Repository*, 13 (1844), pp. 113–23, 466–77, 537–52, 578–603, 641–53.

[71] Marshall Broomhall, *The Chinese Empire* (1907).

[72] W. R. Williams, *Ohio Friends in the Land of Sinim* (Mt Gilead, Ohio 1925).

worshippers were used by Christians since the twelfth century.[73] The language and imagery of Isaiah, particularly in the later chapters, fuel the flames of all kinds of burning attacks on polytheism and idolatry in general, and Hinduism, Buddhism, Islam and Roman Catholicism in particular.

As well as the repetition of a monotheistic formula (e.g. 'besides me there is no God') in verses 5, 6, 14, 21 and 22, and the attacks on idolatry in verses 16 and 20, Isaiah 45 contains other characteristically Isaianic images which were much exploited by the missionary hymn-writers. Victory is depicted in terms of 'gates of brass' and 'bars of iron' yielding before them (cf. 45:2), prisoners being freed (cf. v.13) and foreigners bowing down before Christ (cf. vv.14, 23). The hymn *Lift up your heads, ye gates of brass*, for example, published in 1853 under the title 'China Evangelized', originally contained the line 'To Christ shall Buddha's votaries bow', later amended to 'To Christ shall every nation bow' (cf. Isaiah 45:23).[74] The second verse of Bishop Heber's well-known hymn beginning 'From Greenland's icy mountains', and mercifully omitted from most modern hymnbooks, is another illustration of the arrogant attitude of missionaries towards the peoples of the Third World:

> What though the spicy breezes
> Blow soft o'er Java's isle,
> Though every prospect pleases
> And only man is vile;
> In vain with lavish kindness
> The gifts of God are strewn,
> The heathen in his blindness
> Bows down to wood and stone.[75]

Isaiah's global perspective can be recognized in many of these hymns too, in their frequent use, for instance, of the four points of the compass (e.g. 'That they may know, from the rising of the sun and from the west ...' 45:6; cf. 43:5–6; 49:12; 59:19) and such expressions as 'to the ends of the earth' (42:10; 45:22; 49:6; 52:10).[76] Phrases like 'The isles are waiting' (cf. 42:4; 51:5; 60:9)[77] and 'Ye isles, give ear to me' (cf. 49:1; 41:1)[78] now take on new meaning in a

[73] See pp. 137–40.
[74] Moffatt, *Handbook*, p. 128.
[75] Moffatt, *Handbook*, p. 124.
[76] E.g. *Hills of the North, rejoice: CH* 372, *SOP* 64.
[77] *EH* 551; *CH* 382.
[78] *EH* 548; *CH* 380.

context where missionaries are going forth to preach the Gospel in Ceylon, the East Indies and the Pacific Islands. Not all such passages come from the later chapters of Isaiah. 11:9 and 13:2 also had an important role to play. The first of these, a favourite already of John Wesley as we have seen and familiar as the climax to 'the Peaceable Kingdom' passage (11:6–9),[79] suggested the refrain of the hymn beginning 'God is working his purpose out':

> Give ear to Me, ye continents – ye isles give ear to Me,
> That the earth may be filled with the glory of God,   ·
>   as the waters cover the sea.

This hymn, composed in 1894 by a schoolmaster at Eton, is saturated with images and phrases from all parts of Isaiah.[80]

'Lift ye up a banner on the high mountain', from an unexpected part of the book (13:2 *AV*),[81] was the inspiration for another remarkable missionary hymn. Although the Hebrew word *nes* is common, and other passages where it is translated in the *AV* as 'ensign' or 'standard' (e.g. 11:10), have been much used by Christians down the ages, this is almost the only place where it is for some reason translated 'banner'. The image appears in several hymns. In December 1848 an American bishop composed a hymn in which every verse begins with the cry 'Fling out the banner!'[82]

We end with an extraordinary hymn by another American bishop, Arthur Cleveland Coxe (1818–96), which not only attempts to make sense of a rather awkward Hebrew phrase from Isaiah 52:15, widely assumed by modern scholars to be corrupt, but uniquely applies it to contemporary missionary endeavour. Here are the first and last stanzas:

> Saviour, sprinkle many nations,
> Fruitful let Thy sorrows be;
> By Thy pains and consolations,
> Draw the Gentiles unto Thee.
> Of Thy Cross the wondrous story,
> Be it to the nations told;
> Let them see Thee in Thy glory
> And Thy mercy manifold ...

---

[79] See below.
[80] Moffatt, *Handbook*, p. 126.
[81] It has often been pointed out that chapters 13–23, the 'oracles against the foreign nations' constitute the least fertile part of the book: cf. p. 30.
[82] *EH* 546; *CH* 383.

Saviour, lo! the isles are waiting,
Stretched the hand and strained the sight,
For Thy Spirit new-creating,
Love's pure flame and wisdom's light;
Give the word, and of the preacher
Speed the foot and touch the tongue,
Till on earth by every creature
Glory to the Lamb be sung.[83]

Perhaps we can identify here allusions to other familiar motifs from Isaiah as well as the 'Suffering Servant' in the first stanza and the 'waiting isles' in the last. In view of the general prominence of Isaiah, 'prophet to the nations', in these eighteenth- and nineteenth-century expressions of missionary zeal, one is tempted to recognize also 52:7 ('How beautiful are the feet . . .') and 6:7 ('this has touched your lips') behind the reference to the work of evangelists in the last stanza.

As a final example of nineteenth-century triumphalist uses of Isaiah, we give the last word on the subject to a nineteenth-century English preacher, who tells us that in his day Isaiah was 'a household word everywhere . . . a universal teacher of mankind': 'The wild tribes of New Zealand seized his magnificent strains as if belonging to their own national songs and chanted them from hill to hill, with all the delight of a newly discovered treasure'.[84]

---

[83] *EH* 551; *CH* 382.
[84] Stanley, *Scripture Portraits and Other Miscellanies*, pp. 155, 164.

CHAPTER 9

Isaiah in Literature and Music

We turn now to Isaiah's role in literature and music. As the influence of the Bible spread throughout western culture, the words and images of Isaiah have reached a wide audience in bookshops, libraries and concert-halls, far beyond the immediate context of the life and work of the Church. The dividing line between what appears in this chapter and what is discussed elsewhere, between hymns surveyed in previous chapters, for example, and some of the poems referred to here, or between the *Sanctus* discussed in chapter 3 and *Veni, Veni, Immanuel* or Handel's *Messiah* which appear in this chapter, is not always a hard and fast one. But it was thought there would be sufficient interest in this topic in its own right to devote a separate section to it. There have been several recent studies of the Bible in literature, in which Isaiah naturally figures. Atwan and Wieder, *Chapters into Verse*, for example, an anthology of poetry in English inspired by the Bible, devotes twenty-five pages to a very interesting selection of Isaiah-inspired poems.[1] Jeffrey's very successful *Dictionary of Biblical Tradition in English Literature* has a brief but useful entry on 'Isaiah',[2] and numerous other articles on such words and images as 'Beulah', 'Bruised reed', 'Lilith', 'Lion lies down with lamb', 'Man of Sorrows', 'Swords into Plowshares' and 'Vine, vineyard' which are Isaianic or have Isaianic connections. References to Isaiah can be found in general studies of the 'Bible and Literature' such as those of Roston (1965) and Prickett (1986), and there are some special studies of Isaiah's influence on particular writers.[3] But no exhaustive study of Isaiah in literature – in English, German, French or any other language – or in music, has so far been attempted. Nor can that be

---

[1] Atwan and Wieder, *Chapters into Verse*, pp. 385–410.
[2] Jeffrey, *DBTEL*, pp. 380–1.
[3] E.g. George, 'Reading Isaiah and Ezekiel through Blake'; Carroll, 'Revisionings: echoes and traces of Isaiah in the poetry of William Blake'.

done here. All we shall do is to consider some representative examples, always keeping the text of Isaiah at the centre, in order to get into focus the texts and images from the book that have had the most appeal among writers – some devout religious people, others much less so – over the last three or four centuries.

Neither Isaiah nor his prophecies can be said to have had much direct impact on the language of Shakespeare. But one Isaianic image that does appear in Shakespearean tragedy is that of hands that are 'full of blood' and the longing that they could become 'white as snow' (Isaiah 1:15, 18).[4] In *Hamlet* King Claudius vainly prays that his fratricidal sin can be forgiven in heaven:

> What if this cursed hand
> Were thicker than itself with brother's blood,
> Is there not rain enough in the sweet heavens
> To wash it white as snow?[5]

Macbeth in similar language, appalled by the sight of blood on his hands, doubts whether 'all great Neptune's ocean' can ever wash them clean, despite Lady Macbeth's goading: 'go get some water/ And wash this filthy witness from your hand ... a little water clears us of this deed'.[6]

Isaiah's influence on Milton (1608–74) is greater. The prominent role of Isaiah in the Advent and Christmas lectionaries, together with his famous vision in chapter 6, with its eucharistic associations, were used to good effect by him in his early ode *On the morning of Christ's Nativity* (1629).[7] The words of 9:6–7, familiar to every Christian as an Advent reading, seem to be indirectly alluded to in the first stanza, which explicitly refers to biblical prophecy. The prophet's vision in chapter 6, especially his sense of guilt when confronted with God's heavenly glory, surely inspired the contrast between 'that Light unsufferable,/ and that far-beaming blaze of Majesty' and the 'darksome House of mortal Clay' in the second stanza. The image of God seated 'at Heav'ns high Council-Table ... the midst of Trinal Unity' no doubt owes something to Isaiah's vision as well, in particular to the angelic host's threefold repetition of 'Holy'.[8] Maybe the mention of the 'Star-led wizards' hurrying from the east 'with

4   Cf. Roston, *Biblical Drama*, p. 126.
5   *Hamlet*, Act 3, Scene 3, lines 43–6.
6   *Macbeth*, Act 2, Scene 2, lines 44–65.
7   Darbishire, ed., *Poetical Works*, pp. 395–6.
8   Cf. pp. 59ff.

odours sweet', in the last stanza, comes from Matthew 2:11 rather than directly from Isaiah 60:6. But the poem ends with an explicit reference to Chapter 6, confirming the Isaianic allusions elsewhere:

> Have thou the honour first, thy Lord to greet,
> And join thy voice unto the Angel Quire,
> From out his secret Altar toucht with hallow'd fire.

It was from Isaiah that Milton derived some of his inspiration for the description of the fall of Satan at the beginning of *Paradise Lost*. In a taunting, ironic lament (14:3–20), the prophet portrays the king of Babylon arriving in Sheol, in images more reminiscent of Homer or Virgil or Dante than of any biblical parallel. His arrival stirs up some excitement amongst the inhabitants of Sheol. The ghosts of former world leaders, some apparently still on their thrones, stand up to greet him: 'you too have become as weak as we are, You have become like us!' (verse 10). Their insubstantial, shadowy, colourless existence in Sheol is set against former power and regal splendour. This is the world into which Satan, in Milton's words, was 'hurl'd headlong flaming from th'ethereal sky': 'How you are fallen from heaven, O Day Star (Latin *lucifer*), son of Dawn! ... You said in your heart, "I will ascend to heaven; ... I will make myself like the Most High." But you have been brought down to Sheol, to the depths of the pit' (Isaiah 14:12–15).[9]

George Herbert (1593–1633), in one of many allusions to Isaiah,[10] echoes the sacramental interpretation of Isaiah 63:1–3 so vividly represented in mediaeval Christian iconography,[11] and seems to have structured the stanzas of his poem *The Agony* in the form of a winepress, in a manner reminiscent of his *Easter wings* and *The Altar*. He develops the image in a typical pious and graphic direction: 'Sin is that press and vice which forceth pain/To hunt his cruel food through every vein'.[12] He uses the same image in *The Sacrifice*[13] (lines 161–3) and in another poem, *The Bunch of Grapes*: 'Who of the Laws soure juice sweet wine did make,/Ev'n God himself being pressed for my sake' (lines 26–8). Several collections of hymns contain paraphrases of this famous passage, one of the best known being that of

---

[9] Cf. *Paradise Lost*, Book 1, line 45.
[10] Others include his use of 55:1–2 in a poem on the eucharist, and 58:6–7 in 'Lent': *The Country Parson*, pp. 306, 206.
[11] See pp. 95–98.
[12] Herbert, *The Country Parson. The Temple*, p. 151.
[13] Hutchinson, ed., *The Works of George Herbert*, p. 31.

the American bishop A.Cleveland Coxe (1818–96) in the *English Hymnal* beginning 'Who is this with garments gory'.[14] Another from an earlier period by Friar William Herebert (died 1333), begins with the striking words 'What is he, this lordling, that cometh from the fight?'[15]

An early poem by Gerald Manley Hopkins (1844–89), entitled *Barnfloor and Winepress*, bears an epigraph from 2 Kings 6:27 where the words of the title appear, but is far more dependent on Isaiah to which it contains many allusions. One commentator notes no less than seven, although he somewhat surprisingly omits the main one which is clearly Isaiah 63:1–3.[16] Probably influenced by George Herbert, Hopkins employs the 'winepress' imagery as follows:

> For us by Calvary's distress
> The wine was rackèd from the press;
> Now in our altar vessels stored
> Is the sweet Vintage of our Lord　　　(lines 17–20).

Lord Macaulay (1800–59) incidentally, in a quite different context, uses the gory imagery of Isaiah 63:1–6, almost verbatim, in his poem *The Battle of Naseby*, where he applies the image of the 'Man of Blood ... with his long essenced hair' to the defeated King Charles.[17]

George Herbert's *Easterwings* was probably inspired by Isaiah too:[18] 'But they that wait upon the Lord shall renew their strength; they shall mount up with wings as eagles; they shall run and not be weary, and they shall walk and not faint' (40:31). The same text is used to dramatic effect in the film *Chariots of Fire* (1981), where the Scottish athlete and missionary Eric Liddell, played by the late Ian Charleson, preaches a sermon on it in the Scottish Church in Paris during the 1924 Olympics, a few days before he won the gold medal for the 400 metres, despite his refusal to run on the Sabbath, in world record time.[19] It can be seen too, incidentally, in the RAF Memorial window in Durham Cathedral.

Alexander Pope (1688–1744), struck by the 'remarkable parity' between Isaiah and the fourth *Eclogue* (*Pollio*), wrote a 'sacred eclogue in imitation of Virgil's *Pollio*', entitled *Messiah*.[20] Inspired more by

[14]　*EH* 108.
[15]　Atwan and Wieder, edd., *Chapters into Verse*, pp. 405–6.
[16]　5:1–5; 11:10; 12:32; 16:9–10; 18:56; 28:27–8; 53:5: *Poetical Works*, pp. 26–7, 237–8.
[17]　*ODQ*, p. 322.
[18]　*The Country Parson*, p. 157.
[19]　Cf. Magnusson, *The Flying Scotsman*, p. 49.
[20]　Davies, ed., *Poetical Works*, pp. 31–6.

Isaiah than by Virgil, this early eighteenth-century example of Christian piety pushes the connection as far as it will go:

> The dreams of Pindus and the Aeonian maids
> Delight no more – O Thou my voice inspire
> Who touch'd Isaiah's hallow'd lips with fire!
> Rapt into future times, the bard began:
> A Virgin shall conceive, a Virgin bear a Son!
> From Jesse's root behold a branch arise,
> Whose sacred flower with fragrance fills the skies . . .

The poem is crammed with allusions to Isaiah, and contains one of the few elaborate descriptions of the 'Peaceable Kingdom' that can be dated before Edward Hicks' famous paintings of the subject:[21]

> The lambs with wolves shall graze the verdant mead,
> And boys in flowery bands the tiger lead;
> The steer and lion at one crib shall meet,
> And harmless serpents lick the pilgrim's feet.
> The smiling infant in his hand shall take
> The crested basilisk and crested snake,
> Pleased the green lustre of the scales survey,
> And with their forky tongue shall innocently play   (lines 77–84).

A more recent and more private or domestic example appears in a poem entitled *On falling asleep by firelight* by the American poet William Meredith (born 1919):

> Around the fireplace, pointing at the fire
> As in the prophet's dream of the last truce
> The animals lie down; they doze or stare,
> Their hoofs and paws in comical disuse.
>   . . . the heat
> Turns softly on the hearth into that dust
> Isaiah said would be the serpent's meat.[22]

The last words of the poem just quoted indicate that the images come from Isaiah 65:25 as much as the better known 'Peaceable Kingdom' passage in 11:6–9.

The influence of Bishop Lowth's *Sacred Poetry of the Hebrews* (1753), in particular his use of Isaiah, is evident on both the pre-Romantic and the Romantic poets.[23] The realization that Isaiah the prophet was also

---

[21] See below, pp. 236ff.
[22] The full text is given in Atwan and Wieder, *Chapters into Verse*, pp. 406–7.
[23] Prickett, *Words and the Word*, pp. 114–15.

a poet encouraged them to see in Isaiah a model for them to imitate.[24] Shelley's love for the Bible, especially Job, Psalms and Isaiah, in spite of his atheism, is acknowledged by his wife.[25] But William Blake (1757–1827) is the best example. He had a special admiration for Isaiah: 'as a Prophet and Devil he becomes Blake's "particular friend" ... they "often read the Bible together in its infernal and diabolical sense which the world shall have if they behave well".'[26]

In one of his 'memorable fancies' recounted in *The Marriage of Heaven and Hell*, he tells how Isaiah and Ezekiel dined with him. Given such a unique opportunity, he asked the two prophets three questions, which tell us much about his interest in Isaiah, and how he related him to his own sceptical views of traditional Christianity. The first is about his vision of God in chapter 6, to which he answers: ' "I saw no God, nor heard any, in a finite organical perception; but my senses discovered the infinite in everything, and as I was then perswaded and remained confirm'd that the voice of honest indignation, is the voice of god, I cared not for the consequences but wrote." Then I asked: "but does a firm perswasion that a thing is so, make it so?" He replied: "All poets believe that it does, and in ages of imagination this firm perswasion removed mountains; but many are not capable of a firm perswasion of anything." '[27] Blake clearly interprets Isaiah as an inspired poet like himself, and especially admires his 'honest indignation' against traditional Christianity and its image of God, which in his eyes lacked imagination and was 'not capable of a firm perswasion' of anything.

His second question to Isaiah shows what admiration he had for the Book of Isaiah: 'After dinner I ask'd Isaiah to favour the world with his lost works. He said none of equal value was lost.' The third question focusses on a chapter only Blake could have picked on, out of all the riches of the Book of Isaiah. In it, Chapter 20, Isaiah is, again like himself, at odds with the society in which he lives: 'I also asked Isaiah what made him go about naked and barefoot three years? he answer'd: "the same that made our friend Diogenes the Grecian." ' Blake frequently draws on Isaiah's language and imagery, some of it no doubt at second hand, taken from the Book of Revelation. In *Milton*, he makes much of 'Beulah', one of Isaiah's names for Jerusalem (Isaiah 62:4),[28] and the winepress (63:3) where

---

[24] Roston, *Prophet and Poet*, p. 13.   [25] Roston, *Prophet and Poet*, p. 192.
[26] Erdman, *Blake. Prophet against Empire*, p. 177.
[27] Blake, *Complete Writings*, pp. 153f.   [28] *DBTEL*, p. 87.

'human grapes ... howl and writhe in shoals of torment'. In *Jerusalem* the repeated imperatives 'awake, awake ...' must be influenced by Isaiah (51:9; 52:1) too, as is the extended dialogue with the female figure of Jerusalem. It is probable that his short poem *Jerusalem*, which in its setting by Sir Hubert Parry became almost a second national anthem in England, was inspired by some of the great visions of Zion or the New Jerusalem from Isaiah. This applies to the last four lines in particular:

> I will not cease from Mental Fight,
> Nor shall my Sword sleep in my hand,
> Till we have built Jerusalem
> In England's green & pleasant land.[29]

One commentator sees here an allusion to Isaiah 62:1 ('For Zion's sake will I not hold my peace, and for Jerusalem's sake I will not rest, until the righteousness thereof go forth as brightness ...').[30] In its original context within the preface to his epic *Milton*, it is accompanied with a quotation from Numbers 11: 'Would to God that all the Lord's people were Prophets'.[31] He was thinking no doubt of prophets like Isaiah.

A French example from this period handles a familiar mediaeval tradition, the Jesse tree, with beautiful originality. In his poem *Booz endormi*, Victor Hugo (1802–85) recalls the story of how Boaz, grandfather of Jesse, with Ruth the Moabitess lying at his feet (cf. Ruth 3), dreamed a dream. In the dream he saw an oak tree coming out of his belly, reaching up to the sky, and on it a long line of people, with David at one end and Christ at the other:

> Et ce songe était tel, que Booz vit un chêne
> Qui, sorti de son ventre, allait jusqu'au ciel bleu;
> Une race y montait comme une longue chaîne;
> Un roi chantait en bas, en haut mourait un dieu.

Hugo, no doubt familiar with some of the many Jesse windows in France such as the one in Chartres Cathedral, puts the mediaeval Jesse tree motif back into its original context in the story told in the book of Ruth, but he also combines it, as on the Brougham Triptych and the *Speculum* manuscript described in chapter 5, with the theme of Christ's death on the cross.[32]

[29] *Complete Writings*, pp. 480f.   [30] Moffat, *Handbook*, pp. 221–2.
[31] *Complete Writings*, p. 481.
[32] Lucas, ed., *Oxford Book of French Verse*, pp. 355–8. See pp. 74, 94ff.

Current feminist interest in Lilith from Isaiah 34:14 will be discussed in chapter 10. For the present context it is interesting to note her flourishing role in the Romantic period, where she appears in poems by Dante Gabriel Rossetti (1828–82) and Robert Browning (1812–89) as well as Goethe's *Faust* (1832).[33] The allegorical novel *Lilith* (1895) by the Scottish minister and writer of children's books, George MacDonald, has been described as 'the climax of Lilith's career in English'.[34] In it Lilith is represented as a terrifying demonic character who 'was what God could not have created. She had usurped beyond her share in self-creation and her part had undone His'.[35] The story is about how she finally repents (i.e. conforms to the constraints of a male-dominated society) and is forgiven. Lilith's rebirth is described in a passage written perhaps with some of Isaiah's famous wilderness images in mind: 'For in the skirts of the wind had come the rain – the soft rain that heals the mown, the many-wounded grass, soothing it with the sweetness of all music, the hush that lives between music and silence. It bedewed the desert places around the cottage, and the sands of Lilith's heart heard it and drank it in'.[36] It seems probable that MacDonald, a Calvinist minister whose knowledge and love of scripture cannot be doubted, is alluding here to the familiar images of 'the desert blossoming as the rose', 'the burning sand becoming a pool of water' and 'the redeemed shall walk there' in Isaiah 35. Whether he connected these wilderness images with the appearance of Lilith among the desert creatures of the previous chapter, we cannot say. Chapter 34, incidentally, without the figure of Lilith, provided the inspiration for a belligerent composition by the metaphysical poet Abraham Cowley (1618–67) entitled simply *The 34. Chapter of the Prophet Isaiah.*[37]

The story of Sennacherib's invasion of Judah, recounted in 2 Kings 18–19 as well as Isaiah 36–7, left its mark on literature and art. The poet George Wither (1588–1667) wrote a short two-stanza poem inspired by Hezekiah's prayer in 37:16–20;[38] but the story is best known in English literature from Byron's poem *The Destruction of Semnacherib.*[39] It begins with the memorable lines: 'The Assyrian came down like the wolf on the fold,/And his cohorts were gleaming

[33]   Schell, 'Lilith', p. 455.   [34]   Schell, 'Lilith', p. 455.
[35]   MacDonald, *Lilith*, p. 378.   [36]   MacDonald, *Lilith*, p. 379.
[37]   Atwan and Wieder, edd., *Chapters into Verse*, pp. 393–5.
[38]   Atwan and Wieder, edd., *Chapters into Verse*, p. 396.
[39]   McGann, ed., *Complete Poetical Works*, 3, pp. 309–10.

with purple and gold.' It is the story of Jerusalem's miraculous escape, alone of all the cities of Judah, and of the total destruction of the Assyrian army. The prophet Isaiah, summoned to assist the king as he confronted the Assyrian army, had compared Jerusalem to a young woman bravely dismissing a suitor with a toss of her head (36:22), and, in language reminiscent of earlier Zion faith (cf. 2:3; 7:3), had prophesied that 'a band of survivors' would escape from the besieged city (37:32). In the event the focus is not so much on the escape of Jerusalem herself, as on the dramatic end of Sennacherib and his army. The biblical account, in typically economical style, tells of two spectacular scenes of horror. The first is one verse long: 'And the angel of the Lord went forth, and slew a hundred and eighty five thousand in the camp of the Assyrians; and when morning came, they were all corpses' (37:36). The implication is that the whole army died in their sleep without a blow being struck. Byron fills in the details:

> Like the leaves of the forest when autumn has blown,
> That host on the morrow lay withered and strown ...
> And the eyes of the sleepers wax'd deadly and chill,
> And their hearts but once heaved and forever grew still ...
> And there lay the rider, distorted and pale,
> With the dew on his brow and the rust on his mail.
> And the tents were all silent, the banners alone,
> The lances unlifted, the trumpet unblown ...
> And the might of the Gentile, unsmote by the sword,
> Hath melted like snow in the glance of the Lord!

No doubt readers of Byron's poem, which is dated 19 February 1815, used these dramatic images to celebrate the end of Napoleonic power at Waterloo later that year.[40]

There is a very different painting by Rubens (1577–1640) of the subject in the Alte Pinakothek in Munich, painted in about 1616. In his version of the story, very similar to his *Conversion of St Paul* painted at about the same time, the Assyrians are still alive: 'a wild and raging tumult of flight caused by heavenly apparitions, with men, mostly mounted, fighting against an unearthly enemy; even the horses are beside themselves, and over the whole there pour streams of light and night'.[41] Both these paintings were produced before the beginning of the Thirty Years' War (1618–1648), and in striking

---

[40] McGann, ed., *Complete Poetical Works*, 3, p. 472.
[41] Burckhardt, *Recollections*, p. 84.

contrast to Rubens' later and better-known comment on the horrors of war, *The Allegory of War* in the Pitti Palace in Florence, which dates from 1638.[42]

A phrase from Isaiah 28:15–18 may have suggested an image used by one of the First World War poets. It was used earlier in a 'Resolution adopted by the Massachusetts Anti-Slavery Society on 27 June 1843', where it is attributed to the abolitionist William Lloyd Garrison (1805–79).[43] Isaiah speaks of a 'covenant with death ... an agreement with hell' by which God's enemies, by their lies and falsehood, were 'in league with death' and thought they could escape (28:15,18). Wilfred Owen (1893–1918), applies the image to his own and other soldiers' vain efforts to come to terms with their tragic fate:

> Out there, we've walked quite friendly up to Death;
> Sat down and eaten with him, cool and bland ...
> We whistled while he shaved us with his scythe.
> Oh, Death was never enemy of ours!
> We laughed at him, we leagued with him, old chum
>
> (*The Next War*, lines 1–2, 8–10).[44]

These words of Owen then inspired a poignant moment in Benjamin Britten's *War Requiem* (1962), where they are sung by the two male soloists, laughingly (*allegro e giocoso*), at the heart of his setting of the *Dies Irae*.[45]

Another war poet, Siegfried Sassoon (1886–1967), may have been influenced by some of Isaiah's imagery in his powerful *Babylon*:

> Babylon the merciless, now a name of doom,
> Built towers in Time, as we today, for whom
> Auguries of self-annihilation loom.[46]

The language and imagery of Tennyson's *Babylon* from a hundred years earlier, beginning 'Bow, daughter of Babylon, bow thee to dust!' (cf. Isa.47:1), are almost entirely drawn from Isaiah.[47] In addition to the ironic lament in chapter 47, which was the poet's main inspiration, there are allusions to the winepress (63:1–3), the

---

[42] Burckhardt, *Recollections*, p. 113.
[43] *ODQ*, p. 213.
[44] Lewis, ed., *Collected Poems*, p. 86.
[45] Benjamin Britten, *War Requiem*, op.66, vocal score (Boosey and Hawkes, London, 1962), pp. 37–44.
[46] *Collected Poems*, p. 223; cf. Atwan and Wieder, *Chapters into Verse*, pp. 391–2.
[47] Ricks, *Poems of Tennyson*, vol. 1, pp. 155–7.

victories of Cyrus (45:1–3) and, in the concluding verse, to the scenes of desolation in the wilderness: 'In their desolate houses the dragons shall lie/And the satyrs shall dance and the bitterns shall cry' (cf. 34:14).

A poem by the young American writer Hart Crane (1899–1932) contains an interesting allusion to Isaiah: 'Rush down the plenitude, and you shall see/Isaiah counting famine on this lea'.[48] For Crane, thinking particularly perhaps of Isaiah 5, Isaiah was a prophet of judgement on a sick society's preoccupation with wealth and material comforts. The verse occurs in a prayer placed on the lips of Christopher Columbus, in which he warns King Ferdinand, one of his two sponsors, against seeing the search for the New World as primarily motivated by the desire for wealth.[49] More recently the verse is cited, somewhat cryptically, as an epigraph at the beginning of *The Night Sky of the Lord*, a critique of post-holocaust Christianity by the Anglican priest Alan Ecclestone.[50]

Two more recent American examples are included in Atwan and Wieder's anthology referred to above. Robert Harris gave the title *Isaiah by Kerosene Lantern Light* to a poem criticizing contemporary society in words inspired by one of the prophet's notorious attacks on obduracy and hypocrisy (29:11–14),[51] and the Jewish poet David Rosenberg, translator of Psalms and Job, renders the first two verses of Isaiah 66 ('What is the house you would build for me ... ?') with characteristic terseness and political bite.[52]

We shall look next at two beautiful examples of the use of less familiar passages. The first is to be found in the title chosen by the novelist H. V. M. Prescott for a book she was planning to write shortly before her death in 1972.[53] According to her friends it was to end in joy through tragedy and was to be entitled *The Evening Doves*, brilliantly derived from Isaiah 59:9–15: 'Therefore justice is far from us ... We look for light and behold darkness, and for brightness but we walk in gloom ... We stumble at noon as in the twilight, among those in full vigour we are like dead men. We all growl like bears, we moan and moan like doves ... we look for justice but there is none,

---

48 *Complete Poems*, p. 66.
49 Cf. Lewis, *The Poetry of Hart Crane*, p. 263.
50 See p. 221.
51 Atwan and Wieder, edd., *Chapters into Verse*, pp. 392–3.
52 Atwan and Wieder, edd., *Chapters into Verse*, pp. 407–8.
53 M. B. Fergusson in *Doves & Dons. A History of St Mary's College, Durham*, ed. M. Hird (Durham 1982).

for salvation, but it is far from us'. She no doubt also had the subsequent verses in mind about the Lord's saving intervention (59:16–21), and the familiar imperatives of chapter 60 beginning: 'Arise, shine, for your light is come, and the glory of the Lord is risen upon you'.

The other example is a verse from the somewhat obscure context of an oracle against Moab in Isaiah 15, which nonetheless provided the distinguished Argentinian novelist Eduardo Mallea (born 1903) with the title for his deeply pessimistic study of a woman's isolation, her vain search for happiness and her ultimate despair, *Todo Verdor Perecerá*, published in 1941. It comes from Isaiah 15:6 which is printed in full, along with Ecclesiastes 9:12, as an epigraph at the beginning of the novel: *Las aguas de Nimrim seran consumidas, y secaráse la hierba, marchitaranse los retoños, todo verdor perecerá.* The allusion to the much more familiar words of 40:8 ('the grass withers, the flower fades . . .') is unmistakable, but in the Moab passage used by Mallea, there is no trace of the second half of the verse ('but the word of the Lord will stand for ever'), which, as we have seen, was used to triumphant effect by the German Reformers, and by Brahms in his *German Requiem*.

Finally, if we include personal names derived from Isaiah, his influence, albeit indirect, reaches still further afield. Like most biblical names, *Isaiah* itself appears among seventeenth-century Puritan personal names. It was revived to some extent in the nineteenth century, but is now very rare.[54] *Ariel* from Isaiah 29 appears as an airy spirit in Shakespeare's *The Tempest*, a rebel angel in Milton's *Paradise Lost* (6.371) and chief of the sylphs in Pope's *The Rape of the Lock* (2.53ff.). Twentieth-century poets identify 'Ariel' with poetic imagination: T. S. Eliot called five Christmas poems (1927–54) his 'Ariel poems',[55] and it is the title of the best-known collection of Sylvia Plath's poems, published posthumously in 1965.[56] The first Penguin paperback was André Maurois' *Ariel* (1935), a life of Shelley. Ariel is one of the five major moons of the planet Uranus, discovered in 1851 by the English amateur astronomer William Lassell, while more recently it has become a household word as the name of a well-known brand of washing powder. *Immanuel* (7:14) was a relatively common Christian first name in the eighteenth and nineteenth

---

54 Dunkling and Gosling, edd., *Everyman's Dictionary of First Names*, p. 129.
55 T. S. Eliot, *Collected Poems*, pp. 107–18.
56 Sylvia Plath, *Ariel* (Faber, London 1965).

centuries, but is very rare in modern times. The abbreviated form
Manuel, derived from the Spanish, is known in the English-speaking
world as the name of the comic waiter in the BBC television series
Fawlty Towers, and the French feminine form *Emmanuelle* as the
eponymous heroine of a series of erotic novels.[57] *Mahershalalhashbaz*
(8:1–4) and *Lilith* (34:14) have been mentioned already.[58]

Beulah (Isaiah 62:4) as a personal name is perhaps best known from
Mae West's immortal words 'Beulah, peel me a grape!' in the film
I'm No Angel (1933). But there are also some well-known references to
Beulah as a place-name in John Bunyan, William Blake and Robert
Louis Stevenson. In Bunyan's *Pilgrim's Progress* it is the land that 'lies
beyond the Valley of the Shadow of Death and also out of the reach
of Giant Despair'. For Stevenson it is 'upon the borders of heaven
and within sight of the City of Love'.[59] It was no doubt from such
visions of a better world that the Beulah Roads and Beulah Avenues
in many of our cities got their name. *Hephzibah*, from the same
passage (62:4), has never been a popular name in English, although
one celebrated example is little Eppie in George Eliot's *Silas Marner*
(1861), so-called because Hephzibah was too difficult to pronounce.[60]
The most famous modern example of the name is the distinguished
American pianist Hephzibah Menuhin (1920–1981).

This brings us to the second part of this chapter, a brief survey of
Isaiah in music. We shall for the most part avoid strictly liturgical
music, like the *Sanctus*, the *Rorate* and other hymns, which are referred
to frequently in other chapters, although, as we said at the beginning,
this division of the data is by no means a watertight one. Apart from
a brief but very informative paragraph on 'Isaiah in music' in the
Encyclopedia Judaica,[61] no-one has charted these waters in detail
before. It would obviously be impracticable to survey the whole
corpus of western classical music down to the present, and we have
therefore been, as always, judiciously arbitrary and selective. We
begin with an extended discussion of the most obvious example, and
one which illustrates more than any other composition just how
western audiences and performers, especially English-speaking ones,
have made Isaiah their own.

---

[57]   Campbell, ed., *Bloomsbury Dictionary of First Names*, p. 85.
[58]   See pp. 146, 165
[59]   *DBTEL*, p. 87.
[60]   Dunkling and Gosling, edd., *Everyman's Dictionary of First Names*, p. 120.
[61]   *EJ*, Vol. 9, cols. 69–70.

The first two parts of Handel's *Messiah* are made up almost entirely of direct quotations from Isaiah, in the King James version, brilliantly woven together with other passages of scripture. The words and music are so familiar that their originality and effectiveness are often missed. The story of its composition is a familiar one. In the summer of 1741 Handel was demoralized and thinking of leaving England for good. His last two operas had been dismal failures; he was ill and in debt. At that moment two felicitous things happened: the Duke of Devonshire, Lord Lieutenant of Ireland, invited him to make a visit to Ireland; and the flamboyant and gifted librettist Charles Jennens sent him a libretto entitled *Messiah*. In about three weeks between 22 August and 14 September, Handel composed the world's best-loved oratorio, and next April it was performed in the Music Hall, Fishamble Street, Dublin. It was a spectacular success.

The libretto is certainly brilliant. Charles Jennens was inordinately proud of it, and very critical of Handel's music. He wrote to a friend: 'His Messiah has disappointed me, being set in great haste, tho' he said he would be a year about it. I shall put no more sacred work into his hands.' Later he wrote to the same friend: 'He has made a noble entertainment of it tho' not so good as he might or ought to have done ...' The libretto is actually based on the Anglican Prayer Book, rather than scripture itself, so that the remarkable selection of passages is not quite so original as Jennens claimed. But the three-fold structure is original and impressive: Part I. The coming of the Messiah (mostly Isaiah and Luke), Part II. The suffering, death and resurrection of Christ (including Isaiah 52–3), and Part III. A hymn of thanksgiving incorporating passages from Job, Romans and Revelation, which are familiar as readings prescribed to be read at the Burial Service. I would like to make three observations on this musical interpretation of Isaiah.

First the progression from despair to hope, captivity to freedom, death to life, which is an integral part of Isaianic tradition, cannot be entirely divorced from Handel's own personal circumstances in August 1741. This becomes clear from the overture, which (in spite of Jennens' comments) was in some ways perhaps the most original part of the music. Overtures hitherto were by convention intended to do little more than attract the audience's attention and give them time to settle in their seats. They usually had no thematic connection with what followed. But the overture to Handel's *Messiah* emphatically breaks with this tradition. It has been described as representing 'a mood without hope', first in a slow sighing, mournful elegy, then in an allegro passage which expresses 'the violent, fruitless upward striving of the oppressed'. It is hard to imagine a more perfect, more appropriate context for the opening words of Isaiah 40: 'Comfort ye, comfort ye my people, saith your God ...' Whatever the librettist claimed, it seems that from the very start there is more Handel here than Jennens.

There is a story that, as he was composing the *Messiah*, Handel thought that, like Isaiah, he saw 'the great God himself upon his throne'.[62] Whether or not we believe that he had some mystical experience during those three extraordinary weeks, what is certainly true is that he personally believed in the truth of the words of the libretto, and passionately wanted to communicate them to the people.[63] The first words are 'addressed with real immediacy to the lady in the box and the boy in the gallery: "Comfort ye" '.[64] It is said that he chose the tragic actress and contralto Susanna Maria Cibber to sing five of the most important recitatives and arias at the first performance in Dublin, because of her 'intelligence of the words', her 'native feeling' and her 'powers of expression'. These are all Isaianic: 'Behold a Virgin shall conceive' (7:14), 'O thou that tellest good tidings' (40:9), 'Then shall the eyes of the blind be opened' (35:5, 6), 'And he shall feed his flock' (40:11) and 'He was despised and rejected' (53:3).[65] If we add to these the recitative in part III containing the words 'Death is swallowed up in victory' (Isaiah 25:8, as cited by Paul in 1 Cor.15:5), then all the words given by Handel to Mrs Cibber to sing, set to several of the best tunes, are from Isaiah. Incidentally it is recounted that she sang 'He was despised' so well that the Rev. Dr Delaney was moved to shout 'Woman, for this thy sins be forgiven thee!'.[66]

But there is another very significant factor in Handel's use of these words. As the theologian and musicologist Hamish Swanston points out, both Handel and Jennens, his librettist, were involved in the eighteenth-century controversy over the meaning of biblical prophecy. In this, as in so many other theological contexts, the 'Fifth

[62]   Swanston, *Handel*, p. 97.
[63]   Swanston, *Handel*, p. 96.
[64]   Swanston *Handel*, p. 96.
[65]   Swanston *Handel*, pp. 94–5.
[66]   Robbins, *Handel and his World*, pp. 187f.

Gospel' had a crucial role to play: can the christological interpretation of such passages as Isaiah 7:14 and 53:3–6 be sustained in the
face of the new challenge from the deists? Many writers now
ridiculed those traditionalists who thought they could 'find the New
Testament in the Old'.[67] Jennens' choice of passages for the *Messiah*
has thus to be seen as a contribution to orthodox apologetic. Handel,
who was himself totally convinced of the truth of traditional Christian interpretations of scripture – and not only the prophetic books,
as his *Samson* (1743), *Belshazzar* (1745), *Susanna* (1749) prove – did what
he could to confirm and communicate this in his music.

A third observation I would like to make concerns Handel's
sympathy with and support for the poor. The first performance of
Messiah in Dublin was in aid of charity, and an important subsequent
performance took place in the Foundlings' Hospital chapel in
London in 1750. As a piece of sacred music, it did not go down well
in Covent Garden when it was first performed. It was in churches
and chapels that it was to become a favourite. What I want to
suggest is that one reason for the extraordinary success of Handel's
setting of the Book of Isaiah is the compassion that is common to
both. The tender opening words as we saw are addressed to a
situation of despair and gloom. We could add the lovely arrangement
for alto solo of 40:11: 'He shall feed his flock like a shepherd . . .', and
notice how this is coupled with 35:5–6: 'then shall the eyes of the
blind be opened . . .' Part II poignantly introduces an interpretation
of Chapter 53 with the chorus 'Behold the Lamb of God that taketh
away the sins of the world . . . Surely he hath borne our griefs and
carried our sorrows . . .'. The Gospel of peace comes, in the words of
the soprano aria, from Isaiah 52:7: 'How beautiful are the feet of
them that preach the Gospel of peace' (plural no doubt in reference
to the evangelical preachers of Jennens' time).[68] It may be hundreds
of years and several languages removed from the original Hebrew,
but Handel's *Messiah* faithfully conveys much of the original message
of the Fifth Gospel, I would suggest, and translates it into the idiom
of his own day. It may have been a happy chance that brought Isaiah
and Handel together, but the match was perfect.

A much less well-known eighteenth-century oratorio on *Le profezie
evangeliche d'Isaia* (1729) was composed by Handel's Venetian contemporary, Antonio Caldara (1670–1736). Two great nineteenth-century

---

[67] Swanston *Handel*, p. 93.
[68] See above, p. 137.

religious works, one by Mendelssohn (1809–47) and one by Brahms (1833–1897), contain impressive settings of Isaiah. Mendelssohn's choice of texts for the last arias and choruses of his oratorio *Elijah* (1846), his last major work before he died, is extremely interesting. Apparently influenced by a collection of twenty-three sermons, entitled *Elijah the Tishbite*, by the celebrated Lutheran preacher Friedrich Wilhelm Kruhmacher (1796–1868), Mendelssohn, like Handel, clearly uses the Isaiah texts to express his own faith, and in particular his Christian interpretation of the Elijah story.[69] In one of the two final choruses, he applies three well-known and powerful messianic texts to Elijah as a type of Christ (Isaiah 41:25; 42:1; 11:2). The familiar eucharistic passage beginning 'Ho everyone that thirsteth' from Isaiah 55 is used to similar effect in the quartet that leads into the final chorus, which in turn contains a triumphant verse from chapter 58: 'Then shall your light break forth like the dawn ...'

Brahms' strikingly original *Ein Deutsches Requiem* (1857–68) contains settings of four texts from Isaiah, in Luther's German. The first is the setting of the words of Isaiah 40:6–8 (as cited by 1 Peter 1:24–5) in the second chorus (*Denn alles Fleisch es ist wie Gras* ... 'For all flesh is like grass ...'). By leaving out the sopranos and writing the alto and bass lines at the bottom of their registers, the chorus starts in a uniquely sombre, sepulchral tone, representing human transitoriness at its most tragic and sunless. The passage is repeated twice with James 5:7 (*So seid nun geduldig* ... 'Be patient therefore ...') inserted between. The mood of gloom is then shattered by the triumphant statement of faith so dear to Martin Luther:[70] *Aber des Herrn Wort bleibet in Ewigkeit* ('But the word of the Lord ...'), sung by all four parts. This is then immediately followed by a fugue on a second Isaiah passage, familiar to Christians both from its occurrence in an Advent reading, and from funeral liturgies (35:10; cf. 51:11): it ends with the words ... *und Schmerz und Seufzen wird weg müssen* (' ... and sorrow and sighing shall flee away'). The third text from Isaiah introduced by Brahms into his *Requiem* is one of the few biblical passages in which God is compared to a mother (66:13), and exquisitely appropriate in this context. Addressed to the bereaved, it provides a soothing choral refrain to the soprano solo 'Ye who now sorrow': (*Ihr habt nun Traurigkeit/aber ich will euch wiedersehen*). This verse constitutes, along with 60:19 and 25:8, the concluding

---

[69] Cf. Staehelm, 'Elijah, J. S. Bach and the New Covenant', p. 132.
[70] See pp. 129ff.

paragraph of the Jewish 'Prayer in the house of mourning'.[71] The imagery of Isaiah 25:8, one of Martin Luther's epitaphs[72] ('He will swallow up death for ever …'), comes, by way of 1 Corinthians 15, into Brahms' jubilant chorus on the resurrection of the dead.

Among twentieth-century works based on extended passages of Isaiah, there are several by Jewish composers, including oratorios by Jacob Weinberg (1947) and Alexandre Tansman (1951) and the American Robert Starer's *Ariel. Visions of Isaiah* (1959).[73] There are also works by the English composer Granville Bantock (1868–1946) and the Swiss Willy Burkhard (1900–55), as well as a cantata by Martinu (1890–1959), entitled *The Prophecy of Isaiah*, which was premiered in Jerusalem in 1963. Two 'Motets in Diem Pacis', composed soon after the Second World War by the English composer Wilfrid Mellers (1914–), bear the name of Isaiah at the top, and are settings of a selection of passages from Isaiah in King James' version, for mixed chorus and brass.[74] The apocalyptic words of the first, entitled *The City of Desolation*, come from Isaiah 24:4–14 ('the earth mourneth and fadeth away …'), part of the so-called 'Isaiah apocalypse' (24–27). For the second, *The City not Forsaken*, the composer has selected verses from chapters 61 and 62, beginning with the messianic words 'The spirit of the Lord God is upon me …' and ending with one of the names to be given to the new Jerusalem: 'Thou shalt be called a city not forsaken' (62:4). Composed in September 1945, the words were wonderfully appropriate.

Modern settings of the *Rorate* by John Joubert and Thea Musgrave were mentioned above. One final example of Isaiah's influence on twentieth-century music brings us into the nineties. It is the concerto for percussion and orchestra entitled *Veni, Veni, Emmanuel*, by James MacMillan, a Scottish Catholic, which received its first, and much acclaimed performance at a Promenade Concert, with fellow Scot Evelyn Glennie as soloist, in the Royal Albert Hall, London in August 1992. The composer explains that it was started on the first Sunday in Advent 1991 and completed on Easter Sunday 1992: 'On one level the work is purely abstract in that all the musical material is drawn from the fifteenth-century French Advent plainchant. On another level it is a musical exploration of the theology behind the

[71] Singer, *Authorised Daily Prayer Book*, p. 324.
[72] See chapter 7.
[73] Cf. *EJ* 9, cols.69–70; see also above, p. 104.
[74] Oxford University Press, 1948.

Advent message'.[75] There is no need to mention again Isaiah's central role, from the earliest times, in shaping and inspiring the Advent liturgy.[76]

The highly successful musical *Jesus Christ Superstar* (1976) by Tim Rice and Andrew Lloyd Webber contains a setting of 'Prepare ye the way of the Lord' (Isaiah 40:3 *AV*) which has found its way into the liturgy in some churches as a Gospel acclamation. But we end with a quick reference to another twentieth-century musician, sometimes known as 'Isaiah with a guitar'. Bob Dylan's use of biblical references has been studied in detail elsewhere.[77] *John Wesley Harding* (1967), which Dylan himself described as 'the first biblical rock album', contains over sixty biblical allusions.[78] One of the lyrics in *John Wesley Harding*, 'All along the Watchtower', draws heavily on the account of the fall of Babylon in Isaiah 13–14. In another album, *Infidels*, published sixteen years later (1983), 'there is no song without direct allusion to the Bible'.[79] At an interview published in 1983 Dylan himself talked about his relationship to the biblical prophets: 'Check on Elijah the prophet. He could make rain. Isaiah the prophet, even Jeremiah, see if their brethren didn't want to bust their brains for telling it right like it is, yeah – these are my roots I suppose'.[80]

---

[75] Notes by the composer on the sleeve of the recording (*Catalyst* 09026 61916–4) BMG Music 1993.
[76] See pp. 56f.
[77] Bert Cartwright, *The Bible in the Lyrics of Bob Dylan* (Wanted Man Study Series, 1985).
[78] Clinton Heylin, *Dylan: Behind the Shades* (Penguin 1991), p. 185.
[79] Cf. Heylin, *Dylan: Behind the Shades*, p. 369, citing Cartwright.
[80] Heylin, *Dylan: Behind the Shades*, p. 370.

CHAPTER 10

The Quest for the Historical Isaiah

While the vocabulary and phraseology of Isaiah was spreading to the four corners of the earth, on the lips of ordinary Christian men and women, new historical critical methods were utterly transforming scholars' understanding of the Bible.[1] As the missionary Church of the eighteenth and nineteenth centuries preached and sang about a Saviour who, in Isaiah's words, would 'sprinkle many nations' (52:15),[2] scholars were proving that the Hebrew word does not mean 'sprinkle', the phrase does not refer to Christ, and, naturally, the passage as a whole was not written by Isaiah. Many of the fruits of this new scholarly activity, which was carried out by scholars motivated as much by the secular pursuit of learning as the enrichment of Christian belief or practice, did not at first reach the majority of people that make up the Church, and indeed will in all probability never reach them. But some certainly have had an influence on Christian tradition, especially through modern translations of the Bible and revised editions of prayerbooks and missals, and in any case must be considered an important stage in the history of Isaiah in Christianity.

The Book of Isaiah has been from the start a popular example of the new historical critical approach to the Bible. There seem to be two reasons for this. The first is the same as the reason why he is so prominent in other stages in the history of Christianity: even in the age of historical criticism he remained the 'Fifth Gospel' in all but name. Most of the new scholars working on the biblical texts were Christians or at any rate working within the Christian tradition, even those who were radical critics of it. This is surely one reason why so many of the pioneers of modern biblical scholarship, such as the Dutch Calvinist Campegius Vitringa (c.1659–1722), the Anglican

---

[1]   Cf. Rogerson, Rowland and Lindars, *The Study and Use of the Bible*, Vol. 2, pp. 109–38.
[2]   See above, pp. 156f.

bishop Robert Lowth (1710–87), the German orientalist and lexico-
grapher Gesenius (1786–1842), and Bernhard Duhm (1847–1928),
published outstanding single works on Isaiah. It is also no doubt why
passages like 7:14 and chapter 53 have remained so prominent on the
agenda of biblical scholars, even in the new rational, historical
context in which they work. A glance at any 'Introduction to the Old
Testament' will show this to be the case: a footnote in Eissfeldt's
much-used introduction, for example, refers to no less than fifty
articles on 7:14 published since 1940, and almost as many on the
'Suffering Servant' in chapter 53.

The other reason why Isaiah plays so important a role in general
discussions of historical criticism, is that the new methods, as it
happened, raised some rather obvious questions about traditional
views on the book's authorship and composition, issues almost as
much discussed in the case of the Book of Isaiah as the Mosaic
authorship of the Pentateuch. From mediaeval times it had been
noted that there was an abrupt break, in both style and content,
between chapters 39 and 40. Then in the eighteenth century the
German scholar J. C. Döderlein, in notes on his translation of Isaiah
(1775), worked out some of the details of the theory that chapters 40–
55 may have been written in sixth-century Babylon, and therefore
were not by the eighth-century prophet Isaiah at all. Later commentators developed this hypothesis, which in outline is far simpler and
easier to prove than most of the complex pentateuchal hypotheses,
and the existence of at least a 'Second Isaiah', if not several other
contributors to the book as we have it, is now one of the most widely-
known and generally accepted results of historical criticism: as James
Barr describes it, a 'test-case for the historical critical method'.[3]

It also happens, as we shall see, that comparative philology, a
major part of the new scientific approach to the Bible, proposed
some completely different translations from the traditional ones in
the case of some of the Church's best-loved and most widely-used
texts. Precisely because Isaiah had been so thoroughly Christianized
down the centuries, the new concern to get back to what the original
Hebrew meant, alongside the historical and archaeological quest for
what was actually going on in ancient Israel and who said what, was
especially challenging in the case of Isaiah.

We are concerned here not so much with new theories and

---

[3]   Barr, *Fundamentalism*, p. 304.

discoveries *per se*, but rather with their effect on the development of Christianity. Isaiah, like the Pentateuch and the book of Joshua, was a favourite playground for the modern critical scholars, and, as was pointed out earlier, much of their work remained within the four walls of academia and has had virtually no effect at all on the rest of the world. A text which Augustine frequently cited to give scriptural backing to his belief in the supremacy of faith over reason (7:9),[4] for example, is now used by scholars in a debate about root-meanings in Hebrew.[5] A text used by Christian apologists to prove the divinity of Christ, read in the Christmas liturgy and at masses of the Blessed Virgin Mary, and immortalized in Handel's *Messiah*, is now cited in discussions of the influence of Egyptian royal protocol upon ancient Israelite coronation customs.[6] Chapter 53 is a treasure-house of fascinating philological and textual riddles, rather than a unique account of Christ's passion.[7]

Others presented a challenge to traditional Christianity which had to be faced, and in this chapter we must bear in mind two aspects of this challenge, one negative and the other positive. The negative aspect is this. As a result of the application of new insights from comparative philology, textual and literary criticism, archaeology, the social sciences and the like, texts familiar to generations of Christians were given new meanings and interpretations, many of which bore little or no relation to traditional Christian interpretations. The Church authorities had to decide whether to accept these into their official translations, at the expense of ancient and much-respected tradition, or find some way of avoiding the dilemma. We shall see some interesting examples of how this can be done with varying degrees of success.

On the other hand, these new developments in biblical scholarship, especially the new interest, nourished by the excitement of archaeological discoveries, in what was actually going on in the ancient near east, shed new light on other familiar texts, without affecting the traditional interpretation, and focussed on a new set of texts, many of them scarcely commented on by earlier scholars and preachers. These not only provided a degree of historical realism

---

[4]   See above, pp. 55f.
[5]   Barr, 'Did Isaiah know about 'root-meanings'?'; Sawyer, 'Root-meanings in Hebrew'.
[6]   Cf. Kaiser, *Isaiah 1–12* (first edition, 1972), pp. 128f. Kaiser takes a different view in the second edition (SCM 1983), pp. 1–10.
[7]   See above, chapter 5.

much valued in some branches of the Church: as we shall see, they also brought into Christian Bible study a breath of fresh air which can still be felt today.

Before turning to our main subject, however, there is another reaction to the new historical criticism which must be mentioned, as it affected Isaiah. It was natural that some scholars, spurred on by the excitement of archaeological discoveries from Egypt, Palestine, Iraq and elsewhere, argued that the 'Old Testament', as the product of an ancient Hebrew religion which had now been totally super-seded by Christianity, could no longer be considered fit for use in the Church.[8] It is hard to imagine Christianity without Isaiah, and it must be said that the main thrust of such attacks was not directed at him. More often it was against the 'murderous mentality reflected in the Book of Joshua', for example, or the bloody rituals of animal sacrifice, or the deception of attributing to Moses works known to have been written hundreds of years later'. But Isaiah, along with the other prophets and Psalms, did not escape unscathed from this brand of Christian polemic, as we can see from the following example of an early twentieth-century Assyriologist's radical critique of the 'Old Testament'.[9]

According to Friedrich Delitzsch (1850–1922), the many well-known passages in Isaiah about the love and compassion of God are addressed only to his own people, not to other nations who are often instead the object of savage invective and derision. The universalism in texts much used by the Church to authorize their mission to the gentiles is illusory. He argues, for example, on the basis of passages like Nehemiah 9:2, that Isaiah 56:7 ('My house shall be a house of prayer for all peoples') cannot be taken at face value, or at least presupposes that anyone joining in Jewish worship must accept circumcision and become a Jew. He similarly undermines the tradi-tional Christian interpretation of the famous 'Zion' passage in Isaiah 2:2–4, by pointing out that in the Micah version (4:1–5) it is followed by a verse emphatically dissociating the Jews from the rest of the peoples of the world.[10] It is worth recalling that in another context, not unrelated to the present one, Augustine used a similar method to undermine the Jewish interpretation of this key passage.[11] Delitzsch

---

[8]   Kraeling, *The Old Testament since the Reformation*, pp. 147–63.
[9]   F. Delitzsch, *Die große Täuschung*, 2 vols. 1920–21.
[10] Delitzsch, II, pp. 18f.
[11] See pp. 112f.

had little trouble also in showing how prophecies about the fall of Babylon (e.g. Isa.13–14; 46:1f; 47:9,11) and the return of the exiles to Jerusalem (e.g. 51:11; 52:7–12), like many other prophecies, were proved to have been false.

This kind of attack, stressing discontinuity between the Hebrew Bible and the Gospels, and implying the superiority of Christianity over Judaism which it superseded, has had its supporters from the time of Marcion to the present day, where frequently the term 'Old Testament' itself still carries these damaging overtones.[12] We have devoted some time already to the subject of Christian antisemitism in general, and to antisemitic uses of Isaiah in particular. But our concern here is rather with another aspect of Delitzsch's tirade, namely, his conclusion that the study of the Old Testament as part of Christian theology should be abolished. It should instead be handed over to the secular field of oriental studies and the history of religions. This actually happened in many institutions, where 'Departments of Old Testament Studies', within the wider field of Theology or Divinity, have produced competent semitic linguists, textual critics, ancient near eastern archaeologists, historians, Assyriologists and the like, some of whom had little or no interest in Christian tradition. A similar situation, at a lower academic level, existed in schools as well, where syllabuses focussed to such an extent on the fascinating historical and archaeological material that in some cases students knew more about the Amarna Letters, the Ras Shamra texts and the Dead Sea Scrolls than about the content of the biblical texts themselves.

Of course many devout Christian scholars reacted against these developments. Many preachers, hymn-writers and congregations, although often aware of the new discoveries and excited by them, for the most part continued to understand Isaiah in traditional ways. But the new methodology had a profound effect on the interpretation of Isaiah. We shall look first at examples of how the insights of new historical, linguistic, textual, literary and anthropological methodologies affected one of the most familiar 'Christianized' texts, at times interpreting it in ways that threatened to remove it completely from its well-established position within the liturgy and theology of the Church, at times adding valuable new dimensions to its relevance to Christian beliefs. Then, second, we shall examine examples of how

[12]   See pp. 5f.

archaeological discoveries led to a new interest in the original historical context of Isaiah and focussed on some less familiar parts of the book. This second part of the process raised few problems for traditional Christianity, but rather provided Christians with new material which they could incorporate into their religious beliefs and practices without causing any conflict with tradition.

At a meeting of the British Society for Old Testament Study in the early 1950s, the Chairman quoted part of Isaiah 53:1 ('Who hath believed our report?') to express his incredulity (and presumably that of the audience) at the ingenuity and originality of a lecture just delivered by the distinguished Cambridge philologist D.Winton Thomas, on the last and most familiar of the four Servant Songs (Isaiah 52:13–53:12). His use of these words also provides us with a way into our discussion of new interpretations of familiar texts. It is perhaps particularly applicable to those based on comparative philology, since they were, and often remain, among the most idiosyncratic and controversial. The Old Testament part of the widely used *New English Bible*, for example, first published in 1970 under the chairmanship of another Semitic philologist, the late Sir Godfrey Rolles Driver, contained many radically new philological proposals which remain controversial, and were omitted from the *Revised English Bible* (1990). It is not always easy to decide whether precedence over continuity with tradition should be given to new meanings for Hebrew words, based on the evidence of Arabic or Akkadian or Ugaritic or another Semitic language. Often such meanings are quite unknown to any of the ancient translators and commentators, Christian and Jewish, as far back as we can trace them. The variety in modern translations of the Bible bears this out, as does the seemingly arbitrary way in which some modern suggestions find their way into the official lectionaries, while others do not.

Isaiah has been a popular playground for the linguists and the literary and textual critics of the last two centuries or so. In this, for reasons discussed above, chapter 53 has undoubtedly had pride of place. Let us look first at some examples of the effect of comparative philology on modern interpretations of the chapter. The philological argument runs as follows: Hebrew is a Semitic language like Aramaic, Ugaritic, Arabic, Babylonian, Assyrian and Ethiopic, that is to say, descended from a theoretically reconstructable 'Proto-Semitic'. It should therefore be possible to use the evidence of one of these languages to explain phenomena in another. It so happens that because of the structure of Semitic words it is easier to identify 'roots' throughout the whole language group, than it is in the case of most of the European languages, and from mediaeval times Hebraists have made much use of this branch of comparative linguistics.[13] Its effect on biblical scholarship, especially when the nineteenth-century archaeologists unearthed thousands of tablets in ancient Semitic languages hitherto unknown, has been profound. Countless new meanings for Hebrew words, based on related Arabic, Akkadian, Ethiopic and the other Semitic languages, have been proposed, many of them highly controversial, and many of them representing a complete break with tradition.

Enthusiasm frequently got the better of scholars faced with the new material. Almost as many false etymologies were proposed as correct ones, and more often than not conclusions are no more than probabilities. Let us look at four examples from one of the best-known parts of Isaiah, the 'Suffering Servant' poem in 52:13–53:12. First, an example making use of Akkadian. In the context of early theological discourse and anti-Jewish polemic, we came across the rhetorical question 'Who shall declare his generation?' (53:8 *AV*), where 'generation' (Latin *generatio*) referred to the process of Christ's miraculous birth. The Hebrew word *dor*, however, is not an action word and cannot denote a process of any kind: it means 'generation' in the sense of 'life-time, period of time, age' as in the phrase 'the generations of long ago' (51:9). This meaning is not impossible in 53:8, but has been rejected by many modern scholars, on the basis of a tempting, though unproven, philological argument. The word *dor* in this context, it is argued, is not the normal Hebrew word (*dor* I) but a rare loanword (*dor* II) from Assyrian (another Semitic language) meaning 'fate': thus 'Who gave a thought to his fate?' (*REB*) or 'Who could have imagined his future?' (*NRSV*). Why no-one knew this until the cuneiform tablets of ancient Iraq were deciphered in modern times, is not explained.

Next, comparative philologists have used Arabic to discover two entirely new meanings in this passage, one of them claiming indirect support from the ancient Greek version, the other, like *dor* II, without any trace before modern times. We noted above a missionary hymn beginning 'Saviour, sprinkle many nations' from 52:15. Again the verb translated 'sprinkle' here is well enough known from the priestly

---

[13]   Cf.Blau, 'Grammarians, Hebrew', *ELL* 3, pp. 1474–6.

legislation in Leviticus where it refers to ritual sprinkling with blood or water (Lev.8:11,30; cf. Isaiah 63:3). It is at any rate not correct to state that 'the meaning of the Hebrew word is uncertain' (*RSV*, *NRSV*): strained or far-fetched or difficult maybe, but not uncertain. The Arabic solution depends on a verb meaning 'to jump' (unknown elsewhere in Hebrew), and hence 'he will make them jump (i.e. startle them)'. *REB* has 'so now many nations will recoil at the sight of him' – which is similar to what the ancient Greek version has (*thaumasontai*). It would have been more scholarly to leave the Hebrew meaning in the main text and add the Greek version in the margin, as was done in the case of 7:14.

The third example from this passage involves unearthing an entirely new meaning, once again by means of Arabic, for a common Hebrew word, more frequent even than *dor*, and disposing of one more familiar piece of biblical language in the process. The phrase is 'a man of sorrows and acquainted with grief' in 53:3. Leaving aside the change from 'sorrows' and grief' to the more probable, and more graphic 'pains' and 'disease' which is reflected in many modern versions, it is the word translated 'acquainted' that concerns us here. It comes from the ordinary everyday Hebrew word for 'to know' (*yada'*) and in this context implies, perhaps a little unexpectedly, that 'grief' is personified: the man is, as it were, 'known by Grief, familiar to Grief, one of Grief's companions or acquaintances'. The traditional English translation, 'acquainted with grief' (*AV*), familiar from Handel's *Messiah*, is not quite what the Hebrew has. There is, however, an Arabic word meaning 'to humble, afflict, make submissive', and it was suggested that in Isaiah 53:3 and some other passages (e.g. Judg. 8:16; 16:9; Prov.10:9; Jer.31:19; Job 20:10) we are dealing with another *yada'*, not the very common word *yada'* I., 'to know', but *yada'* II., a word historically related to this Arabic word and meaning 'to afflict, make submissive'. This is how the *REB* translation of Isaiah 53:3 was arrived at: 'painstricken and afflicted by disease'.[14]

There are countless examples of this kind of linguistic activity on the part of modern scholars, concerned to get back to the meaning of the original Hebrew at all costs. Some are effective and tempting alternatives to traditional interpretations, while others are quite gratuitous and unconvincing. Either way, it cannot be too much emphasized that it is possible to give room, even within the confines

---

[14]   Barr, *Comparative Philology and the Text of the Old Testament*, pp. 19ff.

of a single translation, both to the latest and most widely accepted reconstruction of the original meaning, and to the most important traditional interpretation(s), however far apart the two (or more) may be. The *NRSV* at 7:14 is an excellent illustration of how this can be done: it is well known that the original Hebrew has *'almah* 'a young woman', not *bĕtulah* 'a virgin', and the *NRSV* correctly gives 'young woman' in the main text. But in the margin, instead of the unscholarly and tendentious 'or *virgin*' (cf. *RSV*), *NRSV* has 'Greek *virgin*'. All the relevant data must be respected: the Hebrew has 'young woman', the Greek has 'virgin'. Similarly in 53:8 *dor* traditionally meant 'generation', but may originally have meant 'fate' (cf. *REB*). If these safeguards against dogmatism are built in, on the part of the linguists as well as the theologians, there is no scientific reason why the baby of Christian tradition should be lost with the bath water of modern comparative philology.

Like comparative philology, textual emendation has been a major tool in modern biblical research, but, unlike comparative philology, it is available only to those who are unrestrained by the belief that the letters of the Hebrew text as we have it are sacrosanct. Despite the efforts of scribes, meticulously trained and fanatically motivated to preserve correctly every jot and tittle of the inherited text, it is prima facie probable that in some places what we have is not the 'original text'. This is especially so in the case of a difficult and controversial passage like Isaiah 53, and a glance at any modern commentary or the margin of most modern versions will show how many emendations have been proposed. We shall look at two examples which raise theological questions as well as linguistic and textual ones.

The first concerns the 'rich man' in 53:9, identified in Christian tradition with Joseph of Arimathaea. Once again this meaning was considered odd by modern scholars for a number of reasons. Why, for example, should what appears to be a description of ultimate disgrace and death include the reference to a rich man's grave? 'A rich man' is in any case, in Hebrew poetic convention, a somewhat problematical parallel for 'the wicked'. Some therefore, once again on the basis of an Arabic word, suggest 'refuse' (*NEB*) as a better parallel for 'the wicked' and appropriate in the description of a degrading burial. The alternative, proposed by a number of scholars, is to emend the text. By inserting one letter and a space the Hebrew word for 'rich' can be altered to the two words for 'evil-doers' (*NRSV* margin; *REB* 'felons'; cf. Ps.34:16 (Hebrew 34:17); Mal.2:17).

The other is in verse 11. The received Hebrew text begins with four words which may provisionally be translated: 'After his suffering he will see, he will be satisfied'. 'After his suffering', literally, 'from the suffering of his soul', was taken by Jerome to mean 'in return for what he suffered' (*pro eo quod laboravit anima eius*). Either way the two verbs translated 'he will see, he will be satisfied', after the reference to his death and burial in verse 9, seem clearly to refer to his resurrection from the dead. Similar language, traditionally given an eschatological meaning and equally suspect in the eyes of modern commentators, is used at the end of Psalm 17: 'As for me I shall behold thy face in righteousness; When I awake, I shall be satisfied with beholding thy form.' The Isaiah passage reads almost like a shorthand version of this, where the objects of the two verbs 'see' and 'be satisfied (with)' have been omitted, but are understood in the context. By chance we now have a much more ancient Hebrew manuscript of the passage, the Isaiah Scroll A from Qumran, which actually has the word for 'light' after 'see', filling in one of the objects and completing the clause in true Isaianic style (cf. 9:2): 'After his suffering he will see light and be satisfied'. The *New Revised Standard Version* and *REB* both follow this authority. The Hebrew text may not be identical to the 'original Hebrew' but it makes excellent sense as it stands, and, for anyone looking for it, provides an unmistakeable reference to a belief in the rewards that await the righteous after death (cf. Dan.12:1–3).

The question of Hebrew language and images concerning the resurrection of the dead is an issue that inevitably causes tension between scholarly research and the theology and liturgy of the Church.[15] Isaiah has been in the forefront of this too. There are several other passages from Isaiah, as we have seen,[16] which have been much used in both Jewish and Christian contexts to express various aspects of a doctrine of the resurrection of the dead. These include in particular that beautiful verse from chapter 26.[17] Modern versions usually have something like the following (NRSV): 'Your dead shall live, and their corpses shall rise. O dwellers in the dust, awake and sing for joy! For your dew is a dew of light, and on the land of the shades you will let it fall'. Modern scholars argue that no such beliefs had been developed in ancient Israel, and that therefore

[15]   See Sawyer, 'Hebrew terms for the resurrection'.
[16]   See pp. 132ff.
[17]   See p. 133.

this refers to the resurrection of the community after some national disaster, not to individual resurrection. Commentators interpret the verse metaphorically: God gives the people, who are as though dead, new life and illumines the gloom of despair with his radiant dew. The same can of course be applied to the resurrection of the servant in 53:11 where the poem is interpreted collectively.[18] Christian tradition, however, informed by a strong belief in life after death, has found much more here including, in the Hebrew word 'my body' in the first line, another unmistakeable reference to individual resurrection. Jerome has *mei interfecti* for 'my corpses', confirming that this refers to the death of martyrs, and cites the parallel from Daniel 12 where the reward of the righteous is more clearly separated from that of the wicked. The eschatology is even more specific in the LXX which has 'those in the tombs will awake' for 'my corpses will rise'. LXX also has 'your dew will be healing to them', while Tertullian, to stress the idea of bodily resurrection still further, has 'to their bones' instead of 'to them'.[19] What the original Hebrew was and what the original author intended here are not known. Much depends on the date and original historical context: many would date this passage in the Isaiah apocalypse to a period when eschatological ideas were gaining ground, perhaps under Persian influence. Probably the vision of the eschatological feast in the previous chapter when 'death will be swallowed up for ever and God will wipe away tears from all faces' (25:6–8; cf. 1 Cor.15:54; Rev.7:17; etc) comes from the same context. The tension is resolved by recognizing eschatology here but dating the verse to a period long after the time of Isaiah.

Isaiah 53 provides us with a good example of how earlier mistakes in this field are being rectified by more recent research. One of the best-known examples of modern critical scholarship is Bernhard Duhm's proposal that four 'Servant Songs' could be isolated in Isaiah 42:1–6, 49:1–6, 50:4–9a and 52:13–53:12. These four passages had never before been taken together in this way, isolated from their context, and interpreted as telling the single story of an individual. Naturally, although the Christological interpretation had little or no appeal for Duhm, Christians were soon to focus afresh on the identity of the Servant in these passages, and the Christological interpretation, such a casus belli in ancient and mediaeval Christian polemic, received a new lease of life. C. R. North for example, in his

---

[18]   See below.
[19]   *Septuaginta*, XIV. *Isaias*, p. 212.

commentary on 'The Second Isaiah', entitles the third and fourth 'The Gethsemane of the Servant' and 'The Man of Sorrows', even though his commentary is not explicitly Christological.[20] Serious doubt has now been cast on whether Duhm was right to try to take these four passages out of their context.[21] One of the problems was the explicit reference to the community 'Israel' in 49:3. To solve this some, including Duhm, argued that the word 'Israel' was not original, and merely omitted it. Others, attempting to apply current anthropological theory to the problem, accepted H. Wheeler Robinson's theory of 'corporate personality', according to which a 'primitive mentality' such as that underlying the Hebrew Bible did not make a clear distinction between the individual and the community. This 'fluid' interpretation of the Servant Songs was widely accepted until the untenable and distasteful anthropological notions of 'primitive mentality' and 'corporate personality' were finally laid to rest by better field-work and more sophisticated theory.[22]

For this and other cogent reasons Duhm's whole theory has been called into question. But as in other cases, there is a long time lag between the publication of the results of scholarly research and their effect on Christian belief and practice. Not even the gist of Mettinger's *A Farewell to the Servant Songs* has so far reached the churches. Already in the liturgies of both the Catholic and the Anglican Church, the four passages have been prescribed to be read consecutively on Monday, Tuesday, Wednesday and Friday of Holy Week, where they are clearly intended to be understood Christologically. Provided no-one insists that 'the original author intended' that this is how the poems were to be interpreted, there can be nothing academically wrong with incorporating this most recent stage in the history of their interpretation into Christian liturgical practice. But by the same token, it is hard to justify the removal of some of the earlier stages in the process, such as the 'virgin' from 7:14 or the 'rich man' from 53:9, just because they are not 'what the original Hebrew means'.

New developments in literary studies have likewise led to some breaks with tradition, especially in the identification and isolation of new literary units, unknown to earlier generations of readers. It was once assumed that the book of Isaiah was a single work, divinely

[20] North, *The Second Isaiah*.
[21] Cf. Mettinger, *A Farewell to the Servant Songs*.
[22] Cf. Rogerson, 'The Hebrew conception of corporate personality'.

inspired, revealed to Isaiah during his lifetime, that is to say, in the eighth century BC. References to the 'vision which Isaiah saw ... in the days of Uzziah, Jotham, Ahaz and Hezekiah' (1:1; cf. 2:1), and to 'a book that is sealed' (29:11) were taken at face value, as was the instruction to Isaiah to 'seal it among his disciples' (8:16). But modern commentaries, on stylistic criteria, as well as historical and theological, isolated in the Book of Isaiah separate sections, such as the 'oracles against foreign nations' (13–23; cf. Jer.46–51; Ezek.25–32; Amos 1–2), the 'Isaiah apocalypse' (24–27), 'Deutero-Isaiah' (40–55) and the like, as well as smaller literary units such as 'Thanksgiving Psalms' (e.g. 12), 'Salvation Oracles' (e.g. 41:14–16; 43:1–7), 'Woe Oracles' (e.g. 5:8–23), 'Courtroom Speeches' (e.g. 41:21–4), 'Funeral Dirges' (e.g. 1:21–6; 14:4–20; 47), and, perhaps the most widely known example, the four so-called 'Servant Songs' already discussed. Perceptions of Isaiah were drastically transformed by this approach. In the first place, multiple authorship for the book is assumed. Not only must one distinguish clearly between later parts of the book and anything composed by the original eighth-century prophet in whose name it has come down to us, but attention focusses as much on literary style and social context as on any individual author or authors. The book is in effect an anthology of prophetic material, and questions are asked about the original audience of particular parts of the text, rather than about the original author.

Scholars showed that such stereotyped literary forms were conventionally associated with particular situations in ancient Israelite society, in the Temple or in a law court or at a funeral or the like, and the identification of the original *Sitz im Leben* ('life-setting') of a literary unit was an essential stage in the process of interpretation. In several passages, by choosing the style used in funeral orations, for example, like that of David over the bodies of Saul and Jonathan ('How are the mighty fallen ...'! 2 Sam.1:19–27), the prophet adds a peculiarly biting, sarcastic tone to his celebrated taunt against the king of Babylon in chapter 14 – whose death he is scarcely mourning![23] In chapter 1 he uses the same technique against his own people: 'How the faithful city has become a harlot,/she that was full of justice!'

Another style frequently used in the prophets' rhetoric is that of the law court, where witnesses are summoned, the accused cross-

---

[23] See p. 160

examined and judgement is pronounced. This style is all the more apposite where the accused are the prophet's audience, and the Judge in the case is the Lord. Arguably the book of Isaiah opens in this style, with the summoning of heaven and earth to act as witnesses as God introduces his case against the accused: 'Hear, O heavens, and give ear, O earth; For the Lord has spoken: "Sons have I reared and brought up, But they have rebelled against me ..."' (1:2). In another case it is the idol-worshippers who stand accused, challenged to produce evidence of their power (41:21–4). Elsewhere, in a variation on this theme, the crime of God's people is their faithlessness in time of crisis, and the powerful legal metaphor is adduced to reassure them rather than condemn them. In 50:1 they are challenged to produce evidence that they have been abandoned by their God ('Where is your mother's bill of divorce ...?').

Discoveries of ancient near eastern mythological texts often gave new meaning to the use of images. The mythical battle between a deity representing life and justice, on the one hand, and the powers of chaos and death symbolized by monsters like Leviathan 'the fleeing serpent, Leviathan the twisting serpent ... and the dragon that is in the sea' (27:1), on the other, appears several times in Isaiah. Rahab and 'the great deep' (Hebrew *tĕhom*; cf. Babylonian *Tiamat*) appear as the defeated enemies of God, explicitly identified in one case with the Red Sea (51:9–10; cf. 30:7). This powerful imagery combines beliefs about creation, shared with the ancient peoples of Canaan and Babylon, with biblical traditions about divine intervention in history, especially in the Exodus story. In some passages the victorious creator deity is heralded as 'king', another image illuminated by the Canaanite and Babylonian evidence: 'I am the Lord, your Holy One, the Creator of Israel, your King' (43:15). The community's expression of faith in their god is summed up in the formula 'The Lord reigns', familiar from the Enthronement Psalms (Ps.93; 95–100) as well as from texts from Ugarit and Babylon. It appears in Isaiah 52:7.

Whether or not it will ever be proved that an annual ritual existed in Jerusalem, in which the defeat of the monsters and the enthronement of Yahweh were enacted, as was the case in ancient Canaan and Babylon, the language and images are certainly there. The discovery of their ancient near eastern background gave them, in their Christian context, a new dimension, as a popular modern hymn from the 1970s, based on Isaiah 52:7–10 and celebrating the kingship of Christ with the refrain 'Our God reigns', nicely illustrates.[24] The passage has also now found its way into the Catholic lectionary for mass on Christmas Day. Until modern times only the first part of 52:7 ('How beautiful are the feet ...') appeared in the Anglican liturgy in its Pauline form (Rom.10:15) – whence it came to Handel's attention.[25] The whole Isaiah passage is now read on the first Sunday of Advent, illustrating how the insights of modern scholarship can influence the development of Christian worship.

Another example is the 'Salvation Oracle' (German *Heilsorakel*), a literary form identified by the German scholar Joachim Begrich, who argued in an article published in 1934, that it too was derived from ancient ritual.[26] It has been described as one of the 'main literary forms of Deutero-Isaiah's proclamation'.[27] It reads like a response to someone in distress, and the theory is that it was originally designed to be recited on the same occasion as a Psalm of Lament such as Psalm 22. The Book of Psalms contains the worshippers' 'Laments', while 'Deutero-Isaiah' preserves the priest's responses known as 'Salvation Oracles'. Thus for example the Salvation Oracle in Isaiah 41:14 ('Fear not, you worm Jacob') is the response to Psalm 22:6 ('I am a worm and no man ...'). Isaiah 43:1ff. is perhaps the most perfect example, and one that has inspired at least three popular new hymns written in the 1970s.[28] No earlier hymn-writers seem to have made use of the passage. It does not appear in the lectionaries, nor do earlier commentaries find much in it to comment on. It seems likely, though hard to prove, that one of the factors that brought these verses to the attention of Christian worshippers was Joachim Begrich's *Heilsorakel* theory, mediated through popular commentaries to a wider readership in the Church.[29]

From the question of literary form, which largely bypasses matters of date and authorship, we move now to what we may safely describe as the dominant concern of modern scholarship, historicity and historical context. Commentaries over the last two hundred years have devoted more space to such questions, especially the reconstruction of a text's original context, than to almost anything else. One reason for this is that archaeology and ancient history have always

[24] *How lovely are the feet*: *HON*, 224; cf. 223.
[25] See p. 173.
[26] Begrich, 'Das priesterliche Heilsorakel'.
[27] Westermann, *Isaiah 40–66*, pp. 67f.
[28] *HON*, 122, 136, 627.
[29] On twentieth-century Christianity, see further pp. 220f.

tended to capture the imagination of the general public more than any other branch of biblical research, and have often diverted attention from the content of the texts to their history, from questions about what the words and images mean, to when they were written and who wrote them. The study of Isaiah is no exception.

The discovery of inscriptions and other types of documentary evidence from the ancient world drew scholars' attention to some of the proper names in Isaiah. In an article published in 1960, for example, it was suggested that the seal belonging to Isaiah's father Amoz had been discovered in Palestine. From this it could be argued that Isaiah was the son of a scribe, giving us a rare biographical detail about the prophet.[30] The suggestion has not been taken up by many scholars in subsequent commentaries for various reasons, but nicely illustrates the kind of result that frequently emerges from the temptation to relate hard archaeological data which you can handle to the study of the Bible. Another example is the reference in 49:12, according to most modern versions, to 'the land of Syene' (*REB*, *NRSV*). 'Syene' is the ancient Greek form of the name Aswan on the upper Nile, and seems to be written in place of the traditional *sinim* in one of the oldest Hebrew manuscripts of Isaiah that we possess, the Isaiah Scroll A from Qumran. Now we know from archaeological evidence that there was a Jewish military garrison there during the period when the passage was written, and a reference to them in a passage about the people of Israel returning to Zion 'from afar' would make good sense. But once again this is a matter of probabilities and another instance of how archaeology, this time the archaeology of Egypt as well as Palestine, can dictate what to believe. After all it is likely that the reference here to a small Jewish settlement in Egypt, which incidentally was not 'a land', is the result of some kind of scribal activity during the sixth and fifth centuries, which may or may not have been related to the original intention of the author. The intention of the passage as a whole is surely wider and more universal than that. Is it any more convincing than the equally unoriginal *Sinim* 'the land of the Chinese', used by the missionaries discussed in chapter 8?[31]

Most modern commentaries on Isaiah regularly refer to the eighth-century Assyrian documents, discovered in Nineveh, which contain a contemporary account of some of the events referred to in

---

[30]   Anderson, 'Was Isaiah a scribe?'.
[31]   See p. 154.

Isaiah, and to other evidence from later periods which also fills in the background to some of the texts. Thus, for example, from contemporary Assyrian records we know that three of the place-names in the first verse of the famous messianic prophecy in chapter 9, which were applied in early Christian tradition to the Galilean ministry of Christ,[32] refer precisely to three provinces set up by the Assyrian king Tiglath Pileser III in 734 and 732. The Assyrian records also tell of mounting opposition to their hegemony from Palestine, Africa and, closer to home, from Babylon. All these enemies of Assyria figure in Isaiah: the king of Ashdod, crushed by Sargon in 712 (Isa.20:1); the Ethiopians who had conquered Egypt (cf. 18:1–6; 20:3); the Egyptians who sought to persuade Judah to join them in a revolt against Assyria in 705 (30:1–17; 31:1–9); and Merodach Baladan, the Babylonian king, who also entered into diplomatic relations with Judah at the same time (39).

The scene of devastation described in chapter 1, in which 'the daughter of Zion is left like a booth in a vineyard' (v.8) refers to the invasion of Sennacherib in 701, discussed above, and proves that the passage was composed in that year or shortly after.[33] A note in Isaiah 7:8, considered by many to be a later interpolation and bracketed in some versions, refers to an event in 671 when the Assyrian king settled a foreign ruling class in Samaria, another name for 'Ephraim'.[34] The account of Sennacherib's invasion in 701 was probably written during the reign of Josiah towards the end of the seventh century,[35] and then throughout chapters 40–66 there can be found references to sixth-century events, including the destruction of Jerusalem in 587 (e.g. 44:26,28; 49:17), the exile of the people of Judah in Babylon (e.g. 48:20), and the victories of Cyrus, king of the Medes and Persians (44:28–45:1). Passages perhaps reflecting opposition to the rebuilding of the Temple in the years following the fall of Babylon in 538 have been identified (66:1f.), and others from the rather later period of rebuilding and reformation under Ezra and Nehemiah (45:7–10; 51:9–10; 54:5–10).[36] Lastly, historians have found material from still later in the Isaiah apocalypse (24–27), such as the reference to a 'city of chaos' in 24:10, identified by some with

---

[32] See above, p. 34.
[33] E.g. Kaiser, *Isaiah 1–12*, p. 7.
[34] Kaiser, *Isaiah 1–12*, p. 94.
[35] Clements, *Isaiah and the Deliverance of Jerusalem*.
[36] Cf. Vermeylen, 'Le motif de la Création dans le Deutéro-Isaie', pp. 183–240.

Babylon, taken by Alexander the Great in 331, and by others with Carthage, destroyed by the Romans in 146. [37]

The use of this kind of archaeological and historical material to date Isaiah is typical of modern scholarship, and even though there is disagreement on particular passages and sections of the book, the approach is accepted as standard by the vast majority of scholars today. No subject is more hotly discussed in the commentaries. According to many no aspect of biblical research is more fascinating. Until comparatively recently few would challenge the assumption that the original historical context of a passage and its original meaning must be the scholar's chief goal, in sharp contrast to the contexts and interpretations of Isaiah within the history of Christianity which have been the main subject of this volume. These are not often considered worthy of serious scholarly attention. So what are we to conclude?

In the first place much of this kind of historical critical research has no bearing on Christian traditional uses of Isaiah at all. Many of the passages of interest to archaeologists and historians in particular, do not figure at all in the Christian lectionaries, and a good many of their discoveries make only marginal differences to the meaning of familiar texts. It is of purely academic interest, for instance, that the details of the historical background to verses like 9:1 can now be identified. Ancient historians will continue to use Isaiah, and the rest of the Bible, as source material for their research on how things were in ancient Israel, but the majority of the passages that have been so central in the history of Christianity have been unaffected by the discoveries of archaeology. The disproportionate amount of space given to such material in modern commentaries, however, even those designed for use in Christian contexts, is a measure of the distance that exists between the scholars and the Church. It is only in the last decade or two, particularly with the advent of new literary approaches to the text, that this has been appreciated.

Secondly, the world of critical scholarship is a living, developing world. New material still appears from time to time and new methods evolve, which change the scholarly consensus. Occasionally, by the time the Church has incorporated a new theory into the liturgy, scholars have moved on and the theory has been superseded. As was mentioned already, countless examples of this can be found

---

[37]   Cf. Eissfeldt, *The Old Testament. An Introduction*, p. 325.

in the *NEB*, which as the official version has been read in the majority of Anglican churches from 1970 till the present day. Some of these were already removed in the readings printed in the *Alternative Service Book* (1980), while, as already mentioned, many more were rejected by those responsible for the *REB* (1990), but still remain in the lectionary where they are read out, preached on and discussed although the experts are for the most part agreed that they cannot be accepted. Where there is a direct conflict between what the scholars say and what tradition says, as in the case of Isaiah 7:14, we have seen that it is possible and fashionable, as well as scholarly, to preserve both sets of data, each in their own right. The most recent interpretations of the Hebrew text can take their place alongside earlier stages in the process.

We shall end with three examples of recent attempts to allow preaching and up-to-date historical criticism to join forces. They are to be found in a series of lectures given by biblical scholars at the Lutheran Theological Seminary in Philadelphia in Spring 1986, and published under the title *Reading and Preaching the Book of Isaiah.*[38] R. R. Wilson convincingly identifies among the exiles in sixth-century BC Babylon a persecuted minority, possibly priests, as the original social context of Isaiah 40–55. They are the people who are addressed at the beginning of chapter 40 ('Comfort my people . . .'), and whose sense of isolation and abandonment runs through chapters 40–55. They suffer probably partly because they believe that Cyrus is the Lord's anointed (45:1–7), and partly because of their confidence that they are an elite group set apart by God (like priests) for a particular task. This gives added force to such passages as 52:1 and 11 where ritual purity is at stake as much as escape from Babylon, and 53 where their unmerited suffering is understood to 'be redemptive for all of Israel' (p. 68). By reconstructing the social situation in ancient Babylon in which the 'Second Isaiah' and his disciples lived, and attempting to get inside the mentality of a persecuted minority group, Wilson (in his own words) 'helps us to read in a more sophisticated way the texts that the community treasured' (p. 69). But he goes farther, fulfilling the expectations inherent in the book's title *Reading and Preaching*, and concludes with the judgement that the prophet 'gave to the world an understanding of human suffering that would transform the experiences of later

---

[38] Ed. C. R. Seitz (1988).

Jewish and Christian communities. The Second Isaiah community thus became a model that other communities would do well to follow'.

This is of course traditional doctrine, but it is also, according to the writer (or preacher) 'the original meaning of the text', and therefore assumed to carry some kind of special authority over against other doctrines and other interpretations of the same texts. The question as to whether a persecuted minority is the best model for the Church to follow today (especially in the context of prosperous American Protestantism), and whether their beliefs should be given such pre-eminence, is not discussed. Some, while sympathetic to their sufferings, might object to the pietism and elitism present in Wilson's reconstruction, and perhaps fail to be convinced by the universalism which appears, somewhat unexpectedly, near the end of the lecture. Others, in a post-Holocaust theological context, especially the victims, might deplore the traditional view that undeserved suffering can ever be explained or understood as 'redemptive'.[39] As we have seen, there are other ways of interpreting Isaiah 53 and the death of Christ.[40] It cannot be assumed that the reconstruction of how things actually were in ancient Israel, however 'sophisticated', guarantees theological or ethical truth in our own age or in any other.

Paul Hanson's account of the struggling community in which 'Third Isaiah' originated is less elaborate, but his application of the 'last eleven sombre chapters' of the book to the contemporary world, is more extensive and more convincing. The bitterness, anger, violence and radical imagery of these chapters (e.g. 59; 63:1–6; 66:15–16,24) arose in conditions that have 'typically fomented apocalyptic movements': 'In our society, as in that of the struggling community of Third Isaiah, the hopes and expectations of many are raised by glorious promises of prosperity, peace and divine favour only to be dashed on the rocks of marginalization and poverty ... We may not like the rhetoric of millions of militant blacks, strident feminists, revolutionary peasants and radical pacifists, but in their apocalyptic pictures of impending judgment on structures of privilege and injustice we usually encounter a more accurate depiction of

---

[39] Cf. Sawyer 'Le Serviteur Souffrant dans les traditions juives et chrétiennes'. In a later essay the Holocaust is cited as a reason to question traditional thinking on divine promises to the suffering and oppressed: Hanson, p. 97.

[40] See above chapter 6.

the life and death struggles occurring in our world than is given by
those who would like to preserve the myth of manifest destiny and
privilege ... The apocalyptic picture is not the illusion of a sick
mind, but the moral dread arising in the face of a human dereliction
that threatens all life on our planet' (pp. 100f.). Hanson's stout
defence of the moral truth of much of Isaiah 56–66, despite its
extravagant language and imagery, depends very little on a comparison between the original 'struggling community' and those he is
addressing today. His interpretation is not very different from that of
other, less historical, critical writers. Historical reconstruction of how
things were in ancient times, however interesting, actually adds very
little to his argument, apart from the aura of scientific acceptability
demanded by current scholarly opinion.

Finally, there is the editor's own 'canonical critical' contribution,
entitled 'Isaiah 1–66 – Making sense of the whole'. Following D. R.
Jones, R. E. Clements and others,[41] Seitz first surveys examples of
literary and theological continuity in Isaiah. He then identifies a
particular feature which distinguishes Isaiah from Jeremiah and
Ezekiel: 'in the book of Isaiah, God does most of the talking ... the
"retraction of the prophetic persona" permits the Book of Isaiah to
grow as it does without causing obvious readership problems ... and
allows the subject of the story – God – to overshadow so completely
the prophetic mediator or narrative voice' (p. 121). He suggests that a
more accurate descriptive title for the Book would be 'The Drama of
God and Zion' (p. 122). His conclusion is that 'the eschatological
force of the whole book of Isaiah cannot be described or contained
by simple appeal to original historical setting' (p. 123). With these
words we conclude our survey of the advantages and problems of the
quest for the historical Isaiah.

[41] Jones, 'The unity of the Book of Isaiah'; Clements, 'Beyond tradition-criticism: Deutero-
Isaianic development of First Isaiah's themes'; cf. Conrad, *Reading Isaiah*, Williamson, *The Book Called Isaiah*.

CHAPTER II

Women and Isaiah

One of the most radical, and at the same time the most creative, challenges to traditional interpretations of scripture has been in the field of feminist exegesis. It is nearly 100 years since the publication of Elizabeth Cady Stanton's *The Woman's Bible*, 'the original feminist attack on the Bible', but it is only in the last fifteen years or so that the importance of feminist interpretation of the Bible has begun to be fully appreciated within biblical studies. There have been numerous publications since Letty Russell's *Liberating Word. A Guide to Nonsexist Interpretation of the Bible* and Phyllis Trible's *God and the Rhetoric of Sexuality* in the seventies.[1] Standard reference works on the Bible and Biblical interpretation now have articles on the subject.[2] A *Women's Bible Commentary* was published in 1992. The recent Pontifical biblical Commission's document on 'Biblical Interpretation in the Church', with an introduction by Pope John Paul II and a preface by Cardinal Ratzinger, devotes a section to the 'feminist approach', not by any means wholly negative or critical.[3] Apparently the wording of this section was not unanimously approved by members of the commission: a footnote demanded by the minority states that it was accepted by a majority of eleven to four with four abstentions. Elsewhere in this important document, there is a reference to the 'penetrating new views' of the growing number of women exegetes who sometimes 'shed light on aspects that had fallen into oblivion'.[4]

For many women the 'patriarchalism' of the Bible, and of the

---

[1] Cf. Tolbert, ed., *The Bible and Feminist Hermeneutics* (1983); Fiorenza, *Bread Not Stone: The Challenge of Feminist Biblical Interpretation* (1984); Collins, ed., *Feminist Perspectives on Biblical Scholarship* (1985); Bal, ed., *Anti-Covenant. Counter-Reading Women's Lives in the Bible* (1989); Ostriker, *Feminist Revision and the Bible* (1993).

[2] E.g. Middleton, 'Feminist interpretation', *DBI*, pp. 231–4; Sakenfeld, 'Feminism and the Bible', *Oxford Companion to the Bible*, pp. 228–31.

[3] *L'interprétation de la Bible dans l'Eglise* (Libreria Editrice Vaticana, 1993; English translation, ed. J. L. Houlden, SCM Press, London 1995), pp. 58–61.

[4] *L'interprétation de la Bible*, pp. 91–2.

Christian religion in general, is irredeemable, and efforts to 'depa-triarchalize' it pointless. But there have been some successful attempts on the part of those who wish to stay within the Church, to discover or rediscover in the Bible language and imagery which can be used as a basis for alternative forms of Christianity. The prophets, and in particular Isaiah, have played a role in this process. Susanne Heine, for example, an influential Protestant writer on feminist theology, states that 'the strongest statements about the motherhood of God appear in Deutero-Isaiah'.[5] Here, perhaps more than in any other part of our study, we shall see the influence of the reader's viewpoint, 'her sympathy and interpretative frame',[6] on the selection and understanding of the text.

The story begins in the nineteenth century. In her struggle for women's rights, Elizabeth Cady Stanton found in Isaiah only one passage worth including in her *Woman's Bible*, namely the prophet's attack on the 'mincing gait' and 'frivolities' of the wealthy women of his day (3:16–23). Her purpose was to prove that women as indivi-duals are rarely mentioned by the Prophets, and where they are, it is never as human beings equal to men. On the contrary, they are portrayed merely as symbols, the good woman denoting the do-mestic, social and political successes of a society controlled by men, and the wicked woman denoting its failures: 'the idiosyncracies of the sex are constantly used to point a moral or to condemn a sin'.[7] Isaiah's tirade against 'the daughters of Zion', however, provided her with scriptural authority to condemn the bad taste of women in her day, going to church in 'bonnets trimmed with osprey feathers'.[8] As one would expect, this is a passage more often cited by men than by women. The author of the apocryphal and misogamist *Letter of Titus*, composed probably in fifth-century Spain, attributes to Isaiah a reproach against 'the daughters of Zion', which cannot be traced but may well have been suggested by this passage.[9] A painting of the scene by the Victorian Jewish artist Simeon Solomon (1840–1905), a rare reference to the passage from outside of the commentaries, is another example, and Robert Carroll's use of the passage in a collection of essays, *On Humour and the Comic in the Hebrew Bible*, has

---

[5]   Heine, *Christianity and the Goddesses*, p. 26.
[6]   Van Dijk-Hemmes, 'The imagination of power and the power of the imagination', p. 75.
[7]   Cady Stanton, *The Woman's Bible* p. 105.
[8]   Cady Stanton, *The Woman's Bible* p. 102.
[9]   *NTA*, 2,148.

already been mentioned.[10] By selecting this passage of all passages, as her only quotation from Isaiah, Cady Stanton presumably intended to point up the contrast between women like her, who are totally committed to the campaign for equality, and women who are content with the role men have given them.

More recently the radical ex-Catholic feminist Mary Daly likewise has little use for Isaiah. In a discussion of the relevance of the terms 'prophecy', 'prophet', and 'prophetic' to the women's movement, she points out that the prophets as a whole, by definition radical critics of the official priesthoods and hierarchies, have in fact done nothing to lead us 'out of the wilderness of sexism'.[11] In particular she criticizes the biblical prophets for their sexist imagery, and their 'tiresome propensity for comparing Israel to a whore'. Her only reference to Isaiah is to a passage where Zion is spoken of as a harlot (1:21). Like Cady Stanton, Daly recognizes offensive male perceptions and attitudes in the use of 'objectified female sexuality as a symbol of evil'.[12] Another radical feminist, writing on the subject of 'The impossibilities of being a Jewish woman', shows how an even more offensive verse from Isaiah – 'Your hands are full of blood' (1:15) – is sometimes used in traditional Jewish discussions of such topics as menstruation and childbirth and female impurity.[13] Although Mary Daly and others acknowledge the relevance of some aspects of the phenomenon of prophecy for the feminist revolution, and even agree with Max Weber that, unlike priesthood, prophetic religion could theoretically break through patriarchal structures, they point out that this is not what has in fact ever happened in the case of biblical prophecy, and look elsewhere for ways of 're-imaging and re-naming the "world" bequeathed to us'.[14]

Many women, however, have made something of the few texts there are in the Bible which can be read and interpreted as authority for an alternative form of Christianity. Some, like Phyllis Trible, with a professional interest in the Bible, have elected to stay in the Church and to search the scriptures for proof that patriarchal, sexist Christianity is not beyond redemption.[15] Others, like Rosemary

[10] See above, pp. 145f.   [11] Daly, *Beyond God the Father*, p. 162.
[12] Cf. Setel, 'Prophets and pornography', p. 86.
[13] Gilbert, 'When Hitler returns: The impossibilities of being a Jewish woman', pp. 160 and 163.
[14] Daly, *Beyond God the Father*, pp. 164–5.
[15] Cf. Trible, 'Depatriarchalizing in biblical interpretation'; cf. Fiorenza, 'The ethics of biblical interpretation'.

Radford Ruether and Sallie McFague, whose writings are less biblical, nevertheless find appropriate texts and images in the Bible, many of them in Isaiah, and have used them, often with great eloquence and originality, to provide inspiration and authority for Christian feminists today.

We begin with Phyllis Trible's use of Isaiah 53 in her *Texts of Terror*. This is a feminist critique of four biblical texts about women: the stories of Hagar (Gen.16:1–16; 21:9–21), Tamar (2 Sam.13:1–22), 'an unnamed woman' betrayed, raped, tortured, murdered and dismembered (Judg. 19:1–30), and Jephthah's daughter (Judg.11:29–40). One of the most strikingly original features of this study is Trible's application of verses from Isaiah 53 to two of these women. Her epitaph for Hagar, the Egyptian slave woman, is 'she was wounded for our transgressions; she was bruised for our iniquities' (Plate 33);[16] and to Tamar, princess of Judah and victim of rape, she gives the epitaph 'A woman of sorrows and acquainted with grief'.[17] In addition to these texts from the so-called 'Suffering Servant Songs' from Isaiah, she uses others from the Gospel passion narratives and the eucharistic sections of the Pauline epistles, as what she calls 'leitmotifs' guiding us through her retelling of the four 'sad stories'. In this way, by applying familiar texts to situations where women, not men, are suffering servants and Christ-like figures, she hopes to allow scripture to interpret scripture in a radical new way which 'undercuts triumphalism and raises disturbing questions of faith'.[18] The result is a most effective and challenging instance of a new use of Isaiah, not dissimilar to Edwina Sandys' sculpture *Christa* exhibited in 1981 in the Cathedral of St John the Divine in New York, which showed a woman on the cross, wearing the crown of thorns.

Another example of how feminist exegesis throws new light on familiar texts is Rosemary Radford Ruether's use of Isaiah 10:1–2 and 61:1–2 in her discussion of 'Biblical resources for feminism'.[19] Her point is that biblical passages like these, denouncing political and economic oppression, have much to say to women, because women are either specifically mentioned in such passages (e.g.

---

[16] Trible, *Texts of Terror*, p. 8.
[17] Trible, *Texts of Terror*, p. 36.
[18] Trible, *Texts of Terror*, pp. 2–3.
[19] *Sexism and God-Talk*, pp. 22ff.; cf. *Womanguides*, pp. 202–5; on the popularity of Isaiah in liberation theology, see pp. 224ff.

Isa.10:2), or can be readily identified among 'the afflicted ... the brokenhearted ... the captives ... those that are bound ...' (61:1–2). According to Luke 4, this is how Isaiah 61:1–2 was interpreted by Jesus himself when he preached on the text in the synagogue in Nazareth, since the first of his two examples of what Isaiah means by 'the oppressed', is a widow (vv.25–6). She is also a gentile, of course, as is his other example, a Syrian king (v.27), and the usual view is that this is an attack on Jewish particularism. But a feminist interpretation of Luke 4 gives an important new dimension to our understanding of the text, as well as providing scriptural authority for the application of 'the prophetic-liberating principle *to women*. Feminist theology makes explicit what was overlooked in male advocacy of the poor and oppressed: that liberation must start with the oppressed of the oppressed, namely, *women* of the oppressed'.[20] More recently in her *Womanguides. Readings Toward A Feminist Theology*, all the biblical texts chosen to illustrate her section entitled 'The New Earth: Visions of Redeemed Society and Nature', are from Isaiah.[21]

Dorothee Soelle, another Christian feminist and a leader of the German peace movement, in an interesting parallel, begins one of her essays in *The Strength of the Weak. Toward a Christian Feminist Identity* (Engl. transl.1984) by citing Isaiah 58:6–12 in full: 'Is not this the fast that I choose: to loose the bonds of wickedness ... to share your bread with the hungry ...' 'Bible texts are best read with a pair of glasses made out of today's newspaper', she says, and then points out that the 'unjustly imprisoned' referred to by Isaiah are not necessarily the victims of totalitarian regimes elsewhere in the world, but the victims of injustice in our own society.[22] Her example is a woman she knows with eight children in a low-income housing project, whose husband works sporadically and who is bombarded by salesmen she is too weak to resist, until she is eventually jailed for twelve weeks for not paying her bills. Like Ruether, Soelle uses Isaiah to denounce unjust laws, 'laws whose primary purpose is to protect property, laws framed by a society in which the protection of property is far more important than the protection of children'.[23] Like Jesus in Luke 4, Soelle chooses a woman as her first example.

But feminists have found more in Isaiah than these few examples

20 Ruether, *Sexism and God-talk*, p. 32.
21 Ruether, *Womanguides. Readings Toward A Feminist Theology* pp. 202–5.
22 Soelle, *The Strength of the Weak*, p. 155.
23 Soelle, *The Strength of the Weak*, p. 156.

of 'inclusive exegesis', which are not in any case unique to Isaiah. It is a remarkable fact that of all the books of the Bible, once again Isaiah is the one that contains the most developed instances of the application of female images to God, as well as some other interesting and rather exceptional references to women and female imagery. Of the few passages in the Bible where God is compared to a woman, or described as having female attributes, a significant proportion are in the Book of Isaiah.[24] Christian feminist writers like Trible, Ruether, McFague, Loades and others, have made much of these passages, 'searching for lost coins' in an effort to mitigate the exclusively male way in which the biblical God is described and envisaged. Official Church pronouncements such as the Church of Scotland's *Motherhood of God* pamphlet (1984) and Pope John Paul II's apostolic letter *Mulieris Dignitatem*, on the occasion of the Marian Year (1988), quote Isaiah 49:14f., 66:13 and Psalm 131:2 in full, and take seriously texts about God carrying the Chosen People 'within his own womb' (46:3f.) and 'giving birth to it in travail' (42:14). Isaiah 49:14f. provided the inspiration for at least two new hymns, composed in the seventies,[25] one of which, by a Jesuit priest, beginning with the words 'Though the mountains may fall' from Isaiah 54:6, has already become very popular in Catholic congregations.[26] Prayers to God as mother, some consciously Isaianic, are also now widely used.[27] A recent study of women and the British legal system has a Mantegna painting on the front cover, showing two prophets, a man and a woman, apparently discussing a point of law on equal terms.[28] Surely, in view of the prominent role of Isaiah in this context, and in relation to social justice,[29] there can be little doubt as to who the male prophet in this idealized scene must be.[30]

Doubts have been expressed as to whether such passages have any real contribution to make to women's struggle for equality. Are they not further examples of male domination, since what is happening in

[24] The following texts are the most often used in discussions of the female attributes of God: Gen.1:2, 26f., Deut.32:11, 18; Ps.131:2; Isa.31:5; 42:14; 45:10; 46:3f.; 49:14f.; 66:13; Matth.23:37; cf. Luke 13:34.

[25] *I will never forget you* by Carey Landrey (1975) and *Though the mountains may fall* by Dan Schutte SJ (1975): *HON* 265 and 569.

[26] *HON* 569.

[27] Janet Morley, *All Desires Known*, pp. 15, 25.

[28] Helena Kennedy, *Eve Was Framed. Women and British Justice* (Chatto 1992).

[29] See below, pp.

[30] The painting, formerly thought to depict *Esther and Mordechai*, is nowadays given the title *Sybil and Prophet*: cf. Lightbrown, *Mantegna*, pp. 449–50.

a passage like Isaiah 42:14, where God is portrayed as having maternal or 'feminine' characteristics, is that the male God of Christian tradition remains male while taking over female tasks and qualities as well? 'What place is then left for the female? ... if men now have wombs, women are superfluous'.[31] According to this more cynical interpretation, the biblical 'God as mother' passages would then have nothing to say to women today.

Let us look in detail at the passages in question, remembering that in the modern world, within both Catholic and Protestant traditions, 'what the original Hebrew text means' is now more important than it was in earlier periods in the search for scriptural authority, and that feminist writers are in many cases either themselves professional biblical scholars, like Phyllis Trible, or consciously dependent on recent biblical scholarship. The first, and certainly the least effective for the feminist argument, is Isaiah 31:5 ('Like birds hovering, so the Lord of hosts ...'). Already in Jerome's commentary the link is made between the image of God as a bird 'hovering' over its young in this verse and Jesus' poignant cry over Jerusalem: 'How often would I have gathered your children together as a hen gathers her brood under her wings!' (Matth.23:27; cf. Luke 13:35). A parallel from the Song of Moses in Deuteronomy 32 is cited in which the Lord is compared to 'an eagle that stirs up its nest, that flutters over its young ...' (Deut.32:11; cf. Exod.19:4; Ps.91:4). Commentators also cite this verse and Matthew 23:37 in their discussion of Isaiah 66:13, one of the explicit 'God as mother' passages to which we shall be returning shortly. There is also the image of the spirit of God (feminine in Hebrew) 'moving over the waters' (or 'hovering': the same word as the one translated 'flutter' in Deut.32:11) in Genesis 1:2, and descending on Jesus 'like a dove' (also feminine) in the baptism story (Mark 1:10). Much is then made of feminine characteristics attributed to the Holy Spirit in these and other contexts; and at least one person of the Trinity can be envisaged and addressed as female.

There are problems with this use of scripture, however, linguistic, ornithological and theological. In the first place, the Hebrew text of Deuteronomy 32, the key passage which links Isaiah 31:5 with the 'God as mother' passages given above, has nothing feminine in it at all. While in Jerome's Latin the word for 'eagle' *aquila*, like the word for 'hen' *gallina* in Matthew 23, is feminine, the Hebrew word *nesher* is

---

[31]   Hampson, *Theology and Feminism*, p. 95.

not. Secondly, whatever precisely is the meaning of the word *raḥeph*, translated 'flutter' or 'hover', there is no need to assume that it refers to an activity restricted to female birds. In the case of many species, including most birds of prey, the female is the one that sits on the eggs while the male protects her, 'hovering' over or around the nest. The image in the Hebrew text of Deuteronomy 32 in other words does not provide scriptural authority for using female imagery for God, whatever Jerome made of his Latin version of the passage.

Furthermore, in Isaiah 31:5, although the word for 'birds' is feminine, the word translated 'hovering' is not the word used in Genesis 1:2 and Deut.32:11, but simply the regular, neutral word for 'flying'. While it could be argued that, in Isaiah 31:5, the Lord is compared to the female of the species, unlike the image in Deuteronomy 32:11, what he is depicted as doing has nothing specifically female about it. A recent commentator on this passage, however, taking seriously the connection between 31:5 and the preceding verse, as well as the traditional link with the 'God as mother' passages, sees here the powerful, frightening image of a bird of prey, strong, fierce, vigilant, claws ready to attack anyone that dares to approach her young, and reminds us that the image of a mother can be one of superhuman strength and ferocity as well as one of childbearing and suckling.[32]

A second group of texts, used by feminist writers of the seventies and eighties, highlights a semantic connection in Biblical Hebrew between the wombs of women and the compassion of God. It was Phyllis Trible who did the linguistic spadework for this part of the debate in her *God and the Rhetoric of Sexuality* (1978). She starts from the story of the Judgement of Solomon in 1 Kings 3:16–28, where the true mother is identified by her 'compassion': 'because her *raḥămim* [compassion] grew warm, grew tender, or yearned for her son ...' The Hebrew word *raḥămim* is normally translated 'compassion' but in this context can also be translated 'heart' (cf. *RSV*). The singular form *reḥem* actuallly means 'womb, uterus', so it can be argued that in the plural *raḥămim*, as also in the common words *riḥam* 'to show mercy' and *raḥum* 'compassionate', there is a 'semantic movement from the physical organ of the female body to a psychic mode of being ... To the responsive imagination, this metaphor suggests the meaning of love as selfless participation in life. The womb protects

---

[32] See pp. 233f.

and nourishes but does not possess or control. Truly it is the way of compassion'.[33] Trible then goes on to apply this to divine compassion, and her conclusions about the maternal or 'womb-like' qualities of God have been much quoted by subsequent feminist writers.[34]

For present purposes what is interesting is that Trible uses passages from Isaiah at key stages in her discussion. The climax of the first part, in which she examines God's involvement with the functions of the uterus as described in narrative (e.g. Gen.20:1–18; 30:22) and poetry (e.g. Jer.1:5; Job 31:13–15), is her commentary on Isaiah 46:3–4: 'Hearken to me, O house of Jacob, all the remnant of the house of Israel, who have been borne by me from the womb (*beṭen*), carried by me from the womb (*raḥam*); even to your old age I am he, and to grey hairs I will carry you. I have made and I will bear; I will carry and I will save.' She comments that here, as elsewhere, the imagery 'just stops short of saying that God possesses a womb … An organ unique to the female becomes a vehicle pointing to the compassion of God'.[35]

She likewise concludes the second stage of her argument with a discussion of two more passages from Isaiah. The first of these is a passage referred to above as being the inspiration for a popular modern hymn, composed incidentally several years before Trible's book was published and therefore not influenced by her work:

> I will never forget you, my people;
> I have carved you on the palm of my hand.
> I will never forget you;
> I will not leave you orphaned.
> I will never forget my own.
>
> Does a mother forget her baby?
> Or a woman the child within her womb?
> Yet even if these forget,
> yes, even if these forget,
> I will never forget my own   (cf. Isa.49:15–16).[36]

Little use was made of this passage before modern times. It is not in any of the Sunday lectionaries, nor does the imagery figure prominently in hymns before the two recent ones just mentioned.

[33] Trible, *God and the Rhetoric of Sexuality*, p. 33.
[34] E.g. Ruether, *Sexism and God-Talk*, pp. 56f.; McFague, *Metaphorical Theology*, pp. 168ff.; Loades, *Searching for Lost Coins* p. 90.
[35] Trible, *God and the Rhetoric of Sexuality*, p. 38; cf. McFague, *Metaphorical Theology*. pp. 169–70.
[36] Carey Landrey (1975); *HON* 265; cf. 569.

William Cowper's paraphrase, in a famous hymn based on John 21:16 ('Lovest thou me?'), written around 1763, is a conspicuous exception:

> Can a woman's tender care
> Cease towards the child she bare?
> Yes, she may forgetful be,
> Yet will I remember thee.
>
> Mine is an unchanging love,
> Higher than the heights above,
> Deeper than the depths beneath,
> Free and faithful, strong as death'.[37]

Trible points out that in its original context, the 'compassion' of God has already been mentioned three times, each time using the verb *riḥam* (vv.10,13,15), so that the verse which refers explicitly to a mother's 'womb-love' is all the more meaningful.

She turns next to a famous prayer later in the book, in which the following words are addressed to God: 'Where are thy zeal and thy might, the trembling of thy womb and thy compasssion? Restrain not thyself, for thou art our Father ...' (63:7–64:12) This daring translation, recommended by Trible, is James Muilenberg's, to whom she gives much of the credit for her own discoveries. She connects it with her feminist interpretation of Jeremiah 31:20 where the phrase 'the trembling of thy womb' occurs as well. Her point is that the comparison in 49:14f. between a human mother's 'womb-love' and God's is one that can break down because a human mother's love for her baby can conceivably fail, while divine love never fails. Thus we are reminded that the metaphor has limitations: God's 'womb-love' is more than a woman's; the image of God as both male and female (cf. Gen.1:26f.) is beyond human comprehension.

Finally a significant part of Trible's chapter on 'the image of God female', one who 'conceives, is pregnant, writhes in labour pains, brings forth a child, and nurses it' (pp. 60–9), is taken up with her discussion of three more texts from Isaiah: 45:10; 42:14; 66:7–14. She uses the first two of these in her comments on another verse from the Song of Moses, one much used by feminist writers: 'The Rock who gave you birth you forgot, and you lost remembrance of the God who writhed in labour pains with you' (Deut.32:18). Arguing from the structure of the poem, and from Isaiah 42:14 rather than 45:10,

---

[37] *EH* 400, *CH* 417.

she maintains, against some commentators, that both parts of this verse, both images, that of the Rock giving birth and that of God writhing in labour pains, describe God as mother, corresponding to verse 6 which calls God father. 'These birth-pangs of God appear again in Second Isaiah ... Historical chaos has become divine labor pains. Out of God's travail a new creation will emerge (42:5–13) ... now God will cry out, gasping and panting as she gives birth to these new realities in the world'.[38] Notice how in this context, clearly inspired by Isaiah 42:14, Trible refers to God as 'she'.

Among the very few pasages in scripture where God is compared to a woman, none is more explicit than Isaiah 42:14. While the image of God as mother appears elsewhere as we have seen, nowhere is the language so detailed: 'Like a travailing woman I will groan; I will pant. I will gasp at the same time'. This is a woman's translation of the Hebrew.[39] Male commentators since Jerome have not noticed the significance of the language as applied to God. They interpret it as being simply one more passage about God breaking his silence after a long time (cf. Ps.35:22; 83:1; Isa.65:6) and about bringing something new into the world, something that has been hidden from sight till now (cf. 43:19; 65:17–18). They say nothing whatever about the excruciating pain of the process, or about the unique string of words (one of them not attested elsewhere in the Bible) used to describe God's cries. Feminist commentators have opened our eyes to the fact that, while this is a passage about bringing a new Israel into the world, like a child, the implication is that the process is a painful one for God. This is a God who suffers for us as a woman suffers when she brings a baby into the world.

In addition to this striking use of language, the other piece of evidence for this interpretation of Isaiah 42:14 is that there are a number of other images in these chapters of Isaiah which confirm that, in this context, God is not only conceived of as a distant, impersonal figure, outside of and above the human situation (cf. 40:21–26; 55:8–9), but also caught up in it at every turn. These include the remarkable images of God as an apologetic husband (54:1–10), a midwife (66:9), and a warrior limping home from battle, alone, bloodstained to the point of being unrecognizable (63:1–6). As well as the use of a word probably meaning 'stooping' (*NEB*) in verse 1, elsewhere applied only to prostitutes (Jer.2:20), prisoners (Isa.51:14;

38   Trible, *God and the Rhetoric of Sexuality*, p. 64.
39   Trible, *God and the Rhetoric of Sexuality*, p. 64.

Jer.48:12) and gypsies (post-biblical Hebrew), verse 9 gives added force to this interpretation of the passage: 'In all their affliction he was afflicted'.[40] The fact that, according to another passage in Isaiah, not mentioned by Trible in this context, the alleviation of a woman's labour pains is singled out as a feature of the new age, a rare prophetic allusion to the Genesis creation story (Isa.65:23; cf. also 66:7–9),[41] gives feminists further scriptural authority, if they need it, to take seriously the imagery selected by the author of 42:14.

The last of Isaiah's five 'God as mother' passages discussed by Trible comes at the end of the longest and most detailed account of a woman having her first baby and then enjoying the pleasures of family life (66:7–14). The woman is Zion, and the image of her ultimate victory in terms of the pains and joys of having children, is the climax of the 'daughter of Zion' story which will be discussed below. The climax of the passage, however, is the picture of God consoling the people as a mother nurses and comforts her children (66:13), a verse familiar, as we saw, both from Brahms' *German Requiem*, and from the concluding paragraph of the Jewish 'Prayer in the house of mourning'.[42] 'Although the comparison stops just short of calling God mother, it does not stop short of this meaning. Yahweh is a consoling mother to the children of Jerusalem (Plate 31)'.[43]

Of course many passages in these same chapters of Isaiah present God in male images as well. In the verse immediately preceding one of the maternal images, he 'goes forth like a mighty man, like a man of war he stirs up his fury' (42:13). Elsewhere he is compared to an architect (40:12ff.), a potter (45:9) and, as we have already noted, a father (63:16; 64:8). There are also emphatic statements to the effect that God cannot be compared to any human being at all: 'To whom then will you liken God, or what likeness compare with him?' (40:18, 25; cf. 55:8f.) In other words female images have the same logical status as the conventional male ones: with reference to scriptural authority neither can claim to be more theologically acceptable. This explains the significance of Genesis 1:27, according to which both men and women were created 'in the image of God', a verse which

---

[40]   Sawyer, 'Radical images of Yahweh in Isaiah', p. 80; see above, pp. 97f.
[41]   Sawyer, 'The image of God', p. 71.
[42]   See pp. 174f.
[43]   Trible, *God and the Rhetoric of Sexuality* p. 67; Henry, *Biblia Pauperum*, p. 126.

plays such a central role in Trible's discussion: 'like a finger pointing to the moon, our metaphor allows no resting place in the image of God female – nor in the image of God male (cf. Ps.27:10). The One to whom it witnesses is the transcendent Creator going before us to make all things new'.[44] In spite of the limitations of human language about God, in particular the existence in the original Hebrew (and English) of gender-specific personal pronouns, Isaiah provides scriptural authority for addressing God as mother as well as father.

McFague cites Trible's conclusions with approval, recalling three of these Isaiah passages (46:3–4; 42:14; 66:13 – without giving chapter and verse), where 'female metaphors accomplish something male metaphors cannot: the image of God carrying Israel and giving birth in pain, of suckling Israel at the breast'.[45] She contrasts Trible's study with that of a male exegete, who, 'in an otherwise fine book' entitled *The Language and Imagery of the Bible*, published in 1980, lists parts of the body used in images of God without even mentioning parts of the female body.[46]

A common male way of handling the passages discussed above is exemplified by the view, expressed by the Bishop of London and others, that God is never called mother though he may be said to have 'the best female qualities'.[47] Feminine personal pronouns are never used of God in the Hebrew Bible, or the Greek, Latin, German or English versions that have been so influential in the history of Christianity. All the words for 'God' in these languages are masculine. Thus God remains 'Father' in the language and images of the Church, but can be said to have 'feminine attributes'. Jürgen Moltmann's concept of the 'Motherly Father'[48] takes the female imagery more seriously, especially in terms of God's suffering and pain, but does not take the next step demanded by Christian feminists of referring to God as mother as well as, and sometimes instead of, father.

In the late seventies Trible herself rarely referred to God as 'she', no doubt because of her respect for biblical usage. But, as we saw, she does so on at least one occasion. Since then it has become increasingly common in the language of prayer. The following is the

---

44   Trible, *God and the Rhetoric of Sexuality*, p. 69.
45   McFague, *Metaphorical Theology*, p. 169.
46   McFague, *Metaphorical Theology*, p. 170.
47   Furlong, *A Dangerous Delight*, p. 73; cf. Miller, *Biblical Faith and Fathering*, pp. 58–62.
48   Moltmann, 'The motherly father'.

first part of a collect for Mothering Sunday, written to accompany readings from Isaiah:

> God our mother,
> you hold our life within you,
> nourish us at your breast,
> and teach us to walk alone ...
>
>   (Isa.46:3–4; 49:14–16; 66:7–13; Hos.11:1–4).[49]

It has taken many centuries for this dimension of Isaiah to surface in Christian biblical studies, theology and worship. It now has some powerful advocates, who will ensure that it remains there and gives women scriptural authority, if they want it, to build their own alternative to traditional patriarchal Christianity.

Female imagery is also unusually prominent in Isaiah in the way the people of God are described. In other texts they are depicted as God's bride or wife, as for example in Hosea 1–2. But in Isaiah, especially in chapters 49–66, this image is elaborately developed beyond any other biblical parallel. In effect a 'Daughter of Zion' story, telling the story of a woman's life from fear (49:14,24) and barrenness (49:21; 54:1) to marriage (62:4f.) and the birth of her first child (66:7–14), runs through these chapters just as prominently as the more familiar 'Servant of the Lord' image. Furthermore, the people are repeatedly addressed as a woman, 'Zion' or the 'Daughter of Zion', in the second person feminine singular. This is a grammatical feature which is impossible to represent in English, because Hebrew, Arabic and other Semitic languages, unlike English, have different terms for 'you' (feminine) and 'you' (masculine). Thus, for example, the famous passage beginning 'Arise, shine, for thy light is come' is in fact addressed as to a woman. This aspect of the language and imagery of Isaiah has frequently been noticed. Its influence on ancient religious literature has been studied, including Paul's letter to the Galatians and *Joseph and Aseneth*, a work 'permeated by the language and themes of Deutero- and Trito-Isaiah'.[50] Its role in the cult of the Virgin Mary was discussed in chapter 4. In a recent brief 'literary guide' to Isaiah, Luis Alonso Schökel devotes two glowing pages to this aspect of 'Deutero-Isaiah'. On 49:14–26 he says: 'By poetic association, society and history become imbued with an amorous passion in their personal relationship with God – something

---

[49]   Morley, *All Desires Known*, p. 25.
[50]   Pervo,'Aseneth and her sisters', p. 152 note 41.

that the symbol alone is able to capture and bring forth from the ineffable sphere where divinity, humanity, and history are joined.'[51]

Recent interest in this kind of material, and in its place in the history of interpretation, prompted my paper entitled 'Daughter of Zion and Servant of the Lord in Isaiah: A Comparison', read at the Winter Meeting of the British Society for Old Testament Study in January 1989. In it I used the term 'daughter of Zion' as shorthand for the woman who figures in Isaiah 40–66 just as prominently as the man in the Servant of the Lord passages. After tracing the usage back to 1:21–6 where Jerusalem is compared to a harlot, and 37:22 where she tosses her head defiantly at the mighty Assyrian king, I then turned to the concentration of female images in 40–66.

The familiar opening which begins with the words 'Comfort, comfort my people, says your God', gives the feminine form in parallel: 'speak tenderly to Jerusalem'. 'Zion' (or a female herald) is then addressed directly in verse 9: 'O Zion, herald of good tidings' (or 'O thou that tellest good tidings to Zion'). The dialogue with Zion continues in chapter 49 where the chief concentration of female language and imagery begins. In 49:14ff. God comforts Zion like a mother comforting her daughter. In 51 her situation of suffering, rejection and loneliness is described in greater detail, and then 52 begins with a call to shake off the dust and fetters of captivity and stand up, a free woman again:

> Awake, awake, put on your strength, O Zion; put on your beautiful garments, O Jerusalem, the holy city; for there shall no more come into you the uncircumcised and the unclean. Shake yourself from the dust, arise, O captive daughter of Jerusalem; loose the bonds from your neck, O captive daughter of Jerusalem.

54 continues the imperatives ('shout for joy … enlarge your tent-space … do not be afraid'), and portrays Yahweh, with astonishing candour, as a remorseful husband promising never again to leave her or lose his temper with her (54:7–10). 60 and 62 celebrate her wedding with the arrival of gifts from all over the world: her name is changed to Hephzibah ('My-delight-is-in-her') and Beulah ('Married'), and Yahweh rejoices over her as the bridegroom rejoices over the bride (62:5). The climax of the 'story' in 66:7–14 describes in considerable obstetric detail the birth of her first child, and subsequent scenes of domestic bliss in which she feeds her children, carries

---

[51]   Alonso Schökel, 'Isaiah', p. 179.

them on her hip and dandles them on her knee. Again it is significant that in the first of these scenes Yahweh is portrayed as the midwife, humbling himself, as he did in chapter 54, to assist his beloved Zion.

Response to the paper was generally favourable. But there was one criticism, from a feminist perspective. The woman in this 'story' is for the most part weak, dependent on men for her happiness, and apparently content that domestic bliss, a life in which she has babies crawling all over her, should be her one goal in life and crowning achievement. A study of this story, albeit stimulated by feminist developments in the history of the study of the Bible, may help our understanding of the Servant passages and of the book of Isaiah in general, but, like most of the rest of the Bible, it perpetuates the patriarchal attitudes and values that women have suffered from in the Church for centuries. Besides, as an American woman pointed out to me, if we apply the husband/wife image to God's treatment of 'Zion' down to the present century, God is more like O. J. Simpson, the popular American football star, accused of abusing and then murdering his wife, and Zion his helpless victim. Perhaps the only biblical stories about women that can be interpreted as remotely helpful in providing scriptural 'role models' for women today are those about successful independent women like Ruth and Naomi.[52]

Since reading that paper I have thought further about this criticism and now take up the challenge to look again at 'women in Isaiah'. It is true that the choice of female imagery to describe the plight of the people in exile depends not only on the fact that women are physically weaker and often the victims of violence, but also on their traditional social status as totally dependent on men. The story of the daughter of Zion in Isaiah is about a woman made to feel helpless without a husband (54:6) and ashamed of being without children (54:4). It is also true that some of the women in Isaiah, like Immanuel's mother (7:14) and the prophet's wife (8:3), are nameless. Where a woman is given new names, supposed to signal happiness and fulfilment, they are blatantly male creations. *Hephzibah* 'my delight is in her' refers not to *her* happiness but to that of her husband. *Beulah* 'married' is the passive participle of the active verb *ba'al* 'to possess' of which the implied subject is once more the man, her *ba'al*, 'lord, husband'. In both cases she is a passive partner in the relationship. A life of child-bearing and domestic bliss on such terms

---

[52] Cf. Rashkow, 'Ruth: The discourse of power and the power of discourse', in Brenner, ed., *Feminist Companion to Ruth*, pp. 26–41.

is not every woman's idea of a 'happy ending' (66:7–14). The idea of
a society ruled by women is specifically mentioned in Isaiah as a sign
of political chaos (3:12), and the use of the image of a harlot to
denote evil, another male construct, out of sympathy with what
women feel, also occurs in Isaiah (e.g. 1:26).

But on the other hand, there are in Isaiah four passages that
provide scriptural authority for an alternative, in which women
break out of this subordinate, passive role. The images of women
rebuffing a powerful royal suitor with a scornful toss of the head
(37:22), and shaking off the dust and fetters of captivity and enjoying
the luxury of freedom and independence (52:1–2), have been mentioned already, and require little further comment. The first of these,
it must be said, remains very much within a male-dominated society,
where women's reactions are restricted to the occasional defiant
gesture. But the second, albeit metaphorical like the other one,
applied to the liberation of the city of Jerusalem or her people, uses
more powerful, more politically charged language: 'awake',
'strength, power', 'shake off the dust', 'loose' (*JB* 'free'). A close
modern political parallel is the Palestinian Arabic word *intifaḍa*, often
translated 'uprising', but which suggests waking up and shaking off
the dust after a long time asleep. The Isaiah passage is at the very
least a striking exception to normal biblical usage in that here an
author has chosen a female image to express ideas of liberation and
independence, rather than the evil of harlotry or the assumed
perfection of marital bliss. In the light of two further examples we
may be entitled to add these few glimpses of an alternative view of
women to the 'God as mother' passages discussed in the previous
section.

The interpretation of Isaiah 7:14 has probably been more discussed
down the ages than any other passage in Isaiah. In chapter 4, we
looked in some detail at its role in the cult of the Virgin Mary, and it
figured prominently in our discussion of anti-Jewish polemic and
mediaeval disputations in chapter 6. Since the Reformation, scholars
have put forward numerous alternative interpretations of the 'Immanuel sign', looking closely at the original Hebrew and at its
original context in eighth-century BC Jerusalem. But in modern times
few if any have applied feminist exegetical method to it despite the
fact that the subject of the verse is a 'young woman' and the point
seems prima facie to be somehow related to what she does and says.
This is no doubt because interpreters of the verse, who have been

predominantly male, have either used it to uphold their doctrine of the Virgin Birth (cf. Matth.1:23), or focussed their attention on the males in the context, King Ahaz and his son (Hezekiah), or Isaiah and his son (Immanuel), or Immanuel, the woman's son.

Throughout such a history of male attitudes and presuppositions, it would have been hard for an alternative, feminist interpretation to surface. Yet is it not possible that the point of the 'sign' is the contrast between a young woman's faith and the ineptitude and faithlessness of the king? Faith is a key theme in the chapter (cf. vv.4, 9) as also in other passages in Isaiah (e.g. 1:21, 26; 30:15; 53:1). It is generally agreed that the meaning of the name Immanuel 'God is with us' has this significance here (cf. 8:8–10), but the fact that it is on the lips of a young woman has not to my knowledge been sufficiently emphasized.

According to a widely accepted interpretation of the passage, the 'sign' is the shortness of the time between the woman's conception of a child and its birth: in a mere nine months the present crisis will be over and everyone will be celebrating victory over the local threat from the Syro-Ephraimite coalition, some by calling their sons 'Immanuel'. The general gist of this view of the passage as a whole is probably right, but it is typical of a male interpretation in its total disregard for the woman's role. She and her nine months' pregnancy are just a kind of cipher for 'a short time'. The fact that she is the subject of the verse, pointed to by the introductory word *hinneh* 'behold', and that she is the only person in the verse who does anything, is completely ignored. Her role as the one who actually pronounces the keyword 'Immanuel' is of no significance.

The contrast between a powerful king and a mere woman is heightened by the fact that, like other female images in Isaiah, it is set in the context of a social system in which women had no power or independence, and it was thought absurd that they should (cf. Isa.3:12). Also it might be pointed out that, even if she is the centre-piece of the sign, she is very much being used by men for their prophetic purpose. But on the other hand, if the present interpretation is accepted, then Isaiah 7:14 does provide another example of the use of female imagery where the woman in her own right, who calls her son 'Immanuel', stands for faith and strength of character, in contrast to a man whose heart 'shook as the trees in the forest shake before the wind' (7:2).

This brings us finally to one of the most popular images in modern radical Jewish and Christian feminism, that of Lilith, the dangerous and seductive female demon of Jewish legend, who seizes newborn infants and visits men sleeping alone.[53] Isaiah 34:14 is the only place in the Bible where the name 'Lilith' occurs: 'Wildcats shall meet with hyenas, goat-demons shall call to each other; there too shall Lilith repose, and find a place to rest.' It has been customary in Western European tradition, since the Reformation at least, to demythologize this verse entirely by translating Hebrew *lilit* as 'screech-owl' (*KJV*) or 'night-jar' (*REB*) or the like. The verse would not warrant a place in the present study of Isaiah in the history of Christianity, were it not for the fact that some recent translations, including the ecumenical *New Revised Standard Version* (1989) cited above, which is one of the latest and most widely used, and the Catholic *Jerusalem Bible* (1966), actually restore the name 'Lilith'. A footnote in the Oxford Annotated Edition of the *NRSV* to the effect that Lilith is 'a storm demon found in abandoned places', a theory based on the occurrence of a similar name in Assyrian, is hardly going to alter the course of Lilith's exegetical history, least of all in modern feminist writing.

The ancient versions understood the word to refer to a 'witch' (Vulgate *lamia*; cf. Symmachus) or, in classical Greek terms, a 'fury' (*erinus*: cf. Jerome, Comm.). In his very literal Greek translation, Aquila preserves the name 'Lilith', as does the official Christian Syriac version of the Bible. Ancient drawings of her on incantation bowls show her as a Medusa-like creature with dishevelled hair, and in some Aramaic magical texts she is represented as bound with chains and fetters of iron.[54] The *Authorized Version* has 'night monster' in the margin, and the original edition of the *RSV* 'night hag'.

Although only once mentioned in the Bible, Lilith is a well-known character in Jewish folk-lore, much feared as the cause of marital problems and infant mortality. She is less familiar in Christian tradition, although she emerges quite conspicuously in the literature of the Romantic period, including Goethe's *Faust* and poems by Dante Gabriel Rossetti and Browning.[55] The Scottish minister George MacDonald's novel *Lilith* (1895), discussed in an earlier

---

[53] Midrash Rabbah Numbers 9:4–10; cf. Montgomery, *Aramaic Incantation Texts*, p. 190; L .Blau, 'Lilith'; G. Scholem, 'Lilith'; Warner, *Monuments and Maidens*, pp. 221f.; Pagels, *Adam, Eve and the Serpent*, p. 145.

[54] Gordon, 'Two magic bowls in Teheran', p. 310; cf. Duling, 'Testament of Solomon', p. 967, note 5p, p. 966, note 13a.

[55] *DBTEL*, p. 455.

chapter, has been described as 'the climax of Lilith's career in English'.[56] Bram Dijkstra has submitted late nineteenth-century representations of Lilith, ('the world's first virago'), together with her daughter Lamia, to a critical analysis in *Idols of Perversity. Fantasies of Feminine Evil in Fin-de-Siècle Culture*.[57] There are not many paintings of Lilith, but one by Kenyon Cox (1856–1919), reproduced in the American intellectuals' journal *Scribner's Monthly* in 1892, focusses on her love affair with a snake, a recurring theme in this period, where she symbolizes more than anything 'serpentine feminine bestiality'.[58] (Plate 32)

Before looking briefly at how Lilith is used by feminists today, it might be worth looking again, from a feminist viewpoint, at her one biblical appearance. The first thing to note is that she is the only one of all the many creatures in the chapter to be mentioned by name. Outside of prose narrative sections (e.g. 6–9; 36–39), there are relatively few significant personal names in the Book of Isaiah – Abraham and Sarah (51:2), Beulah and Hephzibah (62:4) appear once, and Cyrus twice (44:28; 45:1) – and 'Lilith', a Hebrew form analogous to the name Judith, is one of them. It is therefore not enough merely to group her with the jackals, ostriches, hyenas and other anonymous inhabitants of the desert mentioned in the passage, especially when we know that from ancient times there have been so many colourful stories and traditions surrounding her. It is really a most astonishing fact that she should be mentioned by name in the Hebrew Bible.

Secondly, it is even more astonishing that she is depicted as 'finding rest'. According to Jewish legend, the problem of Lilith begins because she and Adam 'never found peace together for when he wished to lie with her she took offence at the recumbent posture he demanded ...'.[59] By definition Lilith is a restless creature, banished from society but constantly disturbing and threatening it. To depict her at rest is therefore thought-provoking to say the least. The intransitive verb translated 'alight' in the *RSV* occurs in Biblical Hebrew only here and Deut.28:65, but related nouns and adjectives in other contexts (Isa.28:12; Jer.6:16; Ps.35:20) confirm that its

56   *DBTEL*, p. 455; see also p. 165 above.
57   See especially, pp. 306–9.
58   Dijkstra, *Idols of Perversity*, p. 307. see *Scribner's Monthly*, 12 (1892), p. 744.
59   Warner, *Monuments and Maidens*, p. 221.

meaning here is 'find rest, repose' as all the ancient versions and most modern ones agree (cf. *REB, NRSV*).

The other thing that strikes the reader of this chapter is the contrast between the predominantly male violence and aggression of the first thirteen verses, involving rams, wild oxen, young steers and mighty bulls, and the gentler, more restful and predominantly female images that start with Lilith in verse 14b: 'There shall the owl nest and lay and hatch and gather her young in her shadow; yea, there shall the kites be gathered, each one with her mate. Seek and read from the book of the Lord: Not one of these shall be missing; none shall be without her mate'. Without wishing to push this interpretation too far, it does seem as though a major theme in this passage is the destruction of a male society that has gone wrong – as verse 12 puts it, 'they shall name it "No Kingdom There" and all its princes will be nothing' – and the setting up of an alternative society in which the restless outsider Lilith, till now feared and persecuted, can 'find a place to rest'. A comparison with the new society depicted in a more familiar Isaianic vision of a world where 'the wolf shall dwell with the lamb and the leopard shall lie down with the kid' (11:6–9) might be interesting.

However that may be, Lilith has now become important as a feminist 'heroine' and a symbol of woman's experience.[60] Ruether, citing Isaiah 34:14,[61] makes the point that while in Jewish tradition the stories of Adam, Lilith, his first wife who refused to be dominated by him, and Eve who submitted to him, were never taken as 'high theological teaching', Christianity 'elevated the story of Eve's responsibility for the fall of Adam to a position of ultimate theological seriousness'. In the dominant male mythology of western culture, 'the female is seen as the enemy of harmony, good order and felicity in human affairs', and the story that marginalizes and demonizes Lilith as a symbol of that power, has been used to back up traditional beliefs in the superiority and dominant position of men in society and in the family. The six 'Lilith Poems' by the distinguished American feminist critic Alicia Suskin Ostriker are a powerful counter-example.[62] In the eighties, such mythology is being scrutinized with the same urgency and seriousness as the

---

[60]   J.Plaskow, 'The coming of Lilith', pp. 205f.
[61]   Ruether, *Sexism and God-Talk*, p. 168; and see note 7 on p. 278.
[62]   Ostriker, *Feminist Revision and the Bible*, pp. 92–9.

history of the persecution of witches,[63] and a positive side of the Lilith story discovered. Her name appears in at least half a dozen titles of works ranging from collections of poems to studies of women and religion.[64] Feminists have elevated Lilith, instead of Eve, 'to a position of high theological seriousness'. Jewish radical feminists have given her name to a journal published in New York, and she is given a positive interpretation in a recent dictionary of first names.[65]

The legend is that she was created equal with Adam (Gen.1:26–7), and that it was because of Adam's selfish desire to dominate her, in bed as well as everywhere else, that forced her to leave. A brilliant modern apocryphal addition to the legend imagines Eve and Lilith meeting, and telling each other their different experiences with Adam: 'They taught each other many things, and told each other stories, and laughed together and cried over and over till the bond of sisterhood grew between them ... And God and Adam were expectant and afraid the day Eve and Lilith returned to the garden bursting with possibilities, ready to rebuild it together.'[66]

Already in an ancient gnostic version of the story, the roles of Adam's two wives were reversed so that Lilith was the spirit-endowed one and Eve the carnal one.[67] Whether it is conceivable that there could be in the Isaiah reference any sympathy with Lilith, or for the non-patriarchal society where she has found peace, it is certainly remarkable that the one scriptural reference to her contrasts her with the wicked violent rulers of a traditional male society.

Isaiah contains some radical, revolutionary language and images, as we have seen, including some that point in the direction of different ways of thinking about God, and some addressed to the plight of 'captive women'. Before leaving the subject of feminist uses of Isaiah, we may conclude by suggesting that, just as it is only after the rulers of Edom have been destroyed that Lilith finds rest, so there can be no rest in the struggle for liberation (no 'post-feminism'), until the injustices of predominantly male institutions have been removed from every society.

---

[63] Cf. Ruether, *Sexism and God-Talk*, pp. 170f.
[64] Wandor, *Gardens of Eden: Poems for Eve and Lilith* (1984); Chalker, *Lilith: A Snake in the Grass* (1981); Bitton, *Le mythe juif de Lilith* (1988); Bril, *Lilith ou la mère obscure* (1984); de Giovanni, *L'ora di Lilith* (1987); Rigney, *Lilith's Daughters. Women and Religion in Contemporary Fiction* (1982).
[65] Campbell, ed., *Bloomsbury Dictionary of First Names*, p. 153.
[66] Plaskow, 'The coming of Lilith', p. 207.
[67] P. R. Alexander, 'The fall into knowledge' in *A Walk in the Garden*, p. 97.

CHAPTER 12

The Peaceable Kingdom

The unique popularity of the Book of Isaiah in the Church applies as much to the late twentieth century as to any other period. An Anglican clergyman whose popular paperbacks *Church on the Threshold. Renewing the Local Church* (1991) and *Threshold God. Discovering Christ in the Margins of Life* (1992) are peppered with quotations from Isaiah, readily acknowledges his debt to Isaiah ('more than the Gospels', he told me) and speaks of a 'relationship with Isaiah' that goes back to his student days. Cyril Ashton's 'threshold' imagery comes partly from the vision in chapter 6 ('the doorposts and the thresholds shook' *NIV*), and partly from 66:9: 'Do I bring to the moment of birth and not give delivery?' A Catholic writer recently described him as 'the most remarkable of the prophets ... and by far the greatest writer in the Old Testament'.[1] Far more references to Isaiah, especially chapters 40–55, are listed in the 'Scriptural Index' at the end of one of the most widely used modern collections of hymns in English, than to any other book apart from the Psalms and the Gospels,[2] and a high proportion of the many new hymns in such collections, written in the 1970s and 1980s, are musical settings of passages from Isaiah, especially 40–55, taken almost verbatim from the *Revised Standard Version*. Some of these, like Isaiah 55:12 ('You shall go forth with joy ...')[3] and the 'Salvation oracle' in Isaiah 43:1–7, which appears in at least four new hymns,[4] and significantly as a sample devotional text in a paperback best-seller on spirituality,[5] are passages virtually unknown to earlier generations.

---

[1] See above p. 3.
[2] *Hymns Old and New with Supplement*, ed. K. Mayhew (Bath Press, Avon, 1989).
[3] *MP* 281.
[4] *HON* 122, 136, 472, 627; see above, p. 191.
[5] Hughes, *God of Surprises*, pp. 46–9.

The increasing awareness of worldwide social and economic injustice and the experience of two catastrophic World Wars, have changed perceptions of the Church's role in the world, and this is reflected in the selection and interpretation of texts from Isaiah. A good example is the use of a disturbing question from Isaiah 21 – 'What of the night?' – as the starting point for 'a personal reflection on living at this time'. This is how the Anglican priest and writer Alan Ecclestone chose to begin his book *The Night Sky of the Lord* (1980) in which he focusses on the horrors and sufferings caused by Christian antisemitism down the ages, culminating at Auschwitz.

Isaiah's role in Christian writing and preaching about the end of the world is another case in point. In his fascinating study *When Time Shall Be No More. Prophecy Belief in Modern American Culture* (1992), Paul Boyer cites numerous examples from the eighteenth century to the present day. America's doom is expressly foretold in Isaiah 18:1–2 in King James' *Authorized Version* with its explicit references to 'the land shadowing with wings' (that is, the eagle, America's national emblem, or to the US aircraft industry) ... 'a nation scattered and peeled' (that is 'clean shaven' as the US army was reputedly the first to issue a razor to every soldier) ... 'a nation meted out and trodden down' (a reference to the comprehensive Washington geographic surveys).[6]

For dispensationalists the 'Rapture' when the trumpet shall sound and the living and the dead together will be 'caught up in the clouds to meet the Lord' (cf. 1 Thess.4:16–17), is referred to in Isaiah 26:19 and 27:12–13. They also find a reference to the 'Tribulation' which will characterize the world after the 'Rapture' in Isaiah 24:20: 'the earth shall reel to and fro like a drunkard'.[7] 'The glories of the Millennium, that new world in which peace and justice prevail', are more often than not described in Isaianic language too.[8] Since 1970, scriptural texts predicting nuclear accidents, oil spills, global warming and receding rainforests have increasingly been sought out. Isaiah 34:9–10 is one of the most colourful examples: 'And the streams thereof shall be turned into pitch, and the dust thereof into brimstone, and the land thereof shall become burning pitch. It shall not be quenched night nor day; the smoke thereof shall go up for

---

[6] Boyer, *When Time Shall be No More*, pp. 245–6.
[7] Boyer, *When Time Shall be No More*, p. 257.
[8] Boyer, *When Time Shall be No More*, pp. 318–20.

ever; from generation to generation it shall lie waste; none shall pass through it for ever and ever'.[9]

In this context mention must be made of David Coresh, the leader of a break-away messianic sect known as the Branch Davidians, based at Waco, Texas, who took his name from Isaiah 45:1: 'Thus says the Lord to his anointed, to Cyrus (Hebrew Koresh) whose right hand I have grasped, to subdue nations before him ...' The uncompromising tone of this chapter has already been referred to in connection with Christian missionary endeavours[10] ('I will go before you and level the mountains, I will break in pieces the doors of bronze and cut asunder the bars of iron ...'). This provided the sect with scriptural authority to fortify their base, known as Apocalypse Ranch, with a huge armoury of weapons and ammunition, and may be said to have contributed to the violent and bloody showdown with the US forces of law and order, in which there were many casualties and the entire base was destroyed.

Another twentieth-century development in the history of the Church is interfaith dialogue, and here again Isaiah has made his contribution. Neveh Shalom, the ecumenical kibbutz founded by a Dominican in 1979 with the object of bringing together Jews, Christians and Muslims in Israel, received its name from Isaiah.[11] The passage in which the phrase occurs, Isaiah 32:15–20, is prescribed to be read at masses for peace and justice, and prominent in an influential Vatican II pronouncement on social justice, to which we shall return later.[12] In the 1960s a small group of French Dominicans expressly committed to improving Jewish-Christian relations chose to call their house in Agron Street, Jerusalem 'la Maison de Saint-Isaie'.

In a recent volume published in a series concerned with 'the Contact between Christianity and Other Religions, Beliefs and Cultures',[13] Walter Strolz makes extensive use of Isaiah, especially 'Deutero-Isaiah', in an attempt to find a point of contact between biblical religion and Zen Buddhism. He starts with an assessment entirely typical of modern Christian interpretations of Isaiah: 'The prophetic proclamation of biblical Israel reached its zenith in Deutero-Isaiah during the Babylonian exile'.[14] He then finds in these

[9]   Boyer, *When Time Shall be No More*, p. 331.
[10] See p. 155.   [11] Cf. p. 104.
[12] *Gaudium et Spes* (7 December 1965), para.78: see below.
[13] Strolz, 'The incomparability of God as Biblical experience of faith', pp. 106–15.
[14] Strolz, 'Incomparability', p. 106.

chapters appropriate scriptural formulations for every part of his argument, from the 'all-questioning transitoriness' of human existence in 40:7, the incomparability of the God of Israel in 40:18, the radical monotheism of 43:10–11, and the total rejection of dualism in 45:6c-7, to faith and courage in 41:10, 44:2 and 51:7–8, and the 'eternal destiny of man in the irrevocably blessed unity of creation and history' in 45:18 and 51:6.[15] Other Christian writers, concerned to break down the barriers of western prejudice in a multi-faith context and separating themselves both from anti-Catholic propagandists[16] and from the imperialist foreign missionaries of earlier days,[17] even find a way of softening the sharp edge of Isaiah's satirical attacks on idolatry. It is after all, they point out, the Israelites who are addressed in these chapters, not the idol worshippers.[18]

Many other examples could be cited, from the use made of Isaiah by feminist writers[19] and recent settings of the *Rorate* and *Veni Immanuel*, to the following Valentine greeting from Isaiah 35:1 published in a daily newspaper: 'J: The desert doth blossom as the rose. C'.[20] Out of all the many themes, metaphors, images, mottoes and catchwords derived from Isaiah, however, we have selected three as peculiarly characteristic of our own time. First must come social justice and Jesus' so-called 'Nazareth manifesto' summed up in the words of Isaiah 61:1 as 'good news for the poor' (cf. Luke 4:18–19). Of course this emphasis in contemporary Christianity is not new. It has always been there even although it has not always been so conspicuous as it is today. The other two themes of this chapter, the 'swords into ploughshares' motif from chapter 2 (2:2–4; cf. Micah 4:1–3) and the 'Peaceable Kingdom' from 11 (11:6–9), given little prominence in early and mediaeval Christianity, are today probably among the most familiar images from the whole book, as well-known and widely used as the ox and the ass or the Jesse tree in earlier and more traditional contexts. Their frequent occurrence today, not only in hymns, sermons and religious literature, but also in newspapers, political speeches and everyday language, provides one of our best illustrations of the close relationship between Bible use and contemporary culture. It is hard for us nowadays to imagine how earlier

[15] Strolz, 'Incomparability', pp. 107–10.
[16] See pp. 138ff.   [17] See pp. 154ff.
[18] Hooker and Lamb, *Love the stranger*, p. 89.
[19] See chapter 11.
[20] *The Independent* 14 February, 1993, p. 14.

generations of preachers, religious artists and Bible readers could
have failed to make more of these two graphic images. There are
some references to them in mediaeval art and elsewhere; but it is
only now, in the age of world wars and increasing global awareness,
that the full force of these two powerful images has been appreciated
and exploited.

We begin with Isaiah in the context of current concerns for social
justice. In a powerful little monograph, *Option for the Poor. The Basic
Principles of Liberation Theology in the Light of the Bible* (1987), the
distinguished Catholic biblical scholar Norbert Lohfink devotes his
third and final chapter, entitled 'God and the Poor in the Bible', to
Isaiah. The author does not count himself among the liberation
theologians, but as a Jesuit, a parish priest and an active member of
the *Integrierte Gemeinde*, a group of Munich Christians concerned with
biblical, liturgical and community renewal, he is aware of their
struggle and writes for them. He notes that the two texts in the
Gospels where the message of Jesus is called 'a Gospel for the poor'
are both inspired by Isaiah: his reply to John the Baptist's question
'Are you he who is to come?' (Matt.11:4–6; Luke 7:22–3), is made up
of texts from Isaiah 29:18–19, 35:5–6, 42:18 and 61:1; and Luke begins
his account of Jesus' public life with the reading of Isaiah 61:1–2 in
the synagogue at Nazareth (Luke 4:16–30).[21] The phrase 'to bring
good news to the poor' does not originate with Jesus, but comes from
Isaiah 61:1.[22] To find out what 'Gospel for the poor' means, who are
the poor and what exactly is the good news, we therefore have to
consult Isaiah, especially chapters 40–55, where the history of God
with his poor, embodied in the image of a suffering servant, takes
place on a new, worldwide stage (cf. 50:4–6; 53:8–9).[23] God's poor
are to become a model for all societies, 'a light to the nations' (cf.
Isaiah 42:3–4, 6; 49:6; 51:4–5; 55:4–5). Chapters 60–62 ('a midrash
on texts from Deutero-Isaiah') portray a future marked by a 'turning
point from poverty to wealth, as well as the advent of peace and of
just dealing with one another'. 'The book also provided a kind of
hermeneutical key to the praying of the Psalter, at least insofar as the
Psalms present themselves as prayers of "the poor"'.[24]

Isaiah 61:1 has provided several others with authority and inspira-

[21] Lohfink, *Option for the Poor*, pp. 53f.
[22] Lohfink, *Option for the Poor*, pp. 53f.
[23] Lohfink, *Option for the Poor*, p. 68.
[24] Lohfink, *Option for the Poor*, p. 72.

tion in their struggle for justice. Archbishop Desmond Tutu, in a paper on *Church and Prophecy in South Africa Today*, quotes the passage in full, along with 1:14,17, 58:6, chapter 11 and Psalm 72:1–2 ('Give the king thy justice, O God'). He uses these texts to dismiss the argument that 'religion and politics do not mix ... he (the king) was expected to rule as God would rule, showing particular concern for the weak, the hungry, the poor, the marginalised, etc., as God had demonstrated consistently'.[25] *Liberty to the Captives* by Stanley Hope, councillor for a mainly Asian ward in Rochdale and Community Relations Officer, is another example. It is a study of Christianity, racism and the law in Britain, published by the Iona Community. Journalists chose a sermon on Isaiah 61:1 to sum up the religious convictions of Terry Waite, the Archbishop of Canterbury's special envoy, on his release from five years in captivity as a hostage in Lebanon: 'he sent me to bind up the broken-hearted, to proclaim liberty to the captives ...'.[26] Ethiopian Christians ingeniously found a reference to their own country in the Hebrew of this verse: '... he sent me to Ethiopia (*le-ḥabash*), to the broken-hearted ...'[27]

A good instance of the impact Isaiah can have on the media took place at a service in St Paul's Cathedral on 27 March 1990, held to mark the end of the Inner London Education Authority. The leader of the ILEA, Mr Neil Fletcher, in a thinly veiled attack on Mrs Thatcher and her Tory government, substituted a reading from Isaiah for the one he had been asked to read from Luke 2: 'Woe to those who make unjust laws and to those who issue oppressive decrees and deprive people of their rights ... What will you do on the day of reckoning; when disaster comes from afar?' (Isa.10:1–3). The Mayoress of Wandsworth among others got up and walked out. Next day Isaiah was quoted on the front page of *The Times*, and the tabloids had headlines like THE PULPIT HIJACK: OUTRAGE AS LABOUR EDUCATION CHIEF DELIVERS POLITICAL 'LESSON' IN ST PAUL'S.[28] The Bishop of London expressed his views to the press in no uncertain terms. Then in a letter to *The Times* on 30 March Mr Fletcher responded by maintaining that the reading from Isaiah was more fitting than the Luke passage as an expression of 'the deep hurt and

---

[25] *Church and Prophecy*, pp. 21–2.
[26] *The Independent*, 19 November, 1991, p. 3.
[27] In an unpointed Hebrew text *la-ḥabosh* 'to bind up' looks exactly like *lĕ-ḥabash* 'to Abyssinia'. Cf. Ullendorff, 'Jesus in the Hebrew Bible', p. 271.
[28] *Daily Mail*, 28 March, 1990.

anger of Londoners over the ILEA's undeserved abolition ... As the
bishop knows full well that passage (Luke 2:41ff.) is shortly followed
by Luke 4, in which Jesus also runs into opposition from the
establishment at a service in Nazareth by reading from Isaiah.' While
the passage Jesus preached on in Nazareth (Isaiah 61:1ff.) appears
regularly in most of the official lectionaries of the Church (and the
synagogue), the reading chosen by Mr Fletcher does not. It is used,
however, by a Catholic liberation theologian in his discussion of the
relationship between justice and war,[29] which brings us to our next
set of examples.

In the whole revolution within the Catholic Church that followed
Vatican II, Isaiah has played a prominent role, Isaiah the prophet of
justice and peace, that is, not Isaiah the prophet of the Virgin Birth
or the prophet of the Suffering Messiah. Passages central to the
Church in earlier ages are rarely mentioned or given a different
interpretation, while passages hardly noticed before are given a
striking new emphasis. In their pronouncement on justice and peace
(*Gaudium et Spes*), in the 'Pastoral Constitution on the Church in the
Modern World', the cardinals and bishops at the Second Vatican
Council in 1965 focus on just such a phrase.[30] It comes from one of
the three readings from Isaiah now prescribed to be used at masses
for peace and justice. The passage (32:15–20) consists of a beautiful
vision, less familiar than the 'swords into ploughshares' passage (2:2–
4) or 'the wolf lying down with the lamb' (11:6–9), but almost as
effective. It imagines a world where 'justice will dwell in the wilderness and righteousness abide in the fruitful field' (v.15).[31] According
to the Vatican II document, verse 17 contains a unique scriptural
definition of peace in terms of justice: 'Peace is an enterprise of
justice'.[32] In this interpretation of the verse, 'peace' (Hebrew *shalom*)
is the subject of the sentence. The usual view, reflected for example
in the *New English Bible*, is that 'peace' is the predicate: 'righteousness
shall yield peace'. The *Jerusalem Bible*'s 'integrity will bring peace'
similarly has no trace of the 1960s Vatican II interpretation. The
future tenses do suggest that this is an account of how things will
develop in the new age, rather than a definition: the coming of the

---

[29] Miranda, *Marx and the Bible*, pp. 122, 166.
[30] *Gaudium et Spes* (7 December 1965), ed. Flannery, para.78, pp. 986–7.
[31] Cf. Miranda, *Marx and the Bible*, pp. 220ff.
[32] This is the translation given in the 1975 (red) edition of *Vatican Council II. The Conciliar and Post-Conciliar Documents*. The 1981 (green) edition, ed. A. Flannery, blunts the impact of the verse by bringing it into line with the *RSV*: 'the effect of righteousness will be peace'.

Spirit (v.15) makes it possible for justice to flourish in the wilderness (v.16), and the result of that will be peace (vv.17–20). But the interpretation put on these words by the cardinals and bishops is a powerful one, and most significant as an indication of their thinking at the time. By placing the emphasis on the action words in v.17 – *ta erga tes dikaiosunes ... kratesei* (LXX 'the works of righteousness ... will prevail'),[33] rather than on purpose or result, they found in the verse a definition of peace and justice in terms of this-worldly praxis, rather than merely one more description of a messianic kingdom beyond the reach of human achievements. Out of context the Latin *opus iustitiae pax* (omitting the future verb *erit*), translated as 'peace is an enterprise of justice', makes a fine motto, and undoubtedly set the agenda for the discussion of the nature of peace which followed: '(peace) must be actualized by man thirsting after an ever more perfect reign of justice ... peace, justice, love are not private ... internal attitudes, but social realities, implying historical liberation.' The section ends incidentally with the 'swords into ploughshares' text (Isa.2:4).

One liberation theologian, greatly influenced by Isaiah, is the Mexican Church leader José Porfirio Miranda. A glance at the index of biblical references in his *Marx and the Bible* (1977) shows how central Isaiah is to his thinking. Next to Psalms and the Gospels, Isaiah is by far the most often quoted book in the Bible.[34] But what is interesting is his selection of texts. A passage like 7:14 ('A virgin shall conceive') is not mentioned, nor are those verses used in an earlier age to prove the divinity of Christ or the doctrine of the Trinity. Chapter 16 is cited more than once, but not because of any interest in Ruth the Moabitess and the ancestry of the Messiah.[35] Although not now in any lectionary, and submerged in what are dismissed as largely obscure and irrelevant 'oracles against the foreign nations', chapter 16 contains some messianic language and imagery as fine as any in the more familiar passages from chapters 9, 11, 32, and 42. 16:4–5 read as follows: 'When the oppressor is no more, and destruction has ceased ... a throne will be established in steadfast love ... on it will sit in faithfulness one who judges and seeks justice and is swift to do righteousness.' It was the liberation theologians who unearthed the

[33] Cf. Hebrew *ma'aseh tzĕdakah ... àbodat .....* Jerome's *opus iustitiae* misses this dimension of the verse as his commentary shows.
[34] Miranda, *Marx and the Bible*, pp. 322–3.
[35] See above. pp. 69ff.

passage and applied it to our world today. Justice is something that has to be put into practice. In the oppressive regimes of Latin America and elsewhere, Christians found in Isaiah a most eloquent expression of this ideal. Justice, righteousness and even the violent overthrow of oppressors are among the commonest themes in Isaiah, and raise searching questions for those who hear the words of Isaiah read out in their own language at mass.

Isaiah 11 is another example of the contemporary shift in interpretation. In earlier times verse 1, about the root of Jesse, was regularly quoted in the context of the birth and lineage of Christ.[36] In Miranda and other contemporary interpretations, attention switches to verses 3 and 4: 'With righteousness he shall judge the poor and decide with equity for the meek of the earth, and he shall smite the earth with the rod of his mouth.' Already for the author of a mediaeval hymn, as we saw, the rod of justice in verse 4 took precedence over the rod (*virga*) from the root of Jesse in verse 1 which for others pointed to the Virgin Mary (*virgo*) and the royal ancestry of Christ.[37]

Miranda's handling of chapters 11 and 16, however, exposes an alternative way to understand such imagery, clearly reflecting a change in contemporary perceptions of the role of the Church in society. He is also a trained biblical scholar, who knows Hebrew, quotes von Rad, Mowinckel and others, and sees it as his task to get back to the original social and economic context of Isaiah in ancient Israel. In this task he is often highly successful and original. Let me give a few examples. In chapter 1 Isaiah condemns his leaders as 'rulers of Sodom' (v.10). The question as to why he, and also Jeremiah in a parallel passage (23:14), choose this expression is not often seriously considered in the commentaries, but Miranda asks What is the sin of Sodom? and, in line with modern applications of the concept of intratextuality,[38] examines other biblical references to Sodom to answer it. It emerges that Isaiah's choice of Sodom is quite extraordinarily apt. The evidence is in Ezekiel 16:49: 'The crime of your sister Sodom was luxury, opulence, complacency ... they never helped the poor and the needy.'[39] In fact another look at the story of Sodom and Gomorrah itself in Genesis 18 confirms that the sin of Sodom is not to be understood, as it often has been especially within

---

[36] See pp. 74ff.   [37] See above, pp. 78ff.
[38] See above, p. 10.
[39] Miranda, *Marx and the Bible*, pp. 95–6.

the Christian tradition, in terms of sexual sin alone, but in terms of justice and righteousness. Of course Miranda went to the text with a particular bias; he would never deny that. Like the Vatican Council, he was looking for scriptural authority for his view that the Church should be biassed in favour of the oppressed and should fight for justice wherever it appears. But his interpretation of Isaiah is none the less convincing for that.

Another example of an interpretation inspired and informed by Miranda's commitment to justice and freedom is his explanation of the phrase 'evil-doers'.[40] Long ago Mowinckel argued that this expression, which is particularly common in Psalms, was of cultic origin and referred to sorcerers or the like. Miranda convincingly rejects this view, citing Isaiah 58:6–10 where the word for 'evil'('-wickedness' *RSV*) is clearly contrasted with caring for the hungry and has nothing to do with magical spells. His discussion of 53:4 is another example where he rejects ritualistic or mystical interpretations in favour of a concrete practical one. The usual modern translations have 'surely he has borne our pains and carried our sickness' (*RSV*), suggesting something like the atonement ritual in which the scapegoat bears the sins of the people on its back (cf. Lev.16:22). But Miranda quotes Matthew 8:17, where the Isaiah expression is understood to mean, in the context of Jesus' healing miracles, that he actually 'removed our infirmities and carried away our diseases', with no suggestion that he was offering to perform some kind of expiatory sacrifice.[41] Miranda is not a Marxist: the last part of his book is a searching critique of Marxism. But his understanding of the Bible in terms of praxis, in concrete, this-wordly terms, owes as much to his familiarity with Marxist doctrine as to his training as an economist, and throws a good deal of light on the meaning of Isaiah.

Another Catholic theologian from Latin America whose influence on contemporary Christianity has been very great, is Gustavo Gutiérrez. His *A Theology of Liberation. History, Politics and Salvation* (1974) was one of the very first examples of liberation theology to be published in English. It contains some excellent examples of how Isaiah – 'the best theologian among Old Testament writers'[42] – is

---

40 Miranda, *Marx and the Bible*, pp. 100–2.
41 Miranda, *Marx and the Bible*, p. 129.
42 Gutiérrez, *A Theology of Liberation*, p. 154, citing E.Jacob, *Théologie de l'Ancien Testament* (Neuchatel 1954), p. 43, who is referring to 'Second Isaiah' (chapters 40–55).

interpreted in this context. I shall refer to one that is not in itself original but is given new force by the bias of liberation theology. It concerns the relationship between creation and liberation, a theme richly developed in Isaiah. According to 43:1, 44:2, 45:9–11 and many other passages, the liberation of Israel from oppression is described as an act of creation: God is the 'creator of Israel'(43:15). In other words all the rich mythical language and imagery associated with creation is applied to the Exodus and liberation from injustice and oppression. Moreover if Israel is understood as a symbol for the poor and oppressed, then these are eloquent statements about the nature of God and the role of his people in the world, a role which is primarily one of redemption and the liberation of the oppressed.[43]

Charles Elliot is not a Catholic nor a Latin American, but as an economist and theologian and former director of Christian Aid, he confronted some of the same problems as they do, and his interpretation of Isaiah has much in common with Miranda and Gutiérrez. Here are two examples from his little book *Praying the Kingdom. Towards a Political Spirituality* (1985). First, he makes a number of telling points in his discussion of the parable of the vineyard in chapter 5.[44] He reminds us that the whole point of the parable is that it condemns injustice and oppression. The punch-line is the famous wordplay in verse 7: 'He looked for justice (*mishpaṭ*), but behold bloodshed (*mishpaḥ*); for righteousness (*tzĕdaqah*), but behold a cry (*tzĕ'aqah*)!' The wider context, often ignored by commentators before the advent of recent more holistic approaches to the text, makes the point even more explicit. Verse 8 is surely intended to explain what 'bloodshed' and 'a cry' refer to. They refer to the cries for help from the victims of ruthless property-owners and land-speculators: 'Woe to those who join house to house, add field to field … !' Another useful insight emerges from his comparison of the vineyard in Isaiah with the parable of the vineyard in Mark 12. In Isaiah the vineyard is destroyed: 'I will remove its hedge, I will break down its wall, I will make it a waste …' (vv.5–6). In Mark it is the tenants who are destroyed and the vineyard is given to others; and the next verse explains that 'others' refers to the outcasts and the poor ('The stone which the builders rejected has become the head of the corner'). So justice is done; the land is given back to those from whom it had been appropriated.

[43]   Gutiérrez, *A Theology of Liberation*, pp. 154–7.
[44]   Elliot, *Praying the Kingdom*, pp. 82ff.

My other example of Charles Elliot's use of Isaiah is his interpretation of the first seven verses of chapter 52.[45] They consist of two familiar hymns – 'Awake, awake, put on your strength, O Zion' and 'How beautiful are the feet' – separated by a rather odd prose passage between them (vv.3–6). Scholars note that this is the only passage in Deutero-Isaiah (40–55) where Assyria is mentioned, and treat it as a 'marginal gloss'.[46] Elliot, on the other hand, once again in line with current interest among scholars in larger literary units, takes the passage as a whole and sees in it a description of 'the kingdom' in terms of political liberation and economic justice: 'Shake yourself from the dust, arise, O captive Jerusalem! Loose the bonds from your neck, O captive daughter of Jerusalem! (political liberation). For thus says the Lord, "You were sold for nothing, and you shall be redeemed without money" ' (economic justice). It is not hard to relate this to contemporary third world economics, and there is clearly a homiletical purpose about this kind of interpretation. But it does throw some light on a difficult text, and, in particular, it reveals the connection between three short passages usually treated separately. It also illustrates once again how the interpretation of Isaiah is affected by the background and political aims of the interpreter.

We move on now to our second main twentieth-century Isaianic theme, 'swords into ploughshares'. It is an image little used in earlier periods, and where it does appear, as, for example, in Tertullian (c.160–c.220), Athanasius (c.296–373) and St Bonaventura (1221–74), it is used, generally, in a figurative sense.[47] A lively illustration accompanying Isaiah 2:4, in the thirteenth century *Bible Moralisée* shows two blacksmiths working at their anvil while an assistant is keeping them supplied with swords, but the interpretation has nothing directly to do with war. It is about the Church's mission to break through the hardness of human hearts by preaching the word of God. There is also a little-known painting by Jan Brueghel the Elder (1569–1625) (Plate 27),[48] and we mentioned earlier the example of a Scottish writer who, in a 1616 publication, used the phrase to express his view that the reign of King James VI represented a fulfilment of Isaiah's prophecy about the end of wars.[49]

---

[45] Elliot, *Praying the Kingdom*, pp. 119f.
[46] E.g. Westermann, *Isaiah 40–66*, p. 248.
[47] K. Quinsey, 'Swords into plowshares', pp. 746–7.
[48] Ertz, *Jan Brueghel der Ältere*, pp. 383–4, Fig.456.   [49] See p. 135.

An eighteenth-century paraphrase of the whole passage ('Behold the mountain of the Lord/in latter days shall rise')[50] was considered appropriate to be sung at a special BBC service to commemorate the ninetieth birthday of the veteran Methodist peace-campaigner Lord Soper in 1993. A less well-known variation on the theme occurs in a hymn by Charles Sylvester Horne (1865–1914), the influential London preacher and MP for Ipswich:

> All shall be well in his Kingdom of Peace,
> Freedom shall flourish and wisdom increase,
> Foe shall be friend when his triumphs we sing,
> Sword shall be sickle when Jesus is King.[51]

John Ruskin (1819–1900), making the biblical phrase characteristically his own, calls for 'soldiers of the ploughshare as well as soldiers of the sword'.[52]

Since the Second World War the situation has totally changed. The image has become a familiar part of the language of international peace negotiations. In 1959 a statue by the Soviet sculptor Evgeniy Vuchetich, entitled 'Let us beat our swords into ploughshares', was presented by the Soviet Union to the United Nations building in New York and can be seen in the North Garden area (Plate 34). It is about nine feet tall and, true to the violence of the biblical image, shows a man about to strike a huge sword with a hammer. The sword is already buckling in the grip of his left hand, and beneath it the sharp end of a ploughshare appears, already cutting into the soil. The Micah version of the text is inscribed on a wall in another part of the building. The verse appears, in Hebrew and Arabic, on a 'Monument of Peace' set up by the Israelis after the Six Day War in 1967, on the hillside beneath the Scottish Church, facing Mount Zion and the walls of the Old City, where for twenty years barbed wire and machine gun posts had divided the city.[53] A cartoonist used the image to highlight the special twentieth-century problem of disposing of nuclear-weapons, 'beating an ss20 into a ploughshare', even when the superpowers are agreed that they should be got rid of (Plate 35).[54] In the language of daily newspapers a 'swords into ploughshares project' has become a

[50]   *CH* 365.
[51]   *SBSA* 166. In some versions the 'sword shall be sickle' image is omitted: *HAP* 244.
[52]   *Unto this Last*, Essay 3, para.54 (*ODQ* p. 413).
[53]   Vilnay, *Guide to Israel* (19th edition) p. 88.
[54]   *The Independent* 28 December 1991.

shorthand expression used to describe a project 'aimed at converting the nuclear arms laboratories to civilian use'.[55]

In the seventies and eighties a bewildering number of publications, on a variety of contemporary issues, used it in their titles. There are at least half a dozen in the field of international politics and war studies, such as *Disarmament: Nuclear Swords or Unilateral Ploughshares?* by a Catholic peace campaigner.[56] Others include studies of economic problems in the North West of England[57] as well as in the North East,[58] a history of the Catholic Institute for International Relations,[59] a collection of essays in honour of Archbishop Desmond Tutu,[60] and a study of the issues raised for Israelis and Jews by the Intifada.[61] The memoirs of a First World War soldier[62] and the biography of a Welsh educationalist[63] are two more examples. No doubt the list could be longer. It is hard to think of another biblical phrase so much 'in the headlines' over such a precise period of time.

Isaiah has other contributions to make to the subject of global and regional peace. An essay on 'three kinds of peace'[64] finds its scriptural basis for all three in Isaiah. In decreasing order of desperation and fragility, they are the peace of the cauldron necessary in situations of injustice and dire need (26:11–12), the peace of the bird, protecting its young, vigilant and prepared for war (31:5),

[55]   *The Guardian*, 26 May 1994, p. 1.
[56]   Bruce Kent (Macmillan, London 1987); cf. J. A. Stockfisch, *Plowshares into Swords: Managing the American Defense Establishment* (Mason and Lipscomb, New York 1973); A.Wohlstatter, *Swords from Plowshares. The Military Potential of Civilian Nuclear Energy* (Chicago University Press 1979); J. Sandford, *The Sword and the Ploughshare: Autonomous Peace Initiatives in East Germany* (Merlin Press, London 1983); I. L. Claude, *Swords into Plowshares: the Problems and Progress of International Organization* (4th ed. Random, New York 1984); J. Simpson, *Ploughshares into Swords? The International Nuclear Non-Proliferation Network and the 1985 NPT Review Conference* (Council for Arms Control, London 1985); P. H. Folta, *From Swords into plowshares? Defense Industry Reforms in the People's Republic of China* (West View, Boulder, Colorado 1992).
[57]   B. Munske, *Swords into Ploughshares. Trident and Tornado in the North West* (Lancaster University 1985).
[58]   G. Philipson and D. Stevenson, *Aycliffe and Peterlee New Towns 1946–88: Swords into Ploughshares and Farewell Squalor* (Cambridge 1988).
[59]   M. J. Walsh, *From Sword to Ploughshare: Sword of the Spirit to Catholic Institute for International Relations 1940–1980* (London 1980).
[60]   B. Tlhagale and I. Mosala, edd.,*Hammering Swords into Ploughshares. Essays in Honour of Archbishop Desmond Tutu* (Eerdmans, Grand Rapids, Michigan, 1987).
[61]   C. Shindler, *Ploughshares into Swords?* (I. B. Tauris, London 1991).
[62]   W. Carr, *A Time to Leave the Ploughshares. A Gunner Remembers 1917–1918* (Chivers, Bath 1985).
[63]   B. Howells, *Swords into Ploughshares. The Mission of George M. Ll. Davies* (Welsh National Centre for Education, Bangor 1988).
[64]   Armand Abecassis, 'Three kinds of peace: Shalom shĕlomot' in *SIDIC* (Rome 1988), p. 14; cited by U. King, 'The Bible and Peace and War', pp. 153–4.

and finally the peace of the river 'a state of being and dynamic movement' which carries with it prosperity and love (66:12): There is the peace that comes when violence, injustice and trouble are happening to someone else; there is the peace that comes from the power to intimidate and prevent others from harming us; finally there is *shalom* imaged in the river that unites, enriches and fulfils the whole human race.

As the writer is a Catholic, it is significant that, of these three Isaianic images, only one (66:10–14) figures in the official post-Vatican II lectionary.[65] Verses from Isaiah 26:7–19 do appear once, as a weekday reading, but the violent 'cauldron' verse is omitted. A striking feature of Abecassis' use of these verses, as of the examples from Miranda, Elliot and others discussed above, is his careful attention to their literary context. In particular, as we saw in the previous chapter, by taking seriously the connection between 31:5 and the preceding verse, he discovers the much more powerful, more frightening image of a bird of prey. This is a verse sometimes cited alongside 42:14, 49:15, 66:13, Psalm 131:2 and other passages to provide scriptural authority for the image of God as mother, but he reminds us that the image of a mother contains more than references to childbearing and suckling.[66] Similarly the connection which he sees in chapter 26 between verses 11 and 12, but which, as we saw, has been broken by the compilers of the *Lectionary*, gives his interpretation a convincing, practical realism – peace in this imperfect world often demands violence – very much in line incidentally with some 'Marxist' or materialist interpretations of scripture.

We come now to the last of our three main twentieth-century Isaianic themes, 'the peaceable kingdom' from 11:6–9. The picture of ferocious beasts of prey and their vulnerable, timid victims lying down happily together is not only so easy to portray, but also, to our eyes at any rate, such an obvious way to envisage the peace and contentment of a new age, that we cannot but be amazed that it has been so little used till modern times. The Princeton Index of Christian Art, which covers everything up to 1400, lists only five examples, of which three are doubtful and one is no longer extant. A scene on the base of a twelfth-century bronze candlestick from

---

[65]   It is prescribed to be read on the fourteenth Sunday of the year, and also at masses for the Blessed Virgin Mary of Lourdes and St Theresa of Lisieux. See pp. 65f.

[66]   See above, p. 205.

Prague and a piece of fourteenth-century sculpture on Orvieto Cathedral are very indistinct. The appearance of a panther, a boy in a hat and a lion gnawing a bone beside a lamb, in the decorations round a representation of the Annunciation to Anna (or the 'Conception of the Virgin') in a fourteenth-century illuminated missal in the British Museum, can hardly be more than an oblique allusion to Isaiah 11, if that, and the fourth was in a fresco in Milan, described by Ambrose, but now unfortunately destroyed.

This leaves only one unambiguous extant illustration of the passage in the whole of early and mediaeval Christian art. It occurs in the *Bible Moralisée*, a complete, fully illustrated Bible commentary, probably produced by Dominicans in Paris for St Louis in the thirteenth century.[67] Each passage selected for comment and illustration is accompanied by two miniatures, one illustrating the biblical passage and the other the commentary. In chapter 11 four texts are illustrated, verses 1–2 (*egredietur virga*, that is, the 'Jesse tree'),[68] and then three from verses 6–9.[69] The first interprets the 'wolf' as Paul before his conversion,[70] as Jerome had done in his Commentary on Isaiah, the 'lamb' as Peter (cf. John 21:15) and the other animals as 'the wicked', 'the proud', 'the poor' and the like. Also following Jerome, the second understands 'the lion eating straw like an ox' in verse 7 as a reference to this-wordly princes understanding the inner sense of scripture, and the third focusses on the 'asp' and the 'adder' in verse 8, and interprets them as 'Satan' or 'the devil' who holds no terror for the faithful preacher. Thus although the passage is given close attention here, the interpretation is a narrow, inward-looking ecclesiastical one, and the global and political aspects of the vision familiar today are lacking. Furthermore, as part of a Bible in which virtually every chapter is illustrated, these unique mediaeval representations of the 'Peaceable Kingdom' give us no suggestion that the passage held any particular significance for a thirteenth-century audience.

One example survives from the sixteenth century, in an 'emblem book' by the French artist Georgette de Monteney (1540–71).[71] It is a woodcut showing a lion, a lamb and a wolf eating together what

---

[67] *CHB* 1, p. 335.
[68] See above, pp. 74ff.
[69] Laborde, *Bible Moralisée*, fol.109v.
[70] Paul was of the tribe of Benjamin (Rom.11:1; Phil.3:5), described as a 'ravening wolf' in Gen.49:27.
[71] Henkel-Schöne, *Emblemata*, cols.389f.

looks like a sheaf of straw. It bears the title FOEDERE PERFECTO ('The covenant complete'), and is accompanied by the following verses:

> Le loup, l'agneau et le lion furieux
> Paisiblement repairent tous ensemble.
> Le Iuif, le Grec, le doux, le vicieux,
> Au vray repas Dieu par Christ tous rassemble ...

There is also a woodcut by Sebastian le Clerc dated 1695 showing a rustic scene in which a shepherdess appears to have a lion among her flock. There are a few references in literature, especially the lengthy poem by Alexander Pope.[72]

It was without a doubt the paintings of the Quaker preacher-artist Edward Hicks (1780–1849) that gave the passage its popularity, especially in the States.[73] Over a period of about twenty years he painted nearly 100 versions, of which about twenty-five are extant, mostly in American collections and galleries. He originally derived the idea from an illustration by the English artist Richard Westall, which was engraved in contemporary Bibles. Entitled *The Peaceable Kingdom of the Branch*, this was as much an illustration of the first verse of the chapter about the coming-forth of a 'Branch' from the stem of Jesse as of the peaceable kingdom passage itself (vv.6–9). The animals are there – the wolf lying down beside the lamb, the leopard with the kid, and the lion and the fatling together, but the focus is on 'the little child leading them', and on the grapevine in his hand, symbol of the sacrament of the eucharist and of the saving death of Christ.

In Edward Hicks' hands the emphasis eventually changed completely, away from the child, and away from the orthodox Christology and sacramental theology of Westall, to the lion and the other animals as symbols of the warring elemnts in human nature, imagined in this prophecy as coming together in perfect harmony. His earliest versions from the years 1823–5 still retain much of Westall's symbolism, although unlike Westall he dresses the little messianic figure in a jumper suit fashionable among young Friends in the 1820s.[74] But later he saw a different, less Christocentric meaning in the 'Peaceable Kingdom', more in keeping with his Quaker faith. For one thing a little girl replaces the boy. Corner vignettes

---

[72] See above, pp. 161ff.
[73] See especially E. P. Mather, 'A Quaker icon'; cf. also Alice Ford, *Edward Hicks. His Life and Art* (New York 1985).
[74] Ford, *Edward Hicks*, pp. 46–55.

containing the words INNOCENCE, MEEKNESS and LIBERTY in four languages, appear with a dove and an olive branch in each. Four rhyming couplets round the picture make the message clearer still (Plate 36).[75]

Later still, as in 'The Peaceable Kingdom with Liberty', the sacramental vine in the child's hand is replaced by an olive branch,[76] and by the time we reach the final stage and the latest versions, including the group known as 'The peaceable kingdom of the great lion' of 1846–7 (Plate 37),[77] all the details of the next two verses have been included – the cow and the bear, the lion eating straw like the ox, the babies playing beside asps and adders. The emphasis is now entirely on the harmony envisaged by the prophet, even between the most unlikely creatures, and not at all upon the messianic child.

While we can see to some extent the artist's own private spiritual pilgrimage reflected in these paintings, this 'Quaker icon' was also applied by Hicks to contemporary political events. The most familiar of these is the signing of the peace treaty with the Native Americans by William Penn in 1681, which he depicts on the left side of many versions of his painting. In this way he expressed his belief that William Penn, by establishing a Quaker community in Pennsylvania, had gone some way towards setting up the peaceable kingdom here on earth. But there is also a rather tragic group of six of the paintings, known as 'The Peaceable Kingdom of Mourning', dated 1830–2, which show, in place of Penn's Treaty, a hill crowded with Friends, some of whom are clearly recognizable, including George Fox himself preaching. Around them there is a banner with the inscription: 'Behold I bring glad tidings of great joy. Peace on earth and good will to men'. This reflects a bitter controversy within the Society of Friends which took place in 1827, and Hicks used the icon to express his hope that it would be peacefully resolved in favour of religious liberty for all.[78]

The influence of these paintings, especially in the United States, has been enormous. One version appears on the front cover of a Christian Ethics primer entitled *The Peaceable Kingdom* by Stanley Hauerwas (1983).[79] Several other works have the same title, including

75 Ford, *Edward Hicks*, pp. 59ff.
76 Ford, *Edward Hicks*, pp. 140–5.
77 Ford, *Edward Hicks*, pp. 198ff.
78 Ford, *Edward Hicks*, pp. 76–82.
79 Hauerwas, *The Peaceable Kingdom*.

a collection of poems by Jon Silkin published in 1975.[80] The artist
Karen van Heerden used it as the title of a series of greetings cards,
showing animals and birds in a style reminiscent of some of Hicks'
paintings, but later changed the name because she found that people
expected there to be more explicit allusions to Isaiah and the Bible in
a series entitled 'The peaceable kingdom' than she intended, and
wanted to break the connection.[81]

A brightly coloured tract published by the Watch Tower and Bible
Tract Society of Pennsylvania in 1987, entitled *Life in a Peaceful New
World*, brings together Isaiah's vision of the peaceable kingdom in
11:6–9 with his prophecies about 'new heavens and a new earth'
(65:17), where 'nation will not lift up sword against nation' (2:4), the
wilderness will 'blossom as the saffron' (Isaiah 35:1,6,7), 'all will enjoy
the fruits of their own labour' (cf. 65:21–23), and 'no resident will say,
"I am sick"' (33:24). It is illustrated with pictures of little girls and
boys playing with giant pandas and tigers, while deer graze peacefully beside them. A war memorial window in the Reformed Church
in Spaandam, Holland makes the same connection between the
'peaceable kingdom' of Isaiah 11 and the 'new heavens and a new
earth' passage in Isaiah 65 (as quoted in 2 Peter 3:13) (Plate 38).

The motif has proved popular and appropriate in modern Israel,
incidentally too. The Biblical Zoo in Jerusalem at one time boasted
an enclosure in which a wolf, admittedly in a somewhat comatose
condition, lived quite peacefully with a sheep. A series of three
postage stamps was issued to celebrate the Jewish New Year in 1962
depicting three features of Isaiah's 'peaceable kingdom': the wolf
lying down with the lamb, the leopard with the kid and the baby
playing on the hole of the asp.[82] The massive bronze menorah
(seven-branched candlestick) presented by Britain to the young state
of Israel in 1948, and now standing opposite the entrance to the
Knesset in Jerusalem, has a panel uniquely depicting Isaiah surrounded by wild beasts grazing peacefully with lambs, gazelles and
other small animals.[83]

Vegetarians find something else in Isaiah 11:1–9. In his book *The
Forgotten Beginnings of Creation and Christianity*, for example, the German

[80]   Jon Silkin, *The Peaceable Kingdom* (Heron Press, Boston 1975). Another is B. H. Harrison,
       The Peaceable Kingdom (Oxford, 1982).
[81]   Private communication.
[82]   *Stanley Gibbons' Simplified Catalogue. Stamps of the World* (1994), Vol.1, pp. 1037–8.
[83]   Vilnay, *Guide to Israel* (19th edition), pp. 103–4.

vegetarian Christian Karl Anders Skriver (1903–83) finds new meaning in the vision of a world where order is established by the 'rod of his mouth (instead of the sword or stick)', and 'the wolf shall dwell with the lamb ... and the lion shall eat straw like the ox ... because they (humans and animals) shall not hurt or destroy in all my holy mountain'.[84] He argues that the true meaning of Nazoraean, a title given to Jesus by his contemporaries but suppressed or deliberately misinterpreted by the Church Fathers, derives from the Hebrew word *netzer* 'a greening sprout' in verse 1 (cf. Matth.1:23), and thus almost means 'vegetarian'.[85] Skriver suggests that Jesus' opposition to the temple at Jerusalem was thus motivated in part by his abhorrence of animal slaughter, a view vehemently expressed by some of the prophets, not least Isaiah: 'He who slaughters an ox is like him who slays a man; he who sacrifices a lamb like him who breaks a dog's neck ...' (66:2–3; cf. 1:15–17). He concludes that 'therefore, animal murder is equal to human murder'.[86] Another vegetarian writer compares Isaiah's vision of the 'Peaceable Kingdom' with Paul's prophecy in Romans that all creation will be liberated from its 'bondage to decay' and its 'groaning and travail', and eventually share in the 'glorious liberty of the children of God" (Rom.8:19–23) and with 'Vergil's rapturous Fourth Eclogue'.[87]

This brings us finally to some uses to which various other texts from Isaiah have been put by environmentalists. They cite Isaiah 14:4–8 and 24, along with Ezekiel 28 and Ps.82, as scriptural authority for the view that exploitation of the earth is a sin and 'may result in the disorder of God's creation': the earth is also polluted under the inhabitants thereof, because they have trangressed the laws, changed the ordinance, broken the covenant (24:5).[88] The choice of the more ecological-sounding word 'pollute', following the *Revised Standard Version*, in preference to 'defile' (*AV*) or 'desecrate' (*NEB*), makes the text all the more appropriate in such a context. The text in its original context probably has more to do with pollution caused by idolatry or bloodshed, which is how the term is

---

[84] Skriver, *The Forgotten Beginnings*, p. 108.
[85] Skriver, *The Forgotten Beginnings*, pp. 123f.
[86] Skriver, *The Forgotten Beginnings*, p. 100.
[87] B. Wrighton, 'The Golden Age must return: A Catholic's views on vegetarianism' (*The British Vegetarian*, November/December, 1965). On the relationship between Isaiah and the fourth *Eclogue* see also, pp. 47f.
[88] *Survival or Extinction. A Christian Attitude to the Environment*, by HRH the Duke of Edinburgh and the Rt Rev Michael Mann (St George's House, Windsor Castle 1989), p. 46.

used elsewhere in the Bible (cf. Num. 35.33; Jer 3:2, 9), than oil slicks and nuclear waste. But the concept of the sacredness of the earth, and the ethical demands on humankind to protect it, help to bridge the gap between the text and its new application.

We have already discussed, in a more socio-political context, Isaiah's vision of the ideal king in chapter 32.[89] Its reference to 'judgement in the wilderness and righteousness in the fruitful field' (v.16) make it appropriate in an ecological context too, where it is ingeniously placed in juxtaposition with the description of Solomon's legendary knowledge of the natural world (1 Kings 4:29–33).[90] By analogy, human beings, whose kingly status in the world is indicated by other biblical texts (e.g. Gen.1:28), have a duty to 'conserve the order of all Creation, for which we are responsible and answerable to God'.[91]

I have chosen as a kind of epilogue one final ecological example, this time from a service of Dedication and Blessing in the 'Biblical Gardens' at St George's College, Jerusalem in May 1993. The blessing of each of the seventeen newly-planted gardens was accompanied by the reading of an appropriate verse or two from scripture. Three are from Isaiah (more than from any other book): 41:19–20 for the Conifer Garden, 22:8–11 for the Aqueduct Garden and 60:13 for the Library Garden: 'The wealth of Lebanon shall come to you, the pine, fir, and boxwood, all together, to bring glory to my holy sanctuary, to honour the place where my feet rest' (*NEB*).

[89] See above pp. 226f.
[90] *Survival or Extinction*, pp.47–8.
[91] *Survival or Extinction*, p. 48.

CHAPTER 13

Conclusion

In this story of how a text has been used and interpreted down the ages, we have tried to let the participants speak for themselves. From Jesus and Paul in the first century to feminists and environmentalists in the twentieth, people have found in Isaiah an inexhaustible source of language and imagery. Bishops quote him at crucial points in their theological discussions. Writers, artists and musicians have been inspired, directly or indirectly, by him. Missionaries and explorers have taken him with them to the four corners of the earth. Ordinary people have found in Isaiah comfort, hope and, occasionally, comic relief.

A number of questions arise. Is Isaiah unique in the history of the Church? Would a similar study of Genesis or Psalms or Matthew produce so many examples from so many different contexts? Or a study of Isaiah in the history of the Jewish people?[1] My own feeling is that Isaiah probably is unique both in the range of material in the book, and in its popularity in all sections of the Church. But the only way to prove that would be to subject the history of Genesis, Psalms or Matthew in the Church to the same degree of scrutiny as has been done to Isaiah here. One important piece of the story which would obviously be missing in the case of Matthew or any of the other Gospels, would be the complex 'Christianization' process whereby Isaiah in the Church was divorced from Isaiah in the Synagogue: this was undoubtedly one of the most fascinating, if disturbing, topics of the whole subject.

Another question we are tempted to tackle is whether it is possible to construct any kind of unified 'Isaiah'. The unity of the book of Isaiah has recently been the subject of several scholarly discussions,[2] but I am thinking more of the character of the prophet himself as

---

[1] See above, pp. 103–6.   [2] See above, p. 197.

perceived by those who refer to him so regularly. It is hard to find any consistency in the way he is depicted in art. It would be good, for example, if we could recognize a youthful, sometimes clean-shaven Isaiah confidently pointing to the Virgin Mary with the words *Ecce virgo* ... (7:14) on his lips (or his banderol),[3] and an older, more solemn bearded figure, pondering on Christ's Passion (53).[4] But there are too many exceptions. In regal or messianic contexts, he carries a branch from the Jesse tree (11:1) or some symbol of the gifts of the spirit (11:2);[5] elsewhere he has a saw reminding us of his martyrdom.[6] One of the most frequent characteristics of Isaiah, conspicuous in Jewish and Muslim tradition as well as Christian, is his gift for violent abusive language, directed more often than not at his own people. This was why, in Jewish legend, he had his lips scorched by an angel (cf. 6:6–7),[7] and why, in Christian hands, he became such a useful weapon in their incessant onslaught on the Jewish people.[8] It was not until our own century that Christians remembered that his rhetoric was aimed at oppressive regimes and unjust institutions that 'grind the faces of the poor' (3:15), 'call good evil and evil good' (5:20) and 'decree iniquitous decrees' (10:1), irrespective of whether they are Christian or Jewish or Muslim or anything else.

After surveying the whole history of Christianity and Isaiah's role in it, we might also return to one of the questions with which we began, namely, what part did Isaiah play in the earliest origins of Christianity? At the end of our study of Christian uses of Isaiah down the ages, can we conclude, with more confidence than at the beginning, that Jesus was inspired by and dependent on the Book of Isaiah (or at least his earliest followers and biographers were), more than any other part of scripture, for almost every aspect of his teaching? The Gospels give some examples of this as we saw, but are there not many more? The overall 'message' of Isaiah, as perceived by Christians down the ages, is uniquely radical, ethical and anti-Jewish. From the first chapter where sacrifices, festivals and sabbaths are attacked, to the last where the temple is rejected as an unnecessary and immoral institution, there is a radical note reminiscent of Jesus' repeated challenges to contemporary Jewish authority. The (Jewish) people, especially their leaders, are repeatedly condemned as blind (e.g. 6), hypocritical (29:13) and rebellious (65:2). High moral

---

[3]   See above, pp. 66ff.   [4]   See above, pp. 87f.
[5]   See above, pp. 75ff.   [6]   See above, pp. 98f.
[7]   See above, p. 107.   [8]   See above, pp. 106f.

standards, closely related to 'holiness' in chapter 6, and including demands for social justice, are expressed in Isaiah better than anywhere else (e.g. in chaps.1, 9, 11, 16, 32, 42, 58, 61). Isaiah also contains some unique comments on the role of eunuchs and foreigners in the Temple (56), to which may be added the uniquely Isaianic notion of 'a light to the gentiles' (42, 49). Is it conceivable that passages such as Isaiah 2:3 ('the law will depart from Zion'), later interpreted as scriptural authority for the belief that the law will be redundant in the messianic era, were already understood by some radicals in this way at the beginning?

But beyond the more familiar parallels between Jesus and Isaiah there are some other, very striking lines of connection between them. First, the radical anthropomorphism in some of the later chapters of Isaiah opens up new perceptions of both God and humankind. God is actually compared to a woman in childbirth (despite her uncleanness: 42:14), and a midwife (despite her contact with uncleanness: 66:9). Did that affect Jesus' revolutionary attitude to ritual impurity as in his contact with the woman suffering from chronic haemorrhaging? In another text much used in later Christian tradition, God is depicted as a bloodstained warrior, limping home from battle (63:1–3). How early was the connection made between this passage and Christ's Passion? Isaiah also contains some remarkable texts in which a human being is exalted to the ranks of the divine: the Davidic king is named 'mighty God' in one (9:6) and the 'suffering servant' described as 'high and lifted up' (52:13; cf.6:1; 57:15). How soon in the development of Christian doctrine were these texts identified as providing scriptural authority for the belief that Jesus was divine?

Finally two key elements in the Lord's Prayer – his prayer for the 'coming of the Kingdom' – may be said to have come straight out of Isaiah. First, the only scriptural texts in which the term 'Our Father' is applied to God, are Isaiah 63:16 and 64:8; and second, nowhere in scripture is the 'Kingdom' more fully and more memorably described than in Isaiah.[9] As we saw, most of the obvious passages, such as the messianic prophecy in 9:6, the 'Peaceable Kingdom' (11:6–9), the Moabite prophecy (16:1–5), 32:1–8 ('A king will reign in righteousness ...') and 42:1–4 ('Behold my servant ...'), are conspicuous by their absence from early Christian tradition. But of course, the fact that these texts are not quoted verbatim by the earliest

[9]   Cf. Chilton, *God in Strength*, p. 277.

Christian preachers and leaders in our extant documents does not mean that such texts, so familiar and popular throughout later Christian tradition, did not provide the scriptural basis for their notion of the 'Kingdom'. Indeed in the light of the evidence for Isaiah's central role at every stage in the evolution of Christianity, it would be surprising if this recurring Isaianic motif was not one that influenced and inspired many of them, if not Jesus himself.

The two questions I want to end with, however, are rather more fundamental. First, to what extent, if at all, should the history of interpretation be considered an integral part of Biblical Studies; and second, what criteria should we use to evaluate the truth, validity, value or relative importance of one interpretation over against another? In this closing section, we shall use the term 'comparative interpretation', in preference to the 'history of interpretation',[10] in order to shift the emphasis away from historical questions to the contemporary issue of what to do – in writing a commentary or making some kind of official statement on behalf of 'the experts' – when confronted by a plurality of interpretations for one passage.

The book of Isaiah provides an excellent case study. Not only does it, according to Christian tradition, contain the whole story of Christ's birth, death and resurrection, adding details that are not in the Gospels (e.g. 1:3; 19:1; 50:6).[11] As we have seen, it also provides scriptural authority for the sacraments of baptism (e.g. 1:16; 12:3), the eucharist (e.g. 65:13) and penance (55:6–7), for the institution of bishops (60:17b), for the doctrine of the Trinity (e.g. 6:3; 40:12; 42:1), for Augustine's belief in the priority of faith over reason (7:9) and Luther's in the priority of scripture (40:8), for liberation theology (e.g. 16:5; 32:17; 58:6ff.; 61:1ff.) and for the use of female images of God (e.g. 42:14; 49:14–15; 66:13). Should readers of the Bible be warned off this kind of material and urged to take seriously only the 'original meaning' of the Hebrew text? Or is there an alternative approach to biblical studies by which access to it can be made easier and more normal?

There has been plenty of evidence in the least twenty years or so of a heightened awareness among biblical scholars that post-biblical data can be worth studying.[12] 'Late' is not always synonymous with

[10]   Cf. Clines, *What does Eve do to Help?* pp. 20–1.
[11]   See pp. 49ff.
[12]   Cf. Sawyer, 'The "original meaning of the text" and other legitimate subjects for semantic description', pp. 210–12. See above, pp. 9ff.

'inferior'. There has been much interest in 'post-exilic' developments and the history and literature of the Second Temple Period (515 BC – 70 AD). New critical editions of the Apocrypha and Pseudepigrapha are signs of the times too, as is continuing interest in the Dead Sea Scrolls and Nag Hammadi texts. The ancient Jewish and Christian translations of the Hebrew Bible into Greek, Aramaic, Syriac and other languages, are now increasingly being handled as literature in their own right, not merely as a means of getting back to the original Hebrew. Fresh literary approaches to the Bible, focussing on larger units (including whole books) instead of concentrating mainly on isolating separate sources or pericopes, further shift attention from original meanings and authorial intention, as do the notions of intratextuality, reader-response and the plurality of meanings for one text. The 'ethics of reading' has recently been introduced into the field of biblical studies.[13] The study of the Bible as a sacred text within the wider interdisciplinary context of Religious Studies departments is another important factor in the change of attitude among students and scholars to what studying the Bible involves. Whereas in the more traditional 'Departments of Old Testament Language and Literature', for example, students' energies were often primarily directed at mastering a variety of oriental languages, nowadays searching ethical, socio-political and economic questions about the meaning of the texts studied (in the original or in translation) are now raised as a matter of course.

In the light of all these signs of a radical change in scholarly attitudes to the kind of material we have been considering here, it seems to me that the burden of proof is now on those who seek to exclude it from commentaries and teaching programmes. They have to argue the purist case for keeping biblical scholarship, in Elisabeth Schüssler Fiorenza's words, 'detached ... disinterested and dispassionate ... a-political ... unencumbered by contemporary questions'.[14] So, assuming we cannot turn the clock back, and the world is going to demand of its biblical experts that they show some interest in what happened to their texts in the history of western civilization, the answer to my first question must be 'Yes': comparative interpretation must be considered an integral part of Biblical Studies. Students of the Bible must be constantly reminded, at all

---

[13] Young, 'The Pastoral Epistles and the ethics of reading' (1992); 'Allegory and the ethics of reading' (1993).
[14] Fiorenza, 'The ethics of biblical interpretation', pp. 10–11.

levels, that the texts they are working on are not just ancient documents like the lawcode of Hammurabi or the Dead Sea Scrolls, but sacred texts which can be, and have been used in many ways and in all manner of contexts to influence, down to the present day, the lives of real people.

The next generation of commentaries must surely now attempt to record as many theologically and politically important or interesting interpretations of the text from the history of Christianity and Judaism as space will allow.[15] Is there not something seriously defective about a commentary on the book of Isaiah that does not record the fact that a verse in chapter 1 suggested the ox and the ass in Christian nativity scenes or that chapter 6 spawned the antisemitic figure of *Synagoga Caeca* as well as the *Sanctus*, or that Martin Luther's followers had part of 40:8 embroidered on their sleeves ('The Word of the Lord abideth for ever')?

There will be plenty of objections to this. First, there is the practical problem of how such material is to be located in so many diverse sources spanning more than two millennia. This seems at first sight to be particularly difficult just because this dimension of biblical studies has been so badly neglected in modern times and no-one has done the research. But as I hope I have demonstrated here, the problem is not insuperable. There are now many studies and reference works specifically devoted to this area of biblical research. Many of the standard reference works have indices of scriptural references. The same applies to the edited works of most major authors, as well as countless other significant or representative works. Many lectionaries and hymnbooks also have indices of scriptural references. Responsible biblical scholars in their teaching and commentaries will have to do a certain amount of original research themselves, but some of the preliminary work has already been done. So finding the material is not such a problem.

The other problem is more serious: how to decide among all the diverse material what to put in and what to leave out. The main if not the only criterion up till now has been chronological priority: what was the original meaning of the text? 'Late' meant 'inferior' and thus 'not worth including in a work of serious biblical scholarship'. Another criterion sometimes used in existing commentaries, is based on exegetical method: they exclude (or at most make

---

[15] Cf. Coggins, 'A future for the commentary?', pp. 170–5.

derogatory remarks about) any interpretation that is considered to be absurdly contrived or far-fetched. Apart from the subjectivity of such a criterion, this would exclude a large proportion of patristic interpretations which have virtually nothing to do with the original Hebrew, as well as many rabbinic interpretations. If, on the other hand, our aim is to be as comprehensive and descriptive as possible, to let the text and its interpretations speak for themselves, then such criteria cannot be used. Significant examples of antisemitic, imperialistic, oppressive, racist, sexist uses of scripture, whatever their relationship to the original meaning of the text, must be included as well as beautiful, uplifting, liberating interpretations however close to the original author's intention.

The overriding criterion must surely be a quantitative one: a glance at any index of biblical references shows which texts have had a particularly prominent role to play in a given context: e.g. Isaiah 11:1 in mediaeval cathedral architecture, 50:6 in late mediaeval passion iconography, 60:9 in eighteenh- and nineteenth-century foreign missionary enterprises, and 61:1 in twentieth-century liberation theology. Room must be found for interesting and ingenious solutions to problems in the text, such as inconsistencies, ambiguities, obscurities and the like, which have puzzled commentators down the ages, and for which sometimes the pre-critical commentators had the answer.[16] But historical importance must surely be the major criterion: the most common and the most influential interpretations must be given priority, good or bad, beautiful or ugly, orthodox or heretical, repressive or liberating, original or late.

This still leaves us with the question of the truth or validity or moral value of differing interpretations.[17] Our aim to be purely descriptive and to operate a simple quantitative system of selection, is unlikely to be achieved. What criterion can we base value judgments on? Once again chronological priority has usually been virtually the only criterion – the truth or validity of each interpretation has normally been measured against the original meaning. But of course this criterion carries no moral weight when the text in question is from a Latin or German or Spanish or English version in the hands of a Christian writer, worlds away from ancient Israel. As soon as we start taking seriously some of that material, then the way is open to approach the critical task of evaluating differing

---

[16] Cf. Sawyer, 'The role of Jewish studies in biblical semantics'.
[17] Cf. Young, *The Art of Performance*, pp. 4–25, 88–110.

interpretations 'in terms of a religious scale of values'.[18] It may be, for instance, that what is really morally offensive about some interpretations of Isaiah is their antisemitism or their arrogance, and in the face of that kind of value-judgment, the degree to which they can be shown to differ from the original meaning(s) of the texts may be seen to pale into insignificance.

So taking up the notion of comparative interpretation with which we began, I thought it would be interesting to end by comparing different uses and interpretations of Isaiah with a view to arranging them on some kind of religious scale of values. The first example compares two uses of Isaiah's polemic. In the 'original context' of much of this kind of polemic, the speaker was an individual standing up on his own to criticize and condemn his contemporaries, often those in power and often at the risk of his life (cf. 2 Chron.36:15–16; Matt.23:37). By contrast, in many of the worst examples of the Church's antisemitic polemic the Church is the majority, holding all the power, and the victims of their anti-Jewish polemic, not to mention their anti-Jewish legislation, had none. At the beginning of the Tortosa Disputation in fifteenth-century Spain, for example, the Christian spokesman quoted a threatening text from the first chapter of Isaiah.[19] The words were obviously designed to strike terror into the hearts of the Jews present, who knew they were a minority at the mercy of the Christian regime they were living under. By contrast the incident where the leader of the Inner London Education Authority substituted a reading from Isaiah 10, beginning 'Woe to those who make unjust laws ...', for the one he had been asked to read at a civic service, is a case where an individual boldly stands up as Isaiah did, on his own, and attacks those in power.[20] Both uses of Isaiah are surely legitimate in terms of interpreting the text. What is morally unacceptable in the antisemitic example is the Church's abuse of their power over the Jews. The ethical questions raised by the press and others as to whether Neil Fletcher was justified in changing the lesson he was to read in St Paul's, are of a totally different order.

A second comparison highlights a disturbing feature of many Christian interpretations. When Isidore of Seville (c.560–636) used a passage from Isaiah 14 to expand on the infamous verse from Matthew 27 ('His blood be upon us and upon our children'), he

18   Fiorenza, 'The ethics of biblical interpretation', p. 15.
19   See p. 118.   20   See pp. 225f.

changes the third person pronouns ('his sons ... their fathers') of the original Hebrew to second person pronouns ('your sons ... your fathers') to make the application of Isaiah's invective to the contemporary situation more personal and more biting.[21] He also deliberately ignores the fact that the original words were addressed to the King of Babylon, not Judah. But it seems to me that here again the reason why Isidore's version of the text and his use of it are morally despicable, is not that he has changed the text of the original, but that he uses it to castigate a vulnerable minority in his community and whip up popular aggression against them. Once again it would not be sufficient simply to hold up the original Hebrew text as the standard against which to evaluate his interpretation of Isaiah. After all the *NRSV*, representing modern critical scholarship, also changes the grammar of the original Hebrew.

One final example illustrates a rather different point of comparison. Isaiah 16:1, part of a prophecy against Moab, is, from a historical critical point of view, rather obscure and at first sight not very illuminating. Yet the Latin version beginning *Emitte agnum* became a regular part of western Christian language about the Lamb of God, his ancestry in Moab, his coming to Jerusalem and his victory over the world, and was prescribed to be read in the Advent liturgy. Nowadays it is no longer in the Sunday lectionaries, however, nor is its mediaeval interpretation even referred to in most modern commentaries. It is thus an excellent example of a passage whose significance needs to be handled from the perspective of comparative interpretation. We must surely ask which interpretation, within the context of the Christian Church, is more effective or more important: the obscure reconstructed original meaning of a prophecy against a country that no longer exists, or a richly allusive expression of Christian belief about Christ and the establishment of justice and peace? It is certainly a stage in the history of the interpretation of this passage that at the very least deserves a mention in Christian commentaries. Unlike Isidore's behaviour towards the text, the traditional mediaeval interpretation happens to be closer to the original Hebrew than some of the recent versions and does no-one any harm. It seems to me that provided no claim is made that it is the only true meaning, then like countless other beautiful, imaginative allegorical or christological interpretations, it should be treated

---

[21] See pp.113f.

with respect. I have not yet found a single modern commentary that mentions it.

I hope I have succeeded in proving that it is not enough for students of the Bible to steep themselves in ancient languages, archaeology and textual criticism in an effort to get back to the original meaning of the Hebrew text. Far wider and more serious issues are at stake when a text, still sacred to millions, is being handled by experts. Our role in biblical interpretation must surely be more than that of our purist predecessors, whose comments not infrequently add up to: 'We don't know what this originally meant, but it certainly cannot mean that' – despite the fact that it certainly does 'mean that' for millions of Christians and has done for centuries. It may not be what the original author intended, but provided no-one claims that it is, then it can be handled with the same degree of scholarly sensitivity and authority as another part of the data. Surely the next generation of commentaries by the experts must seek to make available to readers of the Bible as many such meanings and uses of the text as possible. What people believe a text means, whatever scribal error or mistranslation or allegorical method or wordplay or free association is involved, may be as interesting and historically important as the original meaning, if not more so.

Bibliography

Abel, F.-M., 'Le commentaire de Saint-Jérôme sur Isaie', *RB* 13 (1916), pp. 200–25

Alexander, P. R., '3 (Hebrew Apocalypse of) Enoch', *OTP* 1, pp. 223–315

Alexander, P. R., 'The fall into knowledge' in *A Walk in the Garden*, edd. Morris and Sawyer, pp. 91–104

Alonso Schökel, L., 'Isaiah' in *The Literary Guide to the Bible*, edd.R.Alter and F.Kermode (London 1987), pp. 165–83

Alter, R., 'A literary approach to the Bible', *Commentary* 60.6 (December 1975), pp. 70–7

Anderson, R. T., 'Was Isaiah a scribe?', *JBL* 79 (1960), pp. 57f.

Andrews, J. S., *A Study of German Hymns in Current English Hymnals* (Peter Lang, Bern-Frankfurt 1981)

Armstrong, H. B. J., ed., *A Norfolk Diary. Passages from the Diary of the Rev. Benjamin John Armstrong, Vicar of East Dereham 1850–88* (Harrap, London 1949)

Ashton, C., *Church on the Threshold. Renewing the Local Church* (Marshall, Morgan and Scott, London 1988; second edition Darton, Longman and Todd, London 1991)

Ashton, C., *Threshold God. Discovering Christ in the Margins of Life* (Darton Longman and Todd, London 1992)

Atwan, R., and L. Wieder, *Chapters into Verse. Poetry in English Inspired by the Bible. 1. Genesis-Malachi* (Oxford University Press, New York 1993)

Aubert, M., L.Grodecki, J.Lafond, and J.Verrier, *Les Vitraux de Notre-Dame et de la Sainte-Chapelle de Paris (Corpus Vitrearum Medii Aevi. France*, vol.1), (Paris 1959)

Augustijn, C., 'The sixteenth-century reformers and the Bible', in *The Bible and its Readers*, edd. W. Beuken, S. Freyne and A. Weiler, pp. 58–68

Bailey, R., *Viking Age Sculpture in Northern England* (Collins, London 1980)

Bal, M., ed., *Anti-Covenant. Counter-Reading Women's Lives in the Bible* (Sheffield 1989)

Bale, J., *God's Promises*, in *The Dramatic Works of John Bale*, ed. J. S. Farmer (London, 1966), pp. 83–125.

Barr, J., 'Did Isaiah know about "root-meanings"?', *Exp. Times* 75 (1964), p. 242

Barr, J., *Comparative Philology and the Text of the Old Testament* (The Clarendon Press, Oxford 1968)

Barr, J., *Fundamentalism* (SCM Press, London 1977)

Barr, J., *Holy Scripture: Canon, Authority, Criticism* (Westminster Press, Philadelphia 1983)

Barrett, C. K., 'The interpretation of the Old Testament in the New' in *CHB* 1, pp. 377–411

Barrett, C. K., *A Commentary on the Second Epistle to the Corinthians* (Harper & Row, New York 1973)

Barth, K., *Church Dogmatics*, Vol.4, Pt. 1 (translated by G.W.Bromiley; T. &. T. Clark, Edinburgh 1956)

Barton, J., *Oracles of God. Perceptions of Ancient Prophecy in Israel after the Exile* (Darton, Longman & Todd, London 1986)

Beadle, R., ed., *The York Plays* (London 1982)

Begrich, J., 'Das priesterliche Heilsorakel', *ZAW* 52 (1934), pp. 81–92

Benisovitch, M. N., 'Un dessin de Jacob Jordaens à la E.B.Crocker Gallery (Sacramento)', *Oudholland* 68 (1953), pp. 56–7

Bernheimer, R., 'The Martyrdom of Isaiah', *Art Bulletin* 34.1 (1952), pp. 19–37

Bernstein, A. E., *The Formation of Hell. Death and Retribution in the Ancient and Early Christian Worlds* (UCL Press, London 1993)

Bertelli, C., *Roma Sottoterranea* (Forma e colore 29), (Florence 1965)

Bettenson, H., *Documents of the Christian Church* (second edition, Oxford University Press, Oxford 1963)

Beuken, W., S.Freyne and A.Weiler, edd., *The Bible and its Readers* (*Concilium* 1991/1, SCM Press, London & Trinity Press International, Philadelphia)

Bevan, E. R. and C. Singer, edd., *The Legacy of Israel* (Oxford 1927)

Bible Moralisée (Paris Bibl.Nat.11560), see Laborde

Biblia Sacra iuxta Vulgatam versionem (second ed. by R.Weber, Stuttgart 1975), 2 vols

Bindman, D. and D.Toomey, edd., *The Complete Graphic Work of William Blake* (Thames and Hudson, London 1978)

Bitton, M., *Le mythe juif de Lilith: de la femininité démonaique au féminisme* (Lille 1988)

Blake, W., *Complete Writings*, ed. G.Keynes (Oxford University Press, Oxford 1966)

Blau, J., 'Grammarians, Hebrew', *ELL* 3, pp. 1474–6

Blau, L., 'Lilith' in *JE* 8, pp. 87f.

Blunt, A., *Guide to Baroque Rome* (Granada, London 1982)

Boitano, P., *The Shadow of Ulysses. Figures of a Myth* (transl. by A.Weston; Oxford 1994)

Bonnard, P.-E., *Le Second Isaie* (Paris 1972)

Bony, J., *French Cathedrals* (Thames and Hudson, London 1951)

Boyer, P., *When Time Shall be No more. Prophecy Belief in Modern American Culture* (Harvard 1992)

Breitenbach, E., *Speculum Humanae Salvationis. Eine typengeschichtliche Untersuchung* (Strasburg 1930)

Brenner, A., ed., *A Feminist Companion to Ruth* (Sheffield 1993)

Breviarium Monasticum Pauli V. et Urbani VIII. SS. Pontificum auctoritate recognitum, pro omnibus sub regula S. Patris Nostri Benedicti militantibus (Mechlin 1901)

Bril, J., *Lilith ou la mère oscure* (Paris 1984)

Broomhall, M., *The Chinese Empire* (London 1907)

Brown, R. E., SS, J. A. Fitzmyer, SJ and R. E. Murphy, OCarm, edd., *The New Jerome Biblical Commentary* (London 1990)

Brueggemann, W., 'Unity and dynamic in the Isaiah tradition', *JSOT* 29 (1984) pp. 89–107

Bultmann, R., 'Is exegesis without presuppositions possible?' in *Existence and Faith. Shorter Writings of Rudolf Bultmann*, ed. S. M. Ogden (London 1961), pp. 289–96

Burckhardt, J., *Recollections of Rubens* (Phaidon, London 1950)

Burkitt, F. C., 'The debt of Christianity to Judaism' in *Legacy of Israel*, edd.Bevan and Singer, pp. 69–96

Burrows, M., ed., with the assistance of J. C.Trever and W. H.Brownlee, *The Dead Sea Scrolls of St Mark's Monastery* (New Haven 1950)

Bynum, C. Walker, *Holy Feast and Holy Fast. The Religious Significance of Food to Medieval Women* (University of California Press, Berkeley, Los Angeles, London 1987)

Bynum, C. Walker, *Fragmentation and Redemption. Essays on Gender and the Human Body in Medieval Religion* (Zone Books, New York 1991)

Byron, Lord George, *Lord Byron. The Complete Poetical Works*, vol. 3, ed. J. J. McGann (Oxford University Press, Oxford 1981)

Campbell, J., ed., *Bloomsbury Dictionary of First Names* (London 1990)

Carpenter, S., 'The Bible in mediaeval verse and drama' in *The Bible in Scottish Life and Literature*, ed. D. F. Wright, pp. 65–78

Carroll, R. P., 'Is humour also among the prophets?' in *On Humour and the Comic in the Hebrew Bible*, edd. Y. T. Radday and A. Brenner, pp. 169–89

Carroll, R.P., 'Revisionings: echoes and traces of Isaiah in the poetry of William Blake' in *Words Remembered, Texts Renewed: Essays in Honour of John F. A. Sawyer*, edd. J. Davies, G. Harvey and W. G. E. Watson (*JSOT Suppl.* 195, Sheffield 1995), pp. 226–41

Chalker, J. L., *Lilith: A Snake in the Grass* (Penguin, Harmondsworth 1981)

Charles, R. H., 'The martyrdom of Isaiah', *APOT* 2, pp. 155–62

Childs, B. S., *Introduction to the Old Testament as Scripture* (Fortress Press, Philadelphia 1979)

Childs, B.S., *Exodus. A Commentary* (SCM Press, London, 1974)

Chilton, B., *The Glory of Israel. The Theology and Provenience of the Isaiah Targum* (Sheffield 1982)

Chilton, B., *A Galilean Rabbi and his Bible. Jesus' Own Interpretation of Isaiah* (SPCK, London 1984)

Chilton, B. D., *God in Strength. Jesus' Announcement of the Kingdom* (Sheffield 1987)

Clemen, P., *Romanische Monumentmalerei in den Rheinlanden* (Düsseldorf 1916)

Clements, R. E., *Isaiah and the Deliverance of Jerusalem* (Sheffield 1980)

Clements, R. E., 'Beyond tradition-critcism: Deutero-Isaianic development of First Isaiah's themes', *JSOT* 31 (1985) pp. 95–113

Clines, D. J. A., *What Does Eve Do to Help? and Other readerly Questions to the Old Testament* (Sheffield 1990)

Coggins, R. J., 'A future for the commentary?' in *The Open Text*, ed. F. Watson, pp. 163–75

Cohen, J., *The Friars and the Jews. The Evolution of Medieval Anti-Judaism* (Cornell University Press, Ithaca & London 1982)

Cohen, J., *'Be Fertile and Increase; Fill the Earth and Master It'. The Ancient and Medieval Career of a Biblical Text* (Cornell University Press 1989)

Cohen, S., ed., *The Soncino Humash. The Five Books of Moses with Haphtaroth* (Soncino, Hindhead, Surrey 1947)

Cohn Sherbok, D., ed., *Using the Bible Today* (Canterbury Papers III: Bellew, London 1991)

Collins, A. Y., ed., *Feminist Perspectives on Biblical Scholarship* (Scholars Press, Chico, California 1985)

Conrad, E. W., *Reading Isaiah* (Fortress Press, Minneapolis, 1991)

Cowan, P., *Rose Windows* (Thames and Hudson, London 1979)

Cowper, W., *The Poetical Works of William Cowper*, ed. H. S. Milford (Oxford University Press, Oxford 1934)

Crane, Hart, *Complete Poems*, revised edition, B.Weber (Bloodaxe Books, Newcastle 1984)

Daly, M., *Beyond God the Father. Towards a Philosophy of Women's Liberation* (Beacon Press,Boston 1973)

Daniélou, J., *Les Symboles chrétiens primitifs* (Editions du Seuil, Paris 1961)

Davies, J. G., 'Lapidary texts. A liturgy fit for heroes?' in *Sociology of Sacred Texts*, edd. Davies and Wollaston, pp. 26–36

Davies, J. G., ed., *Ritual and Remembrance. Responses to Death in Human Societies* (Sheffield Academic Press, Sheffield 1994)

Davies, J. G. and I. Wollaston, edd., *The Sociology of Sacred Texts* (Sheffield Academic Press, Sheffield 1993)

Davies, W. D., *Paul and Rabbinic Judaism* (SPCK, London 1948)

Dean, W., *Handel's Dramatic Oratorios and Masques* (Oxford 1959)

De Wald, E. T., *The Illustrations of the Utrecht Psalter* (Princeton 1933)

Diestel, L., *Geschichte des Alten Testamentes in der christlichen Kirche* (Jena 1869)

Dijk-Hemmes, F. van, 'The imagination of power and the power of the imagination. An intertextual analysis of two biblical love songs, the Song of Songs and Hosea 2', *JSOT* 44 (1989), pp. 75–88

Dijkstra, B., *Idols of Perversity. Fantasies of Feminine Evil in Fin-de-Siècle Culture* (Oxford University Press, London and New York 1986)

Dodd, C. H., *According to the Scriptures. The Sub-Structure of New Testament Theology* (Nisbet & Co., London 1952)

Dodwell, C. R., ed., *St Alban's Psalter* (Warburg Institute, London 1960)

Drabble, M., ed., *Oxford Companion to English Literature* (New Edition; Oxford University Press, Oxford 1986)

Duffy, E., *Stripping the Altars. Traditional Religion in England c. 1400–c. 1580* (Yale University Press, New Haven 1992)

Duling, D. C., 'Testament of Solomon' (*OTP* 1), pp. 935–87

Dunkling, L. and W. Gosling, edd., *Everyman's Dictionary of First Names* (London 1983)

Dyer-Spencer, J., 'Les vitraux de la Sainte-Chapelle de Paris', *Bulletin Monumental*, 1932, pp. 333–407

Ecclestone, A., *The Night Sky of the Lord* (DLT, London 1980)

Eissfeldt, O., *The Old Testament. An Introduction* (transl. by P. R. Ackroyd; Blackwells, Oxford 1965)

Elbogen, I., *Jewish Liturgy. A Comprehensive History* (Translated by R. P. Scheidlin; Jewish Publication Society, New York 1993 = *Der jüdische Gottesdienst in seiner geschichtlichen Entwicklung*, Frankfurt 1913)

Eliot, T. S., *Collected Poems 1909–1963* (Faber, London 1963)

Elliot, C., *Praying the Kingdom. Towards a Political Spirituality* (Darton, Longman & Todd, London 1985)

Engelhardt, H., *Der theologische Gehalt der Biblia Pauperum* (Strasburg 1927)

Erdman, D. V., *Blake. Prophet against Empire*, (Princeton, 1954)

Erefa, H. von and A. Staley, *The Paintings of Benjamin West* (Newhaven 1986)

Ertz, K., *Jan Brueghel der Ältere* (Cologne 1979)

Ettlinger, L. D. & H. S., *Raphael*, (Phaidon, Oxford 1987)

Evans, C. A., *To See and Not Perceive. Isaiah 6:9–10 in Early Jewish and Christian Interpretation* (Sheffield Academic Press, Sheffield 1989)

Fekkes, J, III, *Isaiah and Prophetic Traditions in the Book of Revelation. Visionary Antecedents and their Development* (JSNT Suppl. 93) (Sheffield Academic Press, Sheffield 1994)

Fiorenza, E. Schüssler, *Bread Not Stone: The Challenge of Feminist Biblical Interpretation* (Beacon Press, Boston 1984)

Fiorenza, E. Schüssler, 'The ethics of biblical interpretation. Decentering biblical scholarship', *JBL* 107 (1988), pp. 3–17

Fishbane, M., *Biblical Interpretation in Ancient Israel* (Oxford University Press, Oxford 1985)

Flannery, A., ed., *Vatican Council II. The Conciliar and Post-Conciliar Documents* (Fowler Wright, Leominster, 1981)

Flesseman-van Leer, E., 'Die Interpretation der Passionsgeschichte vom Alten Testament aus', in *Zur Bedeutung des Todes Jesu* (G. Mohn, Gütersloh 1967), pp. 80–99

Ford, A., 'A Quaker icon: the inner kingdom of Edward Hicks', *The Art Quarterly*, Spring/Summer 1973, pp. 84–98

Ford, A., *Edward Hicks. His Life and Art* (Abbeville Press, New York 1985)

Frend, W. H. C., *The Rise of Christianity* (Fortress Press, Philadelphia 1984)

Frerichs, E. S., ed., *The Bible and Bibles in America* (Scholars Press, Atlanta, Georgia 1988)

Furlong, M., *A Dangerous Delight. Women and Power in the Church* (SPCK, London 1991)

Gadamer, H.-G., *Wahrheit und Methode* (third edition, J. C. B. Mohr, Tübingen 1972)

Gager, J. G., *The Origins of Anti-Semitism. Attitudes Toward Judaism in Christian and Pagan Antiquity* (Oxford University Press, Oxford 1983)

Garcia, J. and S. Maitland, edd., *Walking on the Water. Women Talk About Spirituality* (Virago Press, London 1983)

George, D. H., 'Reading Isaiah and Ezekiel through Blake', *NOR* 13 (1986), pp. 12–21

Gibson, J. C. L., 'The Bible in Scotland today: retrospect and prospect' in *The Bible in Scottish Life and Literature*, ed. D. F. Wright, pp. 208–20

Gilbert, M., 'When Hitler returns: The impossibilities of being a Jewish woman' in *Walking on the Water. Women Talk About Spirituality*, edd. Garcia and Maitland, pp. 157–72

Ginzberg, L., *Legends of the Jews* (Jewish Publication Society, New York 1954)

Giovanni, N. de, *L'ora di Lilith: su Grazia Deledda (1871–1936) e la letteratura femminile del secondo novecento* (Rome 1987)

Gordon, C. H., 'Two magic bowls in Teheran', *Orientalia* 20 (1951), p. 310

Grünewald (with an essay by J. -K. Huysmans) (Phaidon Press, Oxford 1976)

Gutiérrez, G., *A Theology of Liberation. History, Politics and Salvation* (SCM Press, London 1974)

Halsall, G., *Prophecy and Politics* (Lawrence Hill, New York 1986)

Hammond, G., *The Making of the English Bible* (Manchester 1982)

Hampson, D., *Theology and Feminism* (Blackwell, Oxford 1990)

Hanson, A. T., *The Living Utterances of God. The New Testament Exegesis of the Old* (Darton, Longman and Todd, London 1983)

Happé, P., ed., *Four Morality Plays* (Penguin, Harmondsworth 1979)

Harper, J., *The Forms and Orders of Western Liturgy from the Tenth to the Eighteenth Century. A Historical Introduction and Guide for Students and Musicians* (Clarendon Press, Oxford 1991)

Hauerwas, S., *The Peaceable Kingdom. A Primer in Christian Ethics* (SCM, London 1983)

Heine, S., *Christianity and the Goddesses* (SCM Press, London 1987)

Hendrix, S. H., 'The use of scripture in establishing protestantism: The case of Urbanus Rhegius' in *The Bible in the Sixteenth Century*, ed. D. C. Steinmetz, pp. 37–49

Henkel, A. and A. Schöne, edd., *Emblemata. Handbuch zur Sinnbildkunst des 16. und 17. Jahrhunderts* (Stuttgart 1976)

Herbert, G., *The Works of George Herbert*, ed. F. E. Hutchinson (Oxford University Press, Oxford 1941)

Herbert, G., *The Country Parson. The Temple*, ed. J. N. Wall, Jr., (SPCK, London 1981)

Hill, C., *The English Bible and the Seventeenth-Century Revolution* (Allen Lane, New York 1993; Penguin, Harmondsworth 1993)

Holländer, H., 'Isaias' in *Lexikon*, ed. E. Kirschbaum, 2, cols. 354–9

Holtz, T., *Untersuchungen über die alttestamentlichen Zitate bei Lukas* (Akademie, Berlin 1968)

Hooker, M., *Jesus and the Servant* (SPCK, London 1959)

Hooker, R. and C. Lamb, *Love the stranger. Christian Ministry in Multi-Faith Areas* (SPCK, London 1986)

Hope, S., *Liberty to the Captives* (Pearce Institute, Govan, Glasgow 1991)

Hopkins, G. M., *The Poetical Works of Gerald Manley Hopkins*, ed. N. H. MacKenzie (Oxford University Press, Oxford 1990

Houlden, J. L., ed., *The Interpretation of the Bible in the Church* (SCM Press, London 1995): this includes an English translation of *L'interprétation de la Bible dans l'Eglise* (Libreria Editrice Vaticana, Rome 1993)

Hughes, G. W., *God of Surprises* (Darton, Longman and Todd, London 1985)

Humfrey, P., *Cima da Conegliano* (Cambridge 1983)

Huysmans, J.-K., 'The Grünewalds in the Colmar Museum' *Grünewald*, pp. 3–12

Johnson, J. W. and J. R., *The Book of American Negro Spirituals* (Viking, London 1925)

Johnson, P., *The History of the Jews* (Weidenfeld and Nicholson, London 1987)

Johnson, S. C., *The Book of Proverbs and Epitaphs* (London 1963)

Jones, D. R., 'The unity of the Book of Isaiah', *Interpretation* 36 (1982) 117–29

Julian, J., ed., *Dictionary of Hymnography*, 2 vols, (revised edition, New York 1907)

Kaiser, O., *Isaiah 1–12* (SCM Press, London 1972; second edition, London 1983)

Katzenellenbogen, A., *The Sculptural Programs of Chartres Cathedral. Christ, Mary, Ecclesia* (New York 1959)

Kelly, J. N. D., *Jerome. His Life, Writings and Controversies* (Duckworth, London 1975)

Kennedy, H., *Eve Was Framed. Women and British Justice* (Chatto, London 1992)

Kerman, J., *The Masses and Motets of William Byrd* (London 1981)

Kerrigan, J., *St Cyril of Alexandria. Interpreter of the Old Testament* (Analecta Biblica 2: Rome 1952)

King, U., 'The Bible and peace and war' in *Using the Bible Today*, ed. Cohn-Sherbok, pp. 145–61

Kirschbaum, E., ed.,*Lexikon der christlichen Ikonographie. Band. 1–4. Allgemeine Ikonographie* (Freiburg im Breisgau, 1968–76)

Klibansky, R., 'Standing on the shoulders of giants', *Isis* 26 (1936), pp. 147–9

Knibb, M. A., 'Martyrdom and ascension of Isaiah',*OTP* 2, pp. 143–76

Knox, J., *The Works of John Knox*, ed. D. Laing (Edinburgh 1846–64)

Kraeling, E. G., *The Old Testament Since the Reformation* (Harper & Row, New York 1955)

Küng, H., and J. Moltmann, edd., *Conflicting Ways of Interpreting the Bible* (*Concilium*, Edinburgh and New York 1980)

Laborde, A. de, *La Bible Moralisée* (Paris 1911–27)

Lee, L., G. Sedden and F. Stephen, edd. *Stained Glass* (London 1976)

Levenson, J. D., *The Hebrew Bible, the Old Testament and Historical Criticism. Jews and Christians in Biblical Study* (Westminster/John Knox, Louisville, Kentucky 1993)

Levine, A.-J., ed., *Women Like This. New Perspectives on Jewish Women in the Greco-Roman World* (Scholars Press, Atlanta, Georgia 1991)

Levinson-Lessing, V. F., ed., *The Hermitage, Leningrad: Medieval & Renaissance* (Paul Hamlyn, London 1967)

Lewis, A. E., ed., *The Motherhood of God* (Edinburgh 1984). A Report by a Study group appointed by the Woman's Guild and the Panel on Doctrine on the invitation of the General Assembly of the Church of Scotland

Lewis, R. W. B., *The Poetry of Hart Crane. A Critical Study* (Princeton 1967)

Lightbrown, R., *Mantegna* (Phaidon, Oxford 1986)

Lindars, B., *New Testament Apologetic. The Doctrinal Significance of the Old Testament Quotations* (SCM, London 1961)

Loades, A., *Searching for Lost Coins* (SPCK, London 1987)

Loewe, R., 'Jewish exegesis', *DBI*, pp. 346–54

Lohfink, N., *Option for the Poor. The Basic Principles of Liberation Theology in the Light of the Bible* (BIBAL Press, Berkeley 1987)

Longenecker, R. N., *Biblical Exegesis in the Apostolic Period* (Eerdmans, Grand Rapids 1975)

Lowth, A., *The Wilderness of God* (Darton, Longman and Todd, London 1991)

Lucas, St. J., ed., *Oxford Book of French Verse* (Oxford and London 1907)

Luther, M., 'The Babylonian Captivity of the Church' in *Three Treatises* (Fortress Press, Philadelphia 1960), pp. 115–260

Macartney, C. E., *The Greatest Men of the Bible* (Abingdon, Atlanta 1941)

Maccoby, H., *Judaism on Trial. Jewish-Christian Disputations in the Middle Ages* (London and Toronto 1982)

Maccoby, H., *Paul and Hellenism* (SCM Press, London 1991)

MacDonald, G., *Phantastes and Lilith* (Eerdmans 1964)

Magnusson, S., *The Flying Scotsman. A Biography* (Quartet Books, London/ New York 1981)

Mâle, E., *L'Art religieux du treizième siècle en France* (Paris 1948)

Mâle, E., *L'art religieux de la fin du moyen âge en France* (revised edition, Paris 1949)

Mâle, E., *L'Art religieux du douzième siècle en France* (Paris 1953)

Mallea, E., *Todo Verdor Perecerá*, ed. D. L. Shaw (Pergamon Press, Oxford 1968)

Manuel, F., *The Broken Staff. Judaism through Christian Eyes* (Harvard 1992)

Marrow, J. H., *Passion Iconography in Northern European Art of the Late Middle*

Ages and Early Renaissance. A Study of the Transformation of Sacred Metaphor into Descriptive Narrative (Van Ghemmert, Brussels 1979)

Mather, E. P., 'A Quaker icon: the inner kingdom of Edward Hicks', *Art Quarterly* (New Series) Vol. 3 (1973)

McFague, S., *Metaphorical Theology. Models of God in Religious Language* (SCM Press, London 1983)

McKane, W., *Jeremiah. Vol. 1. Introduction and Chapters 1–25* (International Critical Commentary; T. & T. Clark, Edinburgh 1986)

McKane, W., *Selected Christian Hebraists* (Cambridge University Press, 1989)

Meistermann, B., *Guide to the Holy Land* (London 1923)

Mettinger, T. S., *A Farewell to the Servant Songs* (Gleerup, Lund 1983)

Meyer, B. F., 'The challenges of text and reader to the historical-critical method' in *The Bible and its Readers*, edd. Beuken, Freyne and Weiler, pp. 3–12

Middleton, D. F., 'Feminist interpretation', *DBI*, pp. 231–4

Miller, J. W., *Biblical Faith and Fathering. Why we call God 'Father'* (Paulist Press, New York 1989)

Mills, D., ed., *The Chester Mystery Plays* (East Lansing Colleagues Press 1992)

Milton, J., *The Poetical Works of John Milton*, ed. H. Darbishire (Oxford 1958)

Miranda, J. P., *Marx and the Bible. A Critique of the Philosophy of Oppression* (SCM Press, London 1977)

Moffatt, J., *The Bible in Scots Literature* (Hodder & Stoughton, London; no date)

Moffat, J., ed., *Handbook to the Church Hymnary* (Oxford University Press, Oxford 1927)

Moltmann, J., 'The motherly father. Is Trinitarian patripassianism replacing theological patriarchalism?' in *God as Father?*, edd. J.-B. Metz and E. Schillebeeckx (Seabury Press, New York 1981)

Montefiore, C. G. and H. Loewe, edd., *A Rabbinic Anthology* (Meridian Books, New York 1963)

Montgomery, J. A., *Aramaic Incantation Texts* (Philadelphia 1913)

Moo, D. J., *The Old Testament in the Gospel Passion Narratives* (The Almond Press, Sheffield 1983)

Morley, J., *All Desires Known* (London 1988)

Morris, P. and D. Sawyer, edd., *A Walk in the Garden. Biblical, Iconographical and Literary Images of Eden* (Sheffield Academic Press, Sheffield 1992)

Mráček, J., 'Rorate chants' in *New Grove Dictionary of Music and Musicians*, ed. S. Sadie (London 1980), Vol. 16, p. 185

Muller, R. A., 'The hermeneutics of promise and fulfilment in Calvin's exegesis of Old Testament prophecies of the Kingdom' in *The Bible in the Sixteenth Century*, ed. Steinmetz, pp. 68–82

Munck, J., *Christ and Israel. An Interpretation of Romans 9–11* (Fortress Press, Philadelphia 1967)

Muraoka, T., 'Bible translation: the ancient versions', *ELL*, pp. 349–51

Neubauer, A. and S. R. Driver, *The Fifty-Third Chapter of Isaiah According to the Jewish Interpreters* (reprinted edition, Ktav, New York 1969)

Neusner, J., *Jews and Christians. The Myth of a Common Tradition* (SCM Press, London 1991)

Newsom, C. A. and S. H. Ringe, edd., *A Women's Bible Commentary* (SPCK, London and Westminster/John Knox, Louisville, Kentucky 1992)

Nineham, D., *The Uses and Abuses of the Bible. A Study of the Bible in an Age of Rapid Cultural Change* (Macmillan, London 1976)

North, C. R., *The Second Isaiah* (Oxford 1964)

Oliphant, M. O. W., *Jerusalem. Its History and Hope* (Macmillan, London 1891)

Ostriker, A. S., *Feminist Revision and the Bible* (Blackwell, Cambridge, Mass. and Oxford 1993)

Owen, W., *The Collected Poems of Wilfred Owen*, ed. C. D. Lewis (New York 1964)

Pagels, E., *Adam, Eve and the Serpent* (Weidenfeld and Nicholson, London 1988)

Pelikan, J., *Jesus through the Centuries. His Place in the History of Culture* (Yale University Press, New Haven and London 1985)

Percy, Lord Eustace, *John Knox* (Hodder & Stoughton, London 1937)

Pervo, R. I., 'Aseneth and her sisters', in *Women Like This. New Perspectives on Jewish Women in the Greco-Roman World*, ed. A.-J. Levine, pp. 145–60

Pickering, F. P., *Literature and Art in the Middle Ages* (Macmillan, London 1970)

Plaskow, J., 'The coming of Lilith: toward a feminist theology' in *Womanspirit Rising. A Feminist Reader in Religion*, edd. C. P. Christ & J. Plaskow (Harper & Row, San Francisco/ London 1979), pp. 198–209

Plath, S., *Ariel* (Faber, London 1965)

Poole, M., *A Commentary on the Holy Bible*, 3 vols. (1700; reprinted by the Banner of Truth Trust, Edinburgh 1979)

Pope, A., *Pope: Poetical Works*, ed. H. Davies (Oxford 1978)

Prickett, S., *Words and the Word: Language, Poetics and Biblical Interpretation* (Cambridge 1986)

Quinsey, K., 'Swords into plowshares', *DBTEL*, pp. 746–7

Radday, Y. T. and A. Brenner, edd., *On Humour and the Comic in the Hebrew Bible* (Sheffield Academic Press, Sheffield 1992)

Rashkow, I. N., *Upon the Dark Places. Anti-Semitism and Sexism in English Renaissance Biblical Translation* (Bible and Literature Series 28; Sheffield Academic Press, Sheffield 1990)

Rashkow, I. N., 'Ruth: The discourse of power and the power of discourse', in *A Feminist Companion to Ruth*, ed. Brenner, pp. 26–41

Réau, L., *Iconographie de l'art chrétien*, 3 vols. (Paris 1955–9)

Renan, E., *Vie de Jésus* (Nelson/Calmann-Lévy, Paris 1938)

Rigney, B. H., *Lilith's Daughters. Women and Religion in Contemporary Fiction* (University of Wisconsin, Madison 1982)

Robbins, H. S., *Handel and his World* (Weidenfeld and Nicholson, London 1984)

Rogerson, J. W., 'The Hebrew conception of corporate personality. A re-examination' *JTS* 21 (1970), pp. 1–16

Rogerson, J., 'Interpretation, history of' in *Anchor Bible Dictionary*, edd. D. N. Freedman and others (New York 1992), Vol. 3, pp. 424–33

Rogerson, J., C. Rowland, and B. Lindars, *The Study and Use of the Bible* (*History of Christian Theology*, ed. P. Avis, Vol. 2) Marshall Pickering, Basingstoke/ W. Eerdmans, Grand Rapids 1988

Rosen, M. and W. Proctor, *Jews for Jesus* (Fleming H. Revell Company, Old Tappan, New Jersey 1972)

Roston, M., *Prophet and Poet. The Bible and the Growth of Romanticism* (Faber & Faber, London 1965)

Roston, M., *Biblical Drama in England. From the Middle Ages to the Present Day* (Faber & Faber, London 1968)

Rowland, C. C., *Christian Origins. An Account of the Setting and Character of the most Important Messianic Sect of Judaism* (SPCK, London 1985)

Royds, T. F., *Virgil and Isaiah. A Study of the Pollio with translations, notes and appendices* (Basil Blackwell, Oxford 1918)

Ruether, R. R., *Faith and Fratricide* (Seabury Press, New York 1974; Search Press, London 1975)

Ruether, R. R., *Sexism and God-Talk. Towards a Feminist Theology* (SCM Press, London 1983)

Ruether, R. R., *Womanguides. Readings Toward A Feminist Theology* (Beacon Press, Boston 1985)

Ruh, K., 'Zur Theologie des mittelalterlichen Passionstraktats', *TZ* 6 (1950), pp. 17–39

Russell, L. M., ed., *The Liberating Word* (Westminster Press, Philadelphia 1976)

Sakenfeld, K. D., 'Feminism and the Bible', *Oxford Companion to the Bible*, pp. 228–31

Salmi, P., *La Pittura di Piero della Francesca* (Novara 1959)

Sanders, E. P., *Jesus and Judaism* (SCM Press, London 1985)

Sanders, E. P., *Paul* (Past Masters Series; Oxford University Press, Oxford 1991)

Sassoon, S., *Collected Poems* (second edition, London 1984)

Sawyer, J. F. A., 'Root-meanings in Hebrew', *JSS*, 12. 1 (1967), pp. 37–50

Sawyer, J. F. A., 'Hebrew terms for the resurrection of the dead' *VT* 23 (1973), pp. 218–34

Sawyer, J. F. A., 'The ruined house in Ecclesiastes 12. A reconstruction of the original parable' *JBL* 94 (1975), pp. 519–31

Sawyer, J. F. A., 'A change of emphasis in the study of the Prophets' in *Israel's Prophetic Tradition*, edd. R. J. Coggins, A. Phillips and M. Knibb (Cambridge University Press, Cambridge 1982), pp. 233–49

Sawyer, J. F. A., 'The role of Jewish studies in biblical semantics' *Scripta signa vocis*, ed. H. L. J. Vanstiphout (Groningen 1986), pp. 201–8

Sawyer, J. F. A., 'Daughter of Zion and Servant of the Lord in Isaiah. A comparison', *JSOT* 44 (1989), pp. 89–107

Sawyer, J. F. A., 'The "original meaning of the text" and other legitimate subjects for semantic description', *Continuing Questions in Old Testament Method and Theology*, revised ed. M. Vervenne, (Leuven 1990), pp. 63–70, pp. 210–13

Sawyer, J. F. A., 'Combating prejudices about the Bible and Judaism' *Theology*, 94 (1991), pp. 269–78

Sawyer, J. F. A., 'The image of God, the wisdom of serpents and the knowledge of good and evil', in *A Walk in the Garden*, edd. D. F. Sawyer & P. Morris (Sheffield 1992), pp. 64–73

Sawyer, J. F. A., ' "My secret is with me" (Isaiah 24: 16): semantic links between Isaiah 24–27 and Daniel' in *Understanding Poet and Prophet: Essays in Biblical Interpretation*, ed A. G. Auld (Sheffield Academic Press, Sheffield 1993), pp. 307–17

Sawyer, J. F. A., 'Radical images of Yahweh in Isaiah' in *Among the Prophets. Language, Image and Structure in the Prophetic Writings*, edd. P. R. Davies and D. J. A. Clines (Sheffield 1993), pp. 72–82

Sawyer, J. F. A., 'Isaiah as a source-book for scriptural texts about death and mourning' in *Ritual and Remembrance. Responses to Death in Human Societies*, ed. J. Davies (Sheffield 1994), pp. 86–102

Sawyer, J. F. A., 'Le Serviteur Souffrant dans les traditions juives et chrétiennes' (unpublished)

Schapiro, M., *Romanesque Art* (London 1977)

Schell, R., 'Lilith' in *DBTEL*, pp. 454–5

Schiller, G., *Iconography of Christian Art*, two vols. (Eng. transl.; Lund Humphries, London, 1972)

Schlauch, M., 'The allegory of Church and Synagogue', *Speculum* 14 (1939) pp. 448–64

Schmidt, P. L., *Die Illustration der Lutherbibel 1522–1700* (Basel 1962)

Scholem, G., 'Lilith' in *EJ* 9, cols. 245–9

Schuerer, E., *The History of the Jewish People in the Age of Jesus Christ (175 BC– AD 135)* edd. G. Vermes, F. Millar and M. Black, 4 vols. (Edinburgh 1979–87)

Scott, R. B. Y., 'Isaiah, the Book of' in *Encyclopaedia Britannica* (1973), Vol. 12, pp. 654–7

Screech, M. A., *Erasmus. Ecstasy and the Praise of Folly* (Penguin, Harmondsworth 1988)

Seccombe, D., 'Luke and Isaiah', *NTS* 27 (1981), pp. 252–9

Segal, A. F., *Paul the Convert. The Apostolate and Apostasy of Paul the Pharisee* (Yale University Press, Newhaven 1990)

Seifert, S. W., *Synagogue and Church in the Middle Ages. Two Symbols in Art and Literature* (Munich 1970; first ed., in German, 1964)

Seitz, C. R., ed., *Reading and Preaching the Book of Isaiah* (Fortress Press, Philadelphia 1988)

Septuaginta XIV. Isaias, ed. J. Ziegler (Göttingen 1939)

Setel, T. D., 'Prophets and pornography: female sexual imagery in Hosea' in *Feminist Interpretation of the Bible*, ed. Russell (Blackwell, Oxford 1985), pp. 86–95

Simpson, E. M. and G. R. Potter, edd., *The Sermons of John Donne*, Vol. 8 (Berkeley and Los Angeles 1956)

Simpson, Rev. J. A., *Holy Wit* (Gordon Wright Publishing, 25 Mayfield Road, Edinburgh 1986)

Singer, I., ed., *Authorised Daily Prayer Book* (London 1892).

Skriver, K. A., *The Forgotten Beginnings of Creation and Christianity* (Vegetarian Press, Denver, Colorado 1990: German original, Lübeck-Travemünde 1977)

Smalley, B., *The Study of the Bible in the Middle Ages* (third edition, Basil Blackwell, Oxford 1983)

Smith, G., *The Life of William Carey: Shoemaker and Missionary* (J. M. Dent, London 1906)

Soelle, D., 'Share your bread with the hungry' in *The Strength of the Weak. Toward a Christian Feminist Identity* (transl. by R. and R. Kimber, Westminster Press, Philadelphia 1984) pp. 154–60 (originally published in *Sympathie*, Kreuzer Verlag, Stuttgart 1978)

Spinks, B. D., *The Sanctus in the Eucharistic Prayer* (Cambridge University Press, Cambridge 1991)

Spurgeon, C., *Sermons* (Sheldon, Blakeman and Co., New York 1857)

Staehelm, M., 'Elijah, J. S. Bach and the new covenant: on the aria "es ist genug" in F. M. Bartholdy's Oratorio *Elijah*', in *Mendelssohn and his World*, ed. R. L. Todd (Princeton 1991), pp. 121–36

Stanley, A. P., Dean of Westminster, *Scripture Portraits and Other Miscellanies* (New Edition, London 1880)

Stanton, E. Cady, *The Woman's Bible* (European Publishing Company, New York 1895, 1898; abridged edition, Polygon Books, Edinburgh, 1985)

Steinmetz, D. C., ed. *The Bible in the Sixteenth Century* (Duke University Press, Durham and London 1990)

Stendahl, K., 'Antisemitism' in *Oxford Companion to the Bible*, edd. B. Metzger & M. D. Coogan (New York/Oxford 1992), pp. 32–4

Stenning, J., *The Targum of Isaiah* (Oxford 1949)

Stewart, J. S., *Preaching* (Edinburgh University Press, Hodder and Stoughton, London 1955)

Strolz, W., 'The incomparability of God as biblical experience of faith' in *On Sharing Religious Experience. Possibilities of Interfaith Mutuality* (*Currents of Encounter*), edd. J. D. Gort, H. M. Vroom, R. Fernhout & A. Wessels (Amsterdam 1992), pp. 106–15

Sugirtharajah, R. S., ed., *Voices from the Margin: Interpreting the Bible in the Third World* (SPCK, London 1991)

Swanston, H., *Handel* (Oustanding Christian Thinkers Series; G. Chapman, London 1990)

Talmage, F. E., *Disputation and Dialogue: Readings in the Jewish-Christian Encounter* (second edition, New York 1975)

Tennyson, A. *The Poems of Tennyson*, ed. C. Ricks, Vol. 1 (second edition, Longman, London 1987)

Thorold, H., *Collins Guide to Cathedrals, Abbeys and Priories of England and Wales* (London 1986)

Tolbert, M. A., ed., *The Bible and Feminist Hermeneutics* (*Semeia* 28 (1983))

Trible, P., 'Depatriarchalizing in Biblical interpretation' *JAAR* 41 (1973), pp. 30–48

Trible, P., *God and the Rhetoric of Sexuality* (Fortress Press, Philadelphia 1978)

Trible, P., *Texts of Terror. Literary-Feminist Readings of Biblical Narratives* (Fortress Press, Philadelphia 1984)

Tutu, D., *Church and Prophecy in South Africa Today* (*Essex Papers in Theology and Society* 3; University of Essex 1991)

Ullendorff, E., 'Jesus in the Hebrew Bible', *JJS* 39,2 (1988), pp. 269–72

Vermes, G., *The Dead Sea Scrolls. Qumran in Perspective* (Collins, London 1977)

Vermes, G., *The Dead Sea Scrolls in English* (third edition, Penguin Press, Harmondsworth 1987)

Vermeylen, J., 'Le motif de la création dans le Deutéro-Isaie' in *La Creation dans l'Orient Ancien* (Lectio Divina 127; Paris 1987), pp. 183–240

Vetus Testamentum Syriace, III.1 Liber Isaiae, ed. S. Brock (Leiden 1987)

Vilnay, Z., *The Guide to Israel* (third ed. Jerusalem 1960; nineteenth ed. Jerusalem 1977)

Waal, H. van de, *Iconclass. An Iconographic Classification System*, ed. L. D. Couprie with E. Tholen and G. Vellekoop (Amsterdam/Oxford/New York 1982)

Wadell, M.-B., *Fons pietatis: Eine ikonographische Studie* (Göteborg 1969)

Wandor, M., *Gardens of Eden: Poems for Eve and Lilith* (Journeyman/Playbooks, London 1984)

Ware, T., *The Orthodox Church* (Pelican, London 1963)

Warner, M., *Alone of All Her Sex. The Myth and the Cult of the Virgin Mary* (Pan Books, London 1985; first published by Weidenfeld and Nicholson, London 1976)

Warner, M., *Monuments and Maidens. The Allegory of the Female Form* (Pan Books, London 1987)

Watson, A., *The Early Iconography of the Tree of Jesse* (London 1934)

Watson, F., ed., *The Open Text. New Directions for Biblical Studies?* (SCM Press, London 1993)

Wesley, J., *Works*, Vol. III, *Sermons*, 1–4, ed. A. C. Outler, (Abingdon, Nashville 1986)

Westermann, C., *Isaiah 40–66. A Commentary* (SCM Press, London, 1969)

Wheeler, M. D., *Death and the Future Life in Victorian Literature and Theology* (Cambridge 1990)

Whittaker, W. G., *The Cantatas of Johann Sebastian Bach. Sacred and Secular*, 2 vols (Oxford 1959)

Wiles, M., *Faith and the Mystery of God* (SCM Press, London 1982)

Williams, W. R., *Ohio Friends in the Land of Sinim* (Mt Gilead, Ohio 1925)

Williamson, C. M. and R. J. Allen, *Interpreting Difficult Texts, Anti-Judaism and Christian Preaching* (SCM Press, London/Trinity Press International, Philadelphia 1989)

Williamson, H. G. M., *The Book Called Isaiah. Deutero-Isaiah's Role in Composition and Redaction* (Oxford 1994)

Wills, G., *Under God. Religion and American Politics* (Simon & Shuster, New York/London/Toronto 1990)

Wilson, D., *The People and the Book. The Revolutionary Impact of the English Bible 1380–1611* (Barrie & Jenkins, London 1976)

Wright, D. F., 'The Bible in the Scottish Reformation' in *The Bible in Scottish Life and Literature*, pp. 155–78

Wright, D. F., ed., *The Bible in Scottish Life and Literature* (St Andrew Press, Edinburgh 1988)

Young, F. W., 'Isaiah and the fourth Gospel', *ZNW* 46 (1955), pp. 215–33

Young, F. W., *The Art of Performance. Towards a Theology of Holy Scripture* (London 1990)

Young, F. W., 'The pastoral epistles and the ethics of reading', *JSNT* 45 (1992), pp. 105–20

Young, F. W., 'Allegory and the ethics of reading', in *The Open Text*, ed. F. Watson, pp. 103–120

Ziesler, J., *Pauline Christianity* (Oxford Bible Series; Oxford University Press, Oxford 1983)

Index of Scriptural references

General index